READING FOR LIFE

PHILIP DAVIS

READING
FOR LIFE

OXFORD

UNIVERSITY PRESS

OXFORD
UNIVERSITY PRESS

Great Clarendon Street, Oxford, OX2 6DP,
United Kingdom

Oxford University Press is a department of the University of Oxford.
It furthers the University's objective of excellence in research, scholarship,
and education by publishing worldwide. Oxford is a registered trade mark of
Oxford University Press in the UK and in certain other countries

First Edition published in 2020

Impression: 2

Published in the United States of America by Oxford University Press
198 Madison Avenue, New York, NY 10016, United States of America

British Library Cataloguing in Publication Data
Data available

Library of Congress Control Number: 2019946475

ISBN 978–0–19–881598–3

Printed and bound by
CPI Group (UK) Ltd, Croydon, CR0 4YY

For *CRILS* and *The Reader*

'The thing is as true as it ever was'
Daniel Doyce in Charles Dickens, *Little Dorrit*, chapter 16

CONTENTS

PERMISSIONS (TEXTS)

Every effort has been made to trace copyright holders and obtain permission to reproduce the relevant material. Please do get in touch with any enquiries or any information relating to rights holders.

John Banville

John Banville, *The Untouchable*, Picador 1998, by permission of Pan Macmillan

John Berger

123 words reproduced from *Confabulations* by John Berger, published by Penguin Books. With permission from Penguin Books Ltd. Copyright © John Berger, 2016.

John Berger, *Selected Essays* ('The Hour of Poetry'), by John Berger and edited by Geoff Dyer, 2001, by permission of Bloomsbury Publishing Plc. and Wylie Agency (UK) Limited.

A Fortunate Man by John Berger, and by permission from Canongate Books, and The Wylie Agency (UK) Limited.

Excerpt(s) from *A Fortunate Man: The Story of a Country Doctor* by John Berger, text copyright © 1967 by John Berger. Used by permission of Pantheon Books, an imprint of the Knopf Doubleday Publishing Group, a division of Penguin Random House LLC. All rights reserved.

Wendell Berry

'The Slip', 27 lines from *The Peace of Wild Things* by Wendell Berry. Copyright © Wendell Berry, 1964, 1968, 1970, 1973, 1977, 1980, 1982, 1994, 1999, 2005, 2016. Reproduced by permission of Penguin Books Ltd.

Copyright © 2012 Wendell Berry, from *New Collected Poems*. Reprinted by permission of Counterpoint Press.

Elizabeth Bishop

Excerpts from 'Cape Breton' and 'In the Waiting Room' from *Poems* by Elizabeth Bishop. Copyright © 2011 by The Alice H. Methfessel Trust. Publisher's Note and compilation copyright © 2011 by Farrar, Straus and Giroux. Reprinted by permission of Farrar, Straus and Giroux.

Philip Booth

'First Lesson', from *Lifelines: Selected Poems 1950–1999* by Philip Booth, copyright © 1999. Used by permission of Viking Books, an imprint of Penguin Publishing Group, a division of Penguin Random House LLC. All rights reserved.

Bertolt Brecht

Raymond Carver

e. e. cummings

Emily Dickinson

T. S. Eliot

Joshua Ferris

668 words from The Unnamed by Joshua Ferris (Viking, 2010). Copyright © Joshua Ferris, 2010. Used by permission of Viking Books, an imprint of Penguin Publishing Group, a division of Penguin Random House LLC. All rights reserved.

From *The Unnamed* by Joshua Ferris, copyright © 2010. Reprinted by permission of Little, Brown and Co., a subsidiary of Hachette Book Group, Inc.

Robert Frost

'Revelation' and 'The Road Not Taken' by Robert Frost. From the book *The Poetry of Robert Frost* edited by Edward Connery Lathem. Copyright © 1916, 1923, 1934, 1969 by Henry Holt and Company. Copyright © 1944, 1962 by Robert Frost. Utilized by permission of Henry Holt and Company. All rights reserved.

From *The Poetry of Robert Frost* by Robert Frost. Published by Jonathan Cape. Reprinted by permission of The Random House Group Limited.

W.S.Graham

W.S.Graham, 'Dear Bryan Wynter', 'Implements in their Places', reproduced by permission of Rosalind Mudaliar, the estate of W.S. Graham.

Elizabeth Jennings

Elizabeth Jennings, 'Friendship' from *The Collected Poems* (Carcanet) by permission of David Higham Associates

Brendan Kennelly

'Begin' from Brendan Kennelly, *Familiar Strangers: New & Selected Poems 1960–2004* (Bloodaxe Books, 2004). Reproduced with permission of Bloodaxe Books.

D. H. Lawrence

'Trust' from *The Complete Poems of D. H. Lawrence* by D. H. Lawrence, edited by Vivian de Sola Pinto and F. Warren Roberts, copyright © 1964, 1971 by Angelo Ravagli and C. M. Weekley, Executors of the Estate of Frieda Lawrence Ravagli. Used by permission of Viking Books, an imprint of Penguin Publishing Group, a division of Penguin Random House LLC. All rights reserved.

Robert Lowell

Excerpts from letter written by Robert Lowell to Elizabeth Bishop dated August 15, 1957 (Castine, ME) from *Words in Air: The Complete Correspondence between Elizabeth Bishop and Robert Lowell* edited by Thomas Travisano with Saskia Hamilton. Writings of Elizabeth Bishop copyright © 2008 by Alice Helen Methfessel. Robert Lowell letters copyright © by Harriet Lowell and Sheridan Lowell. Compilation copyright © 2008 by Thomas J. Travisano. Reprinted by permission of Farrar, Straus and Giroux.

William Stafford

Derek Walcott

Baron Wormser

LIST OF ILLUSTRATIONS

INTRODUCTION

This book is in part a working anthology of poems and of extracts from prose fiction, but also a related series of case-histories of individuals reading, and thinking about their reading lives. Each chapter more or less begins with a literary text that triggers the feeling and the thought of what follows. The text becomes either the scene of a reading group, transcribed and analysed, or an opening into the wider life of its reader, recorded through interview or in reading diaries.

The double format of individual texts and individual readers seeks to enable the reader of this book to collaborate with the readers depicted in it, in a tacitly shared reading of the literary text on offer. My idea is that it may help to see other readers making efforts, perhaps in relation to a poem you do not immediately understand or, understanding, do not connect with; perhaps in order to make what may usually seem to be no more than small and transient verbal details more worthy of a sustained (because implicitly joint) sense of a significant reality on the page in front of us.

In this way *Reading for Life* seeks to provide examples and experiences of what goes into careful and intense literary reading. It tries to show what a more-than-passive form of reading can be like when, in relation to a powerful language in an important area, easy automatic processing no longer serves the purpose. The reading in action revealed and encouraged in this way is 'reading for life' in its first meaning: reading for its vitality and its effects upon vitality, going on alive at a far deeper level of being than information-processing or quick scanning ever can. It is the difference between a literal-minded and a literary-minded feel for words.

This vital difference may be further illustrated by one of this book's leading figures, John Berger, in an essay discussing the activity of translating from one language to another. Conventionally, in the world of technology, says Berger, it means no more than literal word-for-word translation as from the left-hand page in one language to another language on the right. But this operation—which is just like scanning and summarizing and paraphrasing—makes for only mechanically second-rate translation, a mere second-hand copy of the original:

> Why? Because true translation is not a binary affair between two languages but a triangular affair. The third point of the triangle being what lay behind the words of the original text before it was written. True translation demands a return to the pre-verbal. One reads and rereads the words of the original text in order to penetrate through them to reach, to touch, the vision or experience that prompted them. One then gathers up what has been found there and takes this quivering almost wordless 'thing' and places it behind the language it needs to be translated into. And now the principal task is to persuade the host language to take in and welcome the 'thing' that is waiting to be articulated.[1]

Look at the mental work and complex movement described in all these adverbs and prepositions that are around the verbs, in search of that third thing beyond a literal meaning: *behind* and *before*; to return *to* and to penetrate *through*; gathers *up* and places it *behind*; translated *into*, to take *in*. In the risk of trying to get back to where and what the words came out of, truly imaginative translation is for Berger a re-creative model—and a model which serves for more than just translation itself.

That is to say: it is a template for all serious writing, working to-and-fro between pre-language and language itself, translating from the pre-verbal intuition to the verbal formulation that partially recognizes it, as in an act of metaphor. What is more, it is that underlying imagined spirit conveyed within, behind and beneath the letter, which deep literary reading—on the other side of the writing, on the receiving end—also exists to host, to hold, and to translate. Like good translators, good readers do not just literally convert what the writing says, word for word, and think that sufficient for understanding. They co-operate in and learn something of the craft of writing, of why this specific formulation or how this particular turn of phrase has somehow *got* to them. They try to become the readers that their writers seem to be seeking, but more than that, the readers that the writers themselves can be even in the act of their own writing. For writers are also in this sense momentarily readers of themselves—because it is not that writers seek language just for it allow them to speak, to communicate, or to express outwardly, but rather for it also to speak back to them, to reflect back, and answeringly *tell* them something.

For example: at the sudden death of his wife from whom for many years he had been partly estranged even in their living together, Thomas Hardy seems only to have had left to him the resource of writing carefully crafted words on a page. The reader can almost feel him looking down at the lines in the act of arranging them under his hand:

Figure 1. 'Reading Hand'. © Joe Magee, www.periphery.co.uk.

> Never to bid good-bye
> Or lip me the softest call,
> Or utter a wish for a word, while I
> Saw morning harden upon the wall,
>   Unmoved, unknowing
>   That your great going
> Had place that moment, and altered all.
> 'The Going'

Dying alone in her room, she left unannounced and without a word: it felt to him, after, like a silent act of separation, an almost deliberate leaving of him, even at the moment when, as was all too usual he, unsynchronized, was not thinking of her, was unmoved by her. There was nothing left to say, it seems, in that marriage, and so the writing begins where the speaking had failed Now, moved too late, Hardy writes the word or two that she did not say or did not want to ask him for. And as he writes and sees what he has written, he also *hears* for a moment, at the pause of the rhymed line-ending, the '*going*' happening again, coming back to hit him in the impossible shocked instant of death, and in the silent inner cry of his being abruptly bereft. That is the reading of his own writing, the hearing of his own silent script.

'Unmoved, unknowing/That your great going/Had place that moment.' The jolt of 'going' has taken 'place' again on the page, a millisecond before it is realized as having done so, before it becomes fact once more. This is the still quivering 'almost wordless thing' that writer and the reader can innerly feel and hear—and not just see—within the words and between the lines. This is like Berger's imaginative translator reading and re-reading 'the words of the original text in order to penetrate through them to reach, to touch, the vision or experience that prompted them'. Reading for life is—in its second meaning—reading for the sake of re-freeing the life that books hold within them; translating *from* literature, as something more than a self-contained area, back into human beings all that literature saves from being otherwise lost, unrealized or uncreated.

So it is that I want to suggest in these pages that literary thinking, amongst readers as well as writers, is a form of thinking about life not always recognized *as* thinking in the wider world, but here made live and present and specific. This book is concerned with the intuitively emotional—the surprised and excited, the disturbed, and the suddenly autobiographical as crucial initiating involvements; but it is not just about these things, it is about the messages of thought echoing within them for further discovery. This is not a book in favour of using texts merely as excuses for personal confession at the expense of what is being read. Of course a text can withstand undue personal appropriation, and cannot mind it—and perhaps any form of human relief is to be welcomed. But then it is not the literature that does it, when what literature can do is more complicated than that. I will not be arguing that literature can simply offer instrumental answers, novel cures, poetic therapy, or simple self-help effects. All that is too direct and simple a translation. The lives recorded in this book cannot be resolved into simple success stories resulting from very good reading, or they wouldn't be real lives.

Instead *Reading for Life* focuses first on raw moments—whatever may or may not come of them—when readers are suddenly taken aback by fiction. That is to say: when they feel as though they are found out, or attracted by, something that acts almost as an extended part of themselves, or makes them become an extended part of it, in the unclear borderline area between the subjective and objective. One of this book's other great protagonists, William James, describes this near-blind feeling of sudden connection:

> It is as if a bar of iron, without touch or sight, with no representative faculty whatever, might nevertheless be strongly endowed with an inner capacity for magnetic feeling... Such an iron bar could never give you an outward description of the agencies that had the power of stirring it so strongly; yet of their presence, and of their significance for its life, it would be intensely aware through every fibre of its being.[2]

You don't always know in advance what will affect you, and though that may seem back-to-front, I argue that this is the right way round for human beings. Not to know beforehand leads to trying to find out why this has happened, what this still stands for. When a serious reader is, as it were, James's experimental iron bar, that receptive instrument for reading in action, then reading also means going on to try to detect what it is outside that has got you, and what inside is responding to it, looking both ways. Georgina, the reader who is the subject of chapter 9, says:

> When the thoughts just come to you, there is an involuntariness about them that is very easy and a bit beautiful, but it is very difficult to hold onto them. You think or say something, and then say to yourself, 'Where did *that* come from'—exclamation and question mark at once...I want to get to the place where it comes from.

This is a different way of thinking, sudden and flexible, receptive and mobile in the very midst of things, with much that is personally and emotionally at stake in its efforts. The change of level from initial instinctive feeling to the extrication of the thoughts within feeling, without their becoming cold and inert, is vital to the chances for mental life and mental development.

So the chapters that follow seek first of all to disclose, in practice, what may be called 'the literary moment': that otherwise small and transient instant of heuristic realization when readers suddenly do something deep or subtle or moving at a minuscule point within the text, not usually taken into account in more generalized accounts of what reading is. It is like the word 'going' suddenly realized in all its force, in Hardy's poem of that name. It is the point at which, as William James might say, we truly catch reading in the heat and feel of the individual act of doing it. As he tells the audience for his Gifford lectures on *The Varieties of Religious Experience*:

> You can see now why I have been so individualistic throughout these lectures, and why I have seemed so bent on rehabilitating the element of feeling...Individuality is founded in feeling; and the recesses of feeling, the darker, blinder strata of character, are the only places in the world in which we catch real fact in the making, and directly perceive how events happen, and how work is actually done. *Varieties*, pp. 501–2

Reading for Life is not about religious experience as such, but it is about individual acts of triggered contemplation that for some readers have had to become a replacement for religion in the search for human meaning amidst the deeper, darker strata of inner human reality. This book will try to show that the breakthrough into deep and active reading represents a shift from normative ways of thinking into a richer language and a more real understanding of human existence, important to the capacity of lay readers to think the thoughts necessary to them. This goes deeper than therapeutic step-by-step programmes and, as some participants in this book indicate, is arguably more freely therapeutic by *not* being therapy in a directed top-down form. To achieve such a breakthrough, the presence of literature is necessary to act both as a trigger, reaching levels of emotion, memory, and recognition not normally available or easily accessible in daily life, and as a rocket-boost to produce an accelerated excitement of felt intelligence dependent upon the primary prompt of a stimulating text. What is given in these pages then, instead of general top-down theories of 'reader-response', are actual accounts of individual readers, and specific acts of reading, driving towards thought from below upwards, out of the sense of magnetic attraction.[3] Again I hope what you will read here will show, as near live as I can make it, what a more explicit argument cannot always emphasize without interruption to the individual account.

So I need to emphasize here and now that these acts of reading are not only manifested in often subliminal moments of minute change and microscopic attention. Within those micro-moments, like something big exploding within something small, or long-standing within the transient, are also the macro-concerns of the lives of readers featured in this book, brought to their minds by the works they read. This present book does not give and cannot know their whole life-stories: it just reveals momentary fragments of almost involuntary memory. These triggered realizations are more deeply authentic in their sudden heat than conventional narration of personal events or normative explanation of past motives when the reality has begun to fade again into paraphrase. This is reading for life, in a third sense, for the sake of readers' own existences; for the prompting of old and the development of new powers of mind; and in particular, for the glimpsed sense of the books' relation to the lives and thinking of their readers, blending into an almost musical system of interrelated resonances the time of reading in the foreground with the reader's own lifetime in the back, like a poem itself.[4] It is also what prompts a fourth sense: a commitment on the part of some of the subjects of this book to try to hold onto and use the after-effects of their reading, and become lifelong readers in search of meaning. All this is what my colleague Rhiannon Corcoran, a professor of psychology, calls 'literature in practice, psychology in action', with something real and revivifying to say to both the study of literature and the study of psychology when they become too established and static.

*

'The best way to think about reading,' says the literary critic Mark Edmundson, 'is as life's grand.'[5] *Reading for Life* has in the background, for some of its sources, the story of a reading outreach organization that has very much to do with creating those second chances through the realm of literature, or with trying to make a second small world, a warmer human environment, in which to do better thinking.

The Reader, founded in 1997 by Jane Davis, exists to bring the richest possible legacy of serious literature from the sixteenth century to the present day into often hard-to-reach or easy-to-ignore communities.[6] The organization currently delivers over 500 groups per week nationwide, each involving two to twelve participants, in a range of health, educational, and social care settings (community centres, schools, libraries, homeless shelters, facilities for looked-after children, hospitals, offices, doctors' surgeries, prisons, drug rehab units, and care homes for the aged) across the UK. It has partners and associates in Denmark, Belgium, Norway, Sweden, Germany, New Zealand, and Australia. In England in particular, its remit includes people specifically suffering from mental health problems and social isolation—with the emphasis on depression, dementia, and chronic pain. But, more broadly, it is an outreach programme that is not only concerned with what is wrong—with illness and suffering and pain. Rather, it seeks whomsoever it can reach, in whatever way books can find, offering contemplative space for all people whatever their background, known and unknown. Within these local communities, literature is read aloud to those who for a variety of reasons might not otherwise read it, to give glimpses of how life is or might be, should have been or has to be, in a renewed sense of purpose or dignity or concern for themselves. These shared reading groups provide part of the content of *Reading for Life*: in what follows you will find, amongst other evidence taken from elsewhere, both transcripts of group sessions, and interviews with individual participants.

What is important is that these groups are not traditional book clubs whose membership is of limited ethnological range, and where books (normally, recent novels) are read in advance and then discussed, often at the level of opinion, only in retrospect. *The Reader's* model of Shared Reading involves diverse people reading *live*, aloud and together, with intervals for focused analysis and personal reflection. These sessions are led by a project worker—often, a graduate in literature, though increasingly taken from a cohort of trained volunteers—whose role is implicitly educative as well as facilitating. The reader leaders will seek to enable a warm and friendly atmosphere in which the reading aloud of the work helps create a frank and humane atmosphere in the room. But with the text there in front of everyone for eye as well as ear, the group leaders will also push for a careful look at the actual words, the turns and nuances and telling details. They will want people to take the work seriously, personally, and this means allowing free room for mistakes, awkwardnesses, and autobiographical utterances; but they will also regularly re-read the text, aloud, and with care bring participants back into it. The group-work goes on along a spectrum: at one end, an unemotional reading that may respect the text but brings no life out of it; at the other, an emotional response that may leave the text itself too far behind. If anything, the reader leader will far rather risk the latter rather than have the former, but the task is to work within the spectrum, to adjust and realign as the session goes along, rather than rule in or out. Any requirement for simple fixed boundaries in this complex area seems unreasonable. There cannot be utter purity, or tidy abstraction, any more than there is meant to be messy self-indulgence or self-conscious confession. It is about creating an immersed experience, which is the very opposite of knowing-in-advance, by following the processes of reading an often unknown text in all its challenges and bafflements, turns and unpredictabilities. It is about taking literature out of the academy but with the best benefits of academic training, producing through this experiment human effects that should play back into a re-understanding of the role of literature in both the wider world and in the education that should provide for it.

I have said the informal group setting and the act of reading aloud give access to literature to people who may not usually be accustomed to it. Theirs may not be a problem of literacy as such. Depression may prevent people from being able to concentrate sufficiently to bother reading on their own, even if in their better times they are already established readers. Or serious literature from all ages, and in particular poetry, may seem dauntingly elitist or irrelevantly difficult, an unlikely form of human help, for those without experience of reading in this area or at this level. 'Try it' is all the reader leaders say, and then a reader might later respond, as one did, saying, 'You need it, you just don't know that you do.' These lay-readers for the most part would not consider themselves exceptional or even well-educated, but by their very need make for a testing-ground within the norms of life for the effects of literary-inflected thinking.[7]

Those who have less, often give more. But there is no mistaking the effort and faith and persistence required. Alexis McNay running a reading group in a prison on Merseyside describes how it can be amongst the men on the wing, on what he calls the 'razor's edge between positions of brazenness and insecurity'.[8] First, there is often the macho brazenness, defiant and dismissive when confronted with literature often thought of as somehow 'soft':

A very quiet young man, attending his third session, was asked by another member of the group what he thought of the opening of *The Pearl* by John Steinbeck. 'It's shit,' he replied. When I asked him to elaborate, he said, 'It's just about some little Mexicans and their baby...It's boring, I'm not interested.'

But then on this particular occasion something else also happened:

A little piqued, I let my own guard down momentarily: 'Would it be better if it was about you?' I ask. 'No, it would be worse,' comes the immediate reply.

That was the chastening moment, a sense of what might be hidden behind the stance of external rejection. Michael, a prisoner with thirty shared-reading sessions under his belt, and a perceptive intelligence, recognized it and at the end of the session he advised Alexis: 'Persevere with this'—meaning, Alexis thought, both the book and the young man in question. 'There's a lot of front out there; they have to present it. But they see after a while that they don't need to bring it in here: they can leave it out there.' 'In here' and 'out there' *are* very different places, though only a nine-inch wall apart. And 'in here' the young man might begin to let go of his front, for what exists more vulnerably behind it. Alexis did persevere not only by reading every week, but within each weekly session re-reading and repeating the same few lines out loud, as an act of persistence in what he felt was crucial:

One afternoon we're reading Raymond Carver's poem 'Happiness', which describes the simple beauty of the companionship between two boys delivering papers, appreciated at a remove by an onlooker. When we read the lines

> They are so happy
> they aren't saying anything, these boys.
> I think if they could, they would take
> each other's arm.

—then the new young man in the room, uninitiated, and testing the water in mischief more than malice, says, with a nudge and a wink: 'Sounds a bit gay, doesn't it?'

'If they could they would'—but they too can't quite. I'm scrabbling for a response suitably diplomatic—this is John's first contribution, after all—and yet corrective. Before I can sort my Ps from my Qs, Michael raises his own point of order: 'What are you saying that for? This is a serious group, this; we take it seriously—it's not for dickheads.' John, surprised, amused *and* slightly wounded, says defensively, 'I'm not a dickhead!' and Michael completes the exchange: 'Well, don't say dickhead things, then.'

Alexis concludes:

> It is all taken in good spirits, and we segue directly into some really good discussion, but it's been a revelatory moment for me. Not only is it moving to see such a vehement protection of this space, valued for a different kind of interaction, but there's a bigger and more significant implication in the wording of the exchange: that any distinction between the said and the sayer doesn't hold, here in this group. In prison, as in society generally where a lot of people too often 'speak their mind' without much thought as to what they're saying, the idea that one is inseparable from what one says, and should take responsibility for it; the idea that what you say represents you in a fundamental and important way; the potential for this rigour to refine thought itself; and the fact that a group member is demanding it: this makes me realize this can be a great thing here.

It is more dramatic that this is a prison setting, but so often the extreme only reveals what is muffled and hidden in less exposed and more common situations.

If it is hard to make a beginning, it can also be hard to carry on. Another group-leader, Grace Farrington reports on a man she calls Nigel who, diagnosed with personality disorder, is a long-term resident of a high-security hospital supporting the provision of specialist care for forensic psychiatric patients. The group is reading a poem entitled 'Begin' by Brendan Kennelly which you will find in chapter 6, and Nigel, highly intelligent, almost always gets to what is crucially important within seconds of the poem finishing:

> Though we live in a world that dreams of ending
> that always seems about to give in
> something that will not acknowledge conclusion
> insists that we forever begin.

> Nigel: He was saying very roughly that beginnings—like the beginning of the day or the beginning of activity—is something that is built into us. Although it might appear that things are ending, or we may have thoughts of things ending, there's something inside us that always says, you know, begin...I'd have a hard time saying anything else about it.

He has seen it so quickly that there feels as if there is nothing less to say. And Nigel struggles with feelings, which is why perhaps his intelligence is so quick and final. But Grace comments:

> Nigel seems to need the assurance which I was often not fast enough to insert into his rapid train of thought. It was as if he was trying always to be self-sufficient, and

was worried at the idea of coming up short, or even failing himself in some way. But already he has several thoughts to *go* on here, and he had a sense of that insistent 'something'—'there's something inside us that always says...'—which not only powers the poem but suggests a powering of life itself.

Yet always there is this potential obstacle to expansion, even here imaged in small. The thought seems to need to last longer, to warrant more words in becoming bigger. It wants another sentence, more thinking not to let it go short, to establish the possibility of making the 'something' into a genuine subject capable of further development. But if the person who has found it cannot find anything more to say of it, or if no one else will come into the conversation and respond, the danger is that the life of the thought runs out and dies there. Yet that at least can make finding the next word, the extra sentence, something better than polyfilla, when a sense of greater reality, and the need for more of an immediate future, may be urgently at stake.

*

But for all the difficulties, a caveat or corrective here. Though literature deals so much with human struggle and trouble, because (of course) human beings themselves do, not all the participants in these groups or in this book are unusually troubled, ill, or traumatized, and the literary works chosen offer a full range of human responses rather than merely 'problems' or 'examples' or 'cures'. The readers in chapters 6 and 10 make a point of emphasizing this. It is the release of human energy that is important, almost defiantly regardless of whether the subject-matter is itself ostensibly miserable or celebratory, though deeply moved by it. For all the institutional setting, the damaged predicament, even the sometimes painful content of the literature, Peter says of his shared reading group in an addiction centre in London:

> It's real isn't it? It's real. That's me. You can't lie. Why would you go there and lie? It's just so...it's just so pure, there's something beautiful about that group, there's something quite pure going on there. We're being offered a golden afternoon of being ourselves, being allowed to be, be ourselves, aren't we.

Psychologists report that one of the signature symptoms of depression is over-generalized memory—the inner voice that keeps repeating that life is always bad, or I am always terrible; but the force of literature here is to do with a 'real' specificity that in its life fights generalized attitudes, eluding easy categories or prescriptive solutions. And when that force works in these less privileged contexts, there is nothing taken for granted as there might seem to be in more comfortable and blasé settings: it works as if for the very first time again—'real', 'pure', not to have to tell lies but to be me, 'beautiful', 'golden'. As a character in a novel by my old school-master Stanley Middleton puts it, baffled as to why he keeps going to an inferior local musical performance when he could afford to hear it done better elsewhere:

> 'I wonder if it's because seeing something happen at its most humdrum gives you a better insight into its nature.' [9]

It is a Wordsworthian insight that the rough and struggling may offer a more core understanding than the smoothly professional. So in shared reading in a mundane setting we may find a recovery of the roots of why reading literature matters, a recognition of why older literature and a more challenging or unpredictable vocabulary has a vital role, as opposed to either the most apparently 'relevant' novel published this year or a well-intentioned self-help book. What I suggest these case-histories offer is a way of rediscovering the importance of the activity—the thoughtful reading and study of literature—prior to its sometimes professional self-enclosure, through seeing the raw material of its importance to people outside the discipline who nonetheless are involved, however informally, in concentrated reading. For the point here is that with literature anyone, given the opportunity, can get direct access to the original texts. It is not like science or even history, where sources and discoveries must be filtered through secondary descriptions, textbooks of explanation and summary. Reading literature is never first of all a separately specialized activity.[10]

Recording or sitting in on these shared reading groups allows us to see in basic and informal settings what is usually hidden and private: people in the act of thinking about literature. Admittedly this is reading within particular group-contexts rather than people reading silently and alone. But the transcripts of audio-recorded or filmed reading in real time reveal to us, live and spontaneous, at least something of what people actually do when they are reading, and not just what they say or think they do in retrospect. 'Us' here refers to a second organization that helped in forming this book, the Centre for Research into Reading, Literature and Society (CRILS). It is a research unit I set up with Josie Billington and Rhiannon Corcoran in the University of Liverpool from 2010 to take the study of literature out of a literature department, to allow literary specialists to collaborate with psychologists and health professionals within the University's Institute of Psychology, Health and Society. This allowed for a wide variety of overlapping methods of exploration and cross-disciplinary perspectives. In what follows, you will see results from brain-imaging studies; from quantifiable questionnaires and self-reporting measures of psychological health and wellbeing; from interviews; from physiological experiments in measuring changes in heartbeat, cortisol, galvanic skin responses, voice levels, and eye-movements; from thinking in a combination of literary, psychological, and philosophical terms. But above all perhaps, this book is dedicated to exploring the impact of the language of the texts on the actual language of the participants, in the development of a subtler emotional lexicon, a more intricate syntax, even as they think. The analysis of the responses involved collaboration between literary critics, scholars in linguistics, and psychologists in examining these movements in the relation between language and thought. To get beyond the norms of stock responses and reductive vocabulary seemed important not just for literary reasons but for the transferred effect of literature in enabling readers to think their own thoughts inside and outside reading with more dignity and more precision, to take the reality of themselves more seriously.

In this investigation, CRILS also recruited evidence from sources outside shared reading and *The Reader*. The reading-group accounts are supplemented in what follows by more longitudinal accounts gathered from interviews and readings with solitary and private readers—some of whom helped form *The Reader* itself or moved on from its shared group reading (chapters 1, 5, 10); some who quite separately were graduates from (often part-time) degrees combining study with relation to personal or vocational praxis (chapters 2 and 9), and others who from within their own professions as teacher or doctor, as well as poet or novelist, offered us in reading-notes and interviews the nature of their own experience (chapters 2, 6, 7, 11).

What I do think many of these committed readers have in common is their need to create time-out for an inner life, a second world within this world, not in simple retreat from it but for the sake of attempting a better return to it. Reading for them is at once a guided and a spontaneous activity, the one arising within the other. And that is why *Reading for Life* might be also be thought of as reading *for* a second life, or *in* a second life—for two reasons. First, because the idea of second lives, found through books, recognizes the readers' ordinary need to ride upon *other* minds to begin with, enabling their own minds to arise within the minds on the page, into areas suddenly made more open and thinkable by the literary text. And secondly because as the philosopher Hannah Arendt said, all thought that comes out of human experience feels more like after-thought, like something coming second rather than first.[11] For most of us, thinking is not something that feels clever, a rationality in advance of events or even in time with them, but more like personal catch-up, illuminated almost too late in the lag of time. Yet this enhanced capacity for reflective second thought, derived from reading, offers readers access to a partial reclamation of experience at a different level of mental self. In some case-histories, this is felt most powerfully in relation to what is experienced as initially failed or botched attempts at living. But literary reading in itself becomes a second chance by offering for anyone, whatever their condition, another place, a formal holding-ground, for exploring the contents of experience.

It is like something that Jack, a participant in a local library group in Croydon, described in reading Charlotte Brontë's *Jane Eyre*. He is large, gentle man of West Indian extraction thinking here about a little white English girl—and if that seems unlikely and surprising, 'I don't see her as a 10-year-old girl', is what he said at interview. He felt the cruel treatment she received: 'It's not physical, but it is almost like being in a boxing ring with someone. There are certain things that affect your mind, mentally, you know, certain things they say, and it rocks your inner core [*puts fist onto chest*].' He was most moved near the end of chapter 4 when the young Jane, at last free from the tyranny of Mrs Reed's house, decides at the final moment not to leave without saying what she thinks of her treatment under that roof:

> Mrs Reed looked up from her work: her eyes settled on mine, her fingers at the same time suspended their nimble movements.
> 'Go out of the room; return to the nursery,' was her mandate. My look or something else must have struck her as offensive, for she spoke with extreme though repressed irritation. I got up; I went to the door; I came back again; I walked to the window across the room, then close up to her.
> *Speak* I must: I had been trodden on severely, and *must* turn: but how?

Jack loves it that Jane does manage to find her voice: 'Once she knew she was gonna go, she couldn't just be told to go off and [*makes dismissing gesture with arm and hands*] not be heard or anything. So she was on her way out, and then she thought, "No I'm going to tell, to come back and just tell her".' Because she'd been so hurt, 'She feels its impact, and I don't think she thought through whatever she was gonna say but, but she said it.' That is the second chance that literature finds *time* for, to go back even whilst in the midst of going onward. It is the achievement of the girl who is already almost over the threshold and into the future, before she crosses back over it again to do justice to the past. These little oscillating movements contain, like secrets hidden within the apparent continuity, what Henry James calls 'disguised and repaired losses' and 'insidious recoveries'.[12] These can be tiny signs of life looking, backwards and forwards, for some sort of struggling unity with itself.

And that is part of a larger, wider endeavour here, to do with what the pessimist philosopher, Arthur Schopenhauer called the second phase of human life:

> The striving after existence is what occupies all living things and maintains them in motion. But when existence is assured, then they know not what to do with it; thus the *second* thing that sets them in motion is the effort to get free from the burden of existence.[13]

It was the seeking-system in the brain that was the first engine of human evolution, searching the environment for resources necessary to survive and grow, urgently encouraging foraging, exploration, investigation, curiosity, interest and expect-ancy.[14] Its first-order task was to fight for life, to preserve itself, to gain expansion and resist contraction. But now in our second world, says Schopenhauer, in the social human world which follows when physical survival is more or less guaran-teed, the urgent raw fight for life is less obviously needful, and the seeking can shut down. Then this civilized second world becomes more existential and psycho-logical, more concerned with seeking meaning for life than struggling for life itself. At the very point at which basic needs seemed relatively satisfied and readily provided, we become more worried by how the life that is now secured may be actually worth living. That is why Schopenhauer feared that with the closing-down of the primary seeking-mechanism, with the loss of life-and-death actions, the result would be a tamed and passive opposite: melancholy or depression, emotions no longer geared into actions useful for survival but left burdened by an evolved level of inner search for which in the mental domain there was no goal corresponding to survival in the physical. In the second-order social world to which human beings have sensibly adapted, Schopenhauer did not believe in the real possibility of happiness or flourishing.

But *Reading for Life* is about some people's half-abashed, half-defiant search for that 'second thing', even through something as apparently tame as reading. This is why, to take a literary equivalent, all that went into the formation of the realist novel becomes increasingly important in this book. It is not simply because such fiction may seem more 'accessible' to ordinary readers, but because the realist novel—*Great Expectations, Middlemarch, Anna Karenina*, through to *Lord Jim, The Unnamed*, and *The Other Side of You*—marks in literature that immersion in a mundane secular life which may leave the great questions of meaning and purpose awkward and embarrassed, half-abandoned or compromised, and yet never quite avoidable either, to surface in moments of personal crisis.

Books may feel secondary, and at times reading can seem almost shamefully substitutive in relation to a more active, direct, and primary life. But it is worth recalling how this is part of our second task beyond the limit of basic literal needs, in the effort to reincorporate and transmute those needs at another level. Literature is still a form of seeking for life, related to what Jack means by finding an 'inner core' as it is revealed by surprised feeling, in an almost physical version of emergent mentality. It is a form that goes on as a second life within the lives of readers featured in the chapters that follow.[15]

As another CRILS associate, the psychologist Professor Richard Bentall says: 'Literary reading is implicit psychotherapy which is all the more effective in relation to existential problems too often ignored by psychologists, because incurable as such.' Or in the words of the novelist in chapter 11, 'There is no cure for life.'

*

A last word on presentation, in which I want to emphasize two issues.

The first issue has been how best in this book to get out and then reproduce its people's voices. As Georgina put it, 'I want to get to the place where it comes from.'

Jud is another of the unknown highly intelligent people described in this book. In his late 30s, he is beset by psychosis, and after quitting university some years ago, has never since been able to get back on track. His group in a psychosis day-care centre in London was reading a short story, 'Mortals' by Tobias Wolff, on a man who announced his own death to the local newspaper in order that he might read his own (brief) obituary. Jud said:

> If you haven't achieved that much and you are not in a good state at the time of your death, what do you put in an obituary? I mean, people are not going to know about your personal workings are they? And the things that matter to you are always left unreported because they're never said, and an obituary is really about society's view of you...It's a stranger's clinical view of your life, based on criteria of accomplishment.

Then Jud adds what actually it is that, also, literature adds to obituary—the need for the inner story, for a more just representation of the neglected, the lost, and the common:

> This man who reported his own death to read his own obituary—he wants to be acknowledged...he wants everyone to know who he was. And then to correct it and say, actually this is what I'm really about...I think he wanted people to know who he really was...and not in the most shallow sense; he just wanted someone to know who he really was.

That correction is literature, is the second thing.

It is also what the novelist Tim Parks points to, when he says how sick he is of received wisdom. So in a mid-life crisis, your friends tell you it will pass, don't do anything rash, stick with what you have and see it through. And you begin to think, 'This is just me being unreasonable and immature.' It is a conventional sort of second thought that turns back upon you, its apparently reasonableness making you forget or dismiss your individual first thoughts. The advice of those friends and influences, as before with your parents, takes over your own core voice inside:

> For years you accept the logic of this. For years you seek to attach as little value as possible to your experience. Your unhappy experience. It is in your head. Outside your head, *objectively*, you are well off. Happy even. You have a nice house. Your work is going well, or well enough. And of course there are things like children and financial commitments and reputation.[16]

But this is a false objectivity, a denial of what you feel as it flows from within outwards. To hell with it, is Parks's response: it is a false consciousness that ages you and kills your life. Literature can do better that, can restore the sense of lost primacies.

She, he wants to be heard—as to who they really were. So, in trying to replicate on the page the voices of the participants, as independently as possible, I have had to avoid consistency. I have worked tactically instead—according to local context, sometimes providing indented quotations, at others signalling that the story has given way to the protagonist's own words, with or without quotation marks, in the interests of greater immediacy. On many occasions, the thoughts of the participants then become involved in some further thinking that their situation seems to summon or require, or they lead to reports on the wider research arising (in particular in chapter 7). I should also add: most of the participants are given fictional names; some have wanted their own names used, and where this is so, it is indicated; and in some chapters the leading figure is an amalgam of different real-life readers.

But I said there was also a second issue in terms of the organization of this book, which has to do with why I have avoided a conclusion—for which decision I think there are three main reasons.

It is partly to do with trying to let the individuals in each chapter stand somewhat separately, in their own right, in their own detail, as I have said.

Secondly, it is also to do with wanting it to be the reader of this book who finds which chapters most speak to each other. Certain chapters are perhaps more the story of the poem than the story of its readers: chapter 1 on a Shakespeare sonnet, chapter 7 on Renaissance lyrics, chapter 8 on three short lyrics. Some chapters deal with the same poems or the same authors but with different readers: for example, with 'Invictus' across chapters 3 and 4, or in relation to Elizabethan poetics in chapter 2 and chapter 8, or in recurrent references to Wordsworth or George

Eliot, Shakespeare or Tolstoy. And as I have already indicated, the readers themselves are significantly different in age, background, and apparent status. For
example, even at the level of her tastes, the reader of sophisticated modern American poetry in chapter 5, Frances, is very different from the readers in chapters 3, 4, 7,
8, Lesley, Imelda, Donald, Laura, and Evanna, but closer perhaps to the reader of
novels, Georgina, in chapter 9. Then again, certain topics echo across chapters, such
as brain-imaging between chapters 4, 5, and 7, and free indirect discourse between 10
and 11. Or you may perhaps find emergent themes such as 'speaking back' that
resonates between chapter 1 and chapter 5, or the uses of the negative, linking
chapters 1, 7, and 11, or the idea of a future in chapters 6 and 8, in contrast with 10.
Throughout there are signs of what arises out of trauma and the loss of innocence,
out of depression and the loss of meaning, and the competing claims of religious
need and psychological understanding in trying to meet these human difficulties.
Amidst the dense and intricate detail of the involvement, I have tried to break up the
chapters, to offer pauses and provide a variety of both persons and discourses; but
certain chapters may seem to belong more sequentially to those that follow.
Chapter 6 explicitly refers back to chapters 1 and 2. The end of chapter 8 on Bunyan
seems to me to relate to the different journeys undertaken in chapters 9 and 10, and
leads to the end of the book itself through the time-travels of chapter 11.

And yet these are no more than my own suggestions, interests, and impressions,
and as I have said, there is a third reason for avoiding a summary conclusion that
brings all the chapters thematically together. It is that I have not wanted a glib and
pious rounding off on 'the benefits of reading' when the experiences of individuals,
still ongoing in development or jeopardy, are more complicated than such a neat
summary would allow. Much of the initial material for this book is taken from two
research reports, *Cultural Value* funded by the Arts and Humanities Research Council,
and *What Literature Can Do* funded by Guy's and St Thomas' Charity, both of which
may be consulted on the CRILS website.[17] Those reports do offer headings, themes,
findings, and conclusions, the bare bones of which may still be made out in this
book, such as: the importance of felt experience in reading, and the value of the
specific, the small and detailed, and the individual; shared reading as giving a voice
and a language for thought, memory, and emotion; the uses of hesitation, surprise,
uncertainty, and creative inarticulacy; the value of so-called negative experiences
and apparent inabilities; the awakening of new capabilities such as meta-cognition,
reappraisal, and mobility of mind, as against set default patterns and reductive
literalism; shared reading as therapeutic without being a programmed therapy;
the advantages of explorative induction and the working of the executive mind
within genuinely owned neuronal responses from gut or heart, as opposed to

imposed top-down therapies; the value of the group as warm personal community with literature acting as a social glue; the subtle role of the group leader. Further details on this, on case-histories, and methods, may be found in a different context in a companion volume, *Reading and Mental Health*, edited by my long-standing collaborator, Josie Billington, for Palgrave Macmillan.

Instead of a conclusion I do offer a brief afterword, if only to avoid an opposite danger: the danger of shirking the responsibility of saying how important the reading of literature is, and giving some final overall signals of that. I don't want to be mistaken as believing that people who do not read literature are somehow necessarily lesser than those who do. But I believe that the people who in this book do read, are more for have done so, and that that 'more' has to be stood up for.

I am deeply indebted to all the participants here, hoping I have taken no liberties with their generosity, for theirs are acts of reading worthy of respect and admiration in any setting; to members and associates of CRILS, Josie Billington, Rhiannon Corcoran, Chris Dowrick; Richard Bentall, Christophe de Bezenac, David and Helen Constantine, Geoffrey Crossick, David Fearnley, Grace Farrington, Kelda Green, Arthur Jacobs, Kremena Koleva, Esther Harsh, Elisabeth Hill, Phil Jimmieson, Eleanor Longden, Kathryn Naylor, Brian Nellist, Howard Newby, Rick Rylance, Mette Steenberg, Thor Magnus Tangerås, Erin Walsh, and Megan Watkins; but especially to Fiona Magee who helped conduct a large amount of the research and interviewing contained in these pages; to colleagues past and present from *The Reader*, Eamee Boden, Amanda Boston, Katie Clark, Sophie Clarke, Charles Darby-Villis, Ben Davis, Clare Ellis, Penny Fosten, Eleanor McCann, Kate McDonnell, Angela Macmillan, Alexis McNay, and above all the founder of *The Reader*, my wife, Jane Davis. In the world of publishing, my greatest debt is to Jacqueline Norton at Oxford University Press: there too, Eleanor Collins and Aimee Wright were always of great help. There must be a hundred other such dues and influences over the years, I know, but I hope that somehow the debts, conscious and less conscious, are recorded decently in the content of what follows.

CHAPTER 1

NO DEFENCE AGAINST THE WORDS—A STORY OF SONNET 29

Reading this poem, said Keith, suddenly felt like 'reading the writing on the wall'. In rehab for alcoholism—he is in his forties, and at his worst would drink two bottles of whisky a day—he couldn't turn away from the sight of the words before him.

The original for writing on the wall comes from the Book of Daniel at the feast of Belshazzar, the last king of Babylon.

> They drank wine, and praised the gods of gold, and of silver, of brass, of iron, of wood, and of stone.
> In the same hour came forth fingers of a man's hand, and wrote over against the candlestick upon the plaister of the wall of the king's palace: and the king saw the part of the hand that wrote.
> Then the king's countenance was changed, and his thoughts troubled him...
>
> Daniel 5:4–6

Yet the king could not tell what the writing said and called for the wise men of Babylon to interpret it, but they could not. Then his queen told him of a Jewish holy man who many years before had served his father, King Nebuchadnezzar. It is Daniel who is brought forth, only to confront the king with the facts of his drunkenness, sexual debauchery, and worship of false gods: 'and the God in whose hand thy breath is, and whose are all thy ways, hast thou not glorified' (5:23). He then reads aloud the text on the wall which is in Aramaic—'Mene, Mene, Tekel, Upharsin', words to do with currency, weights, and division:

> This is the interpretation of the thing: MENE; God hath numbered thy kingdom, and finished it.
> TEKEL; Thou art weighed in the balances, and art found wanting.
> PERES; Thy kingdom is divided, and given to the Medes and Persians.
>
> 5:26–8

Then, in that night was Belshazzar the king of the Chaldeans slain.

It is like the famous lines written by the twelfth-century Persian poet in *The Rubaiyat of Omar Khayyam*, as translated by Edward FitzGerald between 1859 and 1872:

> The Moving Finger writes; and, having writ,
> Moves on: nor all thy Piety nor Wit
> Shall lure it back to cancel half a Line,
> Nor all thy Tears wash out a Word of it.

What is inscribed in the book of life, even by your deeds, cannot be erased. It is read with a shudder.

The poem Keith saw inescapably on the page in front of him was Shakespeare's sonnet 29, read aloud in a shared reading group set up in a London drug and alcohol rehabilitation centre:

> When, in disgrace with Fortune and men's eyes,
> I all alone beweep my outcast state,
> And trouble deaf heaven with my bootless cries,
> And look upon myself and curse my fate,
> Wishing me like to one more rich in hope,
> Featur'd like him, like him with friends possess'd,
> Desiring this man's art and that man's scope,
> With what I most enjoy contented least;
> Yet in these thoughts myself almost despising,
> Haply I think on thee, and then my state,
> Like to the lark at break of day arising
> From sullen earth, sings hymns at heaven's gate:
>   For thy sweet love remember'd such wealth brings
>   That then I scorn to change my state with kings.

Unlike the king in the Bible, the recovering alcoholic did not need any interpreter or translator beyond himself. The line that first almost literally hit him, Keith says, was *'Yet in these thoughts myself almost despising'*: 'That's the one that really strikes.' It was like seeing so much of what he had previously been doing and thinking, now 'in the light of day'. One of the women in his group thinks there is a bit of hope, a chink of possibility, in that 'almost'—not completely despising, leaving the tiniest space for what 'haply' may bring later in the poem. Keith doesn't think that. He thinks 'almost' is like a sort of terrible gulp on the brink of the next word that can hardly be brought out for being so terrible: 'almost - despising myself'. And he also thinks how impossible it is wholly and truthfully, 100 per cent, to despise yourself, because you who are doing the despising have still to remain being the despised person— unless, that is, you commit suicide. Keith has tried that twice, we learn later.

He admits this during an interview while he watches excerpts of the session from a video recording:

> You read it and it strikes home. I wanted to deny that line when I first read it: I wanted to think that I didn't really despise myself. But...[*he sighs*] no...I did despise myself, and half wanted to and half wanted not to. So now when I see these things in print, they strike home. And once you become aware of something, you cannot turn back, you can't *unknow*.

'Nor all thy Tears wash out a Word of it.'

There is nothing more characteristic of the most heartfelt responses in Shared Reading than that use of the double negative: 'You cannot unknow.' Oona, from another group, reading lines from the American poet Dorianne Laux, 'For the Sake of Strangers'—'No matter what the grief, its weight,/ we are obliged to carry it'—says of her own reluctant feeling of having to carry the burden of widowhood: 'I'm afraid I know that. I can't say I don't know that because I do.' *I cannot say I don't* is how readers may have to approach what lays bare their hurt, backing into it with all the value of what is soberly surprised and almost involuntary. So Keith: 'You can't unknow. When I see these things in print...' It is the very print in its external permanence that 'strikes home', as though something vulnerable and unformulated, hidden away in private behind the reader's forehead, had suddenly appeared, undeniable, in front of his eyes. It is not only the apparently external objectivity of the thing, nor its near-physical effect on the psyche. That word 'home' is also ruefully vulnerable in this context, as though something of yours had come back from a different place for admission to its own again. You try unconsciously to leave some of your worst acts out there in the world to fade away amidst all the other stuff that is happening there, and be forgotten, says Keith: as much as you can you leave the bad things behind you in the past. And then one day they return upon you, come home to roost as we say. Shame and guilt come in, and you think how much you've wasted. That return is what reading can be when you see it written out almost publicly like that.[1] It reflects back on you, like a secret private message just for you:

> ... in disgrace with Fortune and men's eyes,
> I all alone beweep my outcast state,
> And trouble deaf heaven with my bootless cries
> And look upon myself...

You *look upon yourself* (line 4), says someone else in Keith's group, but also *through [other] men's eyes* (line 1). That is how it becomes the shame of 'myself almost despising' (line 9). It seems good and important, somehow, that a reader can do that: not just go serially on from line 1 to 2 and 3 and 4 but put together 4 with 1 and then 9. All our research is about what we call these important-somehows: those little moments of ability that seem bigger or subtler than we quite know. From 'in disgrace with *Fortune*' (line 1) to 'And look upon myself and curse my *Fate*' (line 4): that is how it hardens when what first seemed Bad Luck then becomes your settled Doom. Unless '*haply*' I think of thee (10): a hap against fixed destiny, a chance that seems related to the seemingly lost chance of happ-iness again.

Otherwise I can only 'trouble deaf heaven with my bootless cries'. Group members can feel that terrible interaction between 'deaf' and 'bootless', even if many do not quite know that bootless means 'useless'. One of the other men says, in a plaintive tone himself, 'He's not being *heard*...' Another adds that, even so, 'The crying won't stop, there's no end to it.' Their voices sound different as though the poem has got into them.

Two years later, when we return to see him for a second interview, Keith offers us more of his autobiographical background:

> The poem just gets you. Probably the best way I could describe it is...looking at old photos and having memories come back and going 'I nearly forgot that!' And you can feel a sort of tingle...of the sensation you had at the time. So you might see what?...me and my brothers on the beach and you go 'Ah!' and then you have that half a tingle of joy of running along the beach and you go 'Oh yeah! I forgot about going there...altogether.'
>
> And then in my world I *shape or re-shape it* and go: 'Oh yeah, they was chasing me to beat me up. Yeah, they didn't want me there anyway so they were chasing me', and then I've changed it, to lessen the hurt.
>
> But my first impression I can't lie about. I look at that photo and I feel that tingle and I go 'Oh yeah I...!' [*said excitedly*] but then I'll go 'Oh yeah, now I remember' [*said depressively*]. But the first impression is like a kind of instinct unawares, before all the old secondary stuff comes back to protect or depress me.

Keith's father died when he was six; he was the youngest of four brothers and one sister brought up by the bereaved mother. He was the one who always blushed under accusation, even when he had done nothing wrong. So, he felt he had to be constantly watchful of everything, trying to avert the bad thing that might happen, and then it happens anyway. Keith's reaction to a line of poetry is something like an older version of that blush, though he is seemingly a big rough bloke now. Still it gets through his secondary defences.

The message from the family environment of his childhood was '"Boys don't cry, don't be stupid. If you're gonna do that, we're all just gonna take the mickey and pick on you." So you had to—well you didn't have to—but as a protection mechanism you shut it down, and you go, "No, it doesn't affect me whatsoever. I don't care what you do."' Alcohol later allowed him to cry as 'a release', he says, but it did not solve anything because afterwards he did not feel any better. In the group session he had recalled some of what he calls the wallowing feeling of that time, through that sonnet. The lines about wishing himself 'like to one more rich in hope', 'like him, like him', 'desiring this man's art and that man's scope'—he does not so much paraphrase as act out a self-despising parody of them which in self-pity, he says, he had played out again and again in his own head: '*He's* got everything over there! And look at *her* over here! And then look at *me!* Nobody cares.'

When we had first interviewed him, a few months after the Shakespeare session, he said this about his primary emotional response to the poem:

> What with books and poems, it makes you look at things honestly. And it's harder to tell lies around them....It's about feelings, there's feelings, so you're talking about feelings, *and* feeling them as you do. [In therapy groups] you're talking only about actions or behaviours.

In the addiction therapy group, everything you say often seems no more than plausible. 'In therapy you are being asked questions. You give a ready answer, but you're often not sure if that's even what you really think.' You don't have to be honest, and you don't feel quite honest in any really specific and definite way. You are not '*in* my thoughts' as the poem says, as if they have an inside. 'Yet in these thoughts myself almost despising...' Instead, you can avoid the issue in the therapy sessions, says Keith, and get away with it by using words as distancing substitutes, in a set agenda:

> You can mess about with it. What they want to hear is—well, personally what I thought they wanted to hear was—'Yeah I had a really bad day the other day, I really fancied a drink, but I sat down and I thought No, it won't be just one, it's never just one, so I got through it', and they'll go, 'Oh well done' and I'd walk out of there and go 'Psht'...If I was getting only comfortable thoughts in all the groups that I was going to, I would not change my behaviour.

For Keith, the Shared Reading group was (beneficially) not 'comfortable' because of the abrupt, unexpected, and involuntary emotional involvement that got under his defences. It jump-started his life again, when the words suddenly felt real, and closed the sense of distance.

In Shared Reading it never works if people in the group start talking before feeling or instead of it. That is why the group leaders make sure the poem gets read and re-read, until its felt voice is established in the room as a human presence. And it does not have to provide a comfortable or positive feeling. It is as the American poet Baron Wormser (one of whose poems will figure in chapter 8) polemically puts it:

> People sometimes asked me. 'Are your poems happy or sad, because I don't want to read any sad poems that are going to depress me.' I told them what poetry cared about was feeling. It didn't care about emotional distinctions.[2]

It does care about emotional distinctions but that comes later: the first thing is the immediate liveness of the communicated feeling, before ever it is negotiated or interpreted. That is why group leaders are committed to a three-phase pattern in any session. First phase, Getting In: just trying to get the poem or story alive in the room, trying to get people into its feel. Second, Staying In: reading and re-reading the poem, where repetition is not like it is in other forms of life, getting less and less powerful; but staying with individual lines, phrases, words, so that group members do not get out of the experience through objections or digressions or undue speed but are immersed. And if they can stay in it long enough, then thirdly, something must happen, something must give, in the build-up of feeling, within the saturated solution. That is the final phase, Break-Through: the poem striking home, forcing out thoughts in its readers and a sudden articulation of them. It is not a mechanical procedure: the phases interchange, and sometimes that breakthrough happens almost at once as it did for Keith with one line from sonnet 29. Keith is unusually quick in this. But one thing is reliable in the working of human processes: if you can keep the people immersed in the poem for long enough, something must and will come out.

The 'cannot turn back' and 'can't unknow' condition of change marks the point at which emotions begin to reclaim their evolutionary value as useful. Originally fear, to take the obvious example, would be useful as a warning, in its survival value as indicative of present external danger. In further human development, it may become objectless anxiety and counter-productive. But here in reading, emotions are restored to urgent messages of feeling that usefully tell of a now more internal fact, a psychological reality which, equally, should not be ignored, in the interests of well-being at a higher evolved level of survival. This may be one important reason why reading matters and why it works.

This experience of vital feeling happens still to us, the research team, when we watch the videos, and ourselves feel the poem again, even though already well-known, through the new live responses of the other people we see.

So: sonnet 29 repeated, for example, in another drug and rehabilitation unit, this time in Liverpool rather than London. Seven men at the end each read out-loud two lines of the poem, and apparently by chance it is the physically worst affected in the group, a young man made old with the results of his addiction who reads haltingly and with a slur—as if even so every word is made to matter through the very disability:

> Wishing me like to one more rich in hope,
> Featur'd like him, like him with friends possess'd

'Like him, like him' cries out through the middle of the line. It is what the Elizabethan poet and critic George Puttenham called the underlay or cuckoo spell, like a hidden message of the heart played in momentary counterpoint against the onward movement of the passing line, and it still works.[3] This reader through whose mouth these words come haltingly is so very much not 'like him', not rich in hope, nor with friends possess'd, and we do not know precisely how much he feels and realizes what he has read or how much we would want him to.

But the person running the group is in the midst of it and unlike the researchers watching the video, cannot sit back. In Keith's session, the group leader from *The Reader* wanted still to hold onto that line 'myself almost despising', staying in it, to say:

> **When I think about the times when I have almost despised myself for what I have done ... That's not like, oh damn it how did that happen? It's like truly horrified at myself, and that's a different level of experience.**

Immediately, testing whether that different level is really there, another group member, Peter asks her, 'Are you speaking from experience as well?' It is a crucial moment of silence that follows, which the research team intently watches. If she hesitates now, or evades the issue by retaining her position as facilitator, the situation is lost and the group as a unit of equal human beings is broken. Instead she says—not without pain:

> **Yes! I have despised myself. I remember when I really hurt a friend, I thought: How could I do that, how I could be that person, I don't want to be the person who could do that to somebody. But once you *are* that person, you just have to look at yourself, *look* at yourself 'and curse my fate'.**

In addiction groups where participants have received considerable counselling, one of the challenges for the group leader in Shared Reading is to move group members on from repeated learned responses such as 'Speaking as an addict', or 'This is like addiction'. Through the poetic triggering of sudden feelings and memories, the aim was to stimulate a wider and more spontaneous human discourse that freed people from the set vocabulary of cases in therapy or conditions in recovery. When at that moment the group leader dared to speak like an equivalent bungler herself, the situation was no longer to do with addiction. If in some sense the poem does not care about what feelings it may be responsible for engendering as long as they are alive and felt, it is also that the poem does not know or care whom it is addressing, there are no 'cases'.

Back in the Liverpool rehab unit, a different group leader latches onto another single line:

> Desiring this man's art and that man's scope,
> With what I most enjoy contented least

'This may come as a surprise to you,' she confesses, laughing, 'but I really love *reading!*' (And the men laugh too, feigning incredulity because, as they say, what they have really loved are drugs and alcohol.) 'Yes, I know it's a bit of a shocker...But I went through a time in my life when I suffered a lot of anxiety and I got to the point when I couldn't read. Then the sight of the books made me more unhappy than anything else.' It leads another group member to talk how he loved to take his dog for a walk, and though his dog is still allowed with him in the centre, all he can do is take him for little walks just round and round the institutional garden. 'And I hate it. The same thing over and over again, the repetitiveness. And I used to love it. And I feel the difference.' That is when a person becomes aware of his or her own separateness: when what once made you happy now makes you sad; when something happy in a poem causes sadness in its reader; when mixed feelings do not allow planned and simple responses. On the films the team can almost see and hear at such moments a person's inner sense of individuality, of individual experience, as though the innermost part that recognizes the contrasts and contradictions is what the reading helps to release. Crucially, in the act of reading that higher centre of awareness is generated from below upwards, as a consequence of something no longer able to be easily or automatically integrated by cognitive efficiency. The short-term 'best guess' or 'good enough' description will not do, and the survival-based drive for it is over-ridden by a need to get closer to the heart of things. Keith speaks of almost being forced to the level at which you can actually see what you're thinking, and what you have been doing, rather than just staying in your general feeling about life. It is what the psychologists call the creation of a meta-level of mentality, where metacognition means awareness and understanding of one's own thought processes.

At the first interview he gave us, Keith had already said that sonnet 29 made him more honest and helped keep him straighter, as if the poem said to him that it would have to be the honest way from now on, and he couldn't unknow that. Academics often speak of the multiplicity of interpretations, the indeterminacy of a text. But there is something more urgently demanding here than the luxury of ingenious alternatives. In a therapy session without being *in* the feeling you might say anything plausible, not knowing if it was true or if you really meant it; but for Keith, feelings springing up in response to literature, even within areas of doubt and complexity, have greater immediate personal conviction than he normally has:

> Now I know what I am talking about. In many ways it takes such a burden off, keeping up the pretence or telling the lies. I don't have to remember anything, to cover my story when I am making things up in defence—because I've told the truth. The first thing is the actual thing that *gets* me.

Two years later, he finds himself more willing to stay with the first felt impressions he cannot lie about. He says when he is reading now, he tends not to try to 'shape' what is happening at some second stage that fits better with what he wants or needs it to be. Instead, 'I tend to look at what I've got and rotate it, turn it round and round in my head, adjusting to it.' He actually now likes the fact that the language and their author can resist him, as if resistance was a sign of some other reality, the relief of a reality he has to acknowledge and examine rather than evade or control. 'The Moving finger writes, and having writ,/ Moves on': nothing can 'lure it back to cancel half a line'.

We ask him to explain more of what he means by 'shaping' the text to fit his own preconceptions, in contrast to what has now become, he believes, a more honest way of reading. 'If I'm reading a story,' he explains, 'and—to simplify—it says "Peter thought Malcolm was being a real idiot", then I know what Peter's thinking. You don't get that in real life, you don't get that in film—you might only get someone interpreting. Here, in reading, it seems like you are almost a God-like thing.' That certainly is what the psychologists call a meta-level, but they could see it as a dangerous delusion. When asked to say more about that, Keith responds by saying very quietly, 'It's about *power*', almost not saying this word out loud, and only just doing so, as if it was dangerous to admit the secret.

K: You can see everything. It's *you*. It's exhilarating. You're going 'I know what he's thinking about Malcolm and he don't like Malcolm, and he's saying he likes Malcolm but I know he doesn't, and Malcolm, you are in for a big shock at some stage if you come to know as I do that this guy don't like you.' I can see everything around him. Or, I can see part of it, and I make up the rest of the jigsaw. So the author gives me a part of it and I'll go 'I'm gonna make this complete picture'. And then I may begin to think like I have in the past that I have got all this pegged and sorted.

But then the author will do something, something different, and I'm like 'I'll have to get rid of that picture, have to replace that now, because he's changed it.' Peter's first of all got this look on his face, like 'Ahhhh, I see all through you, Malcolm' and that's me—that hasn't been written in the book. That's me: I'm giving that look. And then the author might go 'And then Peter winked at him' and I'll go 'That wasn't quite the look I was after, so *I'm* going to have to change'.

Interviewer: Because you're not controlling what's written, are you? And yet it seems a strange mix of taking up control and giving up control, all at once?

K: I'm controlling *around* it. And then adapting what the author's given me and if the author changes something, *I* change. It's like when some actor is given a script and they've got a certain licence to ad-lib, and to work out the backstory, but don't go too far off-key in their mind because otherwise the character just goes.

Interviewer: So it's like the reader performs the text, like a sort of real-life actor in his own head, in a mental theatre. I remember myself, as a child, trying to remake on my own, in pretend play, the book I had just been reading...So, in what you describe, you're taking yourself *out* of the equation, by not just shaping the poem or story to what you want it to be; but in a way isn't that also actually putting you back in it more, somehow?

K: I have been very judgemental in my life, including the wallow of passing judgement on myself. It is because I have wanted to see people in black or white, and have made do with that. That is what I mean about getting things pegged and reinforced, already set in concrete. But yes, what gets in the way of that rigidness, through reading, lets something else of me in instead. And I've got to that bit of me more, and can have it more, *and* let it move about more, over the last two years. That is what thinking is like when it *comes back at you*, in the feedback and in the readjustments.

That is complicated, and we ask for an example. Keith remembered reading Somerset Maugham's novel, *The Painted Veil* (1925) over some weeks in the reading group. In it a pretty young socialite Kitty Garstin is persuaded by her mother to settle in marriage for Walter Fane, a bookish and rather cold physician. But not far into the marriage she begins an affair, which Walter only finds out about after it has been going on for two years. The deception, the prolonged dishonesty, makes him almost monstrously cruel towards her. In the group, some of the participants were saying how horrible Walter had become, but Keith had privately identified with him, and so Keith was thinking: 'They are talking about somebody in the book, they don't even know they are talking about me.' And there also was a woman in the group Keith respected, called Sarah, who for her part strongly identified with Kitty. And that, he says, 'forced' him to think more from Kitty's perspective. But he kept trying to come back to the fact that Kitty has had this affair, that she is cheating. 'Come on,' he says to himself, 'just remember the fact. She's cheating. But you can't remember just that, you're getting the different thoughts...' The felt reality of the woman is so powerfully present that the thought of conventional morality is forgotten unless it can be imaginatively recovered at an equivalent deep level. And then feeling less protected, and turning to Walter at his worst, it was for Keith as it had been with 'in these thoughts myself almost despising'—what of ill he saw in Walter, now that he had also to take Kitty seriously, hurt him:

> But he was only fictional and I was real. So I was worse than he was because somebody made him up to show how nasty people can be but I was actually living it.

His mind felt giddy, turned from outside back in, from the fictional to its real counterpart. One moment, you're safe and separately insulated, you can read it as if it were another person, acting as a buffer; the next it's you in some unwritten text you don't want to see spelled out so. But at almost the same time in the thick of things he could also understand why Walter had become the man he was, and feel for him. This was what Keith meant when he said that, immersed in a book, he became 'a sort of...' (and again he hesitated to say it) 'spiritual figure looking over these people, and able to go in and out of them'.

This is what the experience of literary thinking has become like for Keith. There was no longer the simple equivalence of the naming word and the thing it refers to, and an easy passage from one to the other. There is now a *third* thing, a reader aware between the two, trying to work out in his mind the relationship between text and world, going to and fro in various relations between himself and the book, in that area of imaginative feeling that the book had opened up.[4] Keith wants to start a second life: reading has been like a second go at thinking about life.

*

And the second movement of sonnet 29, the sestet, is important in offering an alternative to the shame of the first eight lines.

Initially overwhelmed by the words, Sarah from Keith's group said that, though she normally didn't like Shakespeare and could not understand him, she was glad that the group leader had begun by breaking the poem up into temporary sections, because now she could *follow* it more. Keith said that what really followed, above all, was a huge shift in this second movement, a tremendous weight lifted off the poet's shoulders. And just as that line about self-despising had hit him hard, so now something 'hits the speaker himself on the head—and it's love':

> Yet in these thoughts myself almost despising
> Haply I think on thee, and then my state,
> Like to the lark at break of day arising
> From sullen earth, sings hymns at heaven's gate:
>> For thy sweet love remember'd such wealth brings
>> That then I scorn to change my state with kings.

But there are always failures to feel this. It is painful when some groups can't get there, as happens when they can't get out of the depressed first half of the poem. One young man in the Liverpool rehab group manages it, when suddenly he says: 'A foundation. It lays a foundation, doesn't it, in those rising lines…t-t-t-to be strong from.' But it isn't a foundation, if the other people in the room can find nothing in it to build upon. Then the poem is lost, and made weak and non-existent save as unfulfilled words. And that is not just about the poem, but about what the poem stands for as an area of feeling for human beings to occupy. '"Thy sweet love remember'd": can you think of anything equivalent in *your* lives?' the group leader had to dare to ask the unhappy and perhaps unloved people in her rehab group, fighting for the poem's existence with all the risk of silence or even No in reply. She says later to me, 'To make the old poem real we have to be able to connect it to real lives, to the feeling of a real experience. Only later, when people do this more naturally, can we try to do more abstract literary reading—though I never much want to do that myself, I like staying in the everyday reality. Not Art for Art's Sake but, as D. H. Lawrence said, Art for My Sake. What's hard, however, is constantly making the connection to ordinary reality *and* to complex language.'

In the story of the reading of a poem, one of the roles of the research group, we believe, is to choose the group session, or the single moments within different groups, when amidst all the difficulties of recognition, a poem finds the ones in life who seem most to need it, to be able to feel it and let it be alive again.

So here in relation to the close of sonnet 29 is a group that meets in a mental health drop-in centre in a poor area of Liverpool represented by high levels of deprivation and long-term unemployment. The five members present each have a confirmed diagnosis of depression, with several also struggling with anxiety. Of the three women, one is in her eighties and recently widowed; there is a single mother, depressed and with some learning disabilities whose two children have been previously in care; and also a middle-aged woman who is new to the group and is, she says, an experienced and avid reader. The two men are more self-contained than the women, and appreciate each other's company particularly since they tend to lack confidence in the group context. The oldest woman Beryl, who speaks first, presents herself as a stroppy person, suffering from severe depression but hating the counselling therapy which she is required to attend weekly. She says:

> 'In disgrace, all alone, out-cast.' This man doesn't feel in connection with people, feels outside of everything—But I hate Shakespeare. I can't stand him. No I really don't like Shakespeare.

The group leader asks, 'Why is it you don't like him?'

> I just don't like him, I don't like the verse, I don't like his poetry, I just don't like Shakespeare. When we were doing it at school, it was absolutely boring, I couldn't stand it. And all those teachers and professors making too much of it.

The more experienced reader, Margaret, interjects: 'At the beginning it's really down and out, "*outcast state*", lonely and self-disgusted, and yet at the end, "I scorn to change my *state* with kings"—it's like on top of the world...' And the group leader asks, subtly, '*Where* does it change, do you think?'

Change and the ability to locate the seeds or inklings of it is vital, but it is *where*, not how or why, that is being asked first of all: the *place* first is the rule; the explanation if any, only afterwards. Another member of the group, Lesley whom we will meet again in chapter 3, is the quiet, not very articulate one; but it is she who simply points to the place—and not to the obvious turn of 'Yet' at the beginning of line 9 where the misery actually goes on one step more, even in commencing the sestet, but to line 10:

> There, line 10: Haply I think of thee.
> [*Group leader re-reads:*]
>
> > Yet in these thoughts myself almost despising
> > Haply I think on thee, and then my state,
> > Like to the lark at break of day arising
> > From sullen earth, sings hymns at heaven's gate

'It's there. Can't explain,' Lesley ends by saying, in danger of the things she sees not getting picked up, or not becoming more verbally completed by anyone else. But she is the one who can almost always do that great first thing, by a kind of genius regardless of learning difficulties: she can intuitively but precisely point to the vital place.

It is a sort of coded movement, in poetry's telegraphese or braille-like score. That is to say: 'in these *thoughts myself*' (9) is myself stuck in his thoughts; but these repeated thoughts are released into 'I' suddenly 'thinking'—'I *think*' (10)—and changed by thinking, instead of something else, '*on thee*'. It is what Arthur, a participant from another group, called '*doing* reading' rather than just talking about it:

> It means that your mind is in action. The mind is in action and also your feelings are in action, you're feeling something. It's like when you care for somebody...you don't go 'Oh I think you're wonderful', you express it by the way you are with the person. You might say sometimes 'I love you' but that's not the important thing, it's the way you express by your emotions towards something, the way you do it.

Of course literature is all about language, but as soon as the separate individual words begin to join and work together, in the electrical dance of a line or sentence, it ceases to be simply about naming, communicating, or processing an item-by-item message. There is something to point to that is certainly lodged deep in the language but not just of it; that is the third dimension of meaning arising out of the more visibly literal two dimensions on the page. And Lesley can point to the places where it happens in and between the words. Because that is what language most primally was before ever it got into the formalities of script or print: it was a form of pointing to the world, what in linguistics is called deixis (there! here! this! that! now! then!) subsequently turned into subtler representation through the internal-pointings and self-signallings of grammar on the page.[5] It is like what the poet Les Murray describes in an essay on 'Embodiment and Incarnation' in poetry, remembering a conversation he had about a particular poem with a serious but everyday reader whom he knew well:

> 'I came to that place in the poem,' as a friend said to me once, 'and clunk! my mind turned inside out, quite painlessly. "Huh?" I said, and read that bit again, and it happened again, precisely there, and I couldn't explain it to myself.'[6]

'Precisely *there*' is the act of deixis, pointing however not just to a single name-word but to 'that place' repeatedly created and re-created by the words. That is the first act of reading, to find those places that turn the mind inside-out, or the page outside-in. And interestingly it has to be made non-verbal, or returned to the pre-verbal again, by the very force of what is verbal. It has to go back to wherever it is, in mind inchoately, that the words come from. More articulate explaining comes later, if at all.

Lesley needs the others to follow on if she can't, or she will be left feeling stranded, as if something that should live had died And remarkably, following Lesley, it is Beryl, who has been so constantly saying that she does not like Shakespeare, who now comes back in again and picks up Lesley's baton, and suddenly sounds moved—almost literally moved out of her habitual position, her voice surprised and quite different:

> Isn't that a beautiful verse: happily I think on thee and then my state like the lark at break of day rising. Isn't that lovely, isn't that lovely. I don't really like him—but that is beautiful.

Lesley's pointing action is re-performed here by the demonstrative 'Isn't *that* . . .' The specific focus which this brings allows Beryl momentarily to forget that generally she hates Shakespeare. She hasn't really forgotten, and will stubbornly remind us in her next sentence ('I don't really like him . . .'), but for the moment all she can think about is the beauty of this particular bit, such that rather nicely she misreads 'haply' (= perhaps) for 'happily'. She speaks in a somewhat different tone of voice, more quietly (and we are currently looking for physiological means that can measure such things in their change from the vocal norm), saying repeatedly and rhythmically, half to or in herself: 'Isn't that lovely, isn't that lovely.'

Research into transcripts from reading groups indicates—through changes of tone, vocabulary, heartrate, or body language—that whenever anyone finds something 'beautiful', something good is happening that lifts readers and gives them another, so to speak, cleaner or purer place to be. And with different people on different occasions in different groups, that word 'beautiful' is very quickly associated with a word that frequently follows it: the word is, almost invariably, 'lovely'. It is not just about aesthetics, it is about love. Often with males, particularly in tough settings such as rehab or prison, it is defensively prefaced by the word 'soft'. So, thinking of Shakespeare's lark arising, one of the men says:

> Listen, I'm not being soft, but it if you get up on a cold winter's morning and hear the robin singing outside your room, inside this institution, it is lifting, comforting. It is a change of mind; it's a change of—heart.

Some of these group members from all across the country are undergoing counselling, suffering from depression or chronic pain. But the felt language of the beautiful and—better—the lovely and the loved at such moments replaces the directive language of therapy.

Back in Beryl and Lesley's group:

Group leader: Look at it move across the line:

> 'Like to the lark at break of day arising
> From sullen earth, sings hymns at heaven's gate'

The poem's syntax manages to say of the lark both that it is 'arising/ From sullen earth', from the depressive pull of that sullen-ness, AND 'From sullen earth sings hymns at heaven's gate': it is a double movement by Shakespeare, giving an extra lift.

Beryl: And that's what the lark does, doesn't it, it goes up to heaven, doesn't it; but larks sing right up there, you can't even see them.

Margaret: You can't see the larks when they are so high, but you hear them.

Group leader: 'Sings hymns at heaven's gate' sent out instead of those 'bootless cries' of his own to 'deaf heaven' earlier, when heaven wouldn't even listen.

Between Beryl and Margaret, this is like imagination: that what cannot be seen can be made out in another sense, through hearing, and can be brought to mind in that way. Popular self-help books talk all the time, all too easily, about making 'changes' in your life, urging them upon you. That beautiful lark-rise of the heart— and the recognition of it—already makes a change, without ever demanding a change.[7] It marks the unforced arrival of the lost memory of love and beauty creating a moral shift in the level of being. That a poem could do that—create one mood, the downer of the first eight or nine lines, and then immediately lift it up again—astonishes. 'Haply', by free chance, is not a recovery strategy. But it is a lifting change across the lines—'arising/ from sullen earth', and 'from sullen earth sings hymns'—translating the lark from one sense to another, from sight to hearing; an alternative sense activated in writing for the sake of what is less immediately visible or tangible in life. It is peaceable especially for those who have known little peace of mind.

Keith in his session called it 'an epiphany: a lark-rise in the head'. By the end of the poem, as a result, its speaker no longer wants 'to change his state' with anyone's. The writer Erwin James told the audience at a *Reader* event that it was this poem, sonnet 29, that imprisoned for murder, he had sent from his cell, to his estranged daughter, like a message in a bottle to her, especially in those last five lines. 'I think on thee...'

In contrast, the poet Don Patterson writing a commentary on Sonnet 29 does not feel it personally at all:

> As Shakespearian arguments go, 'whenever I feel awful, I think about you and then I feel much better' isn't up there with his most sophisticated; but it's a pretty enough poem, I suppose. It's really no more than flowery periphrasis. There's very little here to lift it out of the mundane.[8]

Patterson dismisses the poem as unoriginal fluff, as repetitively sentimental. But it is ironic that he finds very little in this poem to *lift* it out of the mundane when actually we have just seen the poem lift people emotionally out of silent depression, precisely because of the lark arising from sullen earth. The poem offers a second chance—which arises when you can think of one person, one thing, still of loving value surviving even the worst.

With all the risks of presumption, we have to help people to *read*, even educated people, and to immerse themselves in a densely emotional communal place, rather than just scan and process, offering paraphrased opinions in which they appear already to know all about whatever it is that is under consideration. So in CRILS's brain-imaging experiments,[9] we have provided as a test a more prosaic example of our sonnet that goes straightforwardly thus:

> Yet though I almost hate myself,
> When I think of you my bad mood lifts
> Like a bird at morning time rising from the ground
> To the sky and singing happily up there

It is always 'on the up'. But in the real poetry:

> Yet in these thoughts myself almost despising
> Haply I think on thee, and then my state,
> Like to the lark at break of day arising
> From sullen earth, sings hymns at heaven's gate

Participants notice how Shakespeare's verse here goes from 'arising', back down again to 'sullen earth', before going up again finally to singing at heaven's gate. The poem's deep 'self-help' message is this: we must not go with the simplest meanings, the easiest routes to apparent progress; we must not know in advance, but follow the meaning through all its unexpected turns and changes, the good and the bad, including the unease and disease. We cannot and should not try to exclude the downers, the sullen earth, the recurrent setbacks. They are a relative part of our experience and human beings must try to use all their time, not just the uppers, the apparently good bits. Any chance of happiness or well-being lies not in trying to forget the sullen earth but in the ability to include it in life's whole meaning. That, and not simple 'positivity' as it is called, is true health.

This is poetry that, nonetheless, can also exist in good prose. There was a shared reading group taking place in London, in a facility for people suffering from psychosis: the participants were often sedated and not all of them literate. They struggled through *Snow Goose*, a novella written by Paul Gallico in 1941, on the unlikely friendship that forms between Philip, a reclusive and disabled artist living in an abandoned lighthouse, and an uneducated young local girl, Fritha, who brings to him for aid a bird, wounded by gunshot. Restored, the bird returns each year for seven years in its migration. Towards the end of the story, Philip takes his small sailing boat to Dunkirk, to evacuate the stranded troops from the German invasion, but after several excursions saving many lives, is finally lost at sea. Then it is that Fritha thinks she recognizes in the bird flying overhead the soul of the artist she has grown to admire and love—as though, now dead, he was taking a last farewell from the sky above her. Jim who had rarely spoken during many weeks, whose vocabulary normally was monosyllabic, suddenly said that, in watching the bird, the girl was 'lifted by her emotion for it'. So for the moment was he: it was not a simple way of formulating it. Then Jim spoke of the work ending with making an 'enormous sky over whatever we most hold dear'; 'the big picture' over and above all the details is what Jim calls it, concluding: 'If you think big, it can take you away from schizophrenia even for a few minutes.' The group leader later read them the Hopkins poem, 'The Windhover', to go alongside the story: 'My heart in hiding/ Stirred for a bird'.

The possibility that something good which people had thought long lost, damaged, or spoiled for ever, even by themselves, could still be retrieved as from the time before the tarnishing: that potential is the opposite of experience seen only as a pattern of ever increasing disillusionment or deterioration.

Sometimes these effects of a work of literature are finally best stored and consummated in a re-energized version of the language of philosophy or psychology, as if the revitalization of a crucial thought for meaning was what the embodied feeling of the poem was reaching for, beyond mere paraphrased message. Sometimes it attaches instead to a personal event which stands as shorthand for it. But sometimes it is *another* work of literature that clinches the meaning, revealing itself in this new usage not just as expressive art in its own terms, but as thought at its most far-reaching.[10] In the story of sonnet 29, the force of 'recovery' for those lifted by their reading is not just in 'moving on' forwards, as the self-help books so often say, but in being able to recover, backwards as it were, the good feeling which long had seemed left behind in disillusionment or ruin. And this potential for life is perhaps best brought back and thought about in the words of George Herbert, in that other great poem of lift from depression, 'The Flower':

> Who would have thought my shrivell'd heart
> Could have recovered greenness? It was gone
> Quite underground...

Question: 'Recovered greenness': it was gone. Who would have thought it? Answer: Not I, certainly, not at heart. Nor could almost anyone. No reasonable human being could expect or predict that. But for George Herbert, as it were: God knows.

*

In Keith's group, Sarah talks of the reading that speaks most to her: 'It's like when I think in my head and I always think, "Someone else has already said that." Some people don't like that feeling, but I really do. When I read a book, it makes me think of what they say: that your life's written in a book.'

But the writing on the wall often strikes home most when it works its message not through identification but through the shock of translation.

When another prophet had to approach another king in admonishment of murder and adultery, he did his work not directly but by parable, that the king might be wakened not to outer anger but to inward penitence. This time it was Nathan who came to King David after he had ordered the murder of his own soldier, Uriah the Hittite, and taken his beautiful wife Bathsheba, whom he had already made pregnant in her husband's absence. Nathan told the king the tale of a traveller who took nothing from the rich man, but instead from the poor man took the one beloved ewe-lamb he had. David was angry at the thought of such a man: he should repay four-fold the loss of the lamb and suffer death. To which Nathan said simply, 'Thou art the man...'

By the riddle, what had seemed safely external was given a sudden turn inward, and the text—spoken or written—had come back at him, as though now from behind his own eyes.

In later days, more secular and lonely, George Eliot writes for the aged clerical scholar Casaubon of the difference when, after his doctor leaves him, the common-place 'We must all die' transforms itself suddenly into the acute personal consciousness 'I must die—and soon' (*Middlemarch*, chapter 42). 'It makes a difference, all the difference, when it is *you*,' a student once said to me on reading this passage, 'And that also includes what it would be like *if* it was you—as it could, may, and will be'. This personal dimension which lifts the poem or story off the page comes with a sudden recognition that words seem to have long held in store for us meanings that are realized only individually. As if the words were like the experience of the race, the DNA of complex vocabulary which we spell out in different ways in different lives. It is strange to find your personal feelings on the other side of what had seemed external and impersonal words. It is as though the words were little minds of help, contained memory networks, bearing traces of what human beings over ages have experienced and thought.

'*Thou* art the man.' Readers discover themselves, back-to-front so to speak, by finding what unpremeditatedly moves them. It is not just straightforwardly liking the poem or identifying with it. It is more like the human subject finding himself or herself through involvement in the sudden object of their concern. Then it is not what the people say they are, or think they are, that is most trustworthy, but what in the act of reading they actually *do*—that is: feel, point at, think, or say, unforeseen in the moment.

Keith knows these processes—feels the change he needs when 'thy sweet love remember'd' comes back on him even in the midst of 'myself almost despising'. One last poem in this chapter, for his reading group, is Robert Frost's 'Revelation'—the first stanza which particularly affected Keith goes:

> We make ourselves a place apart
>   Behind light words that tease and flout,
> But oh, the agitated heart
>   Till someone find us really out.

The place apart is an apparently safe place where the self is within its own self-imposed boundaries. It is a defensive response to the feeling which Sarah describes in relation to other people in her life: 'You're not seeing my pain. Why can't they see I'm in pain, why don't they offer? To invite me, or whatever.' And of course the hurt withdrawal further adds to the impossibility of being recognized. But there are still those attempted 'light words that tease'. The group leader asks Keith a good question, 'Why do we still do that with a good friend?' And he replies, like the child who had to learn the vulnerably canny game: 'Because I think it's a mechanism to check if they still know you. If they can pick up on this, then they *are* a friend.' You need to be known beneath the protective disguises, and are afraid of it happening, and are afraid of it not happening too, especially when you dare try for it. It is the physical hit of the 'Oh' says Sarah—'But oh the agitated heart/ Till someone'—that is like all that hurts and is unspoken, does not want to be admitted and yet is at the very heart. But mainly we try out the smaller, safer, half-version of attempted communication that risks less: you throw out a few lesser words, like tentacular feelers, to see what you get back as feedback in reply.

Literature manages it better, and with form and skill can afford to do it more bravely. There it is not a Keith or Sarah who sends out the few words to see what returns: by a greater version of the same process it is the poem. And what it sends out, on our behalf, is all we don't say and only half want to. It feels as though it is the poem that 'finds us really out', and knows us as we often don't let even friends know us. There is much talk these days of having 'empathy' for this or that character, but what is remarkable is the other way round: when the poem seems to have empathy for us.[11] Yet of course it is not the poem as such that can do it, for the poem is not quite a physical 'someone', even when it is voiced.[12] It is our own silent recognition of the poem that cracks us open, and may even make us speak or cry out from the core, before habitual defences set in again. But we can't do it always on our own. This is psychology in literary action, literature's heart surgery. I need to be cracked open, say the readers.

CHAPTER 2

THE SCHOOLTEACHER

Tom retired a little early from teaching, two years ago, he wouldn't say why when I visited him to talk about his reading life. His departure seems to have been engineered by the new Head, according to Tom a cold, process-driven man who left him feeling not so much indignant as dishonoured and ashamed. It didn't end right is all he says, including some faults of his own that don't allow him to feel it was wholly undeserved: 'And now I have to live on after the ending.' The heavy damage and introspective depression he is trying to fight away makes him think he has no purposive work remaining to him now, through which to reclaim himself. 'I can't get out now,' he says and I didn't know whether he meant the house or the predicament.

He remembers the story of one of his professors at university, a Shakespearian scholar who, unusually for those days, was forced to leave his post because of his drinking. Every day after his dismissal this ageing red-faced man in a blue suit would set off on the train to the university as usual, but never went there. He would take himself off with his sandwiches to the local library where he stayed till his customary home-time. He had never dared tell his wife he had been sacked.

Tom taught literature at high-ranking state and public schools for almost forty years and has been a lifelong maverick reader, never just sticking to the requirements of the school syllabus. He is obsessed in particular with what he calls Tolstoy's blundering fools—Pierre Bezúkhov in *War and Peace* and Constantine Levin in *Anna Karenina*. In the weeks immediately after his own retirement, he spent much of each day, when he couldn't read, absorbed in staring at videos of *War and Peace*, at Anthony Hopkins as Pierre in one version he remembered from 1972, and more recently Paul Dano from another in 2016. It was the hurt young innocence, something also like bungling stupidity, he says, that was so visible on these naive faces. They were like faces that had forgotten to cover things up but were earnestly looked out of, as though unaware of simultaneously being seen.

He loves these baffled, flawed, and earnest types, as though they were someone he had himself lost touch with. There is one sentence to which Tom says he turns regularly, on the page or in his mind. It comes from *War and Peace*, book 1, part 3, chapter 2 where it is said (the translation is Louise and Aylmer Maude's):[1]

Figure 2. Anthony Hopkins (*above*) as Pierre Bezúkhov in the BBC's 1972 adaptation of *War and Peace*; Paul Dano (*below*) played the same role in 2016.

> Pierre was one of those who are only strong when they feel themselves quite innocent...

In the midst of a compromising sexual entanglement, Pierre himself cannot feel basically innocent, and except through painfully demanding acts of will, cannot feel strong without that foundation. In the pathos of not understanding himself Pierre said to that self, 'What am I doing?' He feels guilty and undone. But innocently guilty, Tom says, if that makes sense—as though the innocence was shocked by what it was doing, hurt by what guilt was doing to it, badly wanting to own up to what it has somehow allowed. Tom is always struck by how Tolstoy put it in the preface to *Childhood* when he speaks of his ideal reader: be sensitive, shed some tears for a character you care about, read looking for what grips your heart, and above all, 'You should be an understanding person—one, who when I get to know him, need not have my feelings and inclinations explained, but who I see understands me'. Astonishingly, it is not 'when you get to know me' but when I and my book get to know you—on which outreaching hope it was written. Though for Tolstoy there is no sharp line between the good and the bad, or between the intelligent and the stupid, there is for him one absolute division—between those who are 'understanding' and those who are not.

Tolstoy knows Tom. Tom has always liked to do good, wanted to be good, and suffers when he is not innocent. It is a minor everyday example, but he would walk past the homeless in the street, and it seemed disturbingly arbitrary to him that one day he would turn back in contrition and another he would not. He does not feel strong or innocent any more—not as he thinks he was in those fresher days when he could battle external setbacks with fewer inner doubts. But though weakened by his own life, temperamentally Tom still sides with Tolstoy in the novelist's strong search inside and outside the novels for what to live by. Tom is the sort of reader who would risk wrecking the aesthetic for the sake of some more-than-literary solution, some struggling belief to be won from literature that was more than just an act of reading. But losing self-belief in his latter years, Tom feels he has gradually but increasingly shirked the pressure, has thought himself unworthy of much meaningful purpose, and tried to give up on the need for impossible solutions.

But he still responds to Pierre. There is a Mauriac novel in which the flawed protagonist whose heart feels to himself like 'a knot of vipers', is still told by a grateful innocent that he is a good man: it almost kills him to hear it. Despite everything, and even when he doesn't think so, Pierre, says Tom, is a good man.

But Pierre was never wholly innocent in the first place, of course. There is a more demonic part of Pierre that breaks out in various forms throughout the book, in defiance of guilt even before guilt is felt—in drink, sexual debauchery, mad and violent schemes. For the sake of more life and greater excitement, Tom also in earlier days would experiment in going against his own nature as if to find out what that was. It is in his experience a strange and wildly desperate mixture of freedom and despair together—as though in the exhilaration he was trying to defy the normal rules or test out something beyond them. These purgative binges or occasional acts of idiocy felt like the release of tension and toxicity, a time-out from time that seemed, Tom claims, almost to clean out the blood, a weird sort of purification. Or he needed, he says, some minor threat of chaos to know the need for order again as something other than compliance. Tolstoy calls such risk-taking behaviour 'that vague and quite Russian feeling of contempt for everything, conventional, artificial, and human – for everything the majority of men regard as the greatest good in the world'. And at times, in clumsy rawness, you would throw away all that goody-goody pretence and predictable prudence even if it meant throwing some of yourself away with it:

> It was the feeling that induces a volunteer-recruit to spend his last penny on drink, and a drunken man to smash windows or glasses for no apparent reason and knowing that it will cost him all the money he possesses; the feeling which causes a man to perform actions which from an ordinary point of view are insane, to test, as it were, his personal power and strength, affirming the existence of a higher, non-human, criterion of life.
>
> Book 3, part 3, chapter 27

Non-human is the challenging phrase. There was something wild and untamed in Tolstoy, and in parts of his people, that was primal and pagan, and antecedent to society and to culture. Tom wrote this a long time ago in a reading diary, labelled 'Outlaws', which he got out for me:

> I have been interested in being somewhat out of control in that contemptuous way. That so-called 'Russian feeling' for iconoclasm or debauch. You don't want to remember it afterwards in sober and deflated retrospect, whatever the impulse was. It's then like what it would be if you saw someone else on the binge, from outside: stupidly risky, immature, undignified; certainly not as strong or heroic, unconventional or exciting as the creature thinks it's being, inside. I know this impulsiveness can be a pathological symptom of suffering, an ill-judged escapist reaction against adult suffering that in a vicious circle only causes more of it. Some wild or depressed bit of me is always saying that I have not become what I should have been.

He knows he could never have remained as naive as he was, when a raw student and an idealistic young teacher. He was in need of toughening up, even through the disappointments, mistakes, and compromises. But Tom fears that over the long years he has gone too far the other way, and done too much injury to his own mind ever to be able to think straight again. He says he has been a fool, and worse in many ways. But what he still loves and clings to is a sort of essential stupidity in his Russians.

I told Tom about one of my own university experiences, concerning a poet called Douglas Oliver. In 1974 I heard him read from his recently published long poem *In The Cave of Suicession* in a somewhat coterie poetry society that existed around the Cambridge poet and academic J. H. Prynne. Prynne, the most formidable intellect in the Cambridge English Faculty, had discovered Oliver as a reporter on the local paper and taken him under his wing in the late sixties. That particular night, Oliver read about a man called Q, a quester or questioner, who takes himself, some rations, and his typewriter into a dark abandoned lead mine in the Derbyshire Peak District, known as Suicide or Horseshoe Cave. Oliver had himself done this over many nights for a period of several months, following the death of his son Tom who, born with Down's syndrome, had died of a cot accident in 1969 before his second birthday. In the dark Q spoke and wrote, waiting for a presence called A to answer him back, as oracle. When finally he did answer, A told Q that he was to write the story of a man who has acted so badly as to be unworthy of an oracle. This man must live with his failures, in constant memory of what he cannot do, unless and until he can write something that is (in every sense) good. To do this, Q understood that he must rid himself of himself: which also meant giving up his ambitions for writing some well-formed 'Poetic' text. Instead he must retain all the rawness and roughness of the experience of writing in the dark, under ground.

The point I was trying to make was this: that here on one side of Douglas Oliver, in bad trouble and needing to do something good, was the forbiddingly intellectual Prynne, seeking a new and extraordinarily demanding poetry for a too-cosy England, and on the other the little son whose innocence and kindness had existed without any formal intelligence. Imaginably pitched somewhere between those two ill-matched muses, the following is from a letter of Douglas Oliver's written at the end of 1970, that I now read from my own notebook. Tom and I had agreed in advance to bring some personally important passages to show each other:

> I come down to this fact: there is in me—and I swear in most other people too—an area which is basically stupid, quite unargued, perhaps nineteenth century...It is an area I can easily ignore, for which I have many available antidotes (sometimes they are masks); but ultimately I cannot escape it because its foundation is the necessary impossibility of knowing fully all that we 'know'. You take the current English or American poet. You know damn well that stupidity is there but it never appears in a text that is, in every one of its stages, clever.[2]

This was the nineteenth century that Tom's talk of Pierre and Levin was reminding me of: innocence buried alive in the self-hating consequences of acting badly; the challenge of stupidity in disauthenticating the pretensions and strategies of mere cleverness; yet intelligence still struggling to use and not just mask stupidity.

Show me how, for all their misdemeanours, your people are still innocent, I asked: Give me more instances. We looked through the texts together—the novels, old notes, and reading diaries.

Innocent, said Tom, because when Pierre sees his wife, his valet, or just some peasant woman coming to sell him some embroidery, he 'looked at them over his spectacles unable to understand what they wanted or how they could go on living without having solved the problems that so absorbed him' (book 2, part 1, chapter 1). How *can* they go on? Why aren't they screaming? as Larkin says of the aged. Or as the baffled young Wordsworth says to the imperturbable Leech-gatherer in 'Resolution and Independence', 'How is it that you live, and what is it you do?'

Or then again, innocent like Constantine Levin when he sees a friend who is progressive in thought but conservative in action, and asks himself: What is the 'connection between this man's life and his thoughts'? (*Anna Karenina*, part 4, chapter 8). How can he too bear or manage to go on like that? Tom remembers being that naive sort of young man, like Levin, who couldn't take life for granted. It made him feel very insecure, however, that other people appeared to cope, and that the awkward oddball he must seem to be could not. Now he appears to himself to have become what he calls the 'secondary' older man who carries on without justification, whose life has never matched his ideas.

Only when he reads now, does there return exhilarated feelings from the other, earlier side of his life before his decline. He loves it when Levin stupidly cannot define his own position in comparison with his cleverer half-brother. Compared to the modern social reformer who 'never altered his opinions about the people nor his sympathetic attitude toward them', Levin could not say whether he actually loved or did not love the peasantry, barely understanding the question:

> In the disputes which took place between the brothers when discussing the peasants, Koznyshev was always victorious, just because he had definite views about them, their character, attributes, and tastes; while Constantine had no definite and fixed views, and was often guilty of self-contradiction when arguing on that subject.
>
> Part 3, chapter 1

Levin felt like an inarticulate idiot. He doesn't know, and cannot possibly see from inside the disadvantage, why this honest incomprehension of the theoretical might be admirable. But a reader can, joyous in the celebratory sense of human comedy. If Levin felt like a fool, then—Tom had written in his diary—the novel is a form for people who inadvertently think like fools, think personally, without rationally methodical and consistent views, amidst conflicts and self-contradiction. Saul

Bellow wrote something about not being sure whether a certain character—perhaps his divine fool Herzog—was the world's stupidest clever man or cleverest stupid man. I feel the same, writes Tom, about these people made up of innocence and guilt, not knowing the relation between the two or which was driving the other.

This brings him to another favourite passage, a different instance. If Levin is less consistent than his brother, there is another character in *War and Peace* who is even less consistent than the Levin-type. The peasant-born soldier Platon with whom Pierre is imprisoned 'would often say the exact opposite of what he had said on a previous occasion, yet both would be right':

> Sometimes Pierre, struck by the meaning of his words, would ask him to repeat them, but Platon could never recall what he had said a moment before, just as he never could repeat to Pierre the words of his favourite song: native and birch-tree and my heart is sick occurred in it, but when spoken and not sung no meaning could be got out of it. He did not, and could not, understand the meaning of words apart from their context. Every word and action of his was the manifestation of an activity unknown to him, which was his life. But his life, as he regarded it, had no meaning as a separate thing. It had meaning only as part of a whole of which he was always conscious. His words and actions flowed from him as evenly, inevitably, and spontaneously as fragrance exhales from a flower. He could not understand the value or significance of any word or deed taken separately.
>
> Book 4, part 1, chapter 13

Tom loves this passage, almost as Pierre loves Platon, even though Tolstoy himself was not like this. Tolstoy could never resist his own need to try to hold everything altogether, all at once, in some great whole philosophy of life. But it is the natural freedom of Platon's unbothered thinking that attracts Tom, the way it seems to follow life itself moment by moment. And it is connected with all the clever things Platon can't do, like remember the words of the song without the song itself or recall what he said so differently yesterday. With Platon it was as though thinking could only be a form of unpremeditated *action*, like a leap. Not fitted into the rut and character of what he customarily thought, not in defence of dogged consistency; but something sudden and free and responsive, coming from a lesser-known part of you and revealing it too, as alive. It feels to Tom like the thinking of some poet or novelist.

Perhaps he should have been but Tom is not a writer—not even the minor versions, the academic, the reviewer, or blogger. Instead, he is the sort of thinking reader who likes putting contrasting passages together from different parts of the novel, re-assembling something of the novel's internal dynamics to make it speak itself again through his re-ordering. He used to say to his best students, quoting William James, 'The connecting *is* the thinking'.[3] And the connections were often best when seemingly contrasts, paradoxes or challenges. You create something of the mind of Pierre, he now says, when you put, on either side of him: (1) his admiration for the unsystematic Platon, and yet also (2) his horror at others living on obliviously. Then like an amateur novelist you have to work out the subtler relations and distinctions between the two. Platon does not have to do this. But there are others such as Pierre himself who for better and worse do need to work things out, balancing the unconscious with the conscious, clumsily trying to hold onto life in thought even as it slides past in time.

I ask Tom to carry on with his connections. He recalls the first time Pierre met Platon, in a prison-shed in the midst of war, when they are the luckier captives who were not blindfolded in a row above a pit and shot by the French. Pierre had had to take in the sight of that small massacre:

> From the moment Pierre had witnessed those terrible murders committed by men who did not wish to commit them, it was as if the mainspring of his life, on which everything depended and which made everything appear alive, had suddenly been wrenched out and everything had collapsed into a heap of meaningless rubbish. Though he did not acknowledge it to himself, his faith in the right ordering of the universe, in humanity, in his own soul, and in God, had been destroyed.
>
> Book 4, part 1, chapter 12

In a way, the clause 'though he did not acknowledge it to himself' is like the phrase 'murders committed by men who did not wish to commit them': they are both anomalous extras in their sentences, residual innocencies for which it is now difficult to find room for understanding. At any rate, they mark how Tom and I both know we are reading Tolstoy and not some lesser, more straightforward novelist. Platon then speaks to Pierre:

> 'You've seen a lot trouble, sir, eh?' said the little man.
> And there was so much kindliness and simplicity in his singsong voice, that Pierre tried to reply, but his jaw trembled . . . In his hands he had something wrapped in a rag.
> 'Here, eat a bit, master,' said he, resuming his former respectful tone as he unwrapped and offered Pierre some baked potatoes. 'We had soup for dinner and the potatoes are the grandest!'
> Pierre had not eaten all day, and the smell of the potatoes seemed extremely pleasant to him. He thanked the soldier and began to eat.
> 'Well, are they all right?' said the soldier with a smile. 'You should do like this.'
> He took a potato, drew out his clasp knife, cut the potato into two equal halves on the palm of his hand, sprinkled some salt on it from the rag, and handed it to Pierre.
> 'The potatoes are the grandest!' he said once more. 'Eat some like that!'

Pierre thought he had never eaten anything that tasted better.

'Oh, I'm all right,' said he, 'but why did they shoot those poor fellows? The last one was hardly twenty.'

Book 4, part 1, chapter 12

'But why did they?' is just the kind of incredulous question Pierre would ask, but now in a tone more vulnerable, deep down inside, than a voice of protest could ever be. And incredulous: because his belief in life itself has been destroyed. Yet it being Tolstoy, this is Pierre and the Meaningless Universe and then, within a page, it is also Pierre and the Potato, until it is finally stage three, Pierre and his Question Why?

'But why can Pierre only ask that question *after* he has eaten a potato?' We try out together the obvious, normal explanations: the simple kindliness of Platon, the goodness of the basic food, the being brought back from shock to life again. These 'explanations' are plausible but, seeming less than the feeling the passage gives, are short of what, in the preface to *Childhood*, Tolstoy called true understanding. Tom tries again: Something has to come first before Pierre's question can happen—to do with a renewed context for life, some feeling activated again within a basic ordinariness. You need the feeling there first. It is as though Pierre, Tom goes on, has to start again, with THE most basic things—which have to get to him first through primacy of smell and taste, beneath ideas and thoughts he just cannot answer. It is partly Tolstoy's love of the incongruous juxtaposition of potato and thought, ostensibly small and large, as an image of life's mix, I say. But, Tom replies, it is also like having to begin human life itself again, after trauma, out of the most basic elements, emotions and needs, from below upwards as though repeating evolution. And only then, on the return to something like good normality, does the need for *more*, for a second life mentally, kick in again, out of the unresolved past.

Tom says:

Pierre couldn't just come out with his great childlike cry of wounded innocence— prematurely or too late, whichever it was; he just couldn't come out with it cold. For us as humans, there always has to be something—the potato, some enabling feeling—*beforehand* to allow us to come out real. It can't all be said straight off and direct, as I used to think. Outside books, as well as in them, I have loved those who even for a moment or so have managed to come out with it—have said and done things that have opened up the world just a little more for me. I mean they reminded me of some defiant life that the world around seemed to have made me lose heart in, or not even know properly to exist. And of course in life they don't have to be so well expressed: the existence is everything, the context does it. But this is why I have valued it in books because those moments in books, corrected and well-expressed, were originally the moments in life we should have had more of. What Pierre got from Platon, in the book's imaginary real life, I have got from Pierre.

*

He himself feels he has not much of a human context left him. Tom parted from his wife five years ago. Another reason he can no longer think very well, he feels, is because he doesn't like to remember. He doesn't give details of what led to the divorce but I don't think it was his choice, and their two children have taken their mother's side. Feeling unlovable, he says he doesn't like to think of the details of his life now, though he used to be a man who needed to talk everything out to someone. But now he says, and sometimes fears (since it worries him as a sign), that he is often more excited by abstract ideas than interested in occasional people. Life without the potato, he says.

And there is another thing that troubles him: that his interest in characters in books is like a second life instead of life itself. He also knows full well that in a novel, for him it was a character's specific difficulties that were the profoundest interest; but why then did he so much want to be rid of his own, as if they had never happened? The answer and the irony were in the question.

I had first known him fifteen years ago, at a less troubled and less lonely stage of his life, when he was a mature student on our part-time Masters course. He wrote his dissertation on poet-outlaws, Burns and Byron, and those, such as Samuel Johnson who, from the 'Life of Savage' onwards, resisted temptation and held off demons. The dissolute literary wastrel, Richard Savage, was not only an older friend to the young Johnson adrift in London but, like a human scapegoat, stood for everything in the way of ruinous failure that, later, Johnson himself imagined he too might have become. No wise man could easily presume to say: 'Had I been in *Savage*'s Condition, I should have lived, or written, better than *Savage*'.[4] That is what Johnson's wise man is like—wise enough to fear the dangers, even when he is out of them, and to know the chances of his own vulnerably human stupidity.

I referred back to that thesis of Tom's, and he now told me that he has lately been re-reading Burns, and there was an early poem, unpublished by the young poet, which he hadn't known before and which badly got to him.

It wasn't even, objectively, a particularly great poem, but a draft from a notebook. Yet (as he was to show me in a moment) Tom had found the philosophical work that Burns was reading around the time he wrote the poem, and it was the mix of the writing and the reading that seemed to bring the thinking behind the poem home to Tom. Indeed, it was always the pre-poetic thinking behind the poems—the undignified visceral pangs—that interested Tom, like secret messages partially conveyed from within the power of more dignified forms. It was the author's equivalent to what he picked up as a reader on the other side of the poem: the winces and the repressed memories, the secret cries of recognition, or groans in need of helping thought. At any rate, 'Remorse—A Fragment' is from the poet's notebook of early life, itself a raw ur-text:

> Of all the numerous ills that hurt our peace,
> That press the soul, or wring the mind with anguish,
> Beyond comparison the worst are those
> That to our folly or our guilt we owe.
> In every other circumstance, the mind
> Has this to say, 'It was no deed of mine';
> But when to all the evil of misfortune
> This sting is added—'Blame thy foolish self!'
> Or worser far, the pangs of keen remorse;
> The torturing, gnawing consciousness of guilt,—
> Of guilt, perhaps, where we've involved others;
> The young, the innocent, who fondly lov'd us,
> Nay, more, that very love their cause of ruin!
> O burning hell! in all thy store of torments,
> There's not a keener lash!
> Lives there a man so firm, who, while his heart
> Feels all the bitter horrors of his crime,
> Can reason down its agonizing throbs;
> And, after proper purpose of amendment,
> Can firmly force his jarring thoughts to peace?
> O, happy! happy! enviable man!
> O glorious magnanimity of soul!

Forget the final wishful exclamation marks of the last two lines, Tom warns me. Most of the other lines are more truly the unbearable visceral pangs and gnawings of remorse felt by the drunkard and the philanderer in flight from his own thinking. 'Where we've involved others;/ The young, the innocent, who fondly lov'd us/ ... that *very* love their cause of ruin'. Burns let down some young woman, dependent on him. But his poem allows at least a linguistic admittance of the otherwise unacceptable. And as Tom says, it exists exactly where poetry most powerfully exists—as a message somewhere *between* the private and the published. As such it expresses a part of life that, because it should not exist and wishes it didn't, would not otherwise get turned into human knowledge. Paradoxically this damage Burns has in shame to call Love's work, betraying its own name through seduction, pregnancy, desertion, ruin, even perhaps suicide.

What follows is our thoughts together, re-reading the poem alongside the repertoire of other texts Tom had assembled around it, in informal preparation for my visit and my questions.

Tom brought into the discussion Hannah Arendt, one of his favourite thinkers, who called thinking the work of the 'two-in-one' in a person: the extra one created by having to think in, of, and for oneself.[5] It is hard for those like Burns who have—almost impossibly as well unbearably—to think they have ruined the lives of others, to the ruin (in a different, consciously lesser way) of their own lives too. Arendt argues that the extra one in you who comes to life when you are alert and alone 'is the only one from whom you can never get away—except by ceasing to think' (*Life of the Mind*, p. 188). But suppose you cannot help continuing to think. Suppose, suggests Arendt, that you must go on thinking *after* having violated what Kant called the categorical imperative—the commandment that you should not act in any particular way that you would not be willing to generalize into a universal moral law. Where the properly righteous belong to something that is validating—like a law or a moral universe, the lone wrongdoer can hardly justify himself or his behaviour. Cut off and diminished, he depends upon the chance of a single person (himself) secretly being able to get away with whatever he did, despite the rules and at the expense of the other people. But there is no complete getting away with it; the inner conscience that Freud calls the super-ego, says Tom, is itself cruel.[6] The conscious wrongdoer puts himself into such painful self-contradiction, that he can hardly bear to think of what he has done in particular, compared to what he is meant to believe in general. Then it is, according to Arendt's beloved philosopher Socrates, that by a radical self-contradiction a person has shattered the internal harmony necessary for calm and steady thinking. It's like splitting yourself between would-be good and have-done-bad, says Tom, and then always having to occupy—to be—that damaged crack which lies between them.

For psychological reasons, to do with finding what to live by, Tom has always wanted non-fictional prose alongside poetry. It was partly because what he thought was itself like rough prose in response to polished art. But prose was needed also in the attempt to translate the poetry, and get out more of its compressed thought, in relation to his own real-life situation. In this way he often felt he needed to try to read the abstract prose of the philosophers like Arendt alongside the fiction writers, as if they had to be somehow in conversation, like the general with the particular. Crucially, here then, Burns himself had turned to a Scots philosopher, Adam Smith, on this problem of thinking with remorse. 'I entirely agree with the author of the *Theory of Moral Sentiments* that Remorse is the most painful sentiment that can embitter the human bosom.' This is what in 1783 the young Burns must have read from part 2, chapter 2 of a work first published in 1759, the year of his birth—and it was by this means that Tom said that he imagined the informal working of Burns's mind, reading Adam Smith through the lens of his own private experience:

The violator of the more sacred laws of justice can never reflect on the sentiments which mankind must entertain with regard to him, without feeling all the agonies of shame, and horror, and consternation. When his passion is gratified, and he begins coolly to reflect on his past conduct, he can enter into none of the motives which influenced it. They appear now as detestable to him as they did always to other people. By sympathizing with the hatred and abhorrence which other men must entertain for him, he becomes in some measure the object of his own hatred and abhorrence. The situation of the person, who suffered by his injustice, now calls upon his pity. He is grieved at the thought of it; regrets the unhappy effects of his own conduct, and feels at the same time that they have rendered him the proper object of the resentment and indignation of mankind, and of what is the natural consequence of resentment, vengeance and punishment. The thought of this perpetually haunts him, and fills him with terror and amazement. He dares no longer look society in the face, but imagines himself as it were rejected, and thrown out from the affections of all mankind. He cannot hope for the consolation of sympathy in this his greatest and most dreadful distress.

Perhaps there is no greater turn of one's own thoughts and feelings *against* oneself than this, the very owner of these capacities made 'the object' of them in the tightest of hell's circles. The word 'object' occurs twice in this passage, as if this is what the subject finds himself turned into, even in his own head. Thoughts, questions make it so: How could I ever do that? what does that make me? where does it leave me now? 'The thought of this perpetually haunts him, and fills him with terror and amazement.' That amazement is the last refuge of lost purity, the motives that made him enter into the past conduct no longer present. Even then the resultant regret and penitence are half-cancelled, or made secondary, by the thought of an utterly just condemnation, whatever the self-serving excuses or terror-led apologies. Tom said that reading this as if through Burns's eyes, had left him in pieces. 'O burning hell' in the poem really did also mean burn-in-hell—hell on earth, in mind, unloved and hated. He carefully also noted in particular, within the eighteenth-century formality of his prose, Adam Smith's terrible double-use of that word 'sympathy' here: the wrongdoer sympathizes (in that less usual sense) with those who abhor him, while he himself cannot now expect any straightforward sympathy for even 'the most dreadful' of 'the sentiments that can enter the human breast'. Remorse:

It is made up of shame from the sense of the impropriety of past conduct; of grief for the effects of it; of pity for those who suffer by it; and of the dread and terror of punishment from the consciousness of the justly provoked resentment of all rational creatures.

So many emotions—four or five—almost simultaneously fused together there, catching the man whichever way he turns. Tom said it made him think of bad nights in bed, tossing and turning from thought to thought. He could understand the single elements, the separate feelings and the distinct thoughts each yielded: shame, grief, pity, dread, and so on. What he could never quite figure or wholly bear, especially as he aged, was the combination of them. How could you ever admit it all when it would seem to break your spirit even in confessing to such a past? 'I can't do it. I struggle to survive without doing it.' And all this is what nonetheless must be reasoned 'down', says the poem of Burns's youth, for the rest of a life still to be a life. There in his own poem are the implicit stresses—'Lives there a man so *firm*, who, *while* his heart/ Feels *all* the bitter horrors of his crime,/ *Can* reason *down* its agonizing throbs;/ And, *after* proper purpose of amendment,/ *Can firmly force* his jarring thoughts to *peace*?' And Burns, in his accompanying gloss, then tries to turn his conflict into a prose resolution:

> an ordinary pitch of fortitude may bear up admirably well, under those calamities, in the procurement of which we ourselves have had no hand; but when our follies or crimes have made us wretched, to bear all with manly firmness, and at the same time have a proper penitential sense of our misconduct, is a glorious effort of self-command.

I am not at all sure about that youthful 'glorious', says Tom who is often sceptical of exculpatory names for things, frightened by his own capacity for denial. But 'at the same time'—'to bear all with manly firmness, and *at the same time* have a proper penitential sense of our misconduct', '*while* his heart/ Feels all'—that, he says, I do understand, that needful resolve to hold the split two together. It is the other side of what Smith describes: the sinner, even while regretting 'the unhappy effects of his own conduct' feeling '*at the same time* that they have rendered him the proper object of the resentment and indignation of mankind'.

I said: It is as though Pierre or Levin would ask of Burns what was said of Parolles in *All's Well That Ends Well*, 'Is it possible he should know what he is, and be that he is?' Tom replied: It is possible: you become what you have done. You then have to be what you have become and live out of that. If it is not possible wholly to repent and be otherwise, then 'Lives there a man who . . . after proper purpose of amendment,/ Can firmly *force* his jarring thoughts to *peace*?' Who has sufficient inner resource to continue to be 'and at the same time have a proper penitential sense'? The imagined possibility is to *be the contradiction* and keep it. That is to Tom one of those reading moments of temporary breakthrough that come and go in waves, with the chance of salvaging something from the wreck and holding it together.

It was reading something of Wordsworth's that helped firm up such moments, he said, to see a clue to putting himself back together again. It was another occasional, off-duty utterance in prose, but this time supported by not just a poetic draft but Burns's really achieved poetry. It comes in a 'Letter to a Friend of Burns' written by Wordsworth in 1816 after his reading, with pain, Dr James Currie's exposure of Burns in the first ever biography of him. It is against what we now call transparency but which Wordsworth called superficial knowledge.

To Wordsworth it was as though the biographer thought the momentary poetry was less than the fundamental facts of a whole life's profligacy, and no more than extra evidence of it, a gloss upon it, for a moment from within it. 'If,' writes Wordsworth, 'it were in the power of a biographer to relate the truth, the *whole* truth, and nothing *but* the truth', then indeed

> the friends and surviving kindred of the deceased, for the sake of general benefit to mankind, might endure that such heart-rending communication should be made to the world. But in no case is this possible; and, in the present, the opportunities of directly acquiring other than superficial knowledge have been most scanty; for the writer has barely seen the person who is the subject of his tale...But hear on this pathetic and awful subject, the poet himself, pleading for those who have transgressed!

> One point must still be greatly dark,
> The moving *why* they do it,
> And just as lamely can ye mark
> How far, perhaps, they rue it.

> Who made the heart, 'tis *he* alone
> Decidedly can try us;
> He knows each chord—its various tone,
> Each spring, its various bias.

> Then at the balance let's be mute,
> We never can adjust it;
> What's done we partly may compute,
> But know not what's *resisted*.

> How happened it that the recollection of this affecting passage did not check so amiable a man as Dr. Currie, while he was revealing to the world the infirmities of its author? He must have known enough of human nature to be assured that men would be eager to sit in judgment, and pronounce *decidedly* upon the guilt or innocence of Burns by his testimony...Here, said I, being moved beyond what it would become me to express, here is a revolting account of a man of exquisite genius, and confessedly of many high moral qualities, sunk into the lowest depths of vice and misery! But the painful story, notwithstanding its minuteness, is incomplete,—in essentials it is deficient; so that the most attentive and sagacious reader cannot explain how a mind, so well established by knowledge, fell—and continued to fall, without power to prevent or retard its own ruin.[7]

I repeated the question: How did it happen that 'the recollection' of this poem had insufficient power to affect Currie? Because, said Tom, the poetry was not fully real to Currie—which is to say, he did not 'remember' it in the way that Wordsworth did, imagining it as coming out of Burns's own memory of failing and falling repeatedly. The lines Wordsworth recalls are from the 'Address to the Unco Guid, or the Rigidly Righteous', against the religious moralists 'sae guid yoursel,/ sae pious and sae holy', who by simple condemnation think they *can* explain how a mind, full of knowledge, fell and continued to fall, without power to prevent its own ruin. What makes these mighty condemners differ from the more lowly and fallen, asks Burns? Answer: Easier lives, pride in their so-called purity, but often more than anything else 'your better art o' hiding'. The final lines—on never knowing for sure 'why they do it...how far they rue it'—are not just something in Burns's life, written on a particular calendar day, but they rise from underneath to look over that life from above. High art wrought out of the low depths, poetry achieved, said Tom, *because of* those lows and *despite* them. That is the only essay I would like to write, he went on, to be entitled 'Despite and Because'—just those words, instead of names and themes. And that raised poetry is all the more needed by people who, knowing they are not purely innocent, have few defences against the narrowly self-righteous.

Literary people characteristically love those in-between cases, those complex middles that seem to hold all the world's shades of meaning between too simple black and too clear white. It is as George Eliot was to say of Bulstrode, the banker hiding a discreditable past, at the beginning of chapter 85 of *Middlemarch*—another of Tom's key passages: That it cannot be for the hypocrite Bulstrode as it was for the innocent Faithful in Bunyan's *The Pilgrim's Progress*, undergoing stoning in the face of a hateful crowd of false judges. Faithful is one of those martyrs who can be strong in the inner security 'that what we are denounced for is solely the *good* in us', but for Bulstrode in his public exposure at a town-hall meeting, the difference is that he knows the charges of the mob against him to be substantively undeniable. He could not say he was innocent. He was over-whelmed by disgrace as though there were nothing left solid or good within him against that external shaming. He was defenceless against aggressors tri-umphal in the name of justice though hardly very much better than he perhaps. His own wife, remarkable only in this adversity, could still bring herself to stay loyal to him in his disgrace:

> It was eight o'clock in the evening before the door opened and his wife entered. He dared not look up at her. He sat with his eyes bent down, and as she went towards him she thought he looked smaller—he seemed so withered and shrunken. A movement of new compassion and old tenderness went through her like a great wave, and putting

one hand on his which rested on the arm of the chair, and the other on his shoulder, she said, solemnly but kindly—

'Look up, Nicholas.'

He raised his eyes with a little start and looked at her half amazed for a moment: her pale face, her changed, mourning dress, the trembling about her mouth, all said, 'I know'; and her hands and eyes rested gently on him. He burst out crying and they cried together, she sitting at his side. They could not yet speak to each other of the shame which she was bearing with him, or of the acts which had brought it down on them. His confession was silent, and her promise of faithfulness was silent. Open-minded as she was, she nevertheless shrank from the words which would have expressed their mutual consciousness, as she would have shrunk from flakes of fire. She could not say, 'How much is only slander and false suspicion?' and he did not say, 'I am innocent.'

Middlemarch, chapter 74

Of course, says Tom—thinking of his own broken marriage I supposed—No one has the right to receive this fidelity. It is like renewing vows to a worse version of the man you married. And even this loyal spirit can hardly bear the whole truth. Tom and I haven't actually read this aloud or looked at it, we have only spoken it about it in passing because I was the one who thought of Bulstrode and Mrs Bulstrode at this point. Tom tells me he will never read that passage again. She could *not* ask, 'How much ...?' and he did *not* say, 'I am innocent'.

That is why Burns talks of entrusting ultimate truth and final judgement to what is beyond human capacity, the otherwise impossible balance of judgement and mitigation that must be left to Whomsoever might have made the heart: "tis *he* alone/ Decidedly can try us'. It is all this in Burns that Wordsworth as a reader knows so painfully well: the 'exquisite' so entangled in the 'revolting' as silently to cry 'let's be mute'.

I mention of course that Wordsworth had his own sexual secrets, the woman and child he left in France when he went home from the Revolution. As if that might be a vested interest here, in defence of poets.

I love Wordsworth here, Tom goes on, because his own wounded feelings of pain and sorrow and guilt and compassion are for me just what emotions should be: the messages of core resistance from inside that still plead and protest, fight and stand out for the flawed good, even within—no, especially within—the most negative contexts. (And I think another thing, hardly to be said: That this is when Tom most uses the word 'love' these days, in relation to what is kept through books. And I don't want to spoil that because I think that it is more to do with literature retaining rather than substituting.) 'Like my Russians, even more now I am older, I want the release of feelings, the release of something that punches a hole through ordinary, reticent life—and through me.'

Tom then quietly read me Wordsworth's final sentences aloud as we each looked at our own copies:

> the momentous truth of the passage already quoted, 'One point must still be greatly dark,' &c. could not possibly have been conveyed with such pathetic force by any poet that ever lived, speaking in his own voice; unless it were felt that, like Burns, he was a man who preached from the text of his own errors; and whose wisdom, beautiful as a flower that might have risen from seed sown from above, was in fact a scion from the root of personal suffering.
>
> *Wordsworth Prose Works*, pp. 125–6

That is the good work, and the hard reclaiming work of art that Douglas Oliver meant to do in the dark cave: to make from the root below what seems to have come from seed sown from above. As he wrote his text with careful skill, Burns knew he was also reading in it 'from the text of his own errors'. Texts, says Tom, often feel to me double in that way.

He brings in one other, written by Burns in the same year, 1786. Turning from his defence against the righteous to writing an 'epistle to a young friend', he tells here a different story about guilt. However good love is, illicit love—even when nothing of it is ever disclosed—carries its own punishment:

> I waive the quantum o' the sin,
> The hazard of concealing;
> But, Och! it hardens a' within,
> And petrifies the feeling!

It isn't only criminals who become hardened. And yet Tom is also still hard on himself.

Tom has what I would call a *repertoire* of texts, comprising errors and hearteners, conflicts and triggers, and (perhaps most of all) furtherers that make the glimpsed thought extend and expand into prose thought. They have become a sort of mental map for him, a mix of interrelated languages and voices. But having spent a lifetime with literature, he now says, 'I am at times unsure what it was for, or whether it ever shook down into something':

> That's down to me though. I don't know if all that reading will help me now or even if it should. Sometimes it still feels artificial, even false compared to where I am. Though what is also true is that I am always grateful for the thoughts and feelings literature has enabled me to have.

But he is tired of introspection, weary of thinking about himself. I want to say to him that art comes out of something I only think of afterwards when writing this out: a sentence of F. D. Maurice's in his late nineteenth-century lectures on *Conscience*—'There must be some way of uttering ourselves without talking about ourselves.' [8]

Anyway, he says he is reading Elizabethan lyrics more than anything else these days. He does not quite know why, since he could hardly say that unrequited love—the poetry's major theme for the most part—was an important idea for him now; but he finds there is nothing he more cares to read. Like this sonnet by Edmund Spenser, 1595, in its formal beauty—first stanza:

> Lacking my Love, I go from place to place,
> Like a young fawn that late hath lost the hind,
> And seek each where, where last I saw her face,
> Whose image yet I carry fresh in mind.

Tom: Perhaps I can bear this unrestrained loss only in gentle translation now. I need the cry hidden subtly in the middle of the line, against the grammar – 'seek each where, where last I saw her . . .': 'Where? Where?' it cries in two different senses, as though for a micro-second the line goes backwards, and cannot go on. And I need the feeling to be hidden, beautifully, in the simile: he is looking for the lost woman not like some wildly rampaging lover would but, going further backwards without her, like a child, an offspring, a fawn desperately wanting its mother with what you might have thought was a quite different love. It is a breathtaking innocence, to dare to make that comparison. It brings together a whole life-span of need for love of all kinds, in all a bewildered creature's insecurities and searches.

Stanza 2 goes:

> I seek the fields with her late footing signed;
> I seek her bower with her late presence decked;
> Yet nor in field nor bower I her can find;
> Yet field and bower are full of her aspèct . . .

Tom: It is the movements, the sophisticated turns of words that in themselves are simple and *not* sophisticated; the same lost words, the bare elements. It is almost childlike telegraphese or a sort of braille: seek in field; seek in bower; yet not in field nor bower find; yet field and bower full. I need those last two lines—those two incompatible 'Yets' of life—to be together even if I cannot otherwise hold the two things together. Plus whatever is their relation to that different earlier 'yet': 'Whose image *yet* I carry fresh in mind'. You want that kind of 'yet': even if it hurts, it is there still within the hurt as fresh as a flower and as a wound. I don't actually want to have become hardened.

> But, when mine eyes I thereunto direct,
> They idly back return to me again:
> And, when I hope to see their true object,

> I find myself but fed with fancies vain.
> Cease then, mine eyes, to seek herself to see;
> And let my thoughts behold herself in me.

That is the turn inward at the sonnet's end.

I ask: But why would all that move you? We talk a little about what we had studied together years ago but taking it more personally now—Philip Sidney's late-sixteenth-century *Apology for Poetry*. There Sidney speaks of the 'infected will' that befalls all mortals after the Fall—counterpointed nonetheless by poetry's crafted capacity for an 'erected wit'.[9] That felt intelligence exists to lift what is fallen nearer again to a glimpse of lost Paradise. Or, rather, it is the combination of the two that is most moving—unhappily infected content, raw subject-matter, partly redeemed by beautifully erected form. And only partly so because the form still stays loyal to the human trouble it cares for, which it will not simply magic away. But it *makes* something of it, has done something with it, turning passive to active to combat melancholic helplessness. And as we look at the page together, Tom points again to the careful making of 'place to place', 'where, where', 'lost, last, seek', and finally 'cease seek, let'—as if that is what he has been doing much of his life but is tired of saying so. The seeking is both the problem and at the same time the trying for a way out of the problem...But now Tom answers me in a series of short sentences, with pauses in between them, as though he were talking in lines.

> As if to say: I have only got a few things.
>   And there is something still in them, though it is also missing.
>   And I keep looking where...
>   Where do things go when they are no longer here?
>   Not nowhere, since field or bower re-mind you of them.
>   But they are not in the field or bower.
>   Yet not in your mind without field or bower, their empty sight paradoxically prompting it.
>   That's like a placebo: the power is not in the placebo but in the power of the mind's belief in it; but the mind cannot get at its very own power without that placebo, or without the field or bower to land upon.
>   So Spenser concludes of the missing beloved:

> > Cease then, mine eyes, to seek her self to see;
> > And let my thoughts behold her self in me.

> But I can't do that, cannot keep what is missing held in my mind, even get at my mind to do its work, without a poem to replace field and bower.

*

Sir Philip Sidney thought of poetry as a second nature. I think what I value in Tom is what I would call his second life—though not in the sense he would prefer it. He would want a second chance and a second go at it all, but often feels he has run out of time now. I mean he would like to make something more stable of the second self which is created when he thinks of poems and stories, when by their aid he thinks of himself and of life itself through and in them. But he fears that it is merely a secondary life, because he isn't a poet and seemingly creates nothing.

Yet when I think of Tom, I think that for better and for worse this is a really real human being, deep and hybrid. 'Then at the balance let's be mute. We never can compute it.' The trouble with biographies, wrote John Updike, beset by his own guilty motivations, 'is that they mainly testify to the long worldly corruption of a life', but what they cannot convey is 'the unearthly innocence' that exists 'in the perpetual present tense of living'.[10] Tom's is the story of a man who wanted to be innocent.

CHAPTER 3

THE WOMAN WHO POINTED

E very week the group-leader would turn to her at some stage in the session and say 'Do you *like* that poem, Lesley?' And week after week she would reply by saying very quietly, 'I don't know.'

How was she supposed to know? The reading group had been suggested to her by someone in the local drop-in centre, after her daughter had been taken into care. She didn't know much about books, let alone poetry. It was like a foreign language to her, without rules of translation. Lesley described herself as someone who at the time could not even read properly. And anyway she was in a terrible state of mind.

After a few such unencouraging weeks of Lesley's repeatedly mumbled 'I don't know', the group leader brought in 'Invictus' written by W. E. Henley in 1875 in the midst of a three-year period in hospital when he was in his mid-twenties. Henley had lost his left leg below the knee to tuberculosis of the bone and, still only a young man, was now in danger of losing his right. He had been suffering for nearly fifteen years since catching TB at the age of twelve. A prime example of the colonial Victorian stiff upper lip, one might think, it was this four-stanza poem that in a very different world a hundred years later, Nelson Mandela memorized not from a hospital but in his prison on Robben Island. It opens:

> Out of the night that covers me,
> > Black as the pit from pole to pole
> I thank whatever gods may be
> > For my unconquerable soul.

'Do you like that poem, Lesley?' the group leader had tried as usual. 'Unconquerable' was the word and the tiny syllable she had emphasized in reading it aloud, as if it was added resilience amidst the mix where otherwise it might not have existed at all. 'I like those last two lines,' she replied, liking for the first time, and pointing to the final stanza:

> It matters not how strait the gate,
> > How charged with punishments the scroll,
> I am the master of my fate:
> > I am the captain of my soul

I have to say, for myself 'Invictus' had only been the sort of bluff exhortatory verse I would characteristically read quickly and dismiss. We are not ever the masters of our fate, we are not the captains of our soul, it *does* matter how hard are the surrounding circumstance of life. Yet here were three very different people—Henley, Mandela, and Lesley—who found these stoically defiant lines not to be as hollow as I had thought, but offering hope for a strength they wanted to think of, and needed to be able to speak from. For Mandela, that avid reader, they must have related to the lines he also marked and loved from *Julius Caesar* (Figure 3):

> Cowards die many times before their death:
> The valiant never taste of death but once
> Of all the wonders that I have yet heard,
> It seems to me most strange that men should fear,
> Seeing that death, a necessary end,
> Will come when it will come.
>
> 2.2 32–7

But for him, in the fight against fear, it was 'Invictus' above all.

This is what happens sometimes when a poem that does not move you, moves someone else in a reading group so strongly that you begin to try to imagine it

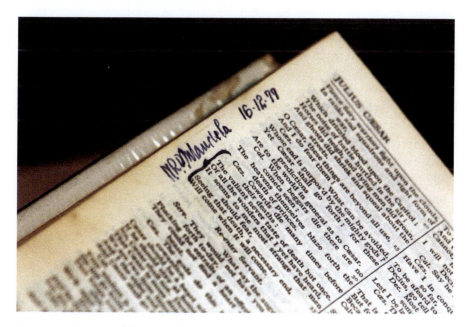

Figure 3. Nelson Mandela's copy of Shakespeare, with a passage from *Julius Caesar* highlighted during the time of his imprisonment on Robben Island.

through their eyes. It then seems that by their feelings and their predicament they had almost *made* the poem, contributing to it beyond its words—by being in their great need almost better, I sometimes think, than is the poem itself. 'I am the master of my fate:/ I am the captain of my soul' meant something to these three, precisely because these people *weren't* masters or captains but, in extremis, needed to imagine that feeling. It came out of their lack of it.

It is not the feeling of being masters or captains that is the real poetry here but the feeling of not being, and wanting to be; of imagining the lift of being such an ideal self, when you still are not. The lines were poignantly a *reverse* expression of the feared amputation or the imprisoned slavery, all the negatives that really lay behind the willed attempt at positive affirmation.

These were the beaten-down people which the poem's second stanza describes:

> In the fell clutch of circumstance
>   I have not winced nor cried aloud.
> Under the bludgeonings of chance
>   My head is bloody, but unbowed.

All those negatives: 'not winced', 'nor cried' 'unbowed', 'unconquerable', 'it matters not'. They are the clue as to how the poem should be read back-to-front. But when it comes to battling through negatives, ordinary people such as Lesley are not obviously martyrs or heroes like Mandela, or poets as Henley was. Yet when she was an eight-year-old child and struggling to learn to tell the time, her father in mad exasperation, she says, smashed a heavy old-fashioned wooden clock against her head. There were other physical abuses too, and she was in and out of care for ten years after that. She believes the whole experience of mental and physical cruelty left her with a form of brain damage. 'My head is bloodied...'

At his trial, years later, she says that her father in his successful defence called her a 'subnormal' child. But afterwards in 2010 she began to attend a shared reading group at a local drop-in centre, though she had considerable learning difficulties in reading and spelling. This included problems in managing clear pronunciation and holding in mind a load of information. By this stage as I have said, one of her own children, a daughter, had been taken into care from the age of twelve as a result of further family abuse in another generation, and Lesley was unable to read or to reply to the relevant paperwork in trying to get her back. She experienced flashbacks, had developed skin cancer, and suffered from depression and anxiety. Lacking trust in people, she had formed, she said, the odd habit of often looking behind herself. The repetition of abuse, the repetition of thoughts about it, made a pattern she wanted rid of.

I don't trust, if anyone hurts me: I can read their minds, I know what they mean. What I mean is: I know in another way they are going to do the same all over again. And I think to myself I am *not* going through that again, I've been down that path, not doing that, not again. So I also have to look at it in another way.

Not, no, not the same all over again, but 'another way' instead. 'Whatever is hidden, if you've got feelings,' she says, 'They've got to come up and out, otherwise your head would explode.'

'My head is bloodied but unbowed.' She wants her real name, Lesley Tilney, to be known and used in this book.

The first complete book that Lesley read with her group—she said she told them they would have to help her with her reading—was Dickens's *Great Expectations*. She identified herself with Pip as though he were real, in place of identifying herself with what her father had called her. As she said years later in an interview for us:

> Pip—Pip was ill-treated, don't forget, wasn't he? He was cheated and I was cheated. It was harsh the way he was ... like mine was harsh. Reading it, I must have cringed at myself.

That last speaks to the sheer physical wince of sensitivity that Dickens himself knew from childhood. The clumsy out-of-place boy in the novel couldn't even manage to play cards well:

> 'He calls the knaves, Jacks, this boy!' said Estella with disdain, before the first game was out. 'And what coarse hands he has! And what thick boots!'
>
> I had never thought of being ashamed of my hands before; but I began to consider them a very indifferent pair. . . . I determined to ask Joe why he had ever taught me to call those picture-cards Jacks, which ought to be called knaves. I wished Joe had been rather more genteelly brought up, and then I should have been so too. . . . I was so humiliated, hurt, spurned, offended, angry, sorry—I cannot hit upon the right name for the smart—God knows what its name was—that tears started to my eyes. The moment they sprang there, the girl looked at me with a quick delight in having been the cause of them. This gave me power to keep them back and to look at her: so she gave a contemptuous toss—but with a sense, I thought, of having made too sure that I was so wounded—and left me.
>
> But, when she was gone, I looked about me for a place to hide my face in, and got behind one of the gates in the brewery-lane, and leaned my sleeve against the wall there, and leaned my forehead on it and cried. As I cried, I kicked the wall, and took a hard twist at my hair; so bitter were my feelings, and so sharp was the smart without a name, that needed counteraction.
>
> *Great Expectations*, chapter 8[1]

Why had Joe Gargery the blacksmith, the one person who really cared for him, taught Pip to say 'Jacks'? Sensitivity does not always come out right, in these places, where shame creates self-distortion and self-diminishment. Through that vulnerability, Miss Havisham and her ward Estella made Pip ashamed of Joe, and all the more so on his second visit to them in chapter 13, when Lesley herself picked on two places which she read aloud, with a little difficulty. First, this in retrospect:

> I am afraid, I was ashamed of the dear good fellow,—I *know* I was ashamed of him— when I saw that Estella stood at the back of Miss Havisham's chair and that her eyes laughed mischievously.

Then this, right at the chapter end:

> I remember when I got into my little bedroom I was truly wretched and had a strong conviction on me that I should never like Joe's trade. I had liked it once, but once was not now.

Pip cringes at the sneers of Estella; cringes again in a different way in that little bedroom, and again and again in later life. Hence Dickens's own winced emphases: 'I am afraid I was ashamed', 'I *know* I was ashamed', as Pip thinks back to what those sneers made him disavow—Joe and his manners and his speech, his class, and even his occupation:

> I had liked it once, but once was not now.

'Stands out that, doesn't it,' says Lesley, '*Once* was not *now*', alert as she always is to the telegraphese of painful change. But she is sensitive also to emotional configurations when she adds: 'Is it that you feel *guilty* of *ashamed*?' The group leader says back to her of the mixed layers of feelings, 'It's a complex, isn't it?' 'That's the way I see it,' she replies.

In the passage from chapter 8 she had especially pointed at the smart of feeling that is felt without a single definitive name for it—'I cannot hit upon the right name ... God knows what its name was'. That was the start of what in this book I am calling *the literary moment*. It comes when words no longer stand in literal one-to-one correspondence with the things they are normally meant to stand for. It comes when they are tried out again and again—'humiliated, hurt, spurned, offended, angry, sorry'—in evocation of 'the more' that they cannot ever wholly match and encompass but can point towards and re-feel.[2] 'Can't have just one feeling,'

Lesley says. 'Emotion full of other emotions in it.' Shame and guilt and anger and embarrassment and sadness and ...

The feeling is also expressed in Dickens through various neo-physical movements back and forth. There is the overpowering nearness of the welling tears, and yet the power of still fighting them off when Pip sees that Estella can see them. Their inevitable return, face against the wall in private when she has gone, and then their conversion into the twisting of his hair and the kicking of the wall—all those feelings of hurt shame, and then the reflection upon them afterwards in a little lonely bedroom. It is a confused fight that Lesley understands:

> I've met more people, been in the reading groups, understand about the books, understand about the poems, and I suppose I've got more chance of doing things haven't I? I might not have had that chance...even though I'm still ill in this, with the mental cruelty and damage...So it's like me fighting that in another way, isn't it?

'Haven't I? Isn't it?': she still has to use question-tags. But for writers and readers, even in doubt and difficulty, literature is that 'other way'—of fighting and asking and understanding. 'People think a book's a book,' Lesley says at interview, 'but there's more to it. Things, personal things, *would* come out.'

My colleague Josie Billington who has read transcript after transcript from Lesley's reading groups says there is no one she would ever trust more than Lesley to pick out and point to the places that first mattered in a text. She observed a session where the group was reading chapter 4 of *Great Expectations* and with help of the group leader, Lesley dwelt for some time on the discomfort of the young Pip amidst the adult company. It is not just because of his guilt in stealing the pie for the convict, or because he was neglected and not allowed to speak '(I didn't want to speak)':

> No; I should not have minded that, if they would only have left me alone. But they wouldn't leave me alone. They seemed to think the opportunity lost, if they failed to point the conversation at me, every now and then, and stick the point into me. I might have been an unfortunate little bull in a Spanish arena...

Lesley was the pointer, the one who most pointed out and repeated phrases within passages as if they were a language for her. But when she said impression-istically of these sentences about Pumblechook and other adults correctively har-assing the little boy, 'That means he is pointing something at him, pointing into me', then it became clear that she was often taking the point of the scene in a more vulnerable and almost physical way. Often what she was pointing at had already made its point, psychically, in her. For her as for many readers, words are *psychoactive* (to use a term applied to drugs that chemically alter brain-function), returning in this medium something you have already dimly experienced, felt or said in another.

Picking up key phrases and resonances, staying quiet for ages in the group, then coming back in with something half-mumbled but insistently repeated that she seems to have been thinking over all the while in between: that is Lesley's pattern, especially in the early days of her time in the group, not taking on too much, daring to say when she does not know a word, but also incisive. 'It's there [*pointing*]. Can't explain' is what she characteristically first says and does, regularly; then if no one picks up on it, she has to stop or does not know how to go on; then seems to look away and go inside, or wait and mull, till she comes back in to say, as though in poetry-code or syllabic shorthand, things such as 'Change rises' or 'Opening up' or 'Going forward and back' or 'Block it out'. She needs short phrases from the text to land upon, like stepping-stones. She was the one who knew where the change first took place in Shakespeare's sonnet 29. It is she who reading Maya Angelou's 'Touched by an Angel' makes the poem the most of what it could be by picking out 'unaccustomed to courage', 'if we are bold', and 'we dare to be brave' in the face of new feeling, and then reads out:

> And suddenly we see
> That love costs all we are

and stops, though the poem has three further and more explicit lines to finish with. But this makes a silence after these lines, the undercurrent of feeling which the poem itself sometimes interferes with. 'Trying to write a poem,' says David Constantine, another of our collaborators, 'The space you are staring into will in the end begin to fill with words. [But] the words taking shape may be the wrong words. They may be *in the way of*, not on the way towards the poem.'[3] It is an emotionally full, not empty, silence which Lesley helps delicately create by interrupting the poem's way, holding there that thought-filled silence she interiorly inhabits before it can go back into making too much further sense. These take-aways or nuggets, a line or two taken out of the apparently finished text and made vibrantly formative again in the reader's head, *are* poetry in action. They come from the sort of mute intuition towards detached fragments that Wordsworth claimed as belonging to what he called 'silent poets'. At that depth, far beneath human appearances, there is amidst the psychological identification something more, a form of intuition that is also wonderfully abstract in Lesley in the form of intact mind, an underlying intellectual resilience that can still be reached and realized.

*

Lesley says of reading *Great Expectations*, 'I can understand *between* the book and meself. With Pip's story and my story, can't I? My own life.' She often uses the word 'between' to mean 'across the space separating'. It makes me want to pause to think further about the experience of a felt match between reader and book.

There is a diagram in a now little-known book entitled *Subjective Criticism* by David Bleich, published in 1978,[4] about what happens in the formation of a mental 'match'. I had not supposed that a diagram could be as exciting as this seemed to me when I first saw it. It set out in a clear but alien medium the shape of what I had dimly always felt I wanted. And perhaps the sense of discovery was freer because Bleich himself did not endorse what he drew, as if it were some old-fashioned belief in realism that was now superseded.

His diagram shows Freud's ideal of how, across a sort of two-way mirror in the mind, a conscious interpretation might meet and fit a dream fashioned from below consciousness, and transform that subconscious dream into conscious understanding. If it seems contrary to the spirit of the humanities to resort to a diagram, it should be remembered (as I hadn't), that even through its etymology, from the Greek—written/marked out in lines—the language of a diagram remains close to the act of symbolic reproduction achieved in both written registers and musical scales, as well as in the use of geometric figures. It is an attempted representation pointing to what may be happening in the invisible processes underlying human response.

Figure 4 is my adapted reproduction of that diagram of Freud's ideal of the power of translation and recognition. It is a doubtless a simplified account but its format represents an urgent sense of the process of connection. On the left, pressurized matter deep in the psyche, half-blindly or dumbly seeking some sort of relieving expression for itself within dream-form or behavioural symptom. The unclear content of that dream-work is then picked up on the awakening right-hand side of the mental mirror, and then passed through some version of psycho-analysis in search of a clearer meaning of what it truly stands for, and of where in the past it originated, until the original underlying feeling re-emerges as thinkable. That is the task for human psychology, to retrieve for consciousness what has long lain latent, lost, denied or distorted, behind it. At its best it feels like unconsciousness itself is come into consciousness, as consciousness carefully turned the delicate dial on the safe in search of the right combination for opening and release. Then they belong

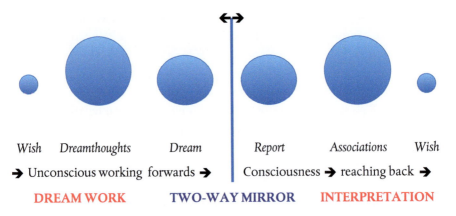

Wish   Dreamthoughts   Dream | Report   Associations   Wish

→ Unconscious working forwards → | Consciousness → reaching back →

DREAM WORK   **TWO-WAY MIRROR**   **INTERPRETATION**

Figure 4. Freud's ideal of the power of translation and recognition, diagram adapted from David Bleich, *Subjective Criticism* (Johns Hopkins University Press, 1978), p. 72.

together, unconscious and conscious and, wonderfully, they heal each other by uniting like a newer recreated version of the old person.

At each stage of investigation—report of dream, account of the associations it now brings—it feels to the person on the right-hand side that he or she is being half led or guided by, and finally matched with, the original repressed material of need and desire on the obscured left. It is an image not merely of *Psycho-analysis* but of what, in relation to all the inchoate ur-matter that needs thinking, *Thought* itself feels like as an act of discovery and resolution. Freud gives as his simple example a son's disturbing dream of a dead father who does not himself *know* he is no longer alive. Interpretation across the mirror says the dream is an inverted image of the son's inability to process and accept the reality of the father's demise. For completion, the son needs to tell his own father, including the father within himself, that he is indeed dead.

The work of the analyst is to help create an interpretation that across the divide meets the dream or the problem, with a click of emotionally felt truth and resultant integration. That feels as though it would be a version of the best form of 'reading': original text on the left, its reader on the right, and despite an often isolating world, each at last finding the ideal of a correspondent kin or host or home in the other.

The sense of recovered connection is something like what Wordsworth felt when he returned home to the Lake District after banishment first in Cambridge, then in London, to find value renewed afresh in what others might think quite ordinary scenes and people:

> Why shine they round me thus, whom thus I love?
> Why do they teach me, whom I thus revere?
> Strange question, yet it answers not itself.

This is from manuscript B of *Home at Grasmere*, reprinted in the wonderful Cornell Wordsworth edition. Manuscript D is still trying to get the emphasis right by rephrasing the first line: 'Why do *They* shine around me, whom I love?'[5] But the point is that these are strange questions which, however simple-looking, do not simply answer themselves. And the role of the poet is to ask those questions as though from the right side of the brain, to try to unlock whatever on the other side is hidden in unconsciousness or in mystery. Asking the question 'Where does this come from, how does this happen?' is just how Wordsworth stays imaginatively naive and baffled, in the best sense. Answer: The people around me do not just shine because I love them (my projection). Answer: I don't just love them because they shine so (my sycophancy). But the love and the shining seem to come separately as well as matching and blending together. They don't just teach me because I revere them, and I don't just revere them because they teach me. The questions are better than those alternative explanatory rationalizations. But Wordsworth did feel at *home* again: there was that profound click between poet and landscape, poet and the people in it.

I feel something of that click of matched satisfaction when I am in a seminar, or watching a video of a shared reading group, and suddenly someone really 'gets' the poem, seeming on the right side of the mirror to reflect what is on the left, the reading bringing the writing to a second life in embodying it. And often at the same time, the literary work feels like some equivalent to a reader's unconsciousness or deeper consciousness, the inkling of something lost or hidden or needed. Nor will the reader stay still, keeping to one side, but crossing over till the divide itself is unclear. And the reader may begin to move into the place of the two-way mirror itself, looking to the poem on one side, and to him- or herself on the other, and sensing the two-way movement back and forth in the richest of thinking. Hence Lesley's sense of her understanding 'between' the novel and herself. Or as Wordsworth puts it, 'the Mind is to herself/ Witness *and* judge', at one moment emotionally reporting back to itself, at another reflecting down upon those reports.[6] There are like different versions of the same reader, as a consequence of reading through different functions and from different perspectives.

But it is time to admit that Bleich himself thought this great model of Freud's verbal cure was a fantasy, offering an impossible and naive objectivity. He could not believe that the right-hand-side interpretation—the report of the dream, the retrieval of its feelings, and the analytic explanation that results—could reliably locate or precisely map onto that obscurely troubled, pre-verbal energy on the left. He was sceptical that the right-hand side could reveal and relieve the other side, through the finding of words that seemed to match the feel of it in translation.

Instead Bleich insisted that any interpretation would always remain subjective. The mirror is not really two-way but is like any other looking-glass in which you only see a reflection of yourself in front, not behind. By definition the unconscious can never be made conscious: it can only be supposed to exist. By a nice twist, however, Bleich actively welcomed the subjectivity, especially in reading. There is, he rightly said, too much rationalized pretence in the world; too great a psychological impulse to resort to claims for a general objectivity; too much suppression of the personal underpinnings that are intrinsically involved in most human undertakings.

This welcome given to subjectivity is as invigorating as the warning of subjectivity is salutary. Shared Reading, for example, cannot work without personal emotions and autobiographical resonances. But the group leaders know that even so in acts of scrupulous reading they must keep *both* things in reciprocal relation, subject and object, the reality of the text as well as the response of the reader. Through experience a leader of a group senses when across the spectrum of possibilities, a group member has gone too far away from the poem or at the other extreme, is only looking at it as an external set of words. And in the time of the session the group leaders must allow these movements and reorientations, because in the human process there can be no easy demarcations, no simple purity, no premature restrictions; yet always nonetheless they go back to the text again and again, to renew its presence, to realign the action. It is because they always want to think that there is something other than subjectivity that, inside and outside, is at once driving and challenging it. They are not just seeking personal confessions for which the text is merely an opportunity and an excuse, the self-indulgence that ironically obscures a deeper more authentic self. They want in their readers the great emotion of verbal seeking—of knowing there is *something* there, an inkling howsoever elusive or resistant, to try for. They want in them the great emotion of verbal finding—because there is no greater gift of your own life given back to yourself than consciousness suddenly informed by the verbal realization of what previously had been too hard to recognize or bear or possess. The risk and the inadequacy are built into the activity, as an honestly struggling part of what is involved in finding literary meaning—in seeking meaning through reading literature. It is better that the personal is never fully sure how much *or* how little it is only subjective, of how much is the book and how much the reader, for only then is it a true venture into the sheer mix of the world. What makes the endeavour vital is not some guarantee that it is wholly possible, but it is the impetus given by its being live and exciting, by readers feeling they are after something, drawn and driven in that quest for meaning which makes for a more activated life. That is what William James meant by 'pragmatism' without any other certainty: only this, that what a suddenly disclosed belief or idea enables you to *do* is the truth it has for you, is what blindly and intuitively works, somehow clicking into place or feeling right.[7]

What readers such as Lesley do is start from the right place, in the right way, pointing to a word or phrase in the midst of the text. It is the kind of basic action that John Henry Newman defended in a University Sermon delivered in Oxford in 1840, entitled 'Implicit and Explicit Reason'. In particular, there is one sentence where Newman says that, in whatever they most deeply think and do, 'All men have a reason, but not all men can give a reason'.[8] Implicit reason is *having* a reason; explicit reason is being able to *give* the reason you have. And the latter, says Newman in his careful syntax and vocabulary, is a valuable but not an initial faculty. Explicit is a later secondary reflection which seeks to bring to conscious articulation, within a more formal and foreign register, some of what was latent and unconscious in a person's initial situation. Some but never quite all. That means that the ontological order of priority in which things are done is vital here and never exhausted. Too often for Newman, especially in educated circles, a secondary faculty does not support but replaces a rawer primary one. Yet what must always come first is implicit reason which is like *acting* on a reason regardless of a later more formal and abstract kind of intelligence. The problem is that the inevitable risk of such intuitive forms of mental action leave people feeling vulnerably stupid when they cannot at once justify themselves before a cleverer objector. They lose confidence and faith, and the natural power that results from them. Of course, thinks Newman, it would be best for such people if instead of feeling naive and unwarranted, they could have *both* the power of implicit reason *and* the capacity to defend and articulate it. But first things are still and always first: implicit reason must always come before explicit reason and be more important than it, if anything is to be done in the world. This is what an intellectual should be, a defender of the value in apparently non-intellectuals and the realm of life they express. 'I am what I am, or I am nothing,' he writes in a magnificent bravery of encouragement which he considers actually unavoidable:

> I cannot think, reflect, or judge about my being, without starting from the very point which I aim at concluding. My ideas are all assumptions, and I am ever moving in a circle. I cannot avoid being sufficient for myself, for I cannot make myself anything else, and to change me is to destroy me. If I do not use myself, I have no other self to use.[9]

It is this *using* of what they have got, even in the discovery of it, that marks the best use of implicit gifts coming into existence through the membership of the reading group. So much in literature, reading or writing, begins from language sounding some chord that lies below consciousness, finding an unconscious nerve struck into feeling.

So what we most think about in CRILS are readers who have not got 'finish' or polish, an explicit set of conscious skills, but are always like starters and re-starters, forgetting their assumptions, vulnerable to being opened up, and working anew from the blank intuitions of implicit thinking. The match between a literary text and a sensitive reader is not smooth for the best readers, is often almost violent—but it is achieved precisely because the words do not automatically turn into meanings: they need the feeling and effort and hazard and surprise that comes out of human imagination.

There was a group reading Robert Frost's 'The Road Not Taken'—a famous poem on all the unknowable might-have-beens on the other side of a life.

> Two roads diverged in a yellow wood,
> And sorry I could not travel both
> And be one traveler, long I stood
> And looked down one as far as I could
> To where it bent in the undergrowth;
>
> Then took the other, as just as fair,
> And having perhaps the better claim,
> Because it was grassy and wanted wear;
> Though as for that the passing there
> Had worn them really about the same

One of the participants, a young woman whom I will call Linda, had suffered neurological damage as a result of an accident with an electrical device in a year of travelling abroad: it affected her concentration, her relation to bright light, and sometimes when under stress her speech itself. The accident changed the course of her young life. If she hadn't taken the opportunity to travel in the first place . . . if she had not had the accident in the second . . . In this session there was one moment, in thinking of turns in the road ahead, which was marked by her greatest stutter, a moment of struggling articulacy. It came as she was reading of those two paths:

> And both that morning equally lay
> In leaves no step had trodden black.
> Oh, I kept the first for another day!
> Yet knowing how way leads on to way,
> I doubted if I should ever come back.

I shall be telling this with a sigh
Somewhere ages and ages hence:
Two roads diverged in a wood, and I—
I took the one less traveled by,
And that has made all the difference.

Then Linda paused over that last phrase 'all the difference', which names but does not specify, requiring something more from its reader. She recognized that she could never know what difference what did *not* happen might imaginably have made. 'I might have been better, I might have been worse some other way, but I will never know. And even if I had gone some other way, I would never know that it had been better or worse than this one—which I would not have taken...' But then of this poem of 'if's, she said, stutteringly: "If ever I have..." five times, like a terrible stutter on the verge of something. 'If ever I have... If ever I have...' and so on, as the listeners hung on painfully, before she could finally utter: 'If ever I have... children...'. She got out what, because of all that happened to her, was now most unlikely ever to occur, though she was still the youngest woman in the group: the word 'children'. Then—if ever, imaginably—she said she would warn those children about the electrical devices and other risks that had affected her.

Quantifiably, we know it was her longest stutter in all the sessions we monitored with her, and the research team is always seeking empirical ways to measure statistically or physiologically these qualitative changes in norms of tone and syntax and vocabulary and fluency. But finally Linda's problem with speech, the very disability, only increased the sense we have in Poetry itself: that to manage to complete a powerful sentence in a sensitive area is one of the greatest of abilities. 'If ever I have children...' Even the accomplished Robert Frost in that last stanza has his own more formal stutter with 'I', across the lines that then determine the finally set meaning: 'and I—/ I took the one less traveled by,/ And that...' The line-endings mark the gaps, the hesitations, the opening possibilities that then close. But this is the paradoxical value of inarticulacy which the poet both summons and overcomes in himself, and which the raw reader feels anyway: that when inarticulacy has to utter itself, it has insufficient secondary resources ready at hand, and has to be creative, genuine, and resourceful. The articulation that aspires to be of first and vital things, or essential but unclear things, is never easy—particularly in poetry and in the reading of poetry. That is why poetry suits the inarticulate reader accordingly. One of the CRILS researchers writes of such moments in informal session-notes:

It is the funny mix of how something that you could describe as tentative is one of the few times your body/mouth/voice goes for certainty... just by *saying* it. But tentative implies you could stop if you wanted. I'm not sure you really can—ok well, maybe you can stop with the voicing of it, but you can't stop with the feeling it. You're not trying to connect with something, you are more likely to be actively trying *not* to, if you can possibly manage it, but then there is some kind of sudden loss of fixed thinking. Suddenly you are not able *not* to speak. And it's not like *you* are being certain... it's more like something certain is coming through you to get out. It is a totally different version of being out of control. And the tentativeness is not like normal uncertainty, apologetic and havering and safe and liberal, but goes *into* an effort as a risked action.

That is what creative can mean. There is a poem Lesley keeps in her folder where she retains what she most likes after the group session, which she brought out when we interviewed her. It is Elizabeth Jennings's 'Friendship', beginning 'Such love I cannot analyse':

> Such love I cannot analyse;
> It does not rest in lips or eyes,
> Neither in kisses nor caress.
> Partly, I know, it's gentleness
> And understanding in one word
> Or in brief letters. It's preserved
> By trust and by respect and awe.
> These are the words I'm feeling for.
> Two people, yes, two lasting friends.
> The giving comes, the taking ends
> There is no measure for such things.
> For this all Nature slows and sings.

'These are the words I'm feeling for', writes the poet, as Pip felt '*for*' the variations on the hurt of 'humiliation', half-blindly, in his own creative inarticulacy. But what makes Lesley sensitively point to this line—line 8—is also, I think, her intuitive aural sense that it has found its quietly right place in the poem. It does so by virtue of the seeming pause just before or inside the rhyme: '—These', as that deictic referent encapsulates the preceding 'trust' and 'respect' and 'awe' and gently gathers them and loves them, within the internal act of writing. 'These are the words...' This happens when a writer in the midst of writing can receive back the words she has given out a moment earlier, as if helped by what she has done and by what the language itself has helped her to do, for herself. But what matters most here is the feeling of 'Friendship' which neither Elizabeth Jennings nor Lesley Tilney want to leave as merely second-best, even though knowing it is not love, committed, married, erotic, or whatever. It is like something that the plain and unmarried Lucy Snowe struggled with in chapter 16 of *Villette*, wondering what she should *do* with 'friends':

I felt that I still had friends. Friends, not professing vehement attachment, not offering the tender solace of well-matched and congenial relationship; on whom, therefore, but moderate demand of affection was to be made, of whom but moderate expectation formed; but towards whom my heart softened instinctively, and yearned with an importunate gratitude, which I entreated Reason betimes to check.

'Not' this, 'not' that, 'but moderate', 'but moderate', instead. Then the very same word 'but' is no longer able to do its works of repression—'but towards whom my heart softened...and yearned...' until so-called 'Reason' is strugglingly summoned to quash the resistance. Friends, says the syntax upfront: what to do with them, how to define them, how much to expect of them in her neediness, when they are not lovers?

Lesley has also brought with her from her folder D. H. Lawrence's poem 'Trust' which is about something bigger than 'the narrow little/ bargaining trust' of personal exchanges, beyond the calculations of analysis or measure. Instead, writes Lawrence, 'I think you may trust/ the sun in me'. Lesley says, 'Between that [*pointing to the Jennings*] and that [*pointing to the Lawrence*] and me, there's a bit of a link, I think.' There is a pause:

Interviewer: But these poems are about—sorry Lesley—from what you told me, what you *didn't* have in your life, especially as a kid.
L: No I didn't.

She knows she finds it very hard to trust people, but these poems 'communicate it in another way' instead:

I never had that when I was a child. I didn't have the love that I was supposed to have. I wasn't brought up with two proper parents, was I?

This is where the thought of *Great Expectations* returns to her.

It's the story, of course, of three parental replacements: Joe Gargery, the husband of Pip's hard-hearted sister; Miss Havisham the twisted old woman who leads Pip to think her the source of his great expectations; and Magwitch, the escaped convict unwillingly helped by the young Pip, who becomes secretly his real benefactor. It had been emotionally painful for Lesley to get through the novel, in addition to the difficulties of reading itself. 'It was that challenge isn't it, against meself. But I wanted to carry on. To see where the book and the story went. You want to see how the story ends of it all. He met that man didn't he, he met the convict again didn't he, and he'd helped him, didn't he? Pip did.' Lesley has been and remains determined to tell her own story, through all the pain of it. The story in Dickens itself offered from the first a model of going on in stamina, step by step, stage by stage with Pip, even as he leaves behind the home he has begun to look down upon for the sake of London: 'and it was now too late and too far to go back, and I went on...and the world lay spread before me' (chapter 19). When one of the participants from another group had become upset in reading of this parting, the group leader had gone so far as to ask whether they should read something else today. The group leader writes:

> But though upset, this woman (I'll call Christine) said, 'No, I want to carry on.' I always find this a moving thing for group members to say, especially in mental-health settings. Very often the reason they are in in-patient care in the first place is because they do not want to carry on, not with anything, not with life. If you can give someone in this position the opportunity to want to carry on with something, even something so apparently small as a single story, is that not a start? A tiny sense of wanting to continue. Of course it occurred to me that we often want to carry on reading because we want to know the end. Often we hope for a happier ending than what's going on mid-story. But it was clear in this case that there could be no completely happy ending, so it was what happens *after* an *unhappy* parting and ending that mattered to Christine who knew it could never now be wholly put right. It seemed like part of her whole struggle is that she is facing up to something, learning to live with a pain, and this was reflected in sticking with the book, even though it hurt.

What is more, even as it drove forward without clear progress, *Great Expectations* was also working backwards into the painful past of its protagonist and its reader.

The culmination comes in old Magwitch's revelation, that he had always thought of Pip as 'my boy' and secretly from a distance in exile had used his own tainted money to further Pip's social elevation, as an alternative life. It is a story that changes the story of the life that Pip thought he had been leading, ever since the rupture with simple, decent Joe Gargery. There is the old Dickensian cringe in Pip and about Pip, as he now discovers the disturbingly low origins of his higher standing, on Magwitch's return to England as a still wanted man:

> He regarded me with a look of affection that made him almost abhorrent to me again, though I had felt a great pity for him.
>
> Chapter 42

And then something else in chapter 54, when Magwitch's own fortunes turn against him:

> For now, my repugnance to him had all melted away, and in the hunted wounded shackled creature who held my hand in his, I only saw a man who had meant to be my

benefactor, and who had felt affectionately, gratefully, and generously, towards me with great constancy through a series of years. I only saw in him a much better man than I had been to Joe.

It is not simply 'a much better man than I had been to *him*'. Though Joe and Magwitch have never actually met save now in Pip's head, the moral link is creatively made back across Pip's life by his recognizing in the feelings of his unattractive benefactor 'a much better man than I had been to *Joe*'. It is characteristic of Lesley that the word 'only' there—'I only saw a man who had meant to be my benefactor…I only saw in him a much better man'—is what would catch her. The utterance still tacitly accepts all that was less good in Magwitch, but marks the determination to concentrate nonetheless on what 'only' should concern Pip: his own conduct across a life. Lesley says, 'It breaks the gap.' Her interviewer begins to talk about whether she means by that 'making links', but then stops herself to ask, 'Breaks the gap?'

> Yeah, that's a proper way of putting it, yours: linking. It *communicates* one thing to another, doesn't it? It breaks the gap…going back here, between that and other things. I'm not explaining meself. Things that have happened can be dangerous. But I can deal with that through the reading groups. Because *that* stops *that*. It breaks that gap because your mind's focusing on something else, concentrating on something else. So that will break that.

Often, and primarily, 'that' in Lesley (as compared to 'other things') seems to mean the almost unspeakable childhood trauma of the past, which Dickens himself knew in his own way when at the age of twelve, as a result of his father's financial stupidity, he had to pawn his collection of books, leave school, and go out to work at the shoe-blacking warehouse, without anyone in his family lifting a finger on his behalf. But for Lesley 'that' here also refers to the literature she points to in the reading group: 'that [stuff in the novel] stops [the primary, traumatic] that'. And 'stops' here seems to mean 'overcomes', to prevent the constant thinking of it; but also refers to what 'breaks the gap' meant: namely, 'puts an end to' and almost 'heals'. Because 'that' is what *Great Expectations* does for Lesley inside, heals the traumatic gap—across the breaks and times and people, across the negative of not being loved as one should have been, 'between that and other things'—through finding some final continuity and future in its story.

> 'Pip's ended up pretty good in the end, got on with his life, didn't he? And I've ended up pretty good in the end, haven't I? Cos I've done more since I went to the

reading group and me voluntary work for *The Reader*. So I've come on. I've gone *forward*, haven't I?'

Reading Pip helped her turn the past forward. When she said, 'Pip's ended up pretty good in the end. And I've ended up pretty good in the end' or 'He was cheated and I was cheated', it reminded me of Silas Marner's bare articulacy when he finds the child at his hearth: 'It's a lone thing—and I'm a lone thing' (*Silas Marner*, chapter 13). But the idiom is even more specific than that: 'pretty well' is a much repeated phrase in *Great Expectations* itself, and those needy question-tags through which Lesley defends and challenges herself even through her problems with trust—'didn't he?', 'haven't I?', 'isn't it?'—are tonally pure Dickens, like Joe Gargery's vulnerably repeated 'Ever the best of friends; ain't us, Pip?' (chapters 7 and 57). These tonal questions seek an answering match, emotionally, from outside in the world. To be Wordsworth here would mean being perfect and at home: 'Why shine they round me thus whom thus I love?'

But most telling in this still developing idiom are the indeterminate dumb pointers to significance and context, the use of deixis, those basic words of orientation within the space, time, and the extra-linguistic situation in which a person is placed. For Lesley these are terms such as 'that' 'something', 'between'. They are what William Barnes, Dorset dialect poet, priest, and philologist, beloved of Thomas Hardy, called 'Thing Mark-words' in his *Outline of English Speech-Craft* (1878) because he wanted to teach English by English, not by words of Greek or Latin origin. Such words *mark* the very movement into language, on the boundary between language and thought: they bear the internal feeling of or for something—without fully knowing it within language, without being able to generate more explicit words for it yet. These are starts towards the turning of implicit into explicit reason. They are not like being told something, fully formed, as by a professional teacher or counsellor, for example.

It is more like the crucial language-movement that Karl Bühler describes in a book recommended to me by another of our collaborators, the psychologist Arthur Jacobs, translated in 2011 from the original German edition of 1934 as *Theory of Language*.

What interests Bühler is a language-shift. It starts out from what he calls the original deictic field, where in real life someone physically and then audibly points to an object of actual perception in the outside world. And from language pointing to the world, there is then in human evolution a shift of register, says Bühler, to a symbolic representation of that world within the written syntax of relationships constructed separately through the medium of the page. It is at that second stage that language does not just point outwards but, displaced, begins, like a person, to develop its own internal resources: namely, its language-*within*-language through its own interconnections, parentheses, and meta-commentaries; its looking forward or turning back on itself, to become reflective upon itself, and create mind there. It is like the evolved form of a more inner pointedness that goes on within the words such as '*then*' and '*too*' in Dickens's sentence: 'I wished Joe had been rather more genteelly brought up, and then I should have been so too'. Or when two clauses come from a different *level* within the same line of writing: as when between 'I was so humiliated, hurt, spurned, offended, angry, sorry—...' and 'that tears started to my eyes', there is the internal reflection in parenthesis, '—I cannot hit upon the right name for the smart—God knows what its name was—'.

This is a new second field—increasingly a literary field—that Lesley, the woman who points, has been learning to develop more and more, when she says that

> the reading group has been what I call a second chance—instead of focusing on...you know...I think I have found my field now, this is probably my path, really.

My *field*—as in Bleich's diagram of Freud or Bühler's account of the development of the autonomous place for linguistic deixis: a place where you feel that consciousness is doing its work from within an area indistinctly marked out as yours by your stimulated pre-consciousness, sub-consciousness, unconsciousness—whatever that resonant, almost recognizable Unknown truly is.

To find your own idiom, the style and the expression of a truer self as opposed to a false one, says the psychoanalyst Christopher Bollas, is to change one's 'fate' into one's 'destiny'. Idiom, he argues, is 'the it' that exists obscurely within people, a core seeking to become more fully 'an I'. 'Its pleasure is to elaborate itself through the choice of objects'—objects like books that, without premeditation or design, seem spontaneously to match 'its' implicit identity and give it further embodiment in human forms. It is 'a joy of living' to find those affinities and in that way to become a more formed 'character' by enjoying the hazard of being affected by an encountered object at a level below deliberate consciousness:

> To be a character, to release one's idiom into lived experience, requires a certain risk, as the subject will not know his outcome; indeed to be a character is to be released into being...puzzled by his itness, yet relieved by the *jouissance* of its choosings.[10]

That is where the finding of a match is the very definition of life happening, of a life being truly lived across and between inside and out.

So Lesley has begun to learn her own idiom: 'That stops that'; 'It breaks the gap between that and other things'; 'I can understand between the book and myself; with Pip's story and my story, can't I? My own life'. It is not just Lesley thinking 'I can relate to that' or 'That's me': there is more *movement* back and forth continuously in dialogue, as though the text were more like an agent for mobile discovery than a template of fixed similarities. She knows she sees things other people don't always, or at least not so immediately. She says she is working from 'different angles' now.

Despite her bad start in childhood, and almost because of it, Lesley feels lucky now, she says, with more chance of being able to describe what's going on in her, and what has gone on in her life. 'So it's like me fighting against that in another way, isn't it? It's like me, challenging meself to have a go at things.'

In standard questionnaires on the value of Shared Reading, this would be called 'increased self-esteem', and group members often speak of increased 'confidence'. But as so often in the literal world, we don't really know much of what those names stand for, and at least Lesley can't put it quite like that. Richard Petty, a professor of psychology at Ohio State University, argues that confidence belongs in the realm of secondary or meta-cognition (where, for example, the act of instinctive pointing and selecting in Lesley would be what is primary).[11] Petty believes that confidence is the bridge that may become increasingly established between thought and action, when people begin to see that they can not only respond to the world but also have some effect upon it. They begin to believe they can get their 'insides outside', as Lesley puts it, feeling there is a home or a match out there, rather than suffer the rejection and neglect that comes in the felt separation between the two. Regularly brought into practice, these increased movements both to and fro—from text to reader, from unconscious to conscious and back again—begin to form a new mental capacity, a mental faculty in humans. And in this process, it is at this point and for this reason that *Ideas* exist, beyond mere intellectualism. They help consolidate implicit reason, to give it memory and confidence. They help people recognize themselves, giving a greater character, permanence, and purpose to whatever it is in a person that may come more alive again through having them. As a landing place for the next stage of development, ideas—if they don't rigidify—can become an instrument for further thinking.

But this chapter remains largely about Lesley, because the models, reflections, and ideas I discuss here are neither irrelevant nor disproportionate to her story. They are what the thought of her prompts, what she herself needs and begins to register in her own terms. She is one of the great beginners, the driving force that incites and requires these further advances in confident and articulate development.

What is finally so interesting with Lesley is that her release through reading is not the same as the involuntariness that in chapter 1 Keith described as crucial to the honesty of his emotional reactions. Lesley says in one session, for example: 'When you know you want to do something, then you know you have to do something.' She is less involuntary, or more committed to what the involuntary is telling her, and in consequence more urgently resolute and indomitable. Her interviewer told me, reporting on this fierceness in her:

> The main thing that struck me about Lesley was her determination to tell her 'story'—the bad bits of her life, I mean, told through fragments of poetry and novels. Because that is what trauma actually feels like, in flashes and broken pieces—more like sudden poetry than an orderly retrospective narrative.[12] If I tried to change the rhythm or pace of our conversation she'd barge through it to say what she needed to say, she'd go back to it, insist on it, she *had* to get it out. Which makes me think about what she said about the personal stuff that it 'would come out'—because it didn't feel accidental or involuntary in that sense. It felt more of a dragging out into the light.

What Lesley fiercely likes about literature is what she said about Shakespeare's sonnet 29 especially when the poem rises almost to the light of heaven's gate: it is 'like as if he is talking to God'. The whole thing finally gets itself said to some listener—even if, as with Pip, it seems to be only your younger to your older self and back again.

> Gives me a boost, doesn't it? Makes me feel better. It gives me a boost what I didn't have. It's like something's inside me [*animated, fists clutched to stomach*] trying to escape. So I'm trying to explore that and the only way I know of exploring everything now is through shared reading in The Reader. So there must be some-thing there, built inside me, that wants to...share whatever's there with others. To help others understand certain things I can see and others can't, but I can't quite say. I never had all that. It's only since I've been going there and in the reading group. It's all strange to me but there is something there. And it's a way of... communicating in another way, isn't it? I didn't have all that there though, did I? So it was hard, hard for me to understand it.

It is all about 'another way'—of seeing, of fighting, of communicating. Lesley has started studying English at a college. She asks again: 'I have done pretty well, I have gone forward, haven't I?'

CHAPTER 4

THE WOMAN WHO
BECAME A POEM

At primary school she had been an elective mute, refusing to speak despite the ability to do so, but she was a compulsive reader. She wanted to live in her own little world. In childhood her parents urged her to stop reading, and go out and enjoy the world. But she wanted to read everything there ever was, and somehow read it all in the right order. Even now she almost physically cannot bear to be without a book.

Hers had been a troubled birth, the mother had Addison's disease, involving damage to the adrenal glands, and the baby suffered a brain haemorrhage. It has always been a story of difficulties. Since the age of thirteen, Imelda has been variously diagnosed with post-traumatic stress disorder (PTSD) and Asperger's syndrome, with attention deficit hyperactivity disorder (ADHD), and a form of obsessive–compulsive disorder called 'pure OCD' in which instead of outward, physical compulsions, there is the obsessive repetition of intrusive thoughts so unwanted as to be monstrously horrific. 'I think there is obviously a fight going on in my head,' she says, now in her mid forties, 'between the labels that have been put on my head.'

Before she started going to Shared Reading groups in 2007, she would be in hospital for up to two weeks out of every month, with problems connected with her brittle diabetes. Once or twice a week she might also ring the local hospital with a knife or matches in her hand, depressed and anxious, sometimes self-harming and suicidal, her head as though on fire. In other group activities she had tried you could sit around and join in the conversation or not; but in the reading group, with the literature, she says:

> You've got to *follow* it. You've got to *stop*, and *think*. And the brain says 'Right, we're doing this now. Concentrate. Switch.'

That overrides what she calls the mental washing-machine of the same terrible thoughts going round and round her tumbling mind. It is why she loves the sheer difficulty of Shakespeare, with his cryptic clues and rapid shifts of perspective, and alongside a friend is now helping to run a group reading the plays. The plays, as she puts it, re-mind her. She is even thinking of trying to translate every Shakespeare play into Scouse dialect to see what they look and sound like in some accessibly rougher version of themselves. She loved first of all *The Winter's Tale*, the tale of redemption after sixteen long years.

Imelda had been in shared reading groups for several years, had even undertaken volunteer training to read one-to-one with an aged neighbour, when one December day—but here are her own words:

> I got a phone call from *The Reader* about doing something in London for them in February 2016 with the poem 'Invictus', though I don't usually leave Merseyside. It was to do with the launch of some other national organization to do with arts and social purpose. I had heard of the poem because I think most people know that story about Nelson Mandela reading it to himself and his comrades in prison. But I must admit I'm not a poetry lover, it's the novel that I want, not the poems—never one really stood out like this one has. And so I started to read it—because what we had to do at this place in London was say a verse each, and then each of us would say the two lines at the end:

> > Out of the night that covers me,
> >   Black as the pit from pole to pole,
> > I thank whatever gods may be
> >   For my unconquerable soul.
> >
> > In the fell clutch of circumstance
> >   I have not winced nor cried aloud.
> > Under the bludgeonings of chance
> >   My head is bloody, but unbowed.
> >
> > Beyond this place of wrath and tears
> >   Looms but the Horror of the shade,
> > And yet the menace of the years
> >   Finds and shall find me unafraid.
> >
> > It matters not how strait the gate,
> >   How charged with punishments the scroll,
> > I am the master of my fate,
> >   I am the captain of my soul.

> A couple of days later, I just started to repeat those last two lines. I kept on thinking 'I *am*'. I've got this thing about people telling me what's best for me: I know what's best for me. No, no: 'I *am* the master of my fate', not you. That was roughly Christmas time, and I don't like Christmas and I don't like certain times of the year, and I found myself, just out of the blue, it was as if a voice … well, this is going

to sound really spooky, but it's as if something said 'Say it. Say it to yourself.' It's as if it gets a hold of me.

'Invictus' has been Imelda's poem, her mantra, for over two years now. She often says it in bed, or walking along the street, and most often in moments of great stress. It makes a difference that she says it out-loud, or even quietly to herself. Taken in that way, it feels more like something she hears, something she receives back, rather than something she just reads on the page. It is language which seems to exist not to go forward and outwards, but back and in—less to express herself than to tell herself something. And the benefit seems to come from that loop of hearing herself saying it. This is something which she believes may have relation to Piaget's famous thoughts about children first developing experimental self-regulation by being able to repeat to themselves, as though from outside, such words as 'Hot, hot', in warning. 'So I kept saying to myself "I am master of my fate, I am captain of my soul". You hear it, don't you, saying it to yourself. I don't know how the body and mind all works but the saying it to myself was like working between those two.'

In what the poem calls 'the menace of the years', W. E. Henley's 'Invictus' has been her steadfast and extended friend, her mate, she says, even soulmate. Though not a cure, it is at least, as she puts it thinking of her diabetes, a form of poetic insulin. She maps herself onto the poem's structure, or recreates it within her: 'This soul on this piece of paper is in the same place as me.' And it offers her an alternative language within which to try to live and think.

It has helped her hold on through varying medical diagnoses and various scans and treatments, in the seemingly endless temporariness of waiting: 'I'm going through something and I just think, well, I hope, that there will be an end. There will be. This just can't ...' If somebody said to her, 'I'm very sorry, but you are going to be like this until the day you die', Imelda thinks she would jump in the river. But instead 'People have said to me that the treatment I'm waiting for *might* not work but that is still a big difference from "no way" it will ... So I just say to myself, right, see this through, see this go a bit further, and a bit further, you just don't know.' She sometimes thinks that more normal people would not survive twenty-four hours with the incessant thoughts she has. She waited two years for EMDR, eye-movement therapy-treatment for trauma, which helped after the first session and subsequently did not. 'And I think well what if, if I killed myself last Saturday and then on the Monday I got the letter through to come to some new treatment, and then everyone would be going, Well if only she'd waited ... just another day. I'm not a big religious person but when you think of that, you think surely, surely there'll be something ...'

Imelda also writes a blog with the verve of her own voice. Second only to reading, writing the blog is a help to her. In it, she seems to feel free to say almost anything regardless of who might read it. It is as if that is what writing is for—to be an extra dimension, between private and public, regardless of the normal social conventions. She never re-reads what she writes, otherwise she would delete everything, begin again, and never complete anything at all. She hardly bothers with punctuation— the only way for her to avoid the perfectionism of editing and re-editing is simply to get it all down raw. But she writes by a sort of rhythm, created through the gaps she leaves between clauses.

On 2 April 2017, after more than a year of constantly repeating 'Invictus' to herself, Imelda wrote in her blog that her repetition of the poem's last two lines 'is more of a scream out   that I am in   charge   not other people'. I, not others, is her motto. In this she relishes the defiant negatives of 'Invictus' before the final lines— 'my *unconquerable* soul', 'have *not* winced *nor* cried aloud' (though she adds, 'Well, I bleeding well have'—), 'find me *unafraid*', 'it matters *not*'. And those stubbornly resistant negatives met something that her PTSD therapist said was central to her: 'No one listening when I say the word "No"!!' That makes sense, she believes, because 'my words of "No I don't want to do that" spark off the physical and mental abuse of my childhood.' No one took notice when she screamed No.

The nature of those negatives is crucial to what two philosophers have noted in the sudden experience of 'being moved'—where the feeling comes from a predominant sense of emotion bursting through 'against the odds', like something deep within a person standing up for herself. 'A common feature' of what these commentators describe as emotion 'making a stand' is '*the presence of the positive in the negative*', achieved 'both *in* and *despite* circumstances'[1] 'In the fell clutch of circumstance...My head is bloody but unbowed.'

Two psychologists have recently followed suit by claiming that this feeling of being moved is 'elicited by core values' such as love or will-power or beauty, which are experienced all the more movingly when emergent through adversity. These hidden but finally defiant core values ('values that are particularly central to being human') manifest themselves in circumstances that are often unfavourable to their existence:

> For example, we expect the value of love to appear stronger when conducted in times of war (unfavourable circumstances) than when conducted in times of peace (favourable circumstances). Likewise, we expect the value of willpower to appear stronger when accomplished by a person with a debilitating disease (unfavourable circumstances) than by a person who is fit and healthy (favourable circumstances).

Moreover, we contend that because unfavourable circumstances make a core value stand out more, they increase the feeling of being moved.[2]

The emotion says, 'It matters not ... how charged with punishments.' Imelda is often unwell, and almost always at war—as if 'ready for a fight' she says. If she had been wired up to some brain-imaging screen, she tells us at interview:

> I think it would have gone off on those last two lines of 'Invictus', straight off. Say your brain's usually going tick, tick, tick; it would go TICK, BANG! You could feel it when you said it. First time you read it, I think *every word* in that: I. Am. The Master. Of *My* Fate. So it is 'I' and 'My'—you can't take them away, it's me; *you* can never take anything. 'Am'—it's in the present tense: so I'm here today and I'm constantly being taken back to thirteen, fourteen years ago, or longer, and I don't want to go there and it's like PTSD says to me: 'You're going there'. But it's today, it's now. I am, it's now. I *am* [bangs table]. And the fact that whatever the fate, it's '*my* fate'.

'Every word', as 'I' and 'am' and 'my' ... To that great founder of psychology William James, this state, whatever the label we might give it, would be like those obsessive emphases of word and voice characteristic of old religious crises. The great example for him was John Bunyan in *Grace Abounding to the Chief of Sinners* (1666).

The sufferer in that memoir had for years ringing in his head a damning Biblical text from Hebrews 12:16–17 which he believed had condemned him, personally, to utter perdition: 'Esau, who for one morsel of meat, sold his birthright: for ye know, how that afterward, when he would have inherited the blessing, he was rejected; for he found no place of repentance, though he sought it carefully with tears'. Just when he would have inherited the blessing, even though he sought it—he was rejected.

Then suddenly from his Bible Bunyan found one day a few brief words from Corinthians come into his mind to take on and fight that lengthy Esau text from Hebrews which he had repeated and repeated, addictively and obsessively:

> But one morning as I was again at prayer, and trembling under the fear of this, *That no word of God could help me*, that piece of a sentence darted in upon me, *My grace is sufficient*. At this, methought I felt some stay, as if there might be hopes. But, oh! how good a thing it is for God to send His word! for, about a fortnight before, I was looking on this very place, and then I thought it could not come near my soul with comfort, therefore I threw down my book in a pet: then I thought it was not large enough for me; no, not large enough; but now it was as if it had arms of grace so wide, that it could not only enclose me, but many more such as I besides.

It is from 2 Corinthians 12:9. Even so, the promise in the text, 'My grace is sufficient' was not a permanent salvation to him. The effect seemed intermittent:

By these words I was sustained, yet not without exceeding conflicts, for the space of seven or eight weeks; for my peace would be in it, and out, sometimes twenty times a day; comfort now, and trouble presently; peace now, and before I could go a furlong, as full of fear and guilt as ever heart could hold. And this was not only now and then, but my whole seven weeks' experience: for this about *the sufficiency of grace*, and *that of Esau's* parting with his birthright, would be like a pair of scales within my mind; sometimes one end would be uppermost, and sometimes again the other; according to which would be my peace or trouble.

It is so specific: four words, up to twenty times a day, over two months, 350 years ago. So it hung, text against text, in the balance of his mind. He still needed two remaining words of the saying from Corinthians:

Therefore I did still pray to God, that He would come in with this scripture more fully on my heart; to wit, that He would help me to apply the whole sentence, for as yet I could not: that He gave, that I gathered; but farther I could not go, for as yet it only helped me to hope there might be mercy for me; *My grace is sufficient*: And though it came no farther, it answered my former question, to wit, That there was hope; yet because *for thee* was left out, I was not contented, but prayed to God for that also. Wherefore, one day, when I was in a meeting of God's people, full of sadness and terror; for my fears again were strong upon me; and, as I was now thinking, my soul was never the better, but my case most sad and fearful, these words did with great power suddenly break in upon me; *My grace is sufficient for thee, My grace is sufficient for thee, My grace is sufficient for thee*, three times together: And oh! methought that every word was a mighty word unto me; as *My*, and *grace*, and *sufficient*, and *for thee*; they were then, and sometimes are still, far bigger than others be.

Paras. 204–6

The sentence 'My grace is sufficient' became fully parsed and complete only when he recalled two further words speaking to him as if from Christ Himself, not stopping short: 'My grace is sufficient *for thee*', endlessly abounding. Four words, then made six words, '*every word* was a mighty word unto me', as though this were no set text but an alphabet of the big words always waiting to be freshly spelt out and re-construed. And Bunyan's own words of physical colloquialism—'come near my soul with comfort', 'darted in', 'felt some stay, as if', 'left out', 'break in', 'that He would come in with this scripture more fully'—bespeak a power of innerly felt construal like almost no other we have known in the history of reading.

And yet for all its extreme intensity on the verge of breakdown, this is not a mind willing to be deluded into a final and total hallelujah. He goes back from the personal voice to the Biblical text he thinks it has come from, to check that the words were really there, objective and true, and not simply a figment created by his own brain. And however desperate he can be, Bunyan remains chastened and precarious in that only '*sometimes ... still*', at the end.

Imelda had in mind a different kind of check-up, which was more modern. She wanted to undergo a brain-imaging scan to find out what was going on in there at moments of crisis, and see the surges of electricity behind the screams.[3] But she couldn't have it, and Imelda reproduced her experience through written sounds instead, in a blog of January 2018, two years on.

She begins by complaining about too easy in-words such as 'triggered' and 'meltdown': 'You may have lost your composure,' she tells her readers, 'but it is not a meltdown like this, with the strength of a monster in my head or brain, the emotions erupting throughout your body ... I know what hell is because I live there.' As a result of mental flashbacks and emotional overload, autistic meltdown means that 'I scream and yell continuously and wreck everything around my teeth clench and I feel the need to bite things anything and have lost various teeth because of the clenching   so you can see how upset I feel when people keep saying they are having a meltdown (Get a grip)'. Normal people only mean by meltdown that life has got on top of them for a while, but Imelda's is something different—as her simulated brain print-out tries now to show through her blog:

> My head is POUNDING I ACTUALLY WORRY IT WILL EXPLODE OVER the floor like what seen on the few horror pictures I have watched!
>
> My jaw is clenched a tooth falls out the memories of past events are in my head BEING TOLD like a dagger stabbing dagger stabbing like fireworks going off try to clench fists instead of mouth as if ready for a fight with no one but myself !!!!
>
> I am screaming I don't want these thoughts in my head they are in control when I never asked them to come in. I DONT WANT THIS I DONT WANT YOU. HAVE BEEN TOLD TO GIVE THE MONSTER A NAME BUT CALLING HIM/HER BILLY SAM FRANK HAS NO EFFECT !!
>
> I RARELY CRY AS THEY HAVE LONG RUN DRY BUT THE FRUSTRATION IN HEAD IT JUST EXPLODES ...
>
> no body can understand this place I am trapped in of hurt and the loss of actual me !!!
>
> LOSS   what is loss it is the loss of control, loss of connection with most people as who else has this monster in the brain so there is total loss of understanding of me and am   passed about like in the game of pass the parcel
>
> If a toddler explodes it is not BECAUSE they are NOT understood it is cos they have no words to describe the feelings that envelope them but as an adult in the same state is frowned at as u turn instantly from an adult to child !!!! ... but there is nothing to show the hurt in your head unlike a child's scrape on a knee 'Shall I kiss it better?' can't do that with a pain in head !!!

She has been told she can be emotionally very like a child, over-excitable and spontaneous, with fast changes of mood; but what children have which she has not, she says, is the gift of living in the present, not the past. She does have the words to express and explain, as infants may not, but it does not help to speak them: no one understands hers as an adult experience. Words are only best for reading and writing. So in the face of these thoughts from her past, she turns in the blog to what she calls her mate 'Invictus', imperfectly reciting it from memory to get the poem inside her, herself inside the poem. I again preserve her spacings and capitals, some of which are perhaps accidents of typing but others forms of expression:

> ahhhh a glimmer of hope take deep breath strong   but laboured just breathe
> like a fish wide and open look at something a tree or a flower come to the
> present turn the rage into uneasy peace yeah u are here today the past has gone
> the relief   is flowing through the body calmer   take a breath AND
> OUT OF THE NIGHT THAT COVERS ME BLACK AS THE PIT FROM POLE TO
> POLE
> I THANK WHATEVER GODS MAYBE   FOR MY UNCONQUERABLE SOUL
> IN THE FELL CLUTCH OF CIRCUMSTANCE I HAVE NOT WINCED OR CRIED
> ALONE
> MY HEAD IS BLUDGEONED BUT UNBOWED
> beyond this place of wrath and tears
> looms but the horror of the shade
> and yet the menace of the years
> finds and shall   find me unafraid
> IT   matters not how strait the gate
> how charged with punishments the scroll
> I am the master of my fate I am the master of my soul
> —wooah hey breathing normally yep survived here as they say to fight another
> day

When the two voices—monster and poem—go against each other like that, Imelda says she feels like a sort of female Job from the Bible, when everything went wrong and it was not known whether it was the Devil or God giving Job a test, each battling over him.

There are noises as well as thoughts and voices. She told us at interview that the repetitive 'bad stuff' in her brain sounds like 'de-de-de-de-de'—fast machine-gun fire. The more routine sentences in life sound only like the reading that a six-year-old does, as with the niece she helps: 'The man went to the pond and then he jumped into the pond and then he . . .' She says this in a linear monotone like a child learning to read, without expression. Then again it can be like this, she says, and this time she bangs hard on the table, without rhythm, but fast, in disturbance. 'But with the *Invictus* you can even turn the words around. I go around and I put it to music sometimes.' It would be like—and now she bangs more softly on the table, rhythmically, humming along with it: 'der der der, der, der der der', like a song. It creates calm out of the other agitated noises. The words change the sound of the voice even as the voice, thinking through them, give the words a depth and resonance.

Imelda can play with the poem, turn the words around, take out single phrases, change their order, not worry if she does not quite remember it correctly, but improvising within its basic script and shelter of words. She goes beyond the merely 'given' in recreating the poem, encouraged by the thought that poets themselves make different versions and revisions. 'I was travelling back home by bus and I could feel the thoughts come back, so picture me on the bus saying OUT OUT out of the night, and repeating each word. I made patterns about saying one word once, then twice, to slow down the wheel of thought.' She doubted if Nelson Mandela ever made such word games with 'Invictus' but then again thought he possibly did. There is a bit of her that is scared of learning it too well, too perfectly, as if it might be all over and done by then.

She only weighs eight stone, but what she is trying to lift, she says, feels like a twenty-five stone person on top of her. She has been given Cognitive Behavioural Therapy and offered other therapeutic advice. 'People have gone mindfulness-mad. And you're supposed to sort of think about what you're doing and living in the moment. Well to me, I could say, and they've said to me, "Think of yourself lifting the coffee mug up" but you see I go "I lift the coffee mug up and I put the coffee in" [*saying this in her child-reading ironic tone*]. Those words "I lift the coffee up, I put the coffee in", they don't feel anything to me, do they? But saying 'Invictus' aloud, you see they are actually words that mean something. "I thank whatever Gods may be for my unconquerable soul".' She says this last almost musically. What CBT offers, she feels, is a surface technique; but the poem as felt and meaningful becomes hers, becomes her, or a companion to her, at her side and in her voice. 'I'll just say the one sentence. Or sometimes I'll just say "Unconquerable Soul" not the whole sum of it, I'll just go "Yes, unconquerable soul".' She even used it during a heart-scan when a tube was put down her mouth, and describes it in her own stream-of-consciousness way (she admires Virginia Woolf):

out of the night that covers me (this pain won't last forever, really it won't) black as the pit from pole to pole (still hurts) I thank whatever gods may be for my unconquerable soul (getting used to looking at screen at my dancing thing in my heart dancing about)...

Sometimes it does not work, sometimes it works less than others, sometimes she despairs and fears its spell has worn out. One time, she writes in her blog, 'the evil bit of me keeps shouting at me, You can repeat Invictus all u like but I am still here...'

This monster voice repeats and repeats and repeats, stuck and incessant, uttering words of obscenity and threat and violence. 'My mum and dad will say to me, "That happened thirteen years ago and you're still telling us about it!" But it's as if it...it's still there. It's still [*gestures an explosion in her head*] !!'

The interviewer suggests to Imelda that the repetition of 'Invictus', with the possibility of improvising off it in changing the words, is the same as the OCD mechanism of repetition but producing a quite different effect. Rhiannon Corcoran, professor of psychology and member of the CRILS team, thinks the alleviation that results is something subtler and more achievable than a 'cure' of obsessive symptoms: the symptoms have not been abolished but they have been used and modified freely to build a meaning and to accomplish something creative. It is a vital adaptation characteristic of the evolution of human capacities. But we also know it is like a poetic form of homeopathy, actually long known though also long forgotten.

In *The Art of English Poesy* (1589), George Puttenham speaks of two kinds of loss. One you may be able to do something about—a run of bad luck, blemished character, loss of money. You may be able to claw something back, receive a second chance, find a remedy that makes the loss, in retrospect, only temporary. For help to make it so, you may go for mending to the adviser, the moneylender, or the physician. But the deeper kind of loss is to do with the irrevocable and the irreversible, loss through death or at war or in unrequited love. These things—in a sense more intrinsic to life—are those which cannot be cured. There we need, argues Puttenham, the force of poetic lamentation, making strong in language what feels so weakened, even by its own power, in life:

> Lamenting is altogether contrary to rejoicing: every man saith so, and yet it is a piece of joy to be able to lament with ease, and freely to put forth a man's inward sorrows and the griefs wherewith his mind is surcharged. This was a very necessary device of the Poet and a fine, besides his poetry to play also the Physician, and not only by applying a medicine to the ordinary sickness of mankind, but by making the very grief it self (in part) a cure of the disease.[4]

What cannot be healed by treatment or medicine or finance may be helped instead by some hidden virtue in words put into song or verse:

> Therefore of death and burials, of the adversities by wars, and of true love lost or ill bestowed are the only sorrows that the noble Poets sought by their art to remove or

appease, not with any medicament of a contrary temper, as the Galenistes use to cure *contraria contrariis*, but as the Paracelsians, who cure *similia similibus*, making one dolour to expel another, and in this case, one short sorrowing the remedy of a long and grievous sorrow.

Art, p. 48

The followers of Galen—the second-century physician, surgeon, and philosopher—had one way, the sixteenth-century followers of the Swiss physician and alchemist, Paracelsus, another. What would the Galenists do? In *The Anatomy of Melancholy* (1628) Robert Burton speaks of *combating* misery by force of opposition—as by humours, a greater heat dispels the cold or a greater cold reduces heat:

> Whatsoever it is that runneth in his mind which so much affects or troubleth him, by all possible means he must withstand it, expel those fears and sorrows... beginning by doing something or other that shall be opposite unto them.... If it be sickness, ill success, or any adversity that hath caused it, oppose an invincible courage, persuade evil for good, set prosperity against adversity.... Force out one nail with another, drive out one passion with another.[5]

In this Galenist camp there are what, in a book about trauma that Imelda has read—*The Body Keeps the Score* by Bessel Van der Kolk—are called 'Firefighters'. They are the desperate people who will do almost anything to try to make the toxic pain go away—impulsively go to a bar to get blind drunk, compulsively pick up a stranger, take another drug to counter the last one, self-harm, destroy the house in order to extinguish the fire, trying somehow to turn the problem into its own solution.

But the way of Paracelsus, says Puttenham, is more sympathetic, working neither by invasive intervention nor by aggressive self-obliteration, but by a kind of homeopathy, a vaccine making the very grief a cure of the disease. Not driving out one passion with another opposing it, but using one short form of sorrow in art to soothe the more lengthily extended sorrow of life. And, though she is a fighter and though her favoured verse contains its own measure of defiance, Imelda instinctively uses her repetition of 'Invictus' to counter the same process of repetition that comes with her intrusive thoughts: 'similia similibus', however much the content is contrary. It is like Brecht in his 'Motto' for poetry, asking whether there will be singing in the dark times, and replying yes, there will be singing, singing *about* the dark times.

Increasingly over the two years Imelda has lived with the poem, it is the lament of the opening two lines to which she has turned:

> Out of the night that covers me,
> Black as the pit from pole to pole...

The lamentation comes 'out' of that deep dark place and still cries from within it, but that word 'out' also looks fractionally forward in Imelda's eyes, to a coming out, a seeking for the way out, in expression of hope: 'I think he's come out of the night and he eventually got free—Nelson Mandela—':

> The night has covered him, and it tells you straight away he's still in this dark place but he's *out* of the night. That gives me some sort of hope. If it started off all sort of happy, that's no good for me, too opposite to me, poems have to go up and down.

It calms her because it contains all that is also not calm. In that way 'Out' is for her like the first word in the third stanza, 'Beyond', pointing forward, 'Beyond this place of wrath and tears':

> *Imelda*: And then you see you've got the third verse haven't you, you've got 'Beyond this place of wrath and tears/looms but the horror of the shade'—so just take that Beyond line by itself. It's not really the whole line, I straight away zoom into 'beyond'. What I think I like about it is if you look at the next line 'Looms *but* the horror of the shade', you could have had something else: it could go 'beyond this place of darkness, there is happiness around the corner!' or something like that. Now to me that is not gonna be... that's gonna do nothing.
>
> *Interviewer*: Why not?
>
> *Imelda*: It's not...to get through something, like what I'm doing, you can't...that will do nothing to me, going 'Right, erm, this happiness is round the corner'. It's not round the corner, it probably will always be, like at the moment, ten miles away or something. I am very wary, you could see me and think oh she's in a great mood but...When we went to London to read 'Invictus' I was absolutely fine the whole time I was in London and I'm thinking oh, I'm better. I've done this before when I first realized what was wrong with me and thought 'Oh, it's gone!' Like a headache, you wake up and it's gone. But then bang, it's back. 'And yet' is, still, the next line.

> Beyond this place of wrath and tears
> Looms but the Horror of the shade,
> And yet the menace of the years
> Finds and shall find me unafraid.

Imelda goes on with this:

> The whole thing is more honest. I don't like these poems where they might start off in a dark place and the next minute you're in Disneyland. I don't think they do much for you. 'The horror of the shade *and yet* the menace of the years finds, and *shall find* me unafraid': now you could *take* that, and this is just for me personally, I'm kind of *used to it*; although it's like hell, but I am kind of used to it. *And yet* is a tiny bit of room for hope to live in. It is hard to read, but also he wedges 'shall find'

between 'finds' and 'me unafraid', determined for the future, even now. And 'unafraid' is like 'I thank whatever gods may be for my *unconquerable* soul.' It is just a word or syllable that's put in, *un*this, *un*that—like it's '*whatever* Gods may be'. It's not saying there is a God, he's not saying either thing, he's saying whatever Gods there *may* be, whether you're somebody who believes or not. And I like the word 'unconquerable' because when I say it over and over—unconquerable soul—I think 'No no no, you can get through this'. 'For my unconquerable soul' it's *my* unconquerable soul, you can get through that.

The interviewer asks her what if it were 'brave soul', wouldn't that be better, for positively and straightforwardly opposing cowardice. Or as Burton puts it, 'Oppose an invincible courage, persuade evil for good, set prosperity against adversity.' But Imelda replies:

> No, I much prefer unconquerable. Because I don't think 'brave' does that much for you if you're mentally ill. You don't want to know. You've got an unconquerable soul so this soul on this piece of paper is in the same place as me. Unconquerable, it's a long word, you can say it yourself a few times, there's a feel in it, even more than 'invincible', which contains and overcomes from inside it the being conquered. It makes you think: you know, I can beat this.

This is Imelda, long practised with this poem, seeing in it what I call literature's second language, inside: that language-*within*-language where, for example, the anaphora 'Out of' and 'Beyond' also tacitly say within themselves 'I am pointing your mind forward, even past what immediately comes next'; or where the insertion of 'un', or 'whatever', or 'shall find' feels like the signal of an implicit intervention made against the odds, holding back an obvious word or too easy sentence to find time and room in which to make some small mark of verbal difference to the way of things. Perhaps these things can only happen en route, in the midst of the way human beings still have to go. But to Imelda they call out, they insert and resist, they honestly doubt, they lament, if you can hear them in their little variations of format, like the inner sound and feel within the word.

I have described how Imelda, fearful of what has happened to her brain, would like a brain scan. In fact, some of the brain-imaging work our research unit has done in relation to the reading of poetry suggests that this idea of a second language in literature is truer than we knew. When the language is not straightforward, there can no longer be simple recourse to automatic information-processing streams. All the practical brain experimentation we have carried out has been about sudden surprises, prediction errors shaking readers out of their norms, to deploy instead at deep neurological levels sudden reappraisal mechanisms that demand change of mind to mirror the inferred change of tense or position or word.[6] So here, for example: not simply 'brave' but 'unconquerable'; not 'finds me unafraid and shall [continue to] find me unafraid', simply spelt out, but 'finds *and shall find* me unafraid', compressed.

What was shown in EEG (electroencephalogram) and fMRI (functional magnetic resonance imaging) studies, as we shall see again in chapter 7, was increased activation in locations beyond those classically activated by typical language-tasks such as Wernicke's area in the left hemisphere of the cerebrum. These newly activated areas lie deep in the mid-brain, in the basal ganglia, such as the left caudate nucleus, and across the hemispheres, the right inferior frontal gyrus, and the right inferior temporal gyrus. And the point is that this is an effect that has also been observed when bilinguals are led to switch from one language to another. That is to say: it is as if we should be thinking of a literary language as indeed a second language, albeit related to our first native language and operating within it. So it is that the second language of 'un' words in 'Invictus' works contrapuntally *down* the lines—unbowed, unconquerable, unafraid—even whilst the first native language carries on making sense *along* them. The second language demands translation, makes its message come home the stronger as a result.

For Imelda there has to be sufficient pain, sufficient bite in the poem such that it contains within itself the adversity it has to deal with, like a language-within-a-language. It can't just be optimistic or soothing. Even the verse-prayer 'Serenity' which she has known for ages won't quite do it for her, though she likes the famous lines on praying to God to grant the serenity 'to accept the things I cannot change', courage 'to change the things I can', and wisdom 'to know the difference'. But, she says, 'Serenity is more like an I-wish poem, though it does open up some choices; but Invictus is more in your face. Serenity is not so good when you fall out with God.'

But she has fallen out with God, so to speak, and gentler poems will not serve that predicament even though their momentary forgetting of that falling-out can be a relief. There was a reading group session in which Imelda read a poem by John Clare on May, its first stanza ending:

> The Sunday paths, to pleasant places leading,
> Are graced by couples linking arm in arm,
> Sweet smiles enjoying or some book a-reading,
> Where Love and Beauty are the constant charm;
> For while the bonny May is dancing by,
> Beauty delights the ear, and Beauty fills the eye.

It feels good for Imelda that 'some book a-reading' is also there, amidst the rest. And she loves the last line. But she has no desire to read the poem countless times—for all the relief in words such as 'pleasant', 'graced' or 'sweet'. She needs more than a holiday for eye or ear.

Her only alternative candidate to 'Invictus' is this by Derek Walcott, 'Love After Love':

> The time will come
> when, with elation
> you will greet yourself arriving
> at your own door, in your own mirror
> and each will smile at the other's welcome,
>
> and say, sit here. Eat.
> You will love again the stranger who was your self.
> Give wine. Give bread. Give back your heart
> to itself, to the stranger who has loved you
>
> all your life, whom you ignored
> for another, who knows you by heart.
> Take down the love letters from the bookshelf,
>
> the photographs, the desperate notes,
> peel your own image from the mirror.
> Sit. Feast on your life.

'I must admit PTSD has more or less destroyed me,' Imelda says in response to this poem; but adds that to accept 'Love After Love' would be a great thing, like welcoming in her 'own' self as the verse suggests. You had too often tried, desperately, to go to other people in your life instead. But 'accepting yourself' now is no longer a cliché here. It involves two people, where one has made the other a stranger—the stranger 'who was your self', from whom you turned away, but who 'has loved you/ all your life' and 'knows you [without cliché] *by heart*'—until amidst all the old furniture, each welcomes the other back in to itself. 'Give back your heart/ to itself', 'You will love again ... who was'—these returns-home are like listening to yourself again, making yourself whole again, rather than just crying out for loves lost or times betrayed. Imelda loves the future happiness in this poem, albeit a yet far future whose arrival at the door of home is offered by the very tone of 'The time *will* come': 'will greet', 'will smile', 'will love again', when the fighting will be over. Voices and their nuances are very important to her; they subtly connect to the physical feel of a meaning. They speak of how being listened to can seem to change the very structure of a brain, the physiology of a body.

And the tone which Derek Walcott here has to try to offer himself is actually taken from his implicit memory of the lost religious tradition, to be found still in the very cadences of George Herbert's poem 'Love (III)'. There it is God, Christ, who is Love:

> Love bade me welcome: yet my soul drew back
> > Guilty of dust and sin,
> But quick-ey'd Love, observing me grow slack
> > From my first entrance in,
> Drew nearer to me, sweetly questioning,
> > If I lack'd any thing.
>
> A guest I answer'd, worthy to be here:
> > Love said, you shall be he.
> I the unkind, ungrateful? Ah my dear
> > I cannot look on thee.
> Love took my hand, and smiling did reply,
> > Who made the eyes but I?
>
> Truth Lord, but I have marr'd them...

Love then replies to the guilty and unwanted one, who is damaged further by the guilt and shame: 'And know you not who bore the blame?' And it is important that the simple, obvious and sacred answer to the riddle—Jesus Christ, by his sacrifice—goes unspoken, that it may go further inside as inner voice. And unnamed, it may now echo on amongst people who would not name themselves religious. 'You must sit down, says Love, and taste my meat:/ So I did sit and eat.' 'Sit here. Eat....,' writes Walcott, 'Sit, Feast on your life.' Whatever you think are your secularized doubts and beliefs, you can feel here in Herbert at the moment of its gentle but insistent voicing what the Grace of the New Testament means just through what it sounds like—even when it is still surprisingly hard for the old guilty Adam to take or receive.

> sweetly questioning
> If I lack'd any thing.

You can feel the unprinted question mark after 'any thing', so much better than if it were the lumpen 'anything'—the offer in its open simplicity of rhyme surviving history, scepticism, and resistance. There is a tone or temper of mind in which a particular idea is held, and the idea here has its own resonance, its own vibration, its own embodied credo. Hold it in the wrong way and the spirit of its meaning may be distorted and violated if not destroyed. Hold it in the right way and the thought and its thinker are united and fulfilled in each other, still across the centuries. That is why it is important that a voice changes as it goes along in the process of reading aloud, in the search to inhabit the feel and tone of a verse. For some thoughts create the right ethos in those who can tune into them.

In contrast, Imelda's counsellor has told her of the primitive mechanisms by which non-physical threats can still have physical effects. This means that so-called illness is often just another term for suffering, but suffering made more seemingly legitimate and acceptable by biomedical accreditation. Yet still psychological threats get secretly bound up within physical dangers. Her counsellor has warned her of how the defence mechanisms originally so vital to survival can at a later evolutionary level damage the very well-being they were originally designed to protect. Like fear at the approach of a wild animal becoming neurosis in the face of intangible modern stresses. Or like the shutting down of the organism—freezing like a deer in the headlights—in order to become less visible, and conserve energy for a chance moment of escape; a natural defence which in the face of trauma becomes turned into a deadened capacity for experiencing live feelings or for switching on key areas of mental activity. She re-explicates this in her blog, referring to the basic reactions of fight and flight and freeze:

> Cavemen had to be alert for most of the time otherwise disaster could strike like a wild animal. If a lion comes near to you your brain reacts with chemicals such as adrenaline and cortisol which is fine if going to be eaten up as you know to run off. But if someone scams you in the internet-world, then the chemicals stay in yr body i reckon that is why i am on alert system all the time and if anyone comes round the corner unexpectedly i over react with a giant scream cos i see any shock as a threat even when it is harm less.

'I have this whole body thing,' she says. In what seems like a partial reversion to primitive ways she feels she has to bite hard on something most of the time, to the ruin of her teeth. A minor disagreement, she feels, can take her back as in some Tardis to the time of cavemen or turn her into something like a raging bull: 'You get ready for a fight, your whole body gets ready, though the people disagreeing with you aren't wanting to have a real fight with you.' That misaligned mistake through instinctive biology, that physiological anachronism is the confusion of reality that makes the psychological blow to esteem feel like a physical blow, registered simply as a blindly felt *hurt*, emotional or physical alike in the very same region of the ancient brain. And yet this is precisely and wonderfully why, on the other hand, by the self-same process literature can have such an intimate visceral effect, as if some deep immediate response did not yet know it was unreal, because affecting the same area that real life had once affected and left vulnerable.

The cognitive scientist Jaak Panksepp thinks language arises out of the calls of distress of a young creature for its mother, being as we are dependent creatures whose survival relies upon on the strength and quality of our social bonds. Poetry, he thinks, in some core sense activates the parts of the brain that react when a child is separated from its mother and feels the loss. In the same way William James said religion arose out the primal human cry, repeated and repeated: Help, help. And Peter Hobson argues that the structure of what is exchanged between child and carer is what begins to shape and form the idea of grammar itself.[7] Imelda knows how the second language that is known as 'the literary' transforms, and makes mature these original cries and screams and calls for help, whilst still maintaining underneath the raw child within the forms of the adult. Readers pick up that rawness still in themselves. The novelist Clive Sinclair remembers a little boy waking from a nightmare in Henry James's *The Turn of the Screw* and calling for his mother—not because he wanted her to comfort him but because first of all he wants her to share the terrible experience he has had: 'In a sense,' writes Sinclair, 'I'm that little boy, calling the reader to me.'[8] I love this sense that beneath the sophistication of literature, and built into it emotionally at base, are primitive forces and childlike needs that are never simply 'got over'.

A child's scrape on a knee, says Imelda, prompts the response 'Shall I kiss it better?'; but with the pain in the mind and the expectation of being mentally grown-up about it, it is a poem that has to serve instead.

*

The psychoanalyst Christopher Bollas is interested in the rift that can take place between what might be solidified into being called a 'self' and what in the same way we may reify as 'mind'.[9] It happens, for example, when a person becomes terrified by her thoughts and identifies herself in contrast to them, in defensive opposition to them. Then I am *not* the master of my fate, I am *not* the captain of my soul. 'The mind is ordinarily at peace with the self until a mental product gets the self to reflect on a content, thereby drawing attention to the mind.' It is then as though 'the mind' knows something disturbing about 'the self' which the self can hardly bear. Then in the midst of mental conflict, the frightened self as a result thinks of 'the mind' as an object, like conscience or trauma. The self may well not want that object inside itself and seek to stifle its growth and impact, trying not to receive or transmit its thoughts. But all too often that rejected mind may return in different ways to get its revenges upon consciousness.

A better relationship, says Bollas, may lie in depicting self-experiencing as going on between 'A thinking part that addresses the naive self as a listener' and 'A listening-experiencing self that emotionally or intuitively tests thoughts' (Bollas, pp. 79–80). When my mind is mastering me, as Imelda's does her, telling her its repeatedly troubling concerns, I don't know if that mind is not sometimes more 'me' than 'I' am. The 'I' of the self may become what tries to work that out. But at best, at its simplest and healthiest, the 'I' that Bollas calls the naive self may venture on ahead of mind, its forward surge towards experience in the world constituting an experimental form of blindness in a continual state of reception and surprise. 'Self is an innocence, the essential naive moment open to experience, as it encounters the complexities of life' (Bollas, p. 86). That new encounter and experience gives rise to endless thoughts, and those thoughts are re-thought and reflected upon within what we call mind, dwelling behindhand, waiting to see and compare and distinguish. In the moment of experience, 'we are always children before our minds' (Bollas, p. 87), ignorant of things until they happen or happen again. 'What was that? What did it mean?' the experiencing self cries to other mental functions. Imelda knows when something tells her to have a monstrous thought or when something else urges her to recall 'Invictus', and that both prompts are somehow still *her*. As she says at interview, 'I think it's just you—you are you in your head aren't you, it's me.' But this is not integrated, it is something at war within itself.

Bollas does not want that 'me' of self to have to feel separate from its mind's thoughts and at their mercy. But neither does he want the mind to be merely a part of the conscious self, like a little inner director safely contained, planning ahead or nagging away inside. It is, he feels, a bigger life if instead it is the other way round and we think of the self as part of the mind, the open receptive part which all the rest feeds from, feeds into, feeds back to. The terms—self and mind, mind and body, conscious and unconscious—may be both clumsy and slippery, but one thing is clear. That so much depends upon getting things into their right place, best order and relation. And that illness itself comes from the sense of an important felt anomaly, an inner trauma, that will not fit the framework in which it arises, and the framework cannot alter around it.

What Derek Walcott offered via George Herbert, which Imelda could not yet wholly take, was some point at which the internal fight would be over.

*

But the poem did not quite fit. Nor on the other hand did Kipling's poem fit either: 'If you can keep your head when all about you/ Are losing theirs...' ('I can't, I haven't' says Imelda). And she used the same phrase again—'doesn't quite fit'—in relation to a final poem she admired but which, even so, could not displace 'Invictus' as her stay.

It is a poem by John Clare much used in the reading groups, which had also come to our minds at a periodic meeting of the research group, for two reasons. First, because of Imelda's partial rejection of John Clare's Maying poem, and the light which that early poem throws on Clare's own precarious mental condition as his life went on. And secondly because of the way that Imelda parsed every word in 'I am the master of my fate,/ I am the captain of my soul', while the great Clare poem we were thinking of can hardly get itself past the first two words. 'I am' was written by Clare at the end of 1844 or beginning of 1845, in Northampton General Lunatic Asylum where he was confined from 1841 until his death in 1864:

> I am—yet what I am none cares or knows;
> My friends forsake me like a memory lost:
> I am the self-consumer of my woes—
> They rise and vanish in oblivious host,
> Like shadows in love's frenzied stifled throes
> And yet I am, and live—like vapours tossed
>
> Into the nothingness of scorn and noise,
> Into the living sea of waking dreams,
> Where there is neither sense of life or joys,
> But the vast shipwreck of my life's esteems;
> Even the dearest that I loved the best
> Are strange—nay, rather, stranger than the rest.
>
> I long for scenes where man hath never trod
> A place where woman never smiled or wept
> There to abide with my Creator, God,
> And sleep as I in childhood sweetly slept,
> Untroubling and untroubled where I lie
> The grass below—above the vaulted sky.

It happens not seldom in reading groups with this particular poem that a person will walk out of the room, as if it is too much for them. In George Puttenham's terms, it would be on the scale of poetic medicine closer to Galen than to Paracelsus—though indeed that final stanza is John Clare's own revulsion from the pain of the first two stanzas' predicament, as if he wanted to walk out on it too. Which could be why he would prefer to be able to write the May poem, the gentler (and indeed earlier) work which does not have to find a place where man never trod or woman never smiled or wept, but can find a youthful rural version of each untroubled together. But the Sunday May verse, for some readers such as Imelda, goes too far the other way on the spectrum, a simple refuge in peace that anaesthetizes what, painfully, might actually make a person desire its ease.

To go back to 'I Am', instead, then: what is most interesting in all this, as far as the reading groups are concerned, is that every time readers have left the room during the reading of this poem, they always take a few minutes outside and then, remarkably, return, come back into the poem and, determined to carry on, at once begin to talk about it. For all the effect of pain, it is also like something that psychologists have noted with very young children, even babies—that at some point in a powerful interaction, they have to look away, go away. In one sense that is obviously because it has become too much, and there is an instinctive need to shut down the over-stimulation and restore equilibrium. But it is also related to the need to *think* however inchoately. So it is when people are in the middle of a busy city and cannot quite orient themselves or remember their directions: for a moment they have to look away, almost close their eyes, in order to think of the physical route, to focus individually inside, and retreat to adapt and recalibrate, instead of being overwhelmed by the uncharted surroundings. This feels related to the origins of thinking: the feedback from the poem, the shock to reality, the withdrawal into separate internal processing—in order to manage and to translate the feeling's message—and then the re-entry into life (the room, the poem) from the different level created after the mental retreat and the mental re-gathering.

So in a drug and alcohol rehabilitation centre, after the mere beginnings of discussion by the rest of the group, a young woman I call Carol suddenly left the room, signalling her need to do so by holding up a single finger, as if to take a moment. She returned nonetheless some minutes later and immediately said to the group amidst restrained tears:

> So—the way this is to me is, I exist at the moment but...I am but I am not—
> [*Another group-member Amy adds, supportively 'Living', amidst the difficulty of sentencing.*]
> I am literally *vapours*, the *nothingness* of what-have-you, and I feel like a *shipwreck*, and things I used to *esteem* in my life are no longer there, and I have been *forsaken* by a lot of people, so like I am a bit of a *memory lost*. Isn't it: no one really cares or wants to know.

It is not just quotation from the poem, the words are repeated in ordinary speech as blows are felt. It is like the poem speaking again through this person. It fitted her; she fitted it.

The group had been speaking about the difference between the first two stanzas and the final stanza when Carol had abruptly left. Some had been the thinking the place offered by the final verse to be beautiful, others a form of suicide. Carol resumes, when she comes back into the room:

And it's interesting what was said about suicide because at the end it is like...I don't want to commit suicide, no, but I want to be at peace...and going back to that innocent childhood, or you know that kind of untroubled place...where also you don't cause trouble...so much trouble as to lose your friends and relations.
So the whole thing really got to me.

The ellipses mark the points where again on the boundary between thought and language, it is hard for this woman to articulate completely, to go forward, or face the painful and complicated thought. The last stanza is the result of that desperation to be without the agitation of all those human feelings and contacts, a single creature simply at peace in the universe, between heaven and earth. It is the peace in the head that Imelda herself might choose at times, though it is close to a sort of pastoral death. But here Carol knows that the word in the final stanza that reveals its reactive relation to the two stanzas preceding it, is the wish not only to be 'untroubled' but also 'untroubling'. That is how grammar (as Peter Hobson indicated) is an index of the mental and emotional turns of relationship in the world, where a person is consciously at once both I and me, subject and object, cause and effect— troubled and troubling. Thus, it is bad enough to be troubled; but it is even worse to feel oneself also at the same time, as a result, the cause of trouble, such as eventually must leave even the 'dearest' to me 'stranger' than all the rest. That is what deep depression is, say the psychologists: the being stuck in felt impossibility between two opposing options neither of which seems bearable alone.[10] As another group member said, thinking of the different alonenesses of the first twelve lines and the last six: 'To be left alone when in this state: that is what you want most—and want least.'

Line 1 goes: 'I am—yet what [not even "who"] I am, none cares or knows'. What could have been self-affirmation, of which there are still residual traces, has become more like the terrible helplessness of an almost meaningless persistence in surviving. For line 6 goes: 'And yet I am, and live'—but then across the stanzas' great gulf, only live '—like vapours tossed/ Into the nothingness of scorn and noise.' This is how 'I am' gets sentenced for John Clare, not as Henley's 'I am the master of my fate/ I am the captain of my soul', but with a persistent dash after it. It is like not being able to get very far with the 'If' with which Rudyard Kipling begins his famous exhortatory poem. 'I am—': What? Incomplete; unable almost to be anything or do anything any more; with 'none' around to know or care. Only with a trapped feeling of 'I-am, yet...' (1) and 'yet-I-am' (6): whichever way round the word 'yet' turns between 'still' and 'however', it is a poetic shorthand for a felt contradiction but also a terrible continuance in it.

Hardly completed utterances. But in truth, nothing in mortal life can be fully said or utterly resolved, and poetry knows that. The poem and its sentences only really get finished when picked up and completed within a reader.[11] So readers spell out what finds them, making the poems and the fragments of poetry a part of their mental repertoire, their psychological grammar and their lexicon for dealing with life. The lines they choose become what Clive Sinclair has called 'an internal dictionary' to provide individual meanings—when, otherwise, a person, knowing the name-word 'grief', still cannot be sure whether that diagnostic label is or is not what he or she is experiencing when not a tear may have been shed.[12] I have asked many readers to send me whatever were their treasured lines and heartfelt excerpts, marking within any given field of predicament or celebration the sheer human range of possible personal responses to tune into. Across that spectrum of taste and need and temperament, three imaginable choices come together in this chapter as representative of one great, varying wavelength: Henley's 'I am the master of my fate'; Clare's 'I am —'—and finally, chosen by many, this major stanza from George Herbert's 'The Flower' on recovering from a long, dark mental winter:

> And now in age I bud again,
> After so many deaths I live and write;
> I once more smell the dew and rain,
> And relish versing. Oh, my only light,
> It cannot be
> That I am he
> On whom thy tempests fell all night.

That is the basic grammar so simply rhymed and parsed, if (as Herbert says later in the poem) we could only spell: 'It cannot be/ That I am he...'. It is as though, through this braille, 'he' who endured that stormy hell were the past tense of this 'I' who is so amazingly recovered now that the two feel utterly different, from completely opposite worlds. But so as to say too: it *cannot* be—and yet (of course; in wonder) it *is*.

I am . . I am the...I am he...So through an unfolding sentence human beings try stutteringly to spell out their situation.

As I write, Imelda is having a very bad time again. Nothing makes anyone invulnerable to events. But of 'Invictus' Imelda still writes, 'Just hoping one day the words will become truth.'

CHAPTER 5

THE BRAIN OF FRANCES

Frances does not mind if she does not immediately understand a difficult poem or know why a delicately quiet and simple one moves her. She does not want paraphrase-able messages, robust lessons, or direct autobiographical identification. She wants it, she says, so that 'the actual art does something to you'. The poem remains itself, won't be used up, or too swiftly translated into something else.

She once spent months, every night, obsessively trying to learn a Marianne Moore poem, 'The Camperdown Elm', word-perfect. That tree is a rare example of a plant that cannot reproduce itself from its own seed, its weeping branches seeming to seek the help it needs from the earth and air, outside it. In a picture by Armand Durand of 1849 (Figure 5), there is depicted a painter Thomas Cole, who died the year previous, and a poet, William Cullen Bryant, standing together as 'Kindred Spirits' in art under the great elm, overlooking a stream 'at the edge of a rockledge'.

> No doubt they had seen other trees—lindens,
> maples and sycamores, oaks and the Paris
> street-tree, the horse-chestnut; but imagine
> their rapture, had they come on the Camperdown elm's
> massiveness and "the intricate pattern of its branches,"
> arching high, curving low, in its mist of fine twigs.
> The Bartlett tree-cavity specialist saw it
> and thrust his arm the whole length of the hollowness
> of its torso and there were six small cavities also.
>
> Props are needed and tree-food. It is still leafing;
> still there. *Mortal* though. We must save it. It is
>   our crowning curio.

It was the gift of Mr A. G. Burgess to Brooklyn's recently created Prospect Park in 1872, a tree that was, as the tree specialists knew, the result of the work of the head forester of the Earl of Camperdown in Dundee in the 1830s, grafting a mutant branch of a Scots Elm onto an ordinary specimen. An uneasy amalgam between human art and unwieldy nature, if it could not reproduce itself, it nonetheless

Figure 5. The painter Thomas Cole and poet William Cullen Bryant under the Camperdown Elm. Armand Durand, *Kindred Spirits* (1849), Crystal Bridges Museum of American Art, Bentonville, Arkansas, 2010.106. Photography by the Metropolitan Museum of Art.

proved resistant to Dutch elm disease, even though still subject to internal decay. Marianne Moore, a poet who never married and apparently was never in love, was devoted to this tree for its meaning to her, forming an action group in the 1960s to save the elm from neglect. 'Props are needed and tree-food.'

Not long released from hospital, for all her efforts in repeating and repeating it, Frances had found she somehow couldn't learn this poem, could not wholly reproduce it in herself either. But then she has always liked poetry that won't simply give in to her. She loves the phrase 'arching high, curving low' like a waterfall, and all those occasional and extraneous details that make 'the mist of fine twigs' also, when you read it aloud, into the mystifying twigs. But above all there is 'Mortal', a word not commonly used of trees so much as humans, and yet, though almost hollow inside, 'still leafing'. 'Still leafing' and yet 'Mortal though'. It means: 'We must save it.'

With Frances, as with the poet, there is more to this than what is commonly meant by aestheticism—which I would usually dismiss, prejudicially, as the mere love of art for art's sake. Over three meetings I try to find out what sort of reader Frances is. 'I feel like that elm,' she eventually tells me.

She is a highly intelligent, conventional-looking woman in her mid-fifties. At our first meeting, she has brought me a slender poem by James Schuyler (1923–91), a friend of Frank O'Hara and John Ashbery in New York—she loves American poetry and its more open, freewheeling forms. The poem is entitled 'The Bluet', after a tiny light-blue flower native to North America; modest spring flowers she tells me, also known as Quaker Ladies perhaps because of a resemblance to the purity of colour of the ladies' dress or to the shape of their hats. It is hardly Marianne Moore's great weeping elm in a Brooklyn park, and yet 'stamina' is almost the first word Schuyler offers for the frail bluet. So much in so little, it is, he writes, 'So small/ A drop of sky' (Figure 6):

> But that bluet was
> the focus of all: last
> spring, next spring, what
> does it matter? Unexpected
> as a tear when someone
> reads a poem you wrote
> for him, "It's this line
> here." That bluet
> breaks me up . . .

It's this line here: something seen that might easily not have been noticed—like Wordsworth's 'violet by a mossy stone' in his poem 'She dwelt among the untrodden ways', a metaphor for the hidden maiden, Lucy, whom there were 'none to praise and very few to love'. Frances loves to find 'the focus' of a half-hidden little line, the bluet that somehow matters. And it makes a great difference that when Schuyler speaks of being unexpectedly broken up by the sight and thought of the frail bluet, the feeling is also related to the effect of a poem when it manages to cross

Figure 6. 'So small/ A drop of sky'. 'Bluet', Kim Smith.

the free gap between the writer and the reader he is writing for. The grateful tear is what comes back to Schuyler as person, from the precious little that as poet he had dared to give out into the world. There may be no better reward for all the work expended upon writing than that return.

It is not that Frances, any more than her poets, only loves the non-human, or cares only for the sort of poetry that artfully refers back only to itself. It is more the other way round: that the poem uses its own technique, like a plant creating its flower, to show through protective analogy the hidden human heart so attached to its nurturing. But in doing it this way, it's as analogical language for what? For inklings of a gentle, understated form of delicate mentality perhaps only achievable through such poetry, though certainly needed beyond it.

Frances loves the idea of poetry as an almost hermetically sealed practice. For the time it lasts, it forms a concentrated little world in which, she says, 'you can move things around'. It is connected to her amused admiration for what she thinks is the weird obsession of the young Nabokov, lepidopterist in years seven to ten, described in chapter 6 of his autobiography *Speak, Memory*—which she leaves with me as one of what she calls 'her things' to read afterwards when we have run out of time.

What Nabokov describes there is the experience of sheer intense concentration on the thing: the insistence on microscopic detail in the butterfly, the shifting combinations of its hues and movements, the structural identification and accurate verbal naming of what is there. And this absorption goes together with an acute desire on his part to be alone, to the dismay of those all around him who would prefer a more normal child who joins in and fits in. Above all, there is the silent and almost timeless immersion in the patterns of the landscape forming and re-forming as the butterflies swarm amongst their food plants, in an excess of beauty and vitality far beyond what Darwinian natural selection might strictly require.

But then, crucially, Nabokov adds another twist, like Schuyler turning his own poem inside-out even from within it:

> I discovered in nature the non-utilitarian delights that I sought in art. Both were a form of magic...

What is involved in that magic are such 'delicate machinations', continues Nabokov, that when at last things come together, as in rhyme or in love, 'not the merest click is audible': there is only the sliding sensation that a pattern is about to form or has just formed, and mundane serial time has turned into a finely tuned system instead.[1]

Frances needs these created forms and formations. She has loved the thought of architecture too—especially in America where she had journeyed with her husband on a freewheeling road trip, early in their relationship: 'I like the idea of lightness over there, as though you could build just where you wanted.' It has made her wonder if somewhere she was more boldly free or wild than her customary caution and anxiety suggested.

*

Our first meeting began with what Frances had to say about George Eliot's *Silas Marner*, the first book she encountered in a shared reading group late in 2014, when she managed to start reading again after a period of great trouble. 'When we were doing *Silas*, the sentences were really demanding—they go on and on, and you don't know what's coming at the end of the sentence, you don't know how it is going to end. Those long sentences made my brain work really hard. Especially when I was reading aloud in the group.'

Long sentences like the one that begins the quotation below on the traumatized Silas, now living in country exile, away from the grim town where he was falsely accused and betrayed:

> Even people whose lives have been made various by learning, sometimes find it hard to keep a fast hold on their habitual views of life, on their faith in the Invisible—nay, on

the sense that their past joys and sorrows are a real experience, when they are suddenly transported to a new land, where the beings around them know nothing of their history and share none of their ideas—where their mother earth shows another lap, and human life has other forms than those on which their souls have been nourished. Minds that have been unhinged from their old faith and love, have perhaps sought this Lethean influence of exile, in which the past becomes dreamy because its symbols have all vanished, and the present too is dreamy because it is linked with no memories.

Chapter 2

Trying to 'keep a fast hold' here is the issue for Frances in the very act of reading the sentence in its motion—holding on to the past 'real' in the face of the suddenly 'new'. But Lethe was the river of unmindfulness in Greek myth, a drink from its waters producing mental oblivion. After his trauma, Silas himself wants to forget and be forgotten, to be dreamy instead of rooted. As the first sentence goes on beyond the familiar, out into living now amongst those who, devastatingly, know nothing of the place he came from, the second, shorter, is glad to be 'unhinged' from the past and lost in present dreaminess. 'You want the sentence to end but you don't want it to end,' says Frances:

> If you're reading aloud you're thinking *Help*, where's this going to end? But you want it to keep going as well. It's a sort of double feeling: relief when it does end in making sense, but exciting when it keeps going into another phase, and then another. I'm not at all used to reading aloud: it is a physical thing, you use different muscles from when you read at home, and the length of the sentence becomes like a physical thing in the mind. Your brain is looking ahead on the page because you've not seen it before. There is a sense of an immediate future ahead of you, to work out.

George Eliot keeps finding more thoughts within one thought, more substance in the depicted life *for* thought: that is why so often it has to be one whole richly interconnected sentence in development.

Frances says that this stretch of mind further accentuated the effect of the shared reading model, one participant reading while the others listen, each person sitting with a copy of the text also in front of them:

> It does something in the *brain* which I can't really put my finger on, looking at the words as the whole reading group goes along together. You know you're not just being read to because you're following the words as well which is different from listening to a spoken book or something on the radio. It must be to do with the audio and visual together, they do something different to what they do when they are separate.

The very process makes your brain work differently, and that affects your mind in turn. 'It engages all your attention, getting your mind off the negative thoughts.' She says it started her brain going again.

We talk about a man I met from another group who had had a course of ECT—electroconvulsive therapy, sending a shock of electric current through the brain—to try to relieve his depression. It left him feeling mentally foggy. He said that in the reading group it was helpful that sentences were being broken down, read slowly through their parts, so that it was like a work-out for mental muscles that have been out of condition.

I asked Frances why she is so interested in the brain.

One reason must be to do with her mother, she says, who is now in her eighties. Unusually for a woman trained in medicine at that time, Frances's mother had been able to go into a new field, neurophysiology, investigating diseases of the nervous system. She had a job-share with another woman so they could both manage their children. Based in outpatients' but increasingly travelling throughout Europe, she worked with technologists to develop EEG, electroencephalography, from its early developmental days in the 1960s, to monitor the electrical activity of the brain by using non-invasive electrodes attached to the scalp. Naturally, she would talk of her work to her daughter. Lines in poetry seem to me like brainwaves, holding the mental wavelength, says Frances: she quotes the poet John Donne on 'putting things into lines to assuage pain' and directs me to Helen Gardner's introduction to the old Penguin selection *The Metaphysical Poets* for the citation. When I check later, it is not there. That often happens, not unpleasingly, when something supposed to be a reference has long become a thought instead. What I do find instead is a reference to George Chapman and his preface to *Ovid's Banquet of the Senses* (1595) where he argues that poetry should not be merely clear but dense with meaning 'to be chewed and digested'.

Frances then mentions she has read something about Alzheimer's, 'that one of the things they've noticed is that people can only cope with short sentences'. This reminds me of something different, a counter to this claim that I suddenly want to share with her, at the risk of digressing. My research team has done some work with shared reading groups in care homes and day centres.

I tell Frances about Patricia, a woman in her sixties with mild-to-moderate dementia, who is part of a reading group in a day-care centre. In one session they read a sonnet by Henry Van Dyke, a popular American poet and story writer, professor of literature and Presbyterian clergyman who died in 1933 in his eighties. The lines seem palpably designed to help the readers through what might otherwise seem very long stretches of sentence, as of time itself:

> Let me but live my life from year to year,
> With forward face and unreluctant soul;
> Not hurrying to, nor turning from the goal;
> Not mourning for the things that disappear
> In the dim past, nor holding back in fear
> From what the future veils; but with a whole
> And happy heart, that pays its toll
> To Youth and Age, and travels on with cheer.
>
> So let the way wind up the hill or down,
> O'er rough or smooth, the journey will be joy:
> Still seeking what I sought when but a boy,
> New friendship, high adventure, and a crown,
> My heart will keep the courage of the quest,
> And hope the road's last turn will be the best.

It is obviously not a great poem, and Frances very much dislikes its sermonizing explicitness about 'Life' (the poem's title), in its blatant attempt to comfort and cheer. She refers instead to a famous poem by Marianne Moore again, called 'Poetry': 'I too dislike it./ Reading it however with a perfect/ contempt for it, one discovers in/ it after all, a place for the genuine.'

But Patricia herself had seemed genuinely to like the Van Dyke poem, repeating the half-line, 'the journey will be *joy*': 'That is brilliant...lovely.' But interestingly when the group leader re-reads the preceding words 'So let the way wind up the hill *or* down', 'O'er rough *or* smooth', Patricia pauses—and I have the film and transcript to show on my laptop:

That's a bit different isn't it.... I'm not sure.... I was just thinking about these things and they don't always do the things, do they, that you want to do, or want them not to do it, you know... [*silence*].

Patricia has aphasia, she has lost names and nouns. But what I had never seen so visibly or nakedly before, amidst the wreckage and showing through it, was the still remaining complexity of her attempted syntax—life and existence not always doing 'the things' you *want* to do, or rather doing the things you want them *not* to do. The pathways are still there in Patricia's brain, the resistant shapes of ill-controlled experience still making their demands through the lines of adaptive thought. She knows when the shape of life is wrong for her. Then, for all the poem's apparent comfort, it is risky for the group leader from *The Reader* to do what she does next: quote in the context of this care home the lines on 'the things that disappear/ in the dim past' and, equally, the fear of 'what the future veils':

> *Patricia*: I don't like that one [*laughs*].
>
> *Group Leader, supportively*: It feels sad . . .
>
> *Patricia*: It is isn't it? You don't quite know what . . . and then you go to say 'I'm not going to take that' and suddenly, and another one, and you can't find out why it's there, you know. I hate that.
>
> *Group Leader*: Not knowing?
>
> *Patricia*: No, you just want things to do nice, comfily, you know, but the inside is that you can't make it like that. Nothing goes like that goes at all. So you just have to get on with it on its own. Basically [*laughs*].

The inside is—that is the place Patricia is thinking from, when she asks why *it* is there—whatever 'it' is now that you have to take or lose, and accept, you don't know why. The group leader repeats 'the things that disappear/ in the dim. . . .' and then says, 'Disappearing, but the poem's kind of holding onto them still.'

> *Patricia*: It is, it is, indeed . . . Anyway I suppose I better get on home . . .
>
> *Group Leader*: I don't think it's time for home yet. We have some more time left, Patricia. . . . But I'm wondering why the past is dim?
>
> *Patricia*: I don't know about that, but it's *there*.
>
> *Group Leader*: Yes, you can still see it but it's dim.

It's there is another insistence of reality, grasped at, even through the bewildering fog. And instead of thinking of retreating back home, Patricia stays now, and goes on:

> Because you're not quite sure what you're going to be doing. In the whole thing you know [*gestures*]. You don't know quite why am I here, who knows me or whatever, and then it goes back again. It's all very, very—I don't know—peculiar [*laughs*].

The 'thing', the 'it': I am unsure there are actually better words, for this is why the poet Wordsworth used such words too and found them basic to his poetry amongst the wanderers and commoners of the Lake District. But speaking through that intuitively ingenious and subtle 'you'—'you don't know quite why I am . . .', Patricia is helped by her syntax to say what she would not more directly, unless she were King Lear himself after his own breakdown: why am I here? who knows me? And then 'it' goes back again into those normalizations, the unfunny laughs and bravely clichéd acceptances of Patricia being normal again.

Frances then tells me the second reason why she is so interested in the brain.

She had eventually been given ECT herself.

Her first period of depression arose when she was fourteen or fifteen, to do with academic pressure at school. She dropped out of the sixth form and went to Art School instead in the late 1970s, without much personal connection to it, taking after that a deliberately menial job with National Express coaches to avoid ambition. On the dole as she fled promotion, she then met the man, also an artist, who became her husband. She took literature-based extra-mural evening classes at Goldsmiths and eventually began a full literature degree course at University College London in the late 1980s. But since adolescence she had always had a sense of something coming, like a hurricane on the horizon. 'Things had started to go well, and that itself created a fear, after things going wrong for so long.' And so just when she felt back on track, as a now mature student, difficulties and worse-than-difficulties followed, breaking this chance of continuity. There was an accidental pregnancy in the midst of her degree and the birth of a daughter who hardly slept in her first years. There was then a terrible stillbirth from uterine infection at twenty-four weeks ('he was alive during the labour but died—I could just tell something had changed—the urgency went out of it'). Then, finally, there was the sudden accidental death of her partner just at the beginning of a difficult third pregnancy in 1997.

It was only years later that all this, cumulatively, seemed finally to catch up with her. 'When it happened I couldn't see how I'd gone on all those years, or why didn't it happen earlier; or why, given that I had gone on in those years, it would be now.' It began physically, with serious stomach problems, failure to eat or to sleep. Then she began to plummet mentally and feel suicidal. 'I thought: I'll get through Christmas, get the presents. Or maybe I'll try jumping off an escalator that I knew someone had fallen off in John Lewis department store in Oxford Street. But I just thought: my children . . .' Alarmed, her own parents moved in and looked after her, her aged mother sleeping on the sofa. But Frances refused medication or hid what she was supposed to take.

Finally in the winter of 2013, having struggled on for years, she was sectioned, terrified that her younger daughter, now aged sixteen, would be taken into care. In what became her psychosis she began to think the whole hospital was a front, the therapist trying to elicit information only to use against her, and all the doctors and nurses fakes who were really trying to kill her. She sat staring at the floor: 'It had a sort of terrazzo pattern, which I used to stare at. I have always been concerned with patterns. But now everything had shrunk down to a few inches. And there was something in the shapes. I could see a mouse. It looked like a sad, sad mouse and it was a sort of companion. It's silly, or hard to describe.' Out of desperation it was her mother who suggested ECT, and after just one session Frances felt immediately better, and shortly after was released. But it was only for the depression to return very rapidly and even more deeply, with a second batch of ECT having no effect. She was given strong antidepressants, which she still takes in lesser dosage. 'I think the illness and the treatment did something to my brain. It's taken a battering.'

She had struggled through her first degree by the early 1990s, with time off for her baby. After a further year off she had then undertaken a Masters in Anglo-American Literary Relations gaining a distinction, despite the stillbirth, though again with a temporary suspension of studies. Though pregnant again, she was even about to undertake a PhD in 1997 when she was suddenly bereaved. And this was when she began to feel that her education had been worth almost nothing—decades behind in the first place, and now more decades gone by. 'Why do you keep doing it to yourself?' her tutor had asked, ruefully not unkindly, during some of the lesser troubles and interruptions. By the time of her eventual breakdown in 2013 she could hardly read or listen to music: 'It only reminded me, when just everything was drained of meaning.' All she could read now was the news. It was an occupational therapist who then took her to a shared reading group and stayed there with her.

She remembered the only poem read at her husband's funeral, Marvell's poem of contemplative retreat, 'The Garden', and especially the lines

> Annihilating all that's made
> To a green thought in a green shade

That was what had left her, or left her to search for: that sort of calm intrinsic thinking.

*

After what had felt like annihilation, for her it had to be thought that mattered, and not story or narrative. Not least because the order of things, the chronology of her life, had always been disjointed, a series of punctuated starts never wholly carried through. And such story as there was in that series of discontinuities was almost unbearable to think of.

She kept circling back to these key dates, gradually amplifying and clarifying, during the course of our several conversations. The worst was 1997. 'I was thirty-six, widowed with two children. I had always been anxious, fearful that when things were good something bad might be on the horizon.' But after her partner's sudden death that year, she felt from then on that she was always running. With the children to bring up, she was unable to stand still, though she never quite got on her feet again. She felt 'pushed and pulled along, with sudden panics coming from behind while trying to keep ahead—until 1997 turned into 2013, a sudden stop where it all caught up.' As I have said, she was baffled: 'Why now? why not earlier?'; but she thinks it was partly triggered by what seemed a sheerly physical illness—hiatus hernia, stomach pain, non-cancerous growths, sleeplessness resulting.

She finally took me back to the circumstances of her husband's death, at our second meeting, to speak more fully of it. What had happened was that her husband had decided he had to go to the funeral of a colleague's young daughter, down in Sussex. There was a lot of discussion as to whether Frances should accompany him but it was early in her third pregnancy—they had only known for five days—and she had started bleeding. She was scared of another miscarriage as with her second pregnancy. She had an urgent appointment at the hospital, and her husband had to decide whether to go with her or to attend the funeral. In the end her mother accompanied her to the hospital. The foetus was still alive, and the medical staff advised that nothing could be done except for Frances to spend as much time lying down as she could, for the long remaining duration of her time. She went back home, suffering with severe cramps.

That evening two policemen came to her door.

After the funeral of the colleague's daughter down in Sussex, some of the gathering of friends had gone swimming, as a sort of release. Her husband was not a strong swimmer, he had a bad arm. The police said he had been swept out and couldn't get back in.

Frances called her mother and then had to tell the news to her daughter who was just seven. So it was that in this terrible chronology of her life's events, she was caught almost incongruously between death and life, late husband and their imperilled pregnancy. 'And all I could think now was *I'm going to lose the baby... I know I'm going to lose the baby*... And they put me to bed and I stayed in bed for weeks, and my mother slept nearby every night on a camp bed. I was as though in another planet, apart from the one our life had been on. This is my last chance ever, I thought, for the baby; there won't be other chances.' The child was born, struggled initially, but still thrived, despite initial learning difficulties.

Just before Frances finally got ill in 2013, she had begun obsessively reading Elizabeth Bishop, copying into her notebooks masses of quotations from poems and correspondence. It was like a sort of drug-induced high, she told me, the poetic injection of another life, and 'I felt I might be somewhat blindly working towards something'. Elizabeth Bishop's mentor was Frances's beloved Marianne Moore: things seemed to be fitting together. But what has stuck with her from back then is another text she has brought to show me at our final interview. It is from the correspondence in friendship between Elizabeth Bishop and Robert Lowell, *Words in Air*, where Lowell confesses that he would have liked to have proposed to her—though almost comically, her letter in reply virtually ignores this.

Do you remember at the end of one swimming and sunning day nearly ten years ago, says Lowell—it was at dinner:

> you said rather humorously yet it was truly meant, 'When you write my epitaph, you must say I was the loneliest person who ever lived.' Probably you forget and any way all that is mercifully changed and all has come right since you met Lota.[2] But at the time everything, I guess (I don't want to overdramatize) our relations seemed to have reached a new place. I assumed that would be just a matter of time before I proposed and I half believed that you would accept. Yet I wanted it all to have the right build-up. Well, I didn't say anything then.... I was so drunk that my hands turned cold and I felt half-dying and held your hand. And nothing was said, and like a loon that needs sixty feet, I believe, to take off from the water, I wanted time and space, and went on assuming, and when I was to have joined you at Key West I was determined to ask you. Really for so callous (I fear) a man, I was fearfully shy and scared of spoiling things, and distrustful of being steady enough to be the least good.... And of course there was always the other side, the fact that our friendship wasn't really a courting, it was really a disinterested (bad phrase), really led to no encroachments. So it is.[3]

But Lowell couldn't quite leave it at that:

> Let me [say] this though and then leave the matter forever; I do think free will is sewn into everything we do. You can't cross a street, light a cigarette, drop saccharine in your coffee without really doing it. Yet the possible alternatives that life allows us are very few, often there must be none. I've never thought there was any choice for me about writing poetry. No doubt if I used my head better, ordered my life better, worked harder etc., the poetry would be improved, and there must be many lost poems, innumerable accidents and ill-done actions. But asking you is *the* might have been for me, the one towering change, the other life that might have been had. It was that way for these nine years or so that intervened; it was deeply buried, and this spring or summer (really before your arrival) it boiled to the surface. Now it won't happen again, though of course I always feel a great blytheness and easiness with you. It won't happen.
>
> *Words in Air*, p. 226

She hands me the excerpt. I read it aloud, then try to guess to her why she has chosen this and given it to me. That seems to be how we are working. I say that the comic and the poignantly meant make for an oblique, ironic style that shows the direct through the indirect—and I know that Frances would like that mix. It is not only Bishop ruefully saying by such means that in his epitaph for her she will have been 'the loneliest person that ever lived'; it is also what Lowell wryly says about the loon needing sixty feet, or about a callous man being suddenly shy, scared and fearful of spoiling things. But what strikes Frances most of all, of course, is 'the might have been' expressed in a letter which has to be rather rambling just because what it describes never became formed or consummated into story. 'I think the thought of other lives,' says Frances, 'I often think *what if my husband had lived? Would I have lost the baby?*' But what if her husband hadn't gone to that funeral and had come with her to the hospital—I ask: Isn't that the bigger if-only, that he wouldn't have died? But Frances also puts it the other way round by saying it might also have made a difference if she had accompanied him to the funeral. He might never have gone plunging into the water. 'Because when some of them went off swimming afterwards, none of the others was a parent, there was no woman there who was a mother to look out for danger.' Every way it turns, there is another turn on the other side:

> I would love to think of parallel worlds going on with every possibility. I think maybe one *is* going on somewhere where he's alive. And then I panic and think, what if there's a world where I've not got my children?

These are strange feelings about reality—irrepressibly *mental* feelings which themselves are not quite able to be real. This is how Frances is so intelligent, I think, and in such a different way.

It was strange too, she said, to think of their youngest daughter never having seen her father, not even once. I had just asked, 'When Elizabeth Bishop speaks to Lowell about being the loneliest, are you thinking about yourself too?' But Frances had answered:

> I think it's more for my children. I think when Elizabeth Bishop says that, it is partly to do with her mother having been committed to an asylum when the child was just five. Her father died when she was just a few months old. So for my children, the father was dead and now the mother going mad.

She spoke of herself as 'the mother' as if from the children's point of view. I try to say something about the loneliness of losing a husband being very different from the loneliness of never having seen your father. 'And I'm not even sure how far my youngest daughter is aware of it, or suffered because of it,' she replies, 'I am the keeper of what she may not know.' 'You look at it as though from her point of view,' I reply, 'though it can't quite be from her point of view because she maybe doesn't feel that as much as you do for her?' And then Frances says:

It's one of those endless puzzles that you can't see how it fits together—it sort of goes round and round. Each time I think of something else. There was never a straight run.

In place of a straight story, it is the various combinations, emphases, and ironies that puzzle her, the sense of a variety of causes, discontinuities, and consequences, interruptions and connections, known and unknown, which she may be still living amidst or leaving still behind, as she goes on. Poems to her are small open versions of that endless puzzle: for her they begin as austere word-puzzles, operating in multi dimensions.

*

There is a memoir Frances mentions by Robert Lowell's step-daughter Ivana which takes its title from one of Lowell's late poems from the collection, *Why Not Say What Happened?* It is a good question, especially when not just rhetorically posed, but rather as Lowell himself speaks it in his pared-down 'Epilogue', the poem that ends his last book:

> Those blessèd structures, plot and rhyme—
> why are they no help to me now
> I want to make
> something imagined, not recalled?
> I hear the noise of my own voice:
> *The painter's vision is not a lens,*
> *it trembles to caress the light.*
> But sometimes everything I write
> with the threadbare art of my eye
> seems a snapshot,
> lurid, rapid, garish, grouped,
> heightened from life,
> yet paralyzed by fact.
> All's misalliance.
> Yet why not say what happened?
> Pray for the grace of accuracy
> Vermeer gave to the sun's illumination
> stealing like the tide across a map
> to his girl solid with yearning.
> We are poor passing facts,
> warned by that to give
> each figure in the photograph
> his living name.[4]

It is another of Frances's key poems, one which she says makes her cry. 'Why are they no help to me now ... ?' asks Lowell of the resources of art, his needed friend when himself in breakdown. Like him, she wants things and people, events and even details, to be given their due, their word and 'living name'. And that is to do with her wanting something more than, or something done with, what is twice called in this poem 'fact'—the merely given. And that is where inert 'fact' is a paralysing problem—for not letting in anything but its now closed-up self. Snapshot, not painting. 'When you are very ill and depressed, everything,' says Frances, thinking of her own time in hospital, 'looks flattened—and garish at the same time.' It is only if, in a better 'alliance', memory can work on fact, as though it were more like imagination, that there is poetry and a second life for life.

Face facts, we say, or you'll find you are only trying to get away from them. Frances might be accused of evasion or avoidance: if true, there would be cause enough for that given all that has happened to her. But what she has actually done, in both horror and disdain of a more literal account of things, has been to make something different out of indirectness, by taking Emily Dickinson's famous line, 'Tell the truth but tell it slant': Frances's is another way of thinking which has to do with the mentality of art itself and how it can be instantiated in a brain.

> Tell all the truth but tell it slant—
> Success in Circuit lies
> Too bright for our infirm Delight
> The Truth's superb surprise
> As Lightning to the Children eased
> With explanation kind
> The Truth must dazzle gradually
> Or every man be blind—

She must not be blinded by the lightning, especially when it has struck with something other than delight or surprise. It is not to do with snobbery that she could not bear 'Invictus' in the direct way that Lesley in chapter 3 and Imelda in chapter 4 love and need it.

It helps understanding when she talks to me about something more simple and rough than poetry, but analogous to it. It is to do with Elvis Presley, another of her American heroes, with whom she was obsessed just before her husband died and for some time immediately after. She thinks Elvis was dyslexic, and that his brain had to compensate for that, in particular through building on the repetition of words and in the different phrasing of them within his singing. His was a sort of live performative *reading* where the intuitive mix of repetition and freedom, text and improvisation, melody and word, is just what she loves, in place of merely dutiful rendition. Elvis might start a song in a lazily stylized rote, lacklustre fashion, she says, 'but then something catches fire, suddenly takes off, often halfway through the material'. She thinks that is his debt to gospel singing. She had chosen for her husband's funeral, 'Precious Lord, Take My Hand'—a version of which was sung by Elvis though on that occasion she had gone for Mahalia Jackson. It was the way her voice floated on the lines, 'precious Lord linger near/ When my light is almost gone', circling the words, changing emphases within them, and returning to them—the crying and the lingering within 'Lord', within 'almost', like a person alone with whatever is her God. Offering an equivalent example from Elvis, she thinks she hears the cadence of take-off, of words taken back to heart, in 'Where No One Stands Alone' when the singer comes to 'not know a thing in the whole *wide* world/ that's worse than being *alone*'. That's when the words come back to him, like neural feedback, as James Schuyler's lines did when he found his words had moved the person for whom he wrote them. And those, she says, were the moments when, from off the basic score, 'Elvis sang himself into a different life.' She wishes she herself could do that in some medium. To cut quite free, to do what one can do, to live in a creative present that is everything for the moment.

Perhaps because it is carried by music, this is a more visceral, direct, and upfront response than Frances customarily allows the caution and sophistication of her intelligence to assume. As we get into more difficult territory again, what I now have to try to do, thinking about Frances as a reader in this closing section, is make signals in the way that I sometimes tell my students to do: at the very least, to leave a marker for significant space, showing what is missing in the account and needs more or better.

Here is one thing that 'seems important'—the words I use as my marker for thoughts that seem still incomplete or unsure. What Frances senses in those live musical improvisations is the arousing exchange of one feeling, usually low and adverse, for another closely neighbouring it in the wiring of mentality, but trumping it. What the hell! the music can say in its transmutation of sorrow by gospel or blues. It is the wild moment that she sometimes experienced when touring America in the early days, or feels now when thinking about the risks of freewheel-ing. Crucially, she tells me: 'The excitement pushes out the worry of the danger sometimes.' It is another kind of homeopathy, using and re-using the same emotional chemicals. For physiologically, in the neurotransmission of noradrenaline or of mesolimbic dopamine in the brain, it is said to be easier to switch from anxiety to excitement than convert from anxiety to calm, as if by sheer speed to miss out any middleman and escape a depressive downer.[5] And this is like her speaking of a drug-like high, though Frances has never been a serious drug-taker, when she read so much of Elizabeth Bishop, copying out hundreds of quotations. This artificial stimulant towards excited effort made her what she calls 'blotted out as a person—in a good way', blocking out her thought of self, her history, to create a different inner world no longer so in thrall to the external or the past one. More than merely a sense of delicious pleasure or reward, it is the *effort* of mental action in the updating of her brain state that provides her with the sense of biochemical change.

There is a Elizabeth Bishop poem she much relishes, 'Cape Breton', which contains more of that transforming injection. The poem figures in its very landscape something of the shifts and transferences vital to this process of recombination. From on high the sea water is seen 'weaving and weaving,/ disappearing under the mist', until 'somewhere the mist incorporates the pulse' of the sea, with the rapid regular beat of a motorboat heard travelling across it. It is a crucial line for Frances, she points to it. For perhaps that is what obscure poetry is for her—a spreading mental mist that incorporates a pulse felt through it. The pulse is taken away from its straightforward human form, only to be returned and reinstated in another subtler one. Or that is my interpretation, my sense of the connections. As often in these talks, Frances is interested when I hazard suggestions as to why she may be taken with a particular verse of phrase, and I don't think she is merely being polite. But she almost always says she had not thought of that—and is surprised not to have done so. I wonder if that is because my connections always seem analytically retrospective, back-formed; whereas what she is always looking to think about is something that, she says, she can 'take forward' in the unfolding of more open meaning. And I have to say, again this seems important.

We talk about the idea of 'carrying forward' which Eugene Gendlin, philosopher and psychologist, inherited from William James's pragmatics. He asks how poets in the midst of composition can ever know which word or phrase will best 'carry forward' the meaning they are struggling to express.[6] They try out one thing and another; across senses and between parts of themselves, to-and-fro, listening into what they see they have written, trying to hear if this combination opens their locked safe. They seek and they refine the way forward—that is to say, in search of an immediate future for their hunch, for their felt sense of a meaning just ahead. Then the present is surging into a future (not The Future, but the very next excited microsecond) which it does not wholly know. When you do know, it's gone. But it is real action here, in quick moments when you instinctively decide to say something or do something, or some decisive thought occurs, or an opening or calling suddenly beckons, with excited liveliness in place of old routine. Then it feels very intimate and interior, a disposition kept both prior to naming and beyond past stereotypes. Gendlin seems to be saying we live most and best in an almost immediate future, not the past. And that immediate future *is* the present, if we called it aright.

'Altogether devoid of knowledge and conscious motive is he when he is heaving into uncreated space' says D. H. Lawrence in his 'Study of Thomas Hardy'.[7] *Uncreated space* in open forms that Frances particularly associates with America history and landscape, with American venture and verse: potential there, stronger than just possibility, works forward and feels forward for the realization of itself.

It is that sort of surge which is achieved when a singer is audibly lifted by hearing his own voice respond to the words, or when through feedback of results in the very midst of process a poet is carried forward by her own formulations. That is why Frances also gave me the fine Frank O'Hara poem on Billie Holiday, 'The Day Lady Died', for its aftermath of memory in those final lines: 'while she whispered a song along the keyboard/ to Mal Waldron and everyone and I stopped breathing.'[8] And now her own breath is gone.

But desire for a new life or a fresh beginning is never where Frances can start from. That would be too directively explicit, too intentionally definite to be true. She starts instead from a text which, like Silas Marner himself, must begin in exile until it comes home again in a new dimension. And as I have said, Frances sometimes likens these texts initially to brain-teasers. 'The way the words are on the page does something to your brain, I think, particularly in the midst of dense poetry. I don't do word-puzzles as such, I am not good at them; but in a way it's a bit like doing a word-puzzle when you're looking at a very demanding or elusive poem. I have been writing my own poetry too of late, and that works your brain.' When asked what is the difference between a word-puzzle and a poem, she replies: 'Some sort of meaning, because even if the meaning seems very slight, a flower, a mist, there are still layers and layers of meaning, and it sends your brain off in different trajectories.'

Always it starts from what she chooses to call brain, instead of mind, as though in need of something below and prior to the normalities of thinking; something on the very boundary between what we call mind and what we call body. Even so, it is a mental feeling that registers itself as more physical than psychological in ways that—perhaps, thanks goodness—can never be fully known; that can change and be altered, without immediate consciousness being able to calculate the precise consequence. I sense some sort of implicit plan in this for someone who emerging from uncompleted starts and abrupt ends, from breakdown and damage, would never dare make plans more definitely. It feels like an attempt to suspend the mind—to halt its automatic habits, its traumatized memory, its psychologically damaged story—through making it (to update George Chapman's terms in the *Banquet of Sense*) bite off more than it can chew—holding more than it can easily accommodate or classify in complex verse or in those long sentences from George Eliot that once set Frances going again. The psyche has then to give way to brain-work, beneath the level of anxious personality, where for her, words seem to work in their rhythmic shapes like stimulating drugs or electrical implants. It is some neurological place which—if anywhere—is relatively, marvellously, or even shockingly unaffected still by all that has happened to the person in which it is lodged. There, in relation to poetic stimuli, at least she can never know whether, or how far, she has been damaged or impaired, in that clumsy way that the conscious human mind will mostly try to explain it. And from there in the nervous system comes the impetus to recreate mind again, anew, out of what the brain's activity is beginning to tell the mind from below upwards. This goes on even to the point at which mind is itself carried forward in search of a character for itself, a life-form that can sustain it. Of course it isn't as simple as that: a version of that mind, of that self is already there, latent but waiting to be re-formed after it has listened long enough to the dense poetic difficulties it takes in. But it seems important that even through her literary sophistication Frances may have retained a naive and inquisitive self almost innocent of her own terrible experience, that can still go venturing forward to a future without knowing its final aim; only following its intellectual reaction to the written neurology of thought.

No wonder that, in all this, Emily Dickinson is another female American poet in whom Frances has taken a passionate interest—because hardly any poet uses the word 'brain' more often, more significantly than she, and in just the way that Frances herself does, to mean the pre-person. 'The Brain is — wider than the Sky —', 'I felt a Funeral, in my Brain', 'I felt a Cleaving in my Mind —/ As if my Brain had split —'. But the poem of hers that Frances particularly brought to my attention was:

This Consciousness that is aware
Of Neighbors and the Sun
Will be the one aware of Death
And that itself alone

Is traversing the interval
Experience between
And most profound experiment
Appointed unto Men—

How adequate unto itself
Its properties shall be
Itself unto itself and none
Shall make discovery.

Adventure most unto itself
The soul condemned to be—
Attended by a single Hound
Its own identity.

The sort of reader Frances is loves the way the fourth line—'And that itself alone'— turns out to have less to do with the preceding third in its own stanza on Death, than with the fifth in the stanza following, by traversing 'the interval', within what is then called 'Experience between'. It is that re-routing of the brain, those turns forwards and backwards across and between the lines, the shift from static to fluid, that distinguishes what is truly reading for her: the 'adventure' of the 'experience between'. It makes a virtue of what at first must seem discontinuous. It is like those em-dashes in 'The Brain is — wider than the Sky —' when Dickinson argues that in that way the Brain is like a version of God for being able to hold the sky within it:

> And they will differ — if they do —
> As Syllable from Sound —

Again, this seems important. For perhaps it is like what Frances is always doing, moving from syllable to sound, from what is written to what is mentally heard again, from one sense to another, brain to mind, score to performance, abstract plan to heavenly creation, or formal notation to felt reality. It is those movements, unsmooth, across dashes, that are again part of 'Experience between', 'And most profound experiment/ Appointed'.

I come across the following later, which seems to me to describe what goes on so to speak between the lines of life, in the transitions from unconscious to conscious, and I send it to Frances, to see if it fits with her as a description of those strange moments when:

> we find ourselves asking 'Who am I? What are these thoughts?' The mood is very apt
> to overtake us while engaged in the commonest acts. In health it is always momentary,
> and seems to coincide with the instant of the transition and shift of our attention
> from one thing to another. It is probably connected with the transfer of energy from
> one set of faculties to another set, which occurs, for instance, on our waking from
> sleep, on our hearing a bell at night, on our observing any common object, a chair or a
> pitcher, at a time when our mind is or has just been thoroughly preoccupied with
> something else.[9]

Written by another pioneering American, John Jay Chapman, a disciple of the visionary Ralph Waldo Emerson, it speaks of those reminders from the midst of life that humans do not command their thoughts. That instead, at such moments of unfamiliar experience, in the loopholes and transitions of being and 'the transfer of energy from one set of faculties to another', what is happening is the realization that thinking is strange, the self-realization of a thinking subject suddenly emergent by reflection upon its own thought-objects. Who am I? What are these thoughts? Frances writes back to me that the Chapman is indeed her sort of thing, and it reminds her of Elizabeth Bishop's 'In the Waiting Room' when self-reflection happens for the first time to a child.

Immersed in reading a disaster-story from the *National Geographic* while she waits for her aunt to undergo dental treatment, suddenly a little girl overhears a feeble cry of pain. She thinks it is her cowardly foolish aunt, but it isn't: it is herself, her own voice she hears. And even then, just short of seven years old, she feels 'you are an I/ you are an Elizabeth' though scarcely daring to look and see what she was:

> I knew that nothing stranger
> had ever happened, that nothing
> stranger could ever happen.

'Such things bring us, as it were, into the ante-chamber of art, poetry and music', writes John Jay Chapman. That is where so many of the readers we have been considering in these chapters place themselves. And in such a place one might find and begin to understand the otherwise enigmatic saying of the poet Valéry: that 'the poet' in the midst of work 'is a transition within a man'—making all those difficult transitions, in the act of essaying human meaning.[10]

So, finally, with Emily Dickinson again:

> How adequate unto itself
> Its properties shall be
> Itself unto itself and none
> Shall make discovery.
>
> Adventure most unto itself
> The soul condemned to be—
> Attended by a single Hound
> Its own identity.

Frances knows what it is to be hounded by identity, and by the misfortunes that may seem to determine it. But she is more concerned with what, in the poem's movement from Brain to Soul, is here only called 'it', 'itself', in between everything and quite alone, testing 'its' own adequacy—'unto', 'unto', 'unto itself'—in the greatest of experiments. She is leading a shared reading group now, she is writing poems. Although she rightly will not say so for fear of hubris, and though she still thinks she is running from behind, and it may all be too late, Frances is carefully and subtly making and re-making a life.

CHAPTER 6

THE DOCTOR

Here speaks Clive, a busy GP in his later forties, responding to my request for reader case-histories:

I have been reading a collection of poems by Denise Riley, drawn to it by its title: *Say Something Back*. It is mainly her grieving over the unexpected death of her adult child Jacob, while abroad, found drowned in his bath in 2008 as a result of cardiomyopathy. I was first struck by the bare-looking epigraph to the book—I looked it up, it's a complete stanza taken out of a longer poem in seventy-four pieces by W. S. Graham, 'Implements in their Places':

> Do not think you have to say
> Anything back. But you do
> Say something back which I
> Hear by the way I speak to you.

It is gentle and intimate. You do not have to say/ anything. But you do/ say something back. Which I/ hear. By the way I speak to you. Even when you do not speak to me. It could be a letter to someone absent but I think of it here the way Denise Riley must have, as an address to the dead. Then 'you' is a forlorn cry: 'you' are no longer here but I cannot yet call you 'him' or 'her' instead. There is another poem of Graham's, 'Dear Bryan Wynter', which I then found, beginning: 'This is only a note/ To say how sorry I am/ You died.' Again it seems poignantly simple, but then strange, to say 'you' here or 'sorry'; strange in a way even to say 'died', as if it was something people did. Even 'he is dead' is odd with that present tense, meaning he just isn't . . . anything. But without these basic simplicities of language, death is unspeakable. Well, it is . . .

This is the way I read. I could tell you I am a very busy man, and it is true; but it is also true that I am anyway a rather lazy, occasional, and disparate sort of reader. I like being given a fragment, a quotation, that someone else has picked out, sending me back to the original. For me it is all about examples, though the good thing is that I may not know what they are examples *of*. Denise Riley handed me a shortcut to W. S. Graham, so that what Graham wrote was no longer just words on the page for me to trawl through, but something passed on through another mind, ready for further adaptation. His lines have an extra human dimension when I can see them through this other reader's eyes and can imagine their effect on her. It's like a little case-history of the use of reading, translated and passed on. And for me poetry here is about that basic need—not just for receiving communication, or for the expression of feeling, but to get *through* to the inside of some reality that might otherwise just pass me by...

'Say something back which I/ hear by the way I speak to you'. The main thing I got from that particular fragment was this. That inevitably for the bereaved, the cry to their dead is met by no voice in return. Missing his wife of fifty years, a patient of mine says, quite typically of many others: 'Even after a good day—especially after a good day—it is the going back to an empty house that is the worst. I used to tell her everything about my day. Now I just hear the silence.' Only now what is suggested through the poem—and this is what I loved, and especially would, had I lost a wife or child—is the presence of that missing voice *within* my own, in 'the way I speak to you'. It's a very minor example, but a new colleague when I first came into this practice said he noticed an immediate change in my tone when quite unexpectedly I came across someone in the surgery I had known years ago at university. Without my being aware of it, my voice at once took on the fact of a friendly relationship though many years had past, and my new colleague could hear the different hue of it.

*

Clive has become part of our informal consultation network—a collection of people from a variety of disciplines and backgrounds to whom we occasionally show films and transcripts, ethically approved, to invite comment and discussion. We are a small unit and need these extra people, especially when they offer a perspective from outside academe. There are two sessions I want to mention here.

One of the case-histories we discussed was that of Keith, the subject of chapter 1 of this book, together with some mention of Tom's reading of Tolstoy, as told in chapter 2. Clive was very much concerned here with the idea of 'recovery' as not so much to do with getting over a trouble and moving on, as recovering through the experience of literature a valued earlier feeling, an innocence or a belief supposed lost or defaced by subsequent trauma or misdoing. He connected it to a group session involved in reading chapter 12 from George Eliot's *Silas Marner*, where the rejected and solitary old miser finds his lost gold replaced by a golden-haired child:

When Marner's sensibility returned, he continued the action which had been arrested, and closed his door, unaware of the chasm in his consciousness, unaware of any intermediate change, except that the light had grown dim, and that he was chilled and faint. He thought he had been too long standing at the door and looking out. Turning towards the hearth, where the two logs had fallen apart, and sent forth only a red uncertain glimmer, he seated himself on his fireside chair, and was stooping to push his logs together, when, to his blurred vision, it seemed as if there were gold on the floor in front of the hearth. Gold!—his own gold—brought back to him as mysteriously as it had been taken away! He felt his heart begin to beat violently, and for a few moments he was unable to stretch out his hand and grasp the restored treasure. The heap of gold seemed to glow and get larger beneath his agitated gaze. He leaned forward at last, and stretched forth his hand; but instead of the hard coin with the familiar resisting outline, his fingers encountered soft warm curls. In utter amazement, Silas fell on his knees and bent his head low to examine the marvel: it was a sleeping child—a round, fair thing, with soft yellow rings all over its head. Could this be his little sister come back to him in a dream—his little sister whom he had carried about in his arms for a year before she died, when he was a small boy without shoes or stockings? That was the first thought that darted across Silas's blank wonderment. *Was* it a dream?. It was very much like his little sister.

This, notes Clive, is recovery in the deepest sense. We watch a videoed session together in which participant Carla notes the abrupt change in Silas Marner, for which he has almost no current framework of explanation, at a moment of sheer transition, 'He doesn't think about the gold *at all*. It had been central to his being until then'.

> *Group Leader* [*re-reading*]: 'and bent his head low to examine the marvel: it was a sleeping child—a round, fair thing, with soft yellow rings all over its head.' ... It's lovely that to his blurry eyesight those ringlets are a bit like the coins: they are round, and golden ... and then it's straight, with no pause, to 'Could this be his little sister come back to him in a dream.' It's funny about it being a dream ... ?
> *Carla*: Well he just cannot ... imagine ... this is reality.
> *Group Leader*: Yes
> *Carla*: It's too wonderful.
> *Group Leader*: Yes, yes.
> *Carla*: And the joy. It's ... he just cannot comprehend.

Rather than being cynically dismissed as 'too good to be true', the really Real in Carla's formulation—'too wonderful', too new and wholly unexpected—is become almost paradoxically that which defies imagination.

> But there was a cry on the hearth: the child had awaked, and Marner stooped to lift it on his knee. It clung round his neck, and burst louder and louder into that mingling of inarticulate cries with 'mammy' by which little children express the bewilderment of waking. Silas pressed it to him, and almost unconsciously uttered sounds of hushing tenderness, while he bethought himself that some of his porridge, which had got cool by the dying fire, would do to feed the child with if it were only warmed up a little.

It is a renewed and restored belief in good things. A single potato for Pierre in *War and Peace*; porridge for the child Silas names after his mother and sister; while across conventional stereotypes of gender, a traumatized old man suddenly has to respond to the infant cry for mammy. This is like what medicine should be, Clive says, porridge, potato: such things add to the gladness of the world, out of all proportion to their material appearance.

In another research meeting, we ask the group to consider alongside Clive's thoughts about W. S. Graham an anonymized case-history we think to be in the same area. The idea is to gather together sufficient examples and evidence to build from ground level upwards potential new themes and ideas. The current example concerns a man reading Christina Rossetti's poem 'Remember' at his mother's funeral. The researcher who interviewed him said that when he repeated his reading of the poem to her, it sounded as if he was speaking to himself through his mother's voice:

> Remember me when I am gone away,
>   Gone far away into the silent land;
>   When you can no more hold me by the hand,
> Nor I half turn to go yet turning stay.
> Remember me when no more day by day
>   You tell me of our future that you plann'd:
>   Only remember me; you understand
> It will be late to counsel then or pray.
> Yet if you should forget me for a while
>   And afterwards remember, do not grieve:
>   For if the darkness and corruption leave
>   A vestige of the thoughts that once I had,
> Better by far you should forget and smile
>   Than that you should remember and be sad.

We asked Clive to read the poem in advance on this occasion and write out his thoughts. He wrote:

That tiny moment between 'half turning to go' and 'yet turning stay' at the close of stanza 1 is to me, somehow, like life itself, happening in its midst:

>   When you can no more hold me by the hand,
> Nor I half turn to go yet turning stay

But that turn is itself 'no more'. Yet though I am a doctor, it is not the death or loss in these verses that primarily interests me. It is more the last six lines when the turn is from 'remember' to 'forget', and in particular the last two.

> Better by far you should forget and smile
>   Than that you should remember and be sad.

The son is not forgetting but remembering her as one who would almost *want* him to forget, out of love.

In another document we had before us, the man who read these verses at his mother's funeral had told our interviewer:

> It's weird that those words on that sheet of paper can create emotion in you. It's not something you can just sit there and do on your own. Poems—I don't know—just bring something up in me that needs...

And then she said he did not finish the sentence but just stopped speaking. He couldn't say *what* it is he needs; just needs... Like other Rossetti poems,[1] added another researcher, in their paradoxically precise sense of the vague, elusive or missing:

> We lack, yet cannot fix upon the lack:
> Not this, nor that; yet somewhat, certainly
>
> Something this foggy day, a something which
> Is neither of this fog nor of today,
> Has set me dreaming...

Something, somewhat, not there... yet... 'Just needs... something.'

Clive is interested in moments when the words run out—the unfinished sentences or leftover silences he often hears with his patients. Kremena Koleva is an expert in linguistics, having worked at the Universities of Leeds and York, and another associate of our team. She calls these uncompleted formulations 'hangings': situations in which speakers abandon a thought or leave it unfinished. Reaching that point, speakers experience a kind of mental emptiness in the face of the unknown or the wanting—what could it be, where it might ever lead. It is no longer a process of linguistic probing for further words, but more like 'a processing halt' at which point silent gestures often have to take over. The readers we think about in these sessions are often people who feel directionless or powerless or stuck, for whom points of change or strong feeling, triggered by a text, were likely to cause hesitancy, stumbling revision, a sense of the important and unfamiliar, or the lost and unattainable. They may not see a future even in their own sentences, let alone their lives. With these linguistic stops and starts, it seems to be that breakthroughs in understanding, if and when they do come, come only in surges. But Dr Koleva's most exciting suggestion is how the to-and-fro of utterance and pause indicates that

> speakers are probably somewhere on the very edge/borderline between language and thought, and there is always a coming back and forth between the two.

That edge is *the* place most crucial to human development.

The research team then shared more information about this son who read Christina Rossetti at his mother's funeral. He had been in a shared reading group, in a rehab centre, after becoming addicted to crack and heroin. The pattern was: got himself back together, went to read English Literature at university for a year; then dropped out; nonetheless found a good job in a different city for the next five years and stayed clean. Only then to relapse to the point at which he lost his job, home, car, family—everything in what had been his second chance at a life, till he was sleeping in a derelict public toilet. Then at the lowest, he returned to the rehab programme back in his home town, including the shared reading sessions again. He would have walked all the way back to it, he said at interview, though actually they paid his bus fare home. Coming back into shared reading: 'It was like you've not seen one of your family for a long while, and then they knock on your door.' It was like that moment at the end of Dickens's *A Christmas Carol* when in stave 5 Scrooge, penitent, goes to the house of the nephew whose invitations he has constantly rebuffed: 'Will you let me in, Fred?' On which note Dickens hesitates for a second: 'Let him in!' And then releases the tension: 'It is a mercy he didn't shake his arm off. He was at home in five minutes.'

He even got some training to help run a small group himself, and did so specifically in a care home because his mother had had dementia, as his father had before her. He got particularly interested when they might do a poem about springtime, sun shining, blue sky, and someone would burst into tears—when they hadn't at all during a sadder piece. It is the *mix* (not just of people but of such feelings) that he most loved when his reading group was going well.

But then his mother had died, long after she was already lost to Alzheimer's, and now he's struggling again, the researcher reported. In alternation with the pattern of addiction, the reading goes away, comes back, goes away again. It is like his Christina Rossetti poem: Remember, forget, remember forgetting. Or the unpredictable group he has helped run: Happy, sad, sad at happy. We're not talking simple or permanent cures or about straight linear progress, but perhaps looking at best for what Rossetti called 'a vestige of the thoughts that once I had' through all the extremes of relapse and recovery. That may be hard to take for people like us, says the researcher: those who loving *Silas Marner* want to believe in a more lasting and stable relation between reading and living, thinking and living, in redemption or a more stable existence.

My interest here comes from my own job as a doctor, Clive concludes, whenever it is that there is no easy remedy and still I must 'say something back'. It is what my patients need.

*

We talk more later about this need *to* reply and *for* reply.

Clive says: the reading that has most helped me here came from my mother's recommendation. She was also a GP, and for the progressivists of her generation in the 60s there was one great book that made her practice personal and humane and holistic, instead of specialist and pathologized. There is now a great surge in books by or about doctors, Clive notes, almost a new literature developed for reasons he cannot quite explain. Perhaps, he suggests, it has to do with the widening of medicine beyond drugs and remedies to take over concern for human areas, in extremis, that otherwise are left stranded by the loss of religion, by the limits of technology. Oliver Sacks, Atul Gawande, Henry Marsh, Gavin Francis, Paul Kalanithi, Sam Guglani... But the first, in 1967, was John Berger's portrait in *A Fortunate Man* of John Sassall, a country doctor in a poor, neglected local community. It wasn't a novel, it wasn't a fixed literary genre, but rather a real-life amalgam, in the rich mixture of non-fictitious facts with the applied skills of a novelist trying to interpret them. Berger was himself like an equivalent doctor offering his own imaginative diagnosis.

In this, Berger was still 'literary' in one crucial respect: that he feared the reductive language of mere 'common sense', that he hated the language of 'normalization'. He'll start an attempted account of why, say, it is so disturbing to witness an adult turned by sobbing into a child, saying: 'This is partly because of social convention...' But then he pushes himself, by adding 'Yet this is by no means the whole explanation'—until he gets to: 'Once more I believe the explanation goes further...' A child cries to a parent for help or in protest; but, says Berger, adults can only cry to themselves, somehow believing that they may regain with the howls and tears the ability to recover like a child: 'Yet it is impossible.'[2] Or to take another example, again beyond the easily conventional and obvious: Why it would be a great mistake to say, tamely and routinely, that what a patient always wants is a 'friendly' doctor? It is more precise and profound even than kindness, said Berger: it is about a doctor who offers *recognition* and *witness*, even when he or she cannot provide cure (*A Fortunate Man*, pp. 68–9).

We look at the relevant pages of *A Fortunate Man* together, this doctor and myself. Sassall's people come to the surgery, says Berger, often feeling themselves to be no more than worried nonentities 'without any confirmation' of themselves 'in the outside world'. But if instead a person 'can begin to feel recognised'

—and such recognition may well include aspects of his character which he has not yet recognised himself—the hopeless nature of his unhappiness will have been changed...

A Fortunate Man, p. 75

How does a doctor begin to make such people feel recognized? Not simply by presenting the face and manner of friendly meeting and greeting, but by trying almost simultaneously to get behind the patients' eyes, to then reflect back to them their own half-articulated thoughts clarified by the doctor's imaginative insights:

> When patients are describing their conditions or worries to Sassall, instead of nodding his head or murmuring 'yes', he says again and again 'I know', 'I know'. He says it with genuine sympathy. Yet it is what he says whilst he is waiting to know more. He already knows what it is like to be this patient in a certain condition: but he does not yet know the full explanation of that condition, nor the extent of his own power.
>
> *A Fortunate Man*, pp. 80–1

He holds on, at the same time seeking to hold the patients' condition and even retain their hope for them, as if he had created between patient and doctor a shared mind.[3] Or the doctor has become for his people, as Berger puts it later, 'the means of translating what they know into thoughts which they can think' (p. 99). Clive loves what, equivalently in literature, Ralph Waldo Emerson wrote in his essay on 'Self-Reliance'—that in every work of genius we recognize our own rejected thoughts returned with interest: 'they come back to us with a certain alienated majesty'.[4] Literature in some cool hands or sceptical circles may have given up on the embarrassingly old-fashioned, nineteenth-century aim of being a great healer or comforter, Clive says: for the moment it may have to be the literature of medics instead that remembers the urgent task of help and recognition, and tries to carry it out now.

Clive gives me two practical examples of creating this mental jointure with his patients. There is the elderly woman who wants to go on having an occasional drink and smoke though her health is very poor and she has limited time left her. She is fearful of the shame of medical disapproval. Then there is the man in the dementia care home who always seemed to be trying to get out of the window, his arms spread wide. He is terribly distressed when the staff try to get him away from this obsession, fearing that he will throw himself out.

With the first, the doctor decided to give up on the warnings—what the hell—and support the decision as a joint collaboration. It made him think of Samuel Johnson when people complained about his giving money to the poor which they would only waste on gin: Why should they be denied 'the sweeteners' of their existence? or looked down upon for seeking whatever might 'gild' the swallowing of life's bitter pill?[5]

In the second case, Clive found out that the man had been a carpenter—that he was not trying to escape but to determine the window's exact size and dimension. The staff were asked to provide him with a tape measure.

The role of the GP in such cases, Clive concluded, was to tap into the subjective core, and try to create the right objective conditions around it. He mentions a favourite poem by Gerard Manley Hopkins, 'Felix Randal', the death of an old big-boned farrier. 'Sickness broke him' and in turn affects the poem's speaker:

> This seeing the sick endears them to us, us too it endears.
> My tongue had taught thee comfort, touch had quenched thy tears,
> Thy tears that touched my heart, child, Felix, poor Felix Randal...

That is the little shared world which the reciprocity of feeling can make.

I told him this creative sharing reminded me of an elderly woman in a care home who hardly spoke much at all any more. But a volunteer read to her group an e.e. cummings poem about the sea:

> and maggie discovered a shell that sang
> so sweetly she couldn't remember her troubles, and
>
> milly befriended a stranded star
> whose rays five languid fingers were

—and she abruptly cried out the single word, 'Bathroom'. The staff assumed this meant a request for the lavatory. But on this occasion, by chance, her daughter was present, and suddenly realized that in the bathroom of the old family home her mum had kept a collection of shells with a starfish mounted on the wall. On her mother's behalf, as though she were her shared mind and extended memory, she was able to explain the connection, and her mother nodded in relief. This act of interpreting and articulating seemed to renew their bond, her mother being grateful for the filling out of her one-word recall into sentences. Thereafter she began to respond more in the reading group, nodding, laughing, talking a little. A few days after the starfish poem, she remembered the name of her daughter's partner for the first time in months.

Clive loves the more unusual treatment, an improvised unorthodoxy in a GP that responds suddenly and humanly to what is there. There is something about the idea of 'health' that Clive does not like when it is too narrowly formulaic, too hygienically sealed. He cites a report on Culture and Heath, subtitled 'A Wider Horizon' which quotes Sartre on being asked when old and blind, whether he regretted having lived such an unhealthy life: 'What's the point of health?'[6] It was and remains a defiantly real question. And Clive also quotes the novelist Daniel Pennac on how it may be best, after all, to use—even use up—a life. '*Acceleration* is everything':

we are not soft-landing missiles; we are cannonballs of consciousness launched on the ever-steeper path of our lives. Whether our carcasses can keep up or not is their business.[7]

Health has to be a means, on the side of launching a life that is defined as being more intrinsically worthwhile than just being-without-disease. If we are here to use up our lives rather than merely prolong them, then we might even drive our own bodies to follow, with speed, whatever it is in our possible future that we are after. 'Whether our carcasses can keep up or not is their business': *our* business is what comes first, if only we can find what it is worth giving our lives to. Patients sometimes want to hear that lift-off instinct confirmed, says Clive, for all the cautions, medications and sticking plasters. 'For what is life, if measured by the space,/ Not by the act?' Ben Jonson says:

> for life doth her great actions spell
> By what was done and wrought
> In season, and so brought
> To light: her measures are—how well
> Each syllable answered, and was formed how fair;
> These make the lines of life, and that's her air.
>
> 'To the Immortal Memory and Friendship of That Noble Pair,
> Sir Lucius Cary and Sir Henry Morison'

Lives feel cut short, as a doctor well knows. And we hardly know how to measure save by length. But, in what Jonson calls the true 'lines of life', 'It is not growing like a tree/ In bulk, doth make man better be':

> A lily of a day
> Is fairer far in May,
> Although it fall and die that night,
> It was the plant and flower of light.

The small brief and beautiful lily then, if that is how it has to be, rather than the stout oak. The poetic lines of life say the 'Although' must turn both ways in thinking about life, forwards and back: fair in May/ *Although* that night it fall and die; but *Although* it fall and die by night,/ It was the plant and flower of light. When we talk about this movement, Clive has what seems to me a wonderful thought about the 'although' and what it stands for on the page and in life: human beings, he says, have basic intractable material to deal with, and what they cannot change, they have to put in as good a place or order as possible, turning it this way and that. That is poetry, so to speak, in real-life practice. Clive finally says, moving from the detail back up to the overall, that he first heard this poem by Jonson read at a funeral for a patient's son who died young, in his twenties. The patient, long-standing, had become a sort of friend over the years, and Clive knew the family history almost as it had happened.

All this variety of involvement, going on in the very midst of his patients' lives, is what being a *general* practitioner most means to Clive in preference to the claims of specialization. That is also how he incorporates his reading and his thinking into his work—by being eclectic and unsystematic, hunting across different fields and disciplines for nuggets of human use or help in the little time he can make free. Being a GP of this kind means a human commitment to a broad irregularity, responsive to the reach of change and variation beyond blanket measures. And it is achieved precisely through *not* defining itself—its aims and its abilities and its reach—too prescriptively, purely, or systematically. Clive is an admirer of Iona Heath, another of Berger's disciples, when she writes: 'There is a specific dualism that characterises medicine, with the body viewed both as a standardised human object, defined by biology, and as a unique human subject, created by biography.'[8] What at best the general practitioner seeks to do, Heath continues, is to *contain* this dualism within herself, in order to try to hold together for each individual patient the scientific knowledge of the object and an imaginative understanding of the subject, and recreate within the practitioner herself a deeply integrated sense of the complexity of human beings. That *is* what a vocation means, Clive believes: it is what a person can be, and through that being, make more existent in the world. And so the GP seeks to occupy and to heal the breach, to be a model of how to make the two—the art and the science, the theory and the praxis, the case and the person— into as near a unity as can be. This is what another of our informal consultants, Alison Liebling, a professor of criminology at Cambridge, calls a tragic rather than a cynical vocation. The cynical way prefers the unequivocal solution—the judgement unchallenged by sympathy or mitigation; the distanced perspective provided without conflict. The tragic view offers the 'total yield of life', and for the sake of all that matters tries not to avoid the pain and fear, the breaches and tensions.[9] By dint of his mission, Berger's John Sassall had to cope with the thought that he had deliberately taken on more than he could cure or even cope with, once he went beyond pills and surgery. He had to bear the class distinction between himself and the poor to whom he wished to dedicate himself. He had to tolerate the paradox that the prestige and value of his role depended upon the very suffering of his patients. And yet, even though it drove Sassall to suicide shortly after the death of his wife, fifteen years after the book was published, Berger still persisted in thinking of this doctor as a fortunate man, without irony. He had always said that his book was deliberately made to be at the mercy of realities he had not invented and could not encompass. And not every endeavour was to be judged solely in the light of its final outcome.

Attempted integration, however difficult, is, it may be concluded, Clive's obsession in his work, and in his reading both for that work and away from it. Above all, the idea that he has found through his patients and their neediness is this: that to speak contains in essence the hope also of being spoken to. 'Say something *back*.'

*

CRILS is currently involved in trying to measure spontaneous variations of voice against a person's default register. The idea is to test if changes in normal modulation overlap with moments of powerfully felt thinking. The poem, the thought it prompts, the imagined or recalled person it suggests, comes into the participants' voice, affects both their tone and their vocabulary or syntax.

Two pieces of poetry act as our models here, connected with 'speaking back'.

In the first, from 'The Shadow on the Stone', Thomas Hardy stares down at the earth plot at the back of his house where his late wife used to do her gardening. Suddenly he sees on the stone in front of him a shadow in human form, seemingly cast from behind him, and then at once, 'I thought her behind my back'. Still facing forward, he blurts out-loud:

> ...'I am sure you are standing behind me,
> Though how do you get into this old track?'
> And there was no sound but the fall of a leaf
> As a sad response...

The second is in contrast and taken from *Hamlet*. It is Shakespeare's Claudius crying out, would-be penitent in his guilt: 'A brother's murder. Pray can I not...O, what form of prayer/ Can serve my turn?'

> 'Forgive me my foul murder'?
> That cannot be, since I am still possessed
> Of those effects for which I did the murder—
> My crown, mine own ambition, and my queen.
> May one be pardoned and retain th'offence?

Finally he rises from his knees:

> My words fly up, my thoughts remain below:
> Words without thoughts never to heaven go.
>
> *Hamlet* 3.3 41, 54–9, 100–1

You can almost hear Hardy's wife (or the affecting thought of her) in Hardy's voice, whatever the long bare after-silence still waiting to be filled. The sensitive cadence of his quiet cry, 'behind me', vulnerably listening out on the receiving end of its own message, is the very touchstone of W. S. Graham's idea of feeling-you-through-how-I-speak-to-you. The proposition is therefore this: That what or whom you speak of, write of, think about, or read, you to some degree *become* in the very act. This is how, at its best, language is emotionally inflected by the imagination of that to which it refers. It is a second go at reaching into the real.

But in Claudius' apostrophe, the reader cannot feel—and worse, Claudius himself cannot feel—the presence of the God he calls upon. 'Forgive me my foul murder' takes on, in the very midst of its being uttered, a self-jeering, parodically disbelieving tone, with that final question-mark against it: Really? His knowledge stands outside himself, as severe as any judge or judgement against him. He is a man barely able to internalize with feeling the terrible thought of what he has done, and of who he has become and must continue to be in consequence. The anonymous 'one' who may not be pardoned because he still retains the fruits of his misdoing, must be hardened back down into again being this self-condemned 'I'—not even saying 'I cannot pray' but more helplessly, 'Pray can I not': 'My words fly up, my thoughts remain below'. What he hears back from what he says is an absence, an emptiness, and a dissociation. He is passing from the tragic back into the cynical.

This is the vital difference for any form of human speech or thought when uttered alone, without answer or company: does it feel to its speaker, even as he or she speaks it, to have still some internal presence and emotional resonance to it, or is it left feeling empty and useless? This is John Berger again:

> The boon of language is not tenderness. All that it holds, it holds with exactitude and without pity. Even a term of endearment: the term is impartial; the context is all. The boon of language is that potentially it is complete, it has the potentiality of holding with words the totality of human experience. Everything that has occurred and everything that may occur. It even allows space for the unspeakable. In this sense one can say of language it is potentially the only human home, the only dwelling place that cannot be hostile to man....
>
> One can say anything to language. That is why it is a listener, closer to us than any silence or any god. Yet its very openness often signifies indifference. (The indifference of language is continually solicited and employed in bulletins, legal records, communiqués, files.) Poetry addresses language in such a way as to close this indifference and to incite a caring. How does poetry incite this caring?[10]

Tenderness is not a given, says John Berger, it has to be made out of material not in itself wholly tender, in palliation or realization of it. This is the definition of a need and a role here: to take that image of indifference, and using its precision at one level, still make a difference to be felt within it. It is worse than horrid when it goes wrong, giving way to a false or automatic note, a failed or a forced utterance: 'for I understand', the poet says, 'that the wrong sound weakens/ what no sound can ever save.'[11]

*

Two things become even clearer still at our follow-up interview. That Clive does not want to stay too much with death and the fear of endings. Nor does he want his whole world to be one of measurable 'outcomes', success or failure rates. This mixture of incurable problems and target imperatives has precipitated an occasional depression which has nearly finished him at times, he says, as a GP. When he reads, he most wants reading-matter that is not escapist as such, but still keeps his spirits up, reminding him of alternatives that may be easily forgotten. He needs to find a world-within-the-world that rescues him from solely being at the mercy of the institutions within which he works.

It is vital to access that second, more inner-related world. People in depression find it difficult to resist the automatic categories of the outer world as though they had given up on their individuality. They may give repeated accounts of life as meaningless or themselves of no value because, psychologists suggest, they cannot access the individual micro-details of life, they cannot benefit from the apparently tiny specifics that are not so easily assimilable into simple gross classification.[12] They have to prefer lumpen generalizations about this person, that job, this situation, all of them pessimistic or cynical. That is why Alison Liebling, again, tries to bring to her interviewing of prisoners what she calls 'appreciative inquiry'. It is not about insistently seeking to draw out the positives in a person and suppress their negative responses, though she does try to get away from always harping on problems and deficiencies. It is rather what she calls the 'heliotropic principle': 'the idea that plants follow the sun, or move in the direction of what gives them life and energy. People and organisations might do the same.'[13] The emphasis is on trying to recall peak moments, to remember strong experiences of specific feeling and encounter, where the energy makes for life, not death, even in experiences that were hard and dark. 'Study elation in order to understand the despair.'[14]

What Clive loves, in his own counselling, are those suddenly emergent fragments of thought that are not immediately part of a set theme or a repeated opinion, but reach below into less controlled and less habitual feelings and memories. That is why literature's vibrant examples, emotional particulars, and anomalies matter to him—precisely because we may not know yet what to do with them; because they may be little bits of sheer life resisting and preventing our general-headed norms.

Clive loved, he says, what a colleague, a psychoanalyst, once told him: 'It is only worth having a past if you have a future—I can't see the point of it otherwise'.

He and I go back to the crucial moment we discussed previously when the usual words and responses run out, as though they could not quite find that future for themselves. I ask him to say more about his interest in incomplete sentences instead of impersonal directives, returning to the example of the Rossetti reader: 'Poems—I don't know—just bring something up in me that needs...' Is that more like a stop or more like a start? I ask. We talk then about a poem we both know and now think of together. It is 'Begin' by Brendan Kennelly, one Clive mentioned in a detailed written response to the question what were his key texts:

> Begin again to the summoning birds
> to the sight of the light at the window,
> begin to the roar of morning traffic
> all along Pembroke Road.
> Every beginning is a promise
> born in light and dying in dark
> determination and exaltation of springtime
> flowering the way to work.
> Begin to the pageant of queuing girls
> the arrogant loneliness of swans in the canal
> bridges linking the past and future
> old friends passing though with us still.
> Begin to the loneliness that cannot end
> since it perhaps is what makes us begin,
> begin to wonder at unknown faces
> at crying birds in the sudden rain
> at branches stark in the willing sunlight
> at seagulls foraging for bread
> at couples sharing a sunny secret
> alone together while making good.
> Though we live in a world that dreams of ending
> that always seems about to give in
> something that will not acknowledge conclusion
> insists that we forever begin.

Does every promise, 'born in light and dying in dark', have to end up being a disappointment, measured only by some narrative account of its eventual result? There is instead here a simple example of our power of invention—that the given sequence of Day into Night within which we seem naturally to live could also become for us, at some key boundary-point hard to identify, the sequence Night into Day instead, without any other change in the order of things. So it was in Claudius' 'Pray can I not' instead of 'I cannot pray': the basic elements in an intractable situation may remain the same but the form—what we may do with them—can be made different. And that is so even if 'Pray can I not' only further realizes the anguish of not being to start again, since it is at least in place of flatly stating the negative fact. Once again, Clive thinks that this change of form if not content suggests some basic paradigm, though he cannot quite say for what. Perhaps (he goes on), for poetry out of the materials of prose, and whatever that stands for beyond poetry itself; for variation and inventive adaptation by getting (what he calls) 'out from under'; for some created room for manoeuvre and discretion in human beings. To Clive, such chinks of possibility offer some hope for mental health, in contrast to the stuck-ness of a world that 'always seems about to give in'.

In fact Clive is interested in how far conceivably we might be able to change the very form in which we do our thinking. In our unacknowledged blindness, something may be very wrong with the current frameworks of understanding, he thinks, which is why he reads literature to find the surprising or uncharted. One form he says he sometimes dislikes, however, is what has been called 'narrative medicine', even though it comes out of the same humanizing movement that looks back to John Berger. He is referring to the common belief that people must be able to have access to their own story, that they suffer without it, and that one way to realize it is by telling it to their physician who won't otherwise recognize their individual depth. The doctor in him knows the value of all this but often as the relating of the story goes on, Clive complains, he finds people losing their initial insight, thinking it down into a more conventionally normalized and stereotyped account of their lives. He knows he still must listen hard and try to interpret the ostensibly banal, but he is waiting for the flashes and discontinuities of insight. 'I want the clue of the lyric glimpse, the vestige or the fragment to *begin* from, not the self-conscious spelling out of an over-clear narrative', he says.[15] In that respect, he notices the little boundary word 'to' in Kennelly poem: 'Begin to' 'Begin again to'. It is that little insertion of 'to' which, less conventionally than normal, opens up the poem. By this means it is not a beginning that almost immediately makes for a closed and foreseeable sense, the forced march to the end of a sentence, but a beginning which greets the free-floating lines of individually good things that do not have to go on to do anything or get anywhere: swans, branches, faces, bridges between forward and back. Clive writes me, later:

I love it whenever anyone starts to do or to say something. There seems no reason they have to, or that it is has to be at that moment. You would not even know if it *didn't* happen. But here it comes: it's fresh life, it's individual, it's what health—a burst of new vitality—means to me. What seems to follow is, actually, often less important, and goes all normal again. I don't want to feel disappointed by that. But what I relish is that initiating moment when you can see thought alive and anew, not yet hardened into a set theme or concept. Thought of that kind is like a mediator doing its thinking between the person and the world.

> Though we live in a world that dreams of ending
> that always seems about to give in
> something that will not acknowledge conclusion
> insists that we forever begin.

For me, writes Clive, even the formal grammar of the lines and sentences exists only to give way to my memory of the little phrases they allow. So, the world *'always about to give in'* is countered by something that *'will not acknowledge conclusion'*, both of them in the same place at the line-end, silently speaking back to each other. Or there is that glimpse of *'something'* that *'insists we forever begin'* where the way 'forever' and 'begin' relate is a paradox I can't quite articulate. (Clive characteristically pauses and stops like this for a moment before going on, like his admired Berger, to have several further attempts at his answer.) It is not ironic, that 'forever begin', he says, like we never really get anywhere, always pushing the heavy stone up the hill and falling back down again; it is more like promise, potential, something always to start from, to start again from. Like Pope famously in his *Essay on Man*: 'Hope springs eternal in the human breast;/ Man never Is, but always To be blest.' It is that non-acknowledging and insistent 'something' in the Kennelly that I look for—'something that will not acknowledge conclusion/ insists'—wherever I am, and especially in my patients. And it comes out of not being a mechanical part of things, however painful it may sometimes be to have to step out of the mechanism:

> Begin to *the loneliness that cannot end*
> since it *perhaps* is what *makes* us begin

'I mean, for me, that's the *poetry*—the accelerated shorthand, the real seeds of thinking—*within* the necessity of sense-making.' So what Clive is interested in is little lonely starts, bits of separation, incomplete fragments and clues with some future to them, even when the world may not quite allow its eventual fulfilment.

I talk to him a little about Henry James describing in some of the prefaces to his fiction how in the origins of novel-writing it is the secret mark of a novelist to take 'nuggets' from real life. These, picked up seemingly by chance, he also calls seeds or grains, germs or even viruses—little imaginative stimuli taken from life that follow the unforeseen principle of growth into the creation of a fully formed novel. In his preface to *The Spoils of Poynton* (1897) he writes of how unthinking life has no such direct sense for 'a subject' as an author has: the little latent possibilities that seem to go unheeded and uncompleted in life, the novelist takes out of the system and rescues for growth within the novel. If these beginnings were not thus thwarted or wasted, if they were already realized and fulfilled, the writer could do less with them, would have no call upon the imagination to make out of them a second life in lieu of the lost first one. But with that, novelists are taken out of the simpler system of known and reported life: 'How do we know when and where to intervene, where do we place the beginnings of the wrong or the right deviation?' The writer, he goes on in the preface to *The Awkward Age* (1899), may therefore find something he had intended to be short, grow long under his hand—beginnings that are suddenly become more than introductory; middles no longer holding the place planned for them. In short, what emerges in this creative forming of things is 'the triumph of intentions never entertained'. What this process means, says Henry James, would be 'a theme for the philosopher'. For to think what is clearly great, what manifestly small, what will lead somewhere or go nowhere, we have no reliable advance-measure in experience. The final lesson a philosopher might grasp from the process of the writer, James concludes, is the absence of any fixed and certain law, by which we may know beforehand 'the just limits and the just extent of the situation, ANY situation'.

So the keen-eyed reader, reading for personal purposes, may be like a novelist but on the opposite, receiving side of art, in turning accomplished forms back into nuggets again. That is to say, in the face of the completed work, the reader is attracted to moments of potential or fragments of bursting value within it, without knowing quite why.

Clive offers me as a test-case one little situation. He was casually reading a theological philosopher who suddenly quoted a passage from a novel, which Clive had never read. Boom, it went off in his hands, he says. The chosen excerpt suddenly seemed more interesting than the book in which he had gratefully found it, the fictional fragment having an unexpected emotional power over him he could not wholly account for—a force it may not even have had if he had been reading the novel more dutifully all through (as subsequently he did). And Clive thinks that is what readers are for—to be almost involuntarily selective, to see what rings bells or causes explosions, and to sort of rip the heart (as they feel it) out of a book.[16] He loves to discard the apparatus of finish and formality—the book covers, the consciousness of a work with an overall design or intention, the whole edifice of publication and education—to find some apparently bare, raw human cry usually concealed within or behind it all. His text-case was this passage taken out of John Banville's novel *The Untouchable* (1997), mainly about the double life of Anthony Blunt, art historian and Soviet spy. He first found it quoted in Richard Holloway's *Looking in the Distance*, about the human search for meaning.

The minimal context necessary for understanding the short excerpt is simple enough: Victor Maskell, the Blunt figure, also the narrator, returns to his childhood home in Ireland to bury his father, a bishop, and comfort his stepmother. But he has also to put his mentally handicapped younger brother, Freddie, into a rather grim care home. Initially Freddie, barely capable of speech, thinks they are just going for a nice drive, but then—'"Come along now, Frankie," the Sister was saying to Freddie, "come along and we'll get you settled in.":

> He had realised at last what was happening, that this was no treat laid on for him, a sort of pantomime, or an anarchic version of the circus, but that here was where he was to be abandoned, the bold corner where, for misdemeanours he could not recall committing, he was to be made to stand for the rest of his life.[17]

This is the preliminary setting, says Clive: I am moved by that insertion 'for misdemeanours he could not recall committing': that is what a writer *is* for me there, someone with the ability to imagine including that extra twist, instead of just 'made to stand in the corner as if he had done wrong'. And most especially, it is the coming home of it all to Freddie himself in his innocent dullness: that 'he had realised at last', like the slow terrible dawning of something other than a fun excursion. And then he clutches at his brother, desperately. But the bit that really kills me is this, as Freddie, calmed by his stepmother, goes to the poor little room that is meant to be his and sits on the bed:

> holding his back very straight, and with his knees together and his hands placed flat on the mattress at his sides. And then, having settled himself, the good boy once more, he lifted his eyes and looked at me where I stood cowering in the doorway, and smiled his most ingenuous, most beatific, smile, and seemed—surely I imagined it—seemed to nod once, as if to say, *Yes, yes, don't worry, I understand.*
>
> *Untouchable*, p. 220

What I have here is the sudden experience of my simply being very, very moved, says Clive. This is even true of Victor also, the older brother, moved despite his harsh mission.

But I ask Clive why he himself finds this so moving: what it speaks back to him, what it tells him about himself. His first reaction as ever is to say—sincerely

I believe—that he doesn't know. That is always where he begins from. The next stages are just that—instinctively made into stages, consisting of try-outs and guesses. He never goes on seamlessly. It is perhaps to do with leaving my patients, he then says: 'Given the bad prognosis, I have seen people have to take the terrible weight of their fate. And a doctor may have to stand by knowing it may well become even more terrible than they can yet imagine…'

After a while I say, 'I think Dickens would have loved this passage, for its twist.' And Clive asks why, and I say because it is someone apparently inferior to you—Freddie—being suddenly better than you in a way. I ask again of what this passage might specifically, personally remind Clive. He casts about emotionally, but doesn't mention his patients this time. Instead he says:

> I remember taking my boy, Samuel, to school the day of some exam and he was only ten. And when I said goodbye to him he turned away and said to himself something in the way of encouragement that I, his adult, might have given him, but didn't for fear of giving him pressure. He said, as he walked away, 'Come on Sam, come on Sam.'
>
> I remember my father dying in the hospital bed, suddenly in the night saying 'Fight, fight, fight, fight', four times together, raising both his fists, like a sort of raging King Lear. And I had to tell him it might be the time to stop fighting. And then seeing him understand.

Across their ages, I had to contain the feeling that both were more than I was, separate from me, but needing me too; needing something, even from themselves when they were almost helpless.

I ask Clive about the father:

> Dad was a reader, but mainly biographies and history. He once told me about the young Keats dying in front of his friend Joseph Severn. It was the greatest example of selflessness my father knew, he said. Keats asked his friend whether he had ever seen anyone die. When Severn said he had not, Keats said, 'Well then I pity you, poor Severn. You must be firm, it will not last long.' I don't think my dad made that up, though he was capable of it.

I then say, in a sort of objection: 'But, Clive, these are examples of the parent, the son, the friend, the doctor too, all in one way or another caring. In the Banville, the older brother doesn't seem to care, or doesn't want to; he wants to get rid of Freddie.'

> I see that. But that is what increases the effect on Victor. It increases also the impact of what for me is fundamental: the shift from one centre, within yourself, to a sense of another separate centre in the person facing you. And then the sense of that

other human centre, outside you, taking over inside you too for the moment, if you see what I mean? The great turning on of a Switch: that is what 'being moved' means to me; it is like being moved mentally *out* of myself whilst obviously having still to remain physically within myself.

I reply that we don't know if Freddie actually had the intention—only *seeming* to nod 'Don't worry, I understand'—or whether Victor just guiltily imagined it, despite himself. What's more, the older brother still goes off after this, refusing to stand in for their father. And the younger still has to stay on, year after year presumably, without that sudden adult moment of understanding, and managing and coping, remaining a steady constant within him. 'I see all that cautious, sceptical stuff,' Clive acknowledges. 'But it is important that Freddie cannot speak, that the literary language here is a mental translation of what was *unspoken* but still tried for in other ways of expression—with all the built-in risk that, yes, it may be only an imagined guess':

> And then, having settled himself, the good boy once more, he lifted his eyes and looked at me where I stood cowering in the doorway, and smiled his most ingenuous, most beatific, smile, and seemed—surely I imagined it—seemed to nod once, as if to say, *Yes, yes, don't worry, I understand.*

Clive then adds: 'It is a goodbye. The improvised formality of that also moves me; the way that as your Henry James said, the beginnings, middles, and ends keep moving around despite our plans, and yet need some place for themselves amidst the indifferent flow of everything. But I like the way, as you say, that there is no subsequent story given to this.' I know Clive is himself suspicious of stories but I still ask why he likes the hanging non-ending, and he replies:

> Because it emphasizes two sorts of transcendence that of course may not last (how could they?). I mean, first the way that Freddie transcends himself, as well as Victor's perception of him, for that moment. It says he is 'the good boy once more' but I also think he is beginning again here, temporarily and even in this moment of ending, to be an adult somewhere at his core. And an adult who in the midst of his own predicament seems to care more for Victor at that moment than Victor cares for him. Which Victor himself knows. (And that made me think of Keats's own selflessness in front of the young man having to witness his dying.)
>
> But that is the second transcendence: something that goes on in the uncaring Victor too for that moment. For all his superiority and his cleverness, he is getting from Freddie the recognition that intelligence cannot for ever rise above the claims of feeling below it. The feelings rise up just as Freddie raises his game: both are no longer for the while merely beneath Victor. You can't overlook in any sense your

own emotions no matter how intelligent you are. That's not a great, new, and original thought, I grant you; but emotionally it brings that back home to me as my own basis.

Do you ever feel like Victor? I ask.

Yes, of course, shamefully often. But in another way I wonder if the connection lies in the thought I could be Freddie too. Because as it says somewhere else in the passage [*and Clive turns to the book to check*], Freddie 'knew something large was expected of him' That is what amazes and moves me, when people, as we say, can rise to the occasion. What bit of them can do that, what bit of them can they somehow find in themselves to do that, even if it cannot consistently stay on...? Well, I feel as if I can remember something of that very temporary self-transcendence in my own case. That immediate sense of something created or recreated in you, by being suddenly responsive to the need for responsibility.

Can you give me an example of what you mean?

Perhaps my first, a simple one. My first time in hospital...I see your look. I know the significance of it being there...Aged about eight, tonsillectomy, not an operation we would advise now. But there were three kids only left on this ward, and I was the oldest, and the one boy. At the end of visiting time, we were all beginning to weep. The father of one of the little girls then urged me to show the girls how not to cry. It was kindly meant. I must have felt flattered because I managed to find a way to carry out that responsibility, as though manly. It was the first time I recall holding back the feeling, swallowing it so to speak, and becoming like an adult. It was learning to get internally strong, learning to become more independent. In a way I think I will look back on it as also one of the worst moments in my life.

Worst—because...?

Because as the poet might say, it is like 'Begin to repression, to being adult'. Begin to trying to overcome dependence. But dependence—the silent plea 'say something back'—is still at core what reminds us we are still only creatures. And though you might say Freddie for some minutes found in himself a moral independence even for the sake of his brother, what still moves me is Victor's recognition of it in turn. '*Yes, yes, don't worry, I understand.*' Victor needs that reassurance, and no one else in the world will ever give it to him again—the reassurance he should have given Freddie himself. But never mind even that now, because there is a bigger point, bigger than guilt. It is this: that the weaker vessel, accepting itself and its situation, looks after the stronger, and the stronger sees it. That unexpected experience of being on the receiving end of 'Don't worry,

I understand'—that is where Victor feels most openly and vulnerably what he still needs, what he can't hope or pray for. It is an acknowledged dependence—like Hopkins's saying of the old man, still, '*child*, Felix'.

'This is the help emotionally we must want or give,' Clive finishes by saying, ' even when it cannot fully help. Because it is the emotional *need* that must be kept alive, regardless.'

CHAPTER 7

EXPERIMENTS WITH RENAISSANCE SCRIPTS

I t was Coleridge and Wordsworth who retrieved the English lyric poem of the sixteenth and seventeenth centuries as foundationally essential to the understanding of the craft of poetry and its creative structures. Like the movement of the Renaissance itself, the Romantic age was dedicated to creating and to releasing new and renewed forces of life.[1]

In his *Preface to Lyrical Ballads* (1800) Wordsworth said that the great creative principle in the making of life was founded upon the perception of 'similitude in dissimilitude, and dissimilitude in similitude'.[2] The subtle mixture of difference and sameness operated within almost everything, he said: from the pleasure of variation in poetic metre, to the to-and-fro passions of sexual appetite. Non-identical repetition—similarity with difference, with recursive modification, and significant variation—is the life-code for the making of Renaissance lyric poetry.[3]

The themes of the Renaissance lyric are very few and generic—above all, love, and especially unhappy, rejected love. Within that range, its workings are themselves very much dependent on minute changes within structural repetitions of line and vocabulary. In his *Defence of Rhyme* (1603) Samuel Daniel called these poems 'orbs of order and form', little rhymed worlds.[4] Within their narrow bounds, the poets then work upon an expansive set of internal repertoires that become a microcosmic script for the generation of life. Like a poetic version of DNA, the basic script offers infinite riches through variations musically created out of a fixed and finite store of generic material enclosed and stabilized by the body of rhyme.

Here is one of those versions of the script or the score or the code, in its modified self-replications. A group of six local people, led by a project worker from *The Reader*, is reading together a mid-seventeenth-century love lyric by Robert Herrick.

> Bid me to live, and I will live
> Thy Protestant to be;
> Or bid me love, and I will give
> A loving heart to thee.

A heart as soft, a heart as kind,
    A heart as sound and free,
As in the whole world thou canst find,
    That heart I'll give to thee.

Bid that heart stay, and it will stay,
    To honour thy decree;
Or bid it languish quite away,
    And 't shall do so for thee.

Bid me to weep, and I will weep,
    While I have eyes to see;
And having none, yet I will keep
    A heart to weep for thee.

Bid me despair, and I'll despair,
    Under that cypress tree;
Or bid me die, and I will dare
    E'en death, to die for thee.

Thou art my life, my love, my heart,
    The very eyes of me;
And hast command of every part,
    To live and die for thee.

It is not an altogether easy poem for modern readers (for example, the word 'Protestant' in the second line punningly refers to one who makes an avowal or declaration of love: that's *his* religion). The person who reads it aloud to the group is Dan, a working-class, middle-aged Liverpool man, unemployed, with few educational qualifications, and suffering from mild depression, though the formal adjective seems rather a mockery. He has never read aloud before. But after five sessions with this shared-reading group, he decides he must volunteer and have a go. Nervous, he reads it very slowly and falteringly, using the lines, like braille, to help guide him through the unfolding sentences. He has only the words to go by, undeclaimed and without interpretation. When he read 'Bid that heart stay, and it will stay', halteringly raw and almost like a child, not yet humanizing it by particular emphases, he was leaving it all there as bare words, just about to relate to each other, at the beginning of the reception of their message. It is somewhat wonderful to think that later another reader may come along and say, 'and it *will* stay', or 'and it will *stay*' (or try to elide between the two) 'to honour thy decree'. Those varyingly possible emphases inside the phrase 'and it will stay' are the tiny elements of barely conscious choice that go on within reading aloud and alive. They are different renditions of the same basic script, the same DNA, and mark the range of individual possibility.

When Dan read it, it sounded like what it was—a slow struggling achievement for him to manage this. One of the group said to Dan afterwards, 'I'll always think of your reading this aloud, whenever I read it again to myself.' 'I wasn't confident,' Dan admits later in interview, 'It was hard for me to say these things, and I think it wasn't easy for the man in the poem to say them either.' His reading made the rest of the group realize all that went into the making of the poetry itself when it was delivered not with a facile elocution and articulacy that knows the route in advance, but hesitantly across the lines, word by carefully repeated word, blindly seeking their code.

The code for the basic scaffolding is this—first 'Bid me/ And I will':

'Bid me to live', 'Or bid me love' stanza 1
'Bid that', 'Or bid it languish' stanza 3
'Bid me to weep' stanza 4
'Bid me despair', 'Or bid me die' stanza 5

—each accompanied by versions of 'I will', with 'to thee' or 'for thee'.
And also this, which receives the 'Bid':

'A loving heart' stanza 1
'A heart as soft, a heart as kind,/ A heart as sound and free' stanza 2
'That heart I'll give' stanza 2
'that heart' stanza 3
'A heart to weep' stanza 4
'my love, my heart' stanza 6.

'Dare' in the middle of stanza 5 is a further variation, where 'death' then takes over from heart.

And then these two streams of repetition—bid/will; heart—come together

at the beginning of stanza 3 'Bid that heart *stay*, and it will stay'.

which is further consolidated in stanza 4: 'yet I will *keep*/ A heart to weep for thee.'

Readers begin to get into that structure as though it were, in its own variations, itself a language. Another member of the group, soon after Dan has finished reading, says something very particular and minute, looking again at those seven repetitions of 'Bid': 'Bid me to live, and I will live', 'Or bid me love, and I will give', 'Bid that heart stay, and it will stay', 'Bid me to weep, and I will weep', 'Or bid it languish quite away,/ And 't shall do so', 'Bid me despair, and I'll despair', 'Or bid me die, and I will dare'. This is Linda, who suddenly hears and sees and says that it is the *comma* of all things which makes a difference in all these iterations; which makes it not just automatic—where automatic would be 'you just tell me and I will'. The punctuation makes it more than the passive obedience of a wimp. Coming as it were a millisecond after the mid-line beat, the comma like a musical notation makes it a weighed commitment. 'And it does even more work, that committed comma', says the group leader excitedly spotting the coded pattern, 'in stanzas 1, 4, and 5, where it occurs not only in line 1 but also in line 3 of each':

> Or bid me love|, and I will give
> A loving heart to thee.

> And having none|, yet I will keep
> A heart to weep for thee.

> Or bid me die|, and I will dare
> E'en death, to die for thee.

'Give', 'keep', 'dare'; 'love', 'weep', 'die': going ever further. And 'I will, "I will", 'I will': that, says another participant, Sarah, is also like '*I do*' in the responses of the marriage service, and the rest nod with pleasure. They are all working together now almost like one extended group mind, each holding a slightly different thought, or, again, like a small orchestra variously performing the score.

We have seen the work of this young woman who spotted the comma, before, in chapter 3. Linda, you may recall, suffered neurological impairment as a result of an accident involving severe electrical shock. This has resulted in problems of memory and concentration, occasional stuttering, and difficulties with eyesight, especially in bright light. When we showed her the clips of this session some time afterwards, and asked her about her suddenly fixing on that little thing the comma, she said she had learnt a lot about the working of the brain in acts of communication since her accident, because she could no longer automatically take it for granted. At the neurological support centre, they had told her about how great a percentage in every act of communication is due to body language and to tone, more than the words themselves. 'But here,' she says, 'you've only got the words on the pages. Which is why you need to be careful if you write a letter or a text. You don't have all the hand gestures; there is a lot more when in person. You only can give clues in the writing, like that comma, as to how it should be heard said':

When something is well written, you head understands all the extra stuff which it looks for in communication, it *reads* from it. But when you're reading something badly written, or too literal, your brain is unable to fill in the blanks. But if it is the right place for a comma, the correct length of the sentence, even saying the same thing in two different ways—all that can totally change things.

It is the sort of precision, almost physically registered, that separates by the thinnest but most vital of differences the mechanical 'Bid me to live-and-I will live' from the voluntary 'Bid me to live, | and I will live'. The version leaves inserted that moment-ary blank space for feeling and voluntary commitment which Linda hears and values. It marks the difference between life and a sort of death, the humanly alive and the inanimate—which is the great literary difference, adding a dimension to the merely flat accounts.

We showed Dan too some clips of the session a few weeks after. Someone predicted he would feel proud of himself, but it wasn't to be as simple as that. The sight and sound of himself moved him, almost tearfully, as though from outside back-in. It was so different from what had become usual with him:

> I've always been so used to my opinion not counting. I feel as if I'm not being noticed. And that's why when I started the group I thought, because a lot of the people read normally, I don't feel as educated as them, being honest. I always feel as if I haven't got anything to say, basically. But because of the group, and how they accepted what I said, the way I was treated made me actually speak, because in other environments I wouldn't usually say anything.

There are negatives in almost every sentence he speaks there. But as a research group we know that when anyone finally volunteers to read, they always say more, then and in later sessions, than they had ever said before: we could statistically measure what was a bit of a breakthrough. On this occasion, at the end of his reading, after the group leader had made a sound of delight, Dan immediately said that it had been hard, that he hadn't done this before, and had been worried. 'See, I would never ever say that, normally,' Dan goes on, as he watches this later, '—about being unconfi-dent or feeling weak; in a group situation I'd never tell anyone that, before.' He had been to group work designed to help people gain employment through interviews. 'As soon as I go in, if they say anything and go: You've got to stand there and say something; I go: No, don't even bother asking me. I'm not doing it.' But this time, in this group, it was different, and the woman who told him she would never forget his reading, also said how softly he had spoken, as though closer to feminine qualities. Dan was brought up in a tough male environment, though he's never quite liked it or felt altogether at home in it. After he and his interviewer look back at the poem together, and quietly repeat parts of it out-loud, he says:

I am, personally, attracted to feminine qualities of nurturing. I just find loyalty and commitment really good things, which I've not had. I had not thought that in the past, but if you say words to me like 'heart as soft', 'heart as kind', kindness, I like those traits. There's certain words there that you've repeated today that touch nerves with me, and that's what I find. See, whatever—'who may command him anything'—he's going to do for her, he is going to look after her if he can, though perhaps he hasn't got much. And even though I'm not that kind of person, I'm usually a cold person.

'You're usually a cold person?' repeats the interviewer.

No, not so much, that's what I try to be, that's what I act, I act like that, that I don't care, when I do care.

One of the other women in the session had wondered if the man in the poem isn't just masochistic. The other male in the reading group, cleverer or more educated than Dan, had added that he wondered if the speaker in the poem wasn't actually trying to manipulate the woman, by being deviously weak. And so reflective scepticism or suspicion began to take over the primary feeling of the poem. That spoilt it for me, Dan replied when asked about that, but he hadn't wanted to argue. Instead he points to the poet saying, if the beloved does not truly want him: 'Bid me despair, and I'll despair'. For all the negative formulations he used (the linguistician in our group later counted ten in just two sentences of Dan's in this interview), it was different when he turned to look at these words, the most apparently negative in the poem, yet still intent on loving blindly, even hopelessly:

See 'weep' or 'despair'? There's a lot of despair that I've got. When I was reading, I was too nervous to be fully conscious of what I was saying. By mistake I didn't read 'Bid that heart stay, and it will stay', but said instead 'Bid that heart stay, and I will stay'. But the group leader said that that was what it meant beneath, and it was great to take it personally. Anyway, since I've gone home and read it again, it's certain words like 'despair' or 'heart as soft' that I'm—not attracted to but—it's like the soft things . . . I just like things that are really soft, see. I do some voluntary work in a youth group with children.

These are still negatives: he is *not* really a cold person; loyalty and commitment are really good things, which he's *not* had, he had *not* thought this in the past but. But they are wholly different negatives from the felt neglect and inadequacy in 'not counting' or 'not being noticed', or from the defensive disguises and stuck resistances in 'I don't care' or 'I'm not doing it'. The imagination is not broken or made cynical in him but appreciates all the more the good things he has not had *because* he

157

has not had them. It is surprising that what is missing is not experienced here as a simple negative, a sadness and lack in his life, a cause of mental ill health or bitterness. It is felt still as an ideal, as a human possibility for love regardless of his own personal unsuccess in that area. At what sometimes seem unpropitious times for belief in sustained feeling, an old language and a strong language can defend vulnerability to emotion in a way that more contemporary languages of cool irony cannot.

It is for Dan—we think later in our own research-group meeting—something of what it was like for Arthur Clennam in *Little Dorrit*, the lonely middle-aged man whose harsh childhood could well have deprived him of feeling:

> He was a man who had, deep-rooted in his nature, a belief in all the gentle and good things his life had been without. Bred in meanness and hard dealing, this had rescued him to be a man of honourable mind and open hand.... And this saved him still from the whimpering weakness and cruel selfishness of holding that because such a happiness or such a virtue had not come into his little path, or worked well for him, therefore it was not in the great scheme, but was reducible, when found in appearance, to the basest elements. A disappointed mind he had, but a mind too firm and healthy for such unwholesome air. Leaving himself in the dark, it could rise into the light, seeing it shine on others and hailing it.
>
> Chapter 13

'All that his life had been *without*': it happens through double negatives. What 'saves' Clennam is his *not* thinking that because some good thing has *not* come into his little path it did *not* exist, anyway independently, elsewhere, for others.

Sometimes only literature itself can best describe again what we find in readers through their reading of literature.[5]

But there is still one more move that was made with Herrick's poem in the group, just before the session-end. Suddenly, looking again at the six stanzas, Sarah notices that two of them do *not* begin with 'Bid', the second and the last. It is, again, the dissimilitude within the similitude, the way that the poem's overall language says, quite tacitly from within its form, 'Notice the difference when I do not begin with "Bid me"'. Cleverly, the group leader asks Sarah to pick them out and then read them together:

> A heart as soft, a heart as kind,
>   A heart as sound and free,
> As in the whole world thou canst find,
>   That heart I'll give to thee.

> Thou art my life, my love, my heart,
>   The very eyes of me;
> And hast command of every part,
>   To live and die for thee.

Sarah listens to what she has just selected, with surprise and delight. It is like finding the naked heart of the poem, she says. Hers is a reading that has gone beyond the passive and the given: the form is not just accepted, it is created again by this reader. This is doing poetry, and she has done it not by saying anything *about* the poem, in extra commentary, but by doing something *with* it—re-creating it through no more than its own words.

The group leader continues it: All those '*or*'s in the poem, she says, counting them: 'Or bid me love' stanza 1, 'Or bid it languish' stanza 3, 'Or bid me die' stanza 5. All those 'Or's, she goes on: 'But they then give way to—', and she pauses to ask, instead of to tell: 'They give way to—what . . . in the *last* verse?' And she re-reads that stanza, for answer, as if the poem's own commitment to love is never exhausted by repeating it:

> And hast command of every part,
>   To live *and* die for thee.

'Or' becomes 'and'! It is the coming together in culmination. 'Thou art my life, my love, my heart,/ The very eyes of me': life, love, heart, eyes, all the stanzas come together in the key words that name them, says the group leader. And all those '*thee*'s at the end of each stanza—but then they are followed by that great quiet cry of '*Thou*' at the beginning of the last. It is the first time he has been able to come out and say 'Thou'. The poem *works*, the group leader says, bringing the session to a culmination. This is the way sessions should end if possible.

'The people who come to evening classes,' says Saul Bellow's Herzog, contemplating his own class, 'are only ostensibly after culture.' What they really want is 'something real to carry home when day is done.'[6]

*

The poem works! And it does so by means of those interrelations between similarity and difference that occur not just along the lines but up and down them, creating back and forth a re-emergent structure that gathers itself cumulatively as the reader goes along. 'Bid/Or', 'heart', 'and I will', to/for thee': these are the words that do the work of catalysts in that constant configuring and re-configuring, blending and deepening of the meanings.

Two issues arise for us, as researchers, in trying to think about this.

First, what is at stake in this is what I have called the *doing* of poetry: the poem's using and re-using of its own words in chains of modified stress and repetition. It is making something out of itself through a second language. And its readers do what poets do when they are not paraphrasing the poem from outside but working within it. That is why we are currently designing a software programme which allows readers to upload to a tablet any poem, and electronically highlight on screen words or phrases that seem instinctively to do work or to stand out. If the readers sense inter-connections and contrasts, similitudes and differences, they can draw lines of force between words, leading forwards or back, revealing the formation of inner structures. In this way, students in schools for example—since the purpose here is also educational—can try interactively to recreate something of the inner mind of the poem without initially having to say anything explicatory about it—without adding more words to words.

Second, there is something subtle that these inner techniques have to say about the nature of change. This is not change as some grandiose and wholesale aspiration in abstract isolation, but as small, swift, and precise micro-changes in the poem's order of things, poetic moves to search out and test for the possibility of larger effects. This is not solely the preserve of the Renaissance lyric, however seemingly fundamental its techniques and practices. It is rather that a lyric such as Herrick's keys into something ever central to the use of language in poetry, to its investigation into the possibilities of somehow changing or deepening our thinking.

Suppose then we travel further on in time, and further away. There is a poem by Brecht translated as 'Everything Changes', written in his troubled exile from Nazi Germany in New York in 1944 and here, first, in John Willett's translation.[7] The historical context is powerful but implicit:

> Everything changes. You can make
> A fresh start with your latest breath.
> But what has happened has happened. And the water
> You once poured into the wine cannot be
> Drained off again.
>
> What has happened has happened. The water
> You once poured into the wine cannot be
> Drained off again, but
> Everything changes. You can make
> A fresh start with your final breath.

The whole poem is based on repeating four phrases:

'*Everything changes*' (or is it not better to translate it as 'is changing' since it never stops?) in lines 1 and 9.

'*You can make/ a fresh start/ with your final breath*, lines 2–3, 9–10 albeit with their different enjambment.

'*What has happened has happened*' on its own at the start of stanza 2 in counterpoint both to 'Everything changes' at the beginning of stanza 1 and to the earlier line 3 'But what has happened has happened', where only retrospectively is the force of 'But' so clear, just as 'but' now intrudes at the end of line 8 before "Everything changes' again.

'*And the water/ You once poured into the wine cannot be/ Drained off again*' lines 3–5 is repeated in 6–8, only now with the 'And' omitted.

This may seem fussy, but together these recursions leave the reader asking: What minute difference in meaning does adding or omitting 'And' or 'But' serve or stand for? What basic, minimal difference do those slightly changed line-endings make? Why—through what implicit attitudinal difference—does saying something a second time no longer make it the same as only saying it the once?

Everything can, does, must change and transform; but equally, 'what has happened' '*has* happened', or, as Tom Kuhn puts it in a recent translation: 'What has been, has been', the second sounding becoming more like an old-has-been.[8] It is better in the original that the line-ending which in English is used in order to say that the water 'cannot be/ drained off' from the wine is in the German, 'kannst du/ Nicht mehr herausschütte'—'can' near the end of one line then closed down again into 'Not' at the beginning of the next. In between the two is everything. So in Tom Kuhn's translation, it goes: 'you can/ Begin anew' (1–2), you can/ Never drain off again' (4–5 and 7–8), and 'You can/ Begin anew with your very last breath' (9–10). That small metaphysical chink given four times after 'can' is also connected to why one might prefer the translation 'latest breath' as compared to 'very last breath' (Kuhn) or 'final breath' (Willetts): almost unimaginably, a person would only know it was indeed the final or last breath in impossible retrospect, after it had happened to make happening itself cease. It is only always the 'latest' which may be the last; mortal uncertainty is continuous right up until the end. And in that complex continuity whenever one thing is put into another—the water into the wine, the words into a sequence, the deed into the world—the two cannot simply be separated out again.[9] That would have to be a miracle. Nonetheless, in terms of making some difference, each element may still be modified within the mix, one affecting another.

Translating is an advanced form of reading. To take another example: in 'Beds for the night', translated by the poet and Germanist David Constantine in the latest

Liveright edition, Brecht questions the value of mitigating charity in an age of fundamental oppression which charity itself inadvertently may only help to prop up. Constantine, another consultative associate for our project, writes by way of introduction that 'though Brecht's political views are well known, his way of thinking-in-poems allows the elements a freer play', and then translates as follows:

> I hear that in New York
> On the corner of 26th Street and Broadway
> A man stands every evening in the winter months
> And begging passers-by
> Gets a bed for the night for the homeless gathered there.
> The world is not changed by this
> Relations between human beings are not improved
> The age of exploitation is not made any shorter.
> But a few men have a bed for the night
> For one night long they are out of the wind
> The snow that was meant for them falls on the streets.
>
> You reading this, do not put down the book.
> A few men have a bed for the night
> For one night long they are out of the wind
> The snow that was meant for them falls on the streets.
> But the world is not changed by this
> Relations between human beings are not improved
> The age of exploitation is not made any shorter.

Even the line 'the world is not changed by this' is not *quite* unchanged when it is repeated at the beginning or end of a stanza. There is a sort of constant turning round and round here, to look at the idea again, and to hold thinking in an austere balance of differing tones and possibilities. That, in its bare selection of some basic elements and the interplay of their varying combinations, *is* poetry, especially where in a minimalist structure the slight differences are felt all the more tellingly. In stanza 2 it goes: '*But* [at least] a few men have a bed for the night'; in stanza 3: '*But* [even so] the world is not changed by this'. A little basic word such as 'But' is like a frozen thought which the poem unfreezes, a fossil brought back into living existence.[10] Some etymologists, after Horne Tooke's *Diversions of Purley* (1786), have said that 'but' may even be a conflation of 'Be Out'—a linguistic signal to the preceding thought that it is to be got out of and left behind by a new clause for thought. Certainly the word stops being automatic here, and whatever makes a difference to the automatic processes which seem to determine the world, says Hannah Arendt, is a minor miracle.[11] It may seem only a little thing, a detail such as a reader seeing the difference that the stanzas without 'Bid me' make in Herrick's little poem. And yet, says Arendt, 'The miracle that saves the world, the realm of human affairs, from its normal, "natural" ruin, is the fact of natality, in which the faculty of action is ontologically rooted' (*Human Condition*, p. 249). How far and in what sense anything short of revolution saves or changes the world is what Brecht's poems partly contest, against the easy rhetoric of humanist pieties. But 'natality' remains a key term: it means the capacity to initiate action, for the birth and re-birth of new interventions by human beings—even in the offer to read aloud for the first time, or to break the silence by offering a doubtful thought—created simply by virtue of their being born. 'Can/Not.'

The Reader favours poems like these of Brecht's because they do not quite offer willed messages, either optimistic or pessimistic, so much as a structure to do thinking in, especially for people who still seek room for some chink of potential amidst their experience of a fixed lack of it.

What is at stake here is also the process of the reading itself, as well as the reading-content that prompts it. It is the type of literary reading that Coleridge described, where the reader is 'carried forward' not by 'merely mechanical impulse', not by automatic and straightforward linear processing, but by a 'to-and fro' motion:

> My readers will have observed how a small water-insect on the surface of rivulets wins its way up against the stream, by alternate pulses of active and passive motion, now resisting the current, now yielding to it. This is no unapt emblem of the mind's self-experience in the act of thinking. There are evidently two powers at work, which relatively to each other are active and passive; and this is not possible without an intermediate faculty, at once both active and passive. In philosophical language, we must denominate this intermediate faculty in all its degrees and determinations, the imagination.[12]

Imagination is here a mental middle-zone allowing movement to-and-fro between active and passive, between structured and unstructured, such that 'at every step the reader pauses and half recedes, and from the retrogressive movement collects the force which again carries him onward' (*Biographia Literaria*, chapter 14). This is why CRILS, in collaboration with Arthur Jacobs and Jana Lüdtke at the Free University of Berlin, and led over here by Christophe de Bezenac and Rhiannon Corcoran, has been conducting eye-tracking experiments simply to see the truth of this complex movement.

We took several examples of four lines of poetry, as compared to control examples which were more prosaic, offering a smoother and more straightforward ease of literal-information-processing, even though put into equivalent poetry-like

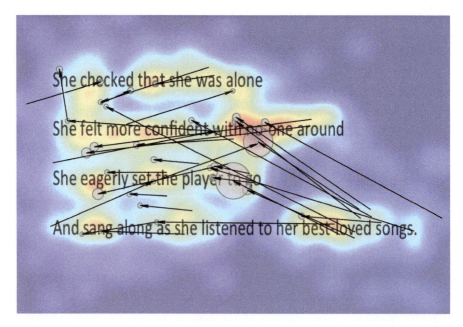

Figure 7. Eye-tracking 1: prosaic processing (non A-HA). 'She checked that she was alone./ She felt more confident with no one around./ She eagerly set the player to go/And sang along as she listened to her best-loved songs.' © Christophe de Bezenac.

lines. In both cases we had examples where the fourth line was a sudden final change (called an A-HA effect) and where it more obviously followed on from the preceding lines (non A-HA). Figures 7 and 8 provide a (non A-HA) heat-map representing for all sixteen participants the total number and location of 'fixations'—the length of relatively stationary visual gaze on a particular word, delaying the pathway of habitual perception. Areas that are more red attracted a greater number of participant fixations; the yellow areas are destination fixations with size representing duration (larger = longer). Overlaid arrows mark the words that effect directional 'regressions' (backward eye movements) before a return to forward movement again.

There are two significant findings.

Initial results indicate that there are longer fixations in the poetic as opposed to the more prosaic texts, as one might expect according to the hypothesis that poetry requires slower and more concentrated reading. But, more significantly, it is in the reading of poetry that there is also more eye movement back and forth, *and* it is quick darting movement, making alerted connections throughout the circuitry.

Secondly, in eye-tracking, the effect of poetry as a whole was greater than any single A-HA effect in either poetry or the prosaic controls: poetry in the act of

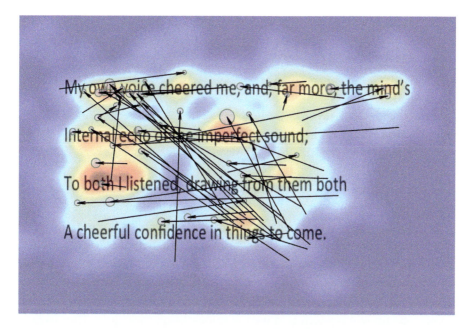

Figure 8. Eye-tracking 2: poetic processing (non-A-HA). William Wordsworth, from Book 1 of *The Prelude*: 'My own voice cheered me, and, far more the mind's/ Internal echo of the imperfect sound;/ To both I listened, drawing from them both/ A cheerful confidence in things to come.' © Christophe de Bezenac.

becoming meaning is more important as a *series* of unpredictable surprises, than in making one big turn of surprise at the end.[13] We will come back to dramatic A-HA movements later. But any poetic movement, against human inertia and dulling habit, creates the speedier mobile brain within the onward linear movement.[14]

This register of speed-within-slowing is a perhaps obvious finding, useful though it is to have such experiential intuitions supported by scientific measures. But it also has a significant implication, which may be related, for example, to Daniel Kahneman's cognitive models in *Thinking Fast and Slow* (Farrar, Straus and Giroux, 2011). For Kahneman there is System 1, fast thinking, which operates automatically, instinctively, and habitually with little effort or voluntary control. Quick and dirty, it is an efficient pathway for responses to the familiar, but liable to error and prejudice when relied on unawares outside of its zone. But System 2 is a later meta-development of the brain, allocating attention to mental activities that in encountering un-straightforward difficulties require greater effort, concentration, and conscious choice. And that last, as a measured corrective and reappraisal, receives the classic Western respect for slow, careful, and judicious rationality.

And yet deep, serious literary reading is, we can see, not simply System 2. Serious literary readers may turn in the first place from a quick scanning system to a slower deeper reading for meaning. *But then* within the slowed-ness they find something happening more *quickly* again, as a relative result. One system—the fast—goes on not instead of, but now suddenly within another—the slowed.

Poetic reading often involves versions of Matthew Arnold's lyric moment, suddenly released from 'The Buried Life': 'A bolt is shot back somewhere in our breast/ And a lost pulse of feeling stirs again./ The eye sinks inward, and the heart lies plain.' Or there is Wordsworth in his 'Preface to Lyrical Ballads' on poetry as emotion recollected in tranquillity, where he argues that the tranquillity allows for a passion arising within it till, by a species of reaction, the tranquillity itself gradually gives way or is formed again in deeper contemplation. (Prose Works, vol. 1, p. 126) This is about re-creating within one system, without quitting it, the capacities of a second and different other. That is what a literary language does, as though it were indeed a second language latent within our normal language: it reminds us, *re-minds* us, that it is not literal, that it is not transparent or straightforward or seamless, but is a translation into words which is in need of re-translation back again. Then literary reading, at the tempo of fast-re-emergent-within-slow, is more like life itself in vitality of spirit and movement; it is more like the very impulses of excitement and insight and survival. It is even a fair bet that the visceral speed of responsive feeling is related to what used casually to be called gut instinct—and which is now designated as a 'second brain', because of the super-fast relation of the enteric nervous system, with its own neurons and synapses, to the brain itself. A thought in the moment of its happening cannot be slow. It is the thinking—the capacity then to think it, use it, mull it, connect it—that needs time.

I have been talking about sudden reading, with its breakthroughs. But what I want also to think about are ways of keeping hold of its spirit, despite the dangers of more and more words of over-explication and over-refined detail. And this makes me offer a proposition: that analytic thinking, in what we rather horribly call 'close' reading, is at its best both excited and exciting, when it is the sudden memory of feeling reconfigured and coming to life through a different mode. Analysis grabs at what it fears to lose—the sudden opening of a meaning, and tries to hold it through spelling it out. So it is when we feel the need to talk more about what a mere comma does, or what a change of pronoun or conjunction achieves, even though aware that, outside this emotional context, talk about commas and pronouns and conjunctions might seem the fiddliest of dry academic exercises. Yet it is not just about detail for detail's sake, though this present book might seem full of minute linguistic details. Inside the kick-start feel of a poem, precise analysis does not mean ponderously losing the fast, the quick, the emotional—on the contrary, analysis becomes passion in disguise or in translation. It is a follow-on trying to live longer and think further in the area of resonance that a literary moment has opened up when the written code explodes into human meaning. Again, it is William James who is a crucial figure here, in terms of pointing to the essential need for hot thinking rather than cold:

> All we know is that there are dead feelings, dead ideas, and cold beliefs, and there are hot and live ones; and when one grows hot and alive within us, everything has to re-crystallize about it. These hot parts are the centres of our dynamic energy, whereas the cold parts leave us indifferent and passive in proportion to their coldness.[15]

This preference for the hot over the cool and cold is not the same as what is criticized when public intellectuals currently complain that unthinking and irrational feeling is taking over the world, that viral contagions of hysterical senti-ment are fuelling over-excited crowd movements.[16] But in the literary context, we are talking about individual feeling arising out of intense focus upon measured words, an overflowing feeling so powerfully triggered by art at a deep level of separate and personal activation as to invoke there the mental need for further articulation and thought. 'Everything has to re-crystallize about it': that is how a hot spot created in the reader's mind by reading begins to have an effect diffusing its warmth of power beyond the immediate occasion, albeit in formations of varying stability and duration. It is not about determinedly creating an identity through inflating an emotion such as willed outrage; it is about a 'centre', as William James calls it, being made or found—a centre whose core existence is disclosed by the sudden experience of an unpremeditated feeling. Around it the person forms again, and re-forms. Analysis re-traces that formation and helps further establish it by knowing more of its reach and meaning.

*

'All we know is that there are dead feelings, dead ideas, and cold beliefs, and there are hot and live ones.'

Again, it was the Romantics who recovered the Renaissance for the sake of a thinking that felt alive not dead. For the Romantic critic and essayist, William Hazlitt, it was Shakespeare who was, as it were, the greatest agent of hot thinking.

In 1805 at the age of twenty-seven, Hazlitt published *An Essay on the Principles of Human Action* which he had hoped would be revolutionary in its account of human nature.[17] It was, as he admitted later, a flawed effort, but it tried to establish that human beings were not, in the first place, as philosophers such as Thomas Hobbes had described them: separated creatures, programmed to be selfish, and increasingly liable to calculate everything coldly in advance, in terms of their own self-interest. These were false models of consciousness, Hazlitt argued, static ideas of the self in ourselves, secondary paraphrases of our primary human text. What human creatures really were, thought Hazlitt, was something originally quicker and more innocently dynamic than that. Our primal feelings snatched at whatever was good and of benefit—*before* ever we knew whether it was for our good or the good of others, prior even to the distinction *between* the two. Identity, the heavy solidification of selfhood comes only later, with backward-projected memory. Action is what comes first, before our constructs.

For Hazlitt the underlying primary impulse that acts within human beings is never to do with the past but always with creating the *future*. And the future is by definition not yet here, is as yet uncreated, if indeed it is to be a genuine future, and not the present or the past in mere continuance. That is why there can be almost *no time* in the movement of our primary impulses: they are instant, barely present save as catalysts, anticipatory between the moment and the future imagined for itself.

It was to reading Shakespeare, to trying to think through Shakespeare and like Shakespeare, that Hazlitt turned to take the place of his failed *Essay*. Shakespeare gives us, said Hazlitt, not paraphrases of human nature but humankind's original text. And in that text, we can hardly say to the future, as Macbeth said to the dagger that seemed to draw him to the murder of Duncan, 'Come let me clutch thee':

> It is a thing of air, a phantom that flies before us, and we follow it, and with respect to all but our past and present sensations, which are no longer any thing to action, we totter on the brink of nothing... We have no presentiment of what awaits us, making us feel the future in the instant.
>
> Hazlitt, vol. 20, pp. 179–80

All we can sense are split-second openings, which if we are not (in every sense) *quick*, may close again in a moment, returning us merely to present established norms. For Hazlitt it was through drama, and above all Shakespearian drama, that thinking was most authentically experienced as taking place in the midst of time. Drama, as Hazlitt's image for vibrant life in the act of being lived, was not founded upon what we already *think* we think, or assume we are, on the secure basis of a past sense of reality. It was about immersion in the midst of action, about imagination reaching not towards some fictitious fabrication but some untried future just ahead of itself that its thinker can then at least try further to actualize.

Why Shakespeare would be the model of live thinking is made even clearer in a work of 1808, Charles Lamb's *Specimens of English Dramatic Poets Who Lived About the Time of Shakespear*. Lamb is talking about *The Two Noble Kinsmen*, a collaboration between Shakespeare and his younger contemporary, John Fletcher, in which Lamb is certain he can tell whose hand is which in the authorship of particular acts and scenes. Fletcher's ideas 'moved slow':

> his versification, though sweet, is tedious; it stops every moment; he lays line upon line, making up one after the other, adding image to image so deliberately that we see where they join.

But Shakespeare is fast and hot, the lines joining into one other 'like a running hand':

> Shakspeare mingles everything, he runs line into line, embarrasses sentences and metaphors; before one idea has burst its shell, another is hatched and clamorous for disclosure.[18]

Fletcher's motion 'is circular, not progressive', 'each line revolves on itself in a sort of separate orbit', 'every step that we go we are stopped to admire some single object'. So in *The Two Noble Kinsman*, Fletcher will write for the two young men imprisoned together: 'We are an endless mine to one another; / We are one another's wife, ever begetting/ New births of love: we are father, friends, acquaintance;/ We are in one another families' (2.2 86–90). But less cumulatively, Shakespeare will have Emilia say of her youthful friendship with Flavina that they two

> were things innocent,
> Loved for we did, and like the elements
> That know not what nor why, yet do effect
> Rare issues by their operance, our souls
> Did so to one another.
>
> 1.3 70–4

With Shakespeare it is about 'elements' 'wanting form' (1.1 120) and finding it for themselves, even ahead of human consciousness: 'And that work presents itself to th' doing./ Now 'twill take form; the heats are gone tomorrow' (1.1 172–3).

Lamb famously felt that Shakespeare was more to be read with the mind, on the page, than staged in the immediacy of eye and ear. But Hazlitt remained committed to theatrical performance, whatever its inadequacies, in the struggle to contain the mental within the physical—intimations of the infinite bursting within the confine of finite physical dimensions, thinking working inside feeling, in the great theatre of experiment. The very constraints of drama were more like life's own, in the fleeting place rescued for the precious little traces of the innerly human. While sympathetic to what Lamb means about the limitations in the staging of Shakespeare in contrast to the recoverable permanence of the written, I am with Hazlitt in also wanting the risk and transience of the dynamic. But of course readers characteristically want both: the live moment and its afterlife—or as the Elizabethan poet Samuel Daniel puts it:

> Take it sudden as it flies,
> Though you take it not to hold.
> When your eyes have done their part,
> Thought must length it in the heart.
> 'Are They Shadows?'

In the past, in the history of reading, perhaps actors more than any others have made manifest what goes on within the performed actualization of a line of a poetry, in the act of reading aloud albeit without a visible text. Hazlitt admired the actor Edmund Kean, but here (because a detailed historic reading is more readily available) is David Garrick, Kean's great predecessor, a generation earlier. He is talking about a moment in his performance of Macbeth when he thinks about the witches' prophecy—that he, Thane of Glamis, will be Thane of Cawdor, and King thereafter. Then suddenly he is made Thane of Cawdor, and he thinks: 'This supernatural soliciting/ Cannot be ill; cannot good': if ill, how comes it true I *am* Thane of Cawdor? if good, why does it give me evil thoughts of the existing King? Garrick then went on:

> My thought, whose murder yet is but fantastical,
> Shakes so my single state of man,
> That function is smother'd in surmise
> *Macbeth*, 1.3 149–51

The sentence should drive its man on across the lines, 'My thought...Shakes *so...*/ *That...*'; but an audience member believed that Garrick paused too long over the adjective 'single', and wrote to him afterwards to criticize his affected delivery. The actor in reply admitted it was a glaring fault if he did indeed go so much against the rhythmic flow and grammar of the lines as to leave the sense imperfect—

> but my Idea of the passage is this—Macbeth is absorb'd in thought, & struck with the horror of the Murder, tho but an Idea (*fantastical*) and it naturally gives him a slow—tremulous—undertone of voice, & tho it might appear I stopp'd at Every word

170

in the line, more than Usual, yet my intention was far from dividing the Substantive from its adjective, but to paint the horror of Macbeth's mind, & keep the voice suspended a little—which it will naturally be in such a situation.[19]

'Shakes so my—*single*—state of man'. It is as though in the midst of this new irresistible career forward, Garrick's Macbeth breaks, tremulously shaken, for a micro-second, to remember what he has lost even in the act of losing it: he has lost a unified mind and even now has to *think* that. It is an arresting moment caught within the nonetheless continuing pull of flow, as the line momentarily oscillates between forward and back. These almost retrospective emphases, extending the word a second after it has been first spoken, are like a minor inner miracle of poetry, in act of reclamation. I spoke 'single', writes Garrick, in an 'undertone of voice'—as if it was to match something in mind that was equivalently forced under. That is the other dimension in which the speaker feels, within a mind that no one else knows, something horrifyingly personal, even as the verse goes on linearly past him like time itself.

In opposition to the stage hams of his day, a line or sentence was not for Garrick a static block to be declaimed with loud grandiloquence regardless of meaning, any more than something to be thrown away in monotonous rote, just to get to the sense-making end. He did not want to act single separate emotions, as if to say: I will pretend now to be 'furious', 'pentitent', 'angry', 'tempted', and so on, but sought instead to reveal how the feelings ran into each other. That is another reason why 'single' was something to say goodbye to. Garrick would not thrash about with his hands: he stood still, forcing the motion into his mind, and holding the emotion he took from his own voicing. Of course, Garrick could always be a show-off still, but actors like him at his best were committed to their script, not just as something for them to say but something for them to be guided by even in the saying, along that uneven journey of the lines. He spoke the words rather than acted the character apart from them. And the guide word for Garrick here was 'natural'—what will 'naturally be in such a situation' to make the scripted line come alive on stage in the moment-by-moment variations of the voice. That's the respect, as Hamlet says in his great soliloquy, 'must give us *pause*', in those micro-seconds when the voice like a singer's is kept 'suspended a little'. It is a voice caught in what Garrick's older contemporary, the dramatist and theatre manager Aaron Hill, marvellously called 'the very instant of the changing passion', within the minute processes of emotional 'transitions'.[20] In those minute transitions, that is where the life is: 'Like a bird's life, our consciousness seems to be made of an alternation of flights and perchings.'[21] We want the perchings, the partial taking stock, the sense of having got somewhere, but it is the flight that is the complex meaning-bearer.

'Bid me to love, and I will love': read it with the implicit stage direction of that transitioning comma, perching only to take flight again, and even though this is not a play, the speaker *becomes* for the moment what he or she is saying. And that is not by deliberate thought or empathy or prior planning—but by that performative tuning-in which is intonation, receiving back the feel of what one's voice is saying even as one says it. Actors, as a public model of how good readers and good reading most matter, are not simply to get used to repeating their lines by default. In the instant, in the midst of transitions, the lines are really channels for working out thinking as it goes along. And on the stage, the genuine use of one's lines marks the dramatic difference between a performance of life itself and the world gone dead again. For it is as though the Elizabethan use of lineation of poetry might be an early-modern version of brain-scanning, of working out the winding pathways of a mind printing itself out across a page. And Shakespeare scanned and wired his lines, like brainwaves, so that if an actor would map himself onto what was there it would be a dynamic template for an existence truly coming to life. That is why reading quietly aloud is so vital, even if sub-vocally so in a reader's mind.

For us at CRILS, research has been no more and no less than what arises out of these tiny examples of practical reading, both past and recent. That research, through the microscopic neural force of one scientific project, is the subject of most of the rest of this chapter.

*

Given that stage was like an original version of shared reading in practice—was shared reading put into more dramatic three-dimensional action—I would often in my own teaching use Shakespeare workshops to bring reading even more off the page, to show the mind of the text working across the different bodies trying to act it out. The praxis revealed even more than usual about the dramatic changes that go on within reading, the almost explosive effect of much going on within little, and of sudden difference emerging from within apparent sameness. This is what the great process philosopher William James said 'mind' truly was: 'a theatre of simultaneous possibilities' (*Principles*, p. 288).

Taking that clue, I wanted to see more of that mental theatre in a different medium again, looking at what was reading through a different method. There was the book ostensibly in two dimensions; there was stage in another dimension, making the act of reading more physical, the actors more like a writer's thoughts made flesh; but there might also be, behind the scenes, a form of mental x-ray, through which to go back inside the mind and show the action within.

It was important that William James was a psychologist as well as a philosopher. In his spirit, I wanted to try out some form of brain-imaging experimentation that would uncover those hot places that James believed lit up in the brain under conditions of strongly felt, mind-changing thought. Granted: neuroscience might often seem modish and could be both hijacked and misapplied for reductive explanations of consciousness. But there was also the chance it gives us of a new dynamic vocabulary of mental happenings, of shifting shapes and changed pathways, instead of the dullness of fixed names and over-solidified nouns. And in an age where science has prestige, science itself may be used to show how it is literature that is a primal form of thinking—revealing the drama of how thinking comes into being with deep effects in creating, charging, and changing the mind. The aim was to find a way to point to what was otherwise invisibly happening, and, in locating it, to try to get a better and longer hold of what by this means might become more of a conscious faculty, to be further tapped into.

In 2005 I had an idea to do with brain-imaging, and knocked on the door with it, the door being that of a neuroscientist—first that of Neil Roberts at Liverpool, then later Guillaume Thierry at Bangor, and most lately my colleague, Rhiannon Corcoran, again at the University of Liverpool. There was nothing to be appalled at here, I believed; it isn't neurological reductivism or determinism to feel that there is something happening in the brain itself in following certain lines of verse. For my idea was that in reading serious literature, the sheer shape of an important sentence in front of your eyes might have an internally dramatic effect on the mental pathways behind your eyes, unlocking and shifting them analogously. This was the alternative to the rigidification of the pathways of the brain when what you think or say becomes all too fixed, mechanically reinforced, repetitive, and predictable. That mental fixity in default mode is the version of dementia we may all already be suffering from, long before we are old. It is a world where 'norms' replace 'reals'—where the predictable and conventional all too often take the place of the sudden, the warm, the unexpectedly live and deep. And it is that over-normalized world—or the mind-set which the deadening world demands—which reading literature can affect.

Can you show this vital difference? I asked my colleagues in neuroscience: Can you show something that is going to *become* thought in its process, in its minute transitions? Will your scanners show the brain's hot spots lighting up a good nanosecond before the thoughts appear in consciousness? Can they reveal these syntax-inspired brain movements happening?

It was Shakespeare I wanted to start from, because of the drama, the mobile density of his language, and the dynamic force of the poetry live. Intuitively, moreover, Shakespeare himself was so unafraid of the brain beneath the mind. He was not interested in what he calls in *Love's Labour's Lost*, 'slow arts', the intellectualism which 'entirely keep[s] the brain' (4.3 320). What compelled him was a passionate force, like sexual love, which

> Lives not alone immured in the brain,
> But, with the motion of all elements,
> Courses as swift as thought in every power,
> And gives to every power a double power,
> Above their functions and their offices.
> *Love's Labour's Lost*, 4.3 324–8

What this means in Shakespeare is that thoughts create and come out of a fundamental neo-physical excitement, as the brain lights up and fires. The experiments we began to design had to depend on the almost microscopic alteration of a little word or so, that had nonetheless 'a double power'. Instruments might be able to catch the 'course' and 'motion' of these things.

For these focal purposes I chose one word—at least, one sort of word—that would embody the very process of what change is in the workings of literature, and would also contain much matter even within what seemed so little. I chose a shape-transforming instrument of language which in linguistics is now technically known as functional shift or word-class conversion.

Functional shift means what happens when suddenly by an almost physical manhandling on the poet's part a word is made to change its function while remaining within the same essential shape. In Daniel's poem, it goes 'thought must *length* it in the heart': noun made into verb, to shove it into life and agency. So in Shakespeare's creative haste, in opposition to the 'slow arts' of spelling it out, an adjective by ellipsis is made a verb when in *The Winter's Tale* heavy thoughts are said to '*thick* my blood' (1.2 172); a pronoun is made into a noun when Olivia in *Twelfth Night* is called 'the cruellest *she* alive' (1.5 230); Prospero turns adverb to noun when he speaks so wonderfully of 'the dark *backward*' of past time in *The Tempest* (1.2 50); or most characteristically of all, noun is made verb as when in *King Lear* Edgar makes a sudden link with Lear himself: 'He *childed* as I *fathered*' (3.6 108). Creation before communication, mind ahead of grammar, is the fast mental priority here. Noun to verb is its characteristic motion: this is reading in action, the brain and mind in drama. There would be none of this tension of thought-coming-into-being, of accelerated and energizing compaction, if Edgar had ponderously said: 'I have a bad father and you have bad children.'

Instead, here is Edgar again on the fall of his father, blind Gloucester—just a few inches on stage though in his own mind hundreds of feet, but then again such that Edgar fears the very imagination of it may have killed him: 'Had he been where he *thought*/ By this had *thought* been past' (4.5 44–5). That is the shift. Or in *Lear* again, there comes the appalled cry: 'A father and a gracious aged man...have you madded' (4.2 44–6): not 'made mad' or even 'maddened', but more suddenly 'mad-ded', a newly activated word of horror appearing by minimal change for the first time in the language. This is what the Elizabethan critic George Puttenham called '*enallage* or the figure of exchange' when the poets did not change one word for another but with powerful economy 'kept the word and changed the *shape* of him only'.[22]

Functional shift was small and tight enough for experimentation. In terms of Shakespeare, it is fast and compressed, it is grammatically free and mobile, it is close in its shift of sense to the dramatist's love of metaphor. In terms of neuroscience, the main cognitive research previously done on the confusion of verbs and nouns had been to do with mistakes made by those who are brain-damaged. Hardly anybody appeared to have investigated the neural processing of a 'positive error' in sudden and useful reappraisal, such as functional shift in normal healthy organisms. We decided to try to see what happens when the brain comes upon these sudden new formulations, the force of a sudden single word.

So for each functional shift we offered three variants, offered randomly to participants to test their reactions. In *Coriolanus*, for example, Shakespeare rather than write 'made a god of', turns 'god' more immediately into 'godded':

A This old man loved me above the measure of a father, nay, deified me indeed.
B This old man loved me above the measure of a father, nay, poured me indeed.
C This old man loved me above the measure of a father, nay, charcoaled me indeed.
D This old man loved me above the measure of a father, nay, godded me indeed.

There are two possible effects in using EEG upon such stimuli (the electroenceph-alogram where electrodes are placed on different parts of the scalp to measure, through electric impulses, brain-events taking place in time). The brain-graph may register what is called an N400 effect, which measures *semantic* violation: it is a negative wave modulation 400 milliseconds after the onset of any critical word that disrupts the *meaning* of the sentence. Alternatively, there is a P600 effect, a parietal modification peaking approximately 600 milliseconds after the onset of a word that upsets *syntactic* integrity, violating *grammar*.

A 'deified' is the standard control or straightforward normal processing: neither N400 or P600.

B is a version where the key verb is perfectly grammatical but nonsensical: 'poured': hence no P600 but N400.

C is an extreme example of shift that does not make sense—neither semantically nor grammatically—'charcoaled' creates both N400 and P600 effects: it is like a sort of mental 'UGH' effect.

D is the true functional shift which is conventionally ungrammatical but remains semantically comprehensible: P600 but no N400, it has more a 'WOW' effect around the surprise word 'godded'.

In D, we also found that the brain is excited for a brief time not only at but *after* the onset of the critical word; the mind's attention-level is lifted by the grammatical surprise into what seems to be a more hesitant and emergent consciousness; yet the overall sense-making requirement will still tolerate what is going on. Between semantics and syntax, it is like two hands on the piano: the basic melody under-lyingly kept going by the left, whilst in counterpoint something experimental is being done with the right to shift the obvious neural pathways.

Some neuroscientists believe there is a specific part of the brain that recognizes verbs and another adjacent part that processes nouns. Suppose this is true for a moment: imagine what happens when for a second the brain is unsure—is it noun, is it verb? The creation of something momentarily *in between* those two employs localization to create a tension precisely so as to rise above localization, calling forth a new level of attentive, excited consciousness. Noun? Verb? In the space and movement between, an executive consciousness is created to intervene and sort out what is momentarily unresolved at the lower neural level. Then the brain is working at a higher level of evolution, *undetermined* by the very structures of localization it still works from.

I was also told by my neuroscientist colleagues that when the brain registers the word 'knee', the part of the brain to do with moving the knee actually fires, albeit less powerfully than in the physical action itself. Imagine again what happens when the brain is invaded with 'Fall down and *knee/* the way into his mercy' from *Coriolanus* and noun becomes further animated as verb.

Functional shift—the same word turned within itself into a different function—thus operates in a way that the prosaic alternatives 'Fall down and beg for mercy' or 'This old man made a god of me' cannot. The difference is between the literary and the literal, where the literary is more than a matter of ornamental style. Instead it is like thinking the thing, in language, for the first time again.

This is just one of many writerly techniques that seem to prime the alerted brain to go *on* to higher levels of active attention, to a pathway shifted more lastingly out of the norm. As if the verbal signal said to the mind via the brain: get ready for—get alive to—something deeper, stranger, more excitedly affecting. And what this means in Shakespeare is that thoughts come live out of a fundamental physical excitement—stimulating a pre-conceptual excitement that is always in excess of any subsequent conceptualization of it. That is why I want to keep a sense of those deep primal UGHs and WOWs, in the wonderful democratizing paradox of raw feelings being released by sophisticated language.

At the same time as conducting these experiments we asked a writer, David Constantine again, as poet but also short-story writer and translator, to test this technique outside the lab from the point of view of both practitioner and reader. He set himself to work on *Macbeth*, recording twenty-five examples, checking the new usages with the *Oxford English Dictionary* to confirm that they were the first coinages. '*Sleek* o'er your rugged looks' (adjective as verb, 3.2 27), '*Scarf* up the tender eye of pitiful day' (noun as verb, 3.2 47), 'Nought that I am,/ Not for their own demerits, but for mine,/ *Fell* slaughter on their souls (4.3 225–7, verb containing the weight of both noun and adjective, as later 'my fell of hair' (5.5.11). These, he reported, are forms of verbal alchemy and of verbal explosion, working in transition, causing retrospective re-emphases, thwarting the obvious, and densening the world. 'Amidst the frequent deferring of the completion of sense across the lines, and with the almost constant lateral and up-and-down expansion of the text, it is as though, like the light in the play, its language frequently *thickens* (Macbeth 3.2 50),' writes Constantine. It is like the syntax so intricately involved in the thick of lines like 'The eye wink at the hand. Yet let that be,/ Which the eye fears, *when it is done*, to see' (1.4 52–3) or 'Come, thick night,/ And pall thee in the dunnest smoke of hell/ That my keen knife *see not* the wounds *it makes*' (1.5 48–50). For Macbeth, the poet concludes, 'palpably his life clogs up with horrors. The poetic line has an intrinsic moral force, which is latent and the reader makes it actual.'

To examine this small but powerful effect further, we next transferred the experiment to fMRI (functional magnetic resonance imaging, involving immersion in

Figure 9. Eye-tracking 3: A-HA surprise change from lines 3 to 4. Adapted from David Constantine, 'Watching for Dolphins' when certain passengers rose from their seats on board: To watch for dolphins. [One saw them lose/ Every other wish.] Even the lovers/ Turned their desires on the sea, [and a fat man/ Hung with equipment to photograph the occasion/ Stared like a saint, through sad bi-focals;] others,/ Hopeless themselves, looked to the children for they/ Would see dolphins if anyone would…' © Christophe de Bezenac.

full-body tunnel-like brain-scanners), which tracks not the time of happening as in EEG but its location by means of oxygen movement in the brain.

We experimented first in functional shift, and later also tried for a wider form of unfolding surprise in poetry. For this we created some stimuli (re-used, as I have said, in eye-tracking experiments), where a set of poetic four lines were contrasted with more prosaic four-liners, and where in both cases, there might or there might· not be a surprise turn from third into fourth line, producing a mental A-HA. One of these mini-poems was itself adapted from David Constantine's own work, with the poetic effect and A-HA effect working together in brain imaging. Figure 9 shows what that looked like, equivalently, in the eye-tracking experiment where you can actually trace the density of the interconnections, and see the lovely moves even from 'hopeless', as it looks towards 'children' and 'if anyone' instead, and is not insurmountable. The overall outcomes for the various brain-imaging experiments may be summarized.

Neuroimaging results showed that sentences featuring functional shift elicited significant activation beyond the regions usually automatically activated by typical language tasks. Results suggest that the concept of felt 'shift' behind the functional shift extends to the domain of functional neuro-anatomy, since it also leads to an actual shift in activation from traditional Left Hemisphere structures (Broca's area, language production) to Right Hemisphere 'additional' networks usually involved in processing non-literal aspects of language, releasing emotion and autobiographical memory, and relating to go/no go actions for either risk-taking or inhibition, for taking ways forward or not. This was also true in terms of our comparison between poetic and more literal/prosaic four-liners: it was the poetry that en route and in the very midst of reading linearly, most shifted the mind away from automatic processing (though this can also be the poetry that goes on, more hiddenly, within the creative prose of a novel or short story).

Example 1—a more literal/prosaic control with the A-HA shift from line 3 to line 4:

> An eye-sore in the modern landscape.
> The diggers and giant hammers arrive
> People gather to see the demolition
> But an old man cries to see his childhood home destroyed.

Example 2—Wordsworth and the more poetic A-HA:

> She lived unknown, and few could know
> When Lucy ceased to be;
> But she is in her grave, and, oh,
> The difference to me!

What we discovered in particular through all our experiments was increased activity in the deep middle areas at the centre of the brain, in the basal ganglia in activation of their learning function[23]—and in particular, the left caudate nucleus, the right inferior frontal gyrus, and the right inferior temporal gyrus (all of them involved in clinching single updated meaning across multiple possibilities), whose work of reappraisal was then consolidated in the hippocampus (Figure 10). What is perhaps most exciting is that this increased activity in the basal ganglia, resulting from disruption of automatic integration of syntax and semantics, is an effect also observed when bilinguals are led to switch from one language to another. That is to say: what is being created is thus a second (literary) language in the very midst of

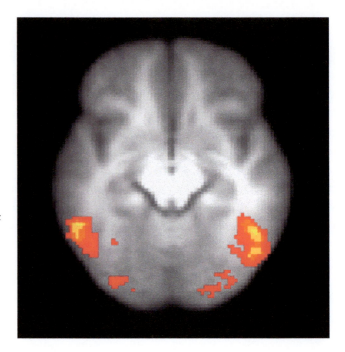

Figure 10. Activation created by A-HA moments in *both poetic and prosaic versions.* (a) Inferior temporal gyrus; (b) Hippocampus: consolidation of new information. © Christophe de Bezenac, Noreen O'Sullivan, et al.

the first.[24] So it is that the shift works at every level—it works in the language, it works through the neurological underpinnings, it works psychologically and experientially.

But above all poetic shifts and turns, in words and across lines, work against the cold of stuckness, deadness and automaticity. All this is related to what are called, according to the development of the probability theory created by the eighteenth-century mathematician, Thomas Bayes, 'prediction errors' in the face of reasonable expectations. That is to say, to take just the example of reading, it is reasonable to expect adjectives to call for nouns, verbs for adverbs, subjects for verbs, verbs for objects, and so on: it is what William James calls a 'foreboding of the coming grammatical scheme', the tendencies arising before they are actualized (*Principles*, vol. 1, p. 254). These predictions in all areas of life are fundamental to our very survival, in the capacity to foresee and plan and economize on effort by the ability to create safe habits of established normality. But when they do occur, like warning signs, prediction errors are not errors at all but new responses to somewhat unforeseen situations at new levels of existence.[25] They arise as felt signals, as intrinsic messages, when suddenly the brain recognizes that hitherto automatic expectations and default mechanisms, which previously served so well our

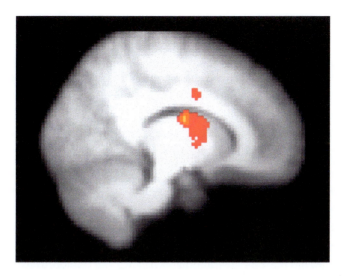

Figure 11. Increased activation associated with the need to update understanding *in poems over and above prose*. Left caudate: poetic updating appears more 'rewarding'—important in context of depression. © Christophe de Bezenac, Noreen O'Sullivan, et al.

assurance of safety, no longer obtain in this specific instance. By a form of quick feedback, they warn that a conscious reappraisal, re-adaptation, and revitalization is required in the face of what, in excited uncertainty, is no longer simply straightforward. At this level it is not that we are required to think about 'trying to change', as the books of popular psychology urge us, but that the brain is already lightningly alert in its sensitivity to minute but significant changes now actually happening. It is, as it were, *doing* change, even in undoing what has become a rigidity. This is why we wanted further experimentation on the journey taken by mind and eye over four lines of text in various formations.

And now here is the tiniest version of the change. Converging evidence suggests that the left caudate in particular may be recruited when a language task cannot be accomplished using solely automatic processing streams. What is more, it was the activation of the left caudate nucleus that was specifically to distinguish the effect of poetic A-HAs from that of the non-poetic ones (see Figure 11). Both types of stimuli—poetic and prosaic—had effects in response to the disruption of mechanical norms and linear predictability, but the poetic effect on this tiny point of the brain—the left caudate nucleus—was distinctive.

Moreover, if the left caudate nucleus is indeed a part of the brain that especially recognizes that prediction errors have been made, it is also, my colleagues know, an area of the brain that is under-activated in those suffering from depression, people too often passively stuck in blind circles of reinforced repetition—so different from repetition in and of poetry. The caudate nuclei are shaped like a sea horse, and when recognition takes place at the dorsal or head part, what is simultaneously offered at the ventral end, its tail, is a sense of reward. That this is so, in small but fundamental form at the micro-level of neurology, is somewhat wonderful: it is not a matter of *First, Do well* to recognize an exception in the patterns of meaning, and *Then Feel good* about having noted it, like the plodding sequence of cause and effect, or conscious utilitarian effort encouraged by the bribe of a sweet reward. In the brain, the two effects occur dynamically as one, electrically charged at the self-same time, the sense of excited existence intrinsic to the action in the very speed of life happening there. That is Shakespeare's own untamed linguistic speed—his fast art—and the density of simultaneous meanings concentrated within it. In Lamb's words: 'before one idea has burst its shell, another is hatched and clamorous for disclosure.'

We do not know all that goes into reading or that comes out of it. Until, through as many means and levels as possible, we know more of what these processes are—in literature, and the practices of writing, and reading and acting, via eye and voice and brain—we may not appreciate how to use these agencies more fully nor see how they can be transferred for use elsewhere outside the world of words. But for sure what without pretension, I hope, we may call 'literary thinking' is a work of mind that activates, figures, and represents some vital qualities of excited human being, in contrast to our all too automatic and mechanical default systems. 'What I want to know,' David Constantine concludes in his informal report

> is whether there is any transferable good in this excitement, truly whether consciousness might be shifted by poetic language into a disposition that would enliven, empower, and enlarge us as citizens. I do hold—cling sometimes—to that belief, I suppose because of my writerly bad conscience, because I can't write in a way that will ever mend the world. So I think of the writing of poetry and equally the reading of it as a state of more human engagement that most of us are capable of most of the time.

*

For the sake of that engagement in real, I want to close, accordingly, with a return from brain studies to the human level of the reading groups in praxis.

In a psychosis ward, Jud, an extraordinarily intelligent man in his thirties, is in a group reading Tobias Wolff's short story, 'Bullet in the Brain'. In it, by a kind of quirky black comedy, an acerbic literary critic, named Anders, is shot through the head—for pedantically correcting a robber's vocabulary and grammar.

The end of the tale gives a slow-motion account of the brain's final movements when the dying literary man has a last flashback to a moment in his youth when he was playing baseball. It was specifically when another kid, whom he saw once and never again, chose the position of 'shortstop', saying, 'Short's the best position they is'. The critic never forgot that phrase, the music of the last two words, and the shifted inversion. For all his compunctions about grammar, this was for him a sort of natural poetry, the words coming to his brain at the moment of entry like a poetic bullet. *They is, they is, they is.* 'The bullet is already in the brain,' Jud reads: 'In the end it will do its work...But for now Anders can still find time, make time...' Then Jud says:

> The first time, when this boy makes a grammatical mistake 'Short's the best position they is', he might usually want to correct him, even back then, show him up; but he doesn't. Instead he actually enjoys it. And repeats it. And now, near death, it is the last and most thing he remembers. I guess that's where his innocence is still intact, his childishness, his humanity because he's not bitter and twisted at that time, or cynical. He sees a beauty in everything. Even someone else's mistake. I guess he wanted to stay there as long as possible. It's as close as he's ever going to get to Heaven, that moment in the past, when he was happy, happy, and you know, he wants it to last forever.

Jud knows his own propensity for bitterness and cynicism, not unreasonable in the face of his own hard life, living with psychosis and depression. But he makes this imaginative extension into another mind, into another brain—against his own now usual mindset—in a transformation that emotionally imitates the character's own. Despite illness and trauma, somewhere in the hurt brain 'his innocence is still intact'.

CHAPTER 8

ABOUT TIME — THREE
LITTLE POEMS

There was of late a poet who was always more interested in what he called the 'power of beginnings' than in anything else, 'accepting the beginning line, the glimmer of an idea, the clumsy opening'.[1] He customarily rose early each morning at 4 a.m., before the rest of his family was about, to complete his writing stint around dawn. He would often begin with 'recent news from his own life', before trying to come to deeper things. It wasn't that, lazily, he did not seek to give as much craft and finish to his poems as he could. But he did not quite believe in making his poems seem like complete and polished ends in themselves. Entering the realm of writing meant feeling the gestation of a thought *before* ever it became dauntingly formalized into 'Poetry' or 'Philosophy' or anything else too easily nameable in the ordinary world. It didn't wholly matter how good a writer he was or not, even if he could have known for certain. His love was for the process of the ordinary man becoming a poet anew with the beginning of each poem. 'Poet' there meant no more and no less than seeking a voice that seemed more like his own, in those early hours before full day. The poems are slipped into the interstices of life and time.

My life as a writer, he concluded, comes in two parts, 'like two rivers that blend': the normal current of times, events, people, and everyday routines, and a second story beneath and within it which 'hardly belongs to the place where I'm living' but may belong instead to a more primary consciousness always looking for some place for itself in the world.[2]

It was as though in that place where he was living every day, he wanted someone to ask him something, hidden and important, to break the usual mould, even though he might not be able to find a reply. 'Ask Me' is a late poem by this American poet, William Stafford (1914–93):

> Some time when the river is ice ask me
> mistakes I have made. Ask me whether
> what I have done is my life. Others
> have come in their slow way into
> my thought, and some have tried to help

or to hurt: ask me what difference
their strongest love or hate has made.

I will listen to what you say.
You and I can turn and look
at the silent river and wait. We know
the current is there, hidden; and there
are comings and goings from miles away
that hold the stillness exactly before us.
What the river says, that is what I say.

'Ask me whether/ what I have done is my life' is where the second, inner life may hardly belong to 'what I have done' in the first more outward one. The poet's son Kim, in his memoir refers to the director Jean-Luc Goddard saying that every film should have a beginning, a middle, and an end—but not necessarily in that order. Changing the order of time, 'Ask Me' looks forward to some future—'Some time ask me … and I will answer'—from which to look back on 'now' and all the past behind it. When he thinks of his late father's sense of overlapping time, particularly in his last poems, Kim Stafford asks whether those poems are left to act not so much as end or beginning but rather as 'a middle, a hinge-point between before and after' (*Early Morning*, p. 11).

It is the creation of that middle, that imagined stopping-point, that so interests a reading group filmed by CRILS in a drug and alcohol rehabilitation centre.

Those line-endings, says Peter: 'ask me/mistakes' 'ask me whether/what I have done', 'ask me what difference':

Are they vulnerable or resolute?

Both: the poet helping the man.

There are risks taken in this reading group—in the fear of shame and exposure, under threat of difficult thoughts and admissions—but Peter says later:

The risk started with the author putting his thoughts out there, opening it up. If the poet risked it, I am more able to do so also, in response.

What interests Peter is how a writer opening up an area of feeling allows others, called readers, to follow on in. In our research we in turn follow these participants into areas where it no longer matters if the thoughts have been thought before, because they are thought again for the first time here by these readers. And they can and will be thought again and again in other settings, anew. Abstract literary study of a text requires (at least the semblance of) originality within its specialist discipline. But what matters here is that even as risky guesses and flawed interpretations, our *own* thoughts as investigators (looking at the film, reading the transcripts) now have practical application to the shared reality of that reading in a drug and alcohol rehab unit and, however deficient, feel wanted or needed in response, occasioned to be real and necessary again, as thoughts truly should be in life.

So it is that 'Ask Me' stills the river of time described in Matthew Arnold's great poem 'The Buried Life'. Arnold wrote about how something he calls 'Fate' providentially kept our own human identity hidden from itself, a 'buried stream' deep in 'the unregarded river of our life', so that we could not get to fiddle or tamper with it too much. But just occasionally 'A man becomes aware of his life's flow,/ And hears its winding murmur':

> And then he thinks he knows
> The hills where his life rose,
> And the sea where it goes.

Then, despite the imperative not to be over-consciously meddling with identity, the poem reminds its readers of the counter-need: the need, nonetheless, to be still in touch with ourselves at some deep level.

The holding space created in 'Ask Me' is an image of that need. In the rehab reading group, along with Peter there is Keith whom we also met in chapter 1, and Lionel who has cirrhosis of the liver and now lives in danger of fatally bursting the veins in his oesophagus. After a number of relapses through alcohol addiction, Lionel now has no real choice but to give up the drinking or else die. There is for him a sort of terrible relief in finally reaching the verge of that extreme future disaster. In pulling himself back into the sober present, he feels changed in one part of himself, and yet with another part for ever left physically irreparable by his past.

The three men note how in the poem it is ice, the hard form given to the water, that is necessary to arrest the flow. Thinking cannot always be hot, feel warm. 'It doesn't feel joyful, does it, this ice-coldness?' says the group leader. 'It's not joyful but it's not painful,' Lionel replies, carefully, 'It is a different experience, it is neither stagnant calmness nor the onward rush of the river':

It's almost artificially silent, but it is not artificial, it is just a different state, a third state between calm and tidal.

Not 'x', not 'y' but something in the difference of the words themselves: that is what literary thinking is like, where words and meanings are no longer simply one-for-one, but create a space for thought to work in:

> *Others*
>
> have come *in their slow way into*
>
> my thought, and *some* have tried to help
>
> *or to hurt:* ask me what *difference*
>
> their strongest love *or* hate has made.

The mental concentration this kind of thinking requires, Lionel says later at interview, replaces the bad form of total concentration that was his addiction. This third state in the middle of things, neither wholly calm nor utterly wild, is like the poem itself, or it is also like the group. It is the place where the men notice the two slightly different 'theres' in

> We know
> the current is there, hidden; and there
> are comings and goings from miles away
> that hold the stillness

—the second 'there' re-activating the familiar first beneath the surface.

A hold between the comings and goings: it makes for an area of not knowing without the usual fear that accompanies it. Brain-scientists use the term 'entropy' to describe the degree of unpredictability registered in brain activity. Rhiannon Corcoran comments that higher entropy is reflected in conditions going all the way from mental flexibility into mental chaos, from divergent and creative thinking to dopamine-fuelled addiction and psychosis. Normal waking consciousness, typically more structured, is associated with lower entropy, and characterized by rigid and bounded thinking. In its lowest form, it is reflected within obsessive-compulsive disorder and medicated depression when only the barest information-processing can be managed, often repetitively.[3]

The setting here is, significantly, a drug and alcohol rehabilitation unit where these conditions are most pertinent in their entire range. The aim, as always in shared reading, is always first to 'get into' the poem and then to 'stay in' it, and stay in it, until something comes out. What the readers here are sensing in 'Ask Me', and recreating from within it, is what Rhiannon calls a zone of sustained criticality—pitched on the verge between high and low entropy—in which individuals can do thinking-work across active and passive, unorganized and organized states of mind. That immanence—a bounded instability that is neither chaotic nor routine—might well be a poem, she says, and the reading that then goes on within it. It is a good place to be, at the centre of whatever we are capable of.

Group Leader: I love in that second verse: 'we know/ the current is there, hidden; and there/ are comings and goings from miles away/ that hold the stillness exactly before us.' I love those extra-precise little words that are put in—'hidden', 'away' ...

Keith: And 'exactly': 'exactly before us'. There's a stillness about it, so you can stop and pause, and allow time in, in a different way. 'You and I can turn and look/ at the silent river and wait. We know ... ' You know there's things going on around you, comings and goings, before and ahead. But you can stay in one place of asking for a while, and go 'I know I can think'. Otherwise all of it will just roll on by. We need it to make a place for itself. And you'd want to try to make this place speak a bit more for you. Then 'what the river says, that is what I say.'

Group Leader: The place is the river, held at this point; or in other words it is the poem itself. And it is this gathering of past, present, and future there that makes you *think*: contemplate calmly as you couldn't when it all went along.

Lionel: That is thinking, when times get held together like that—till they say something of your whole life.

William Stafford wrote, 'For me an artist is someone who lets the material talk back' (*Revise Your Life*, p. 21). Those contracted little insertions of thought—'exactly'—into the dense saturated solution of the poem, themselves speak of bigger things, as if they were the beginnings of what needs, or becomes, philosophic thought. Without the act of thinking, without the human thinker, adds a philosopher, 'there would be no difference between past and future', no sense of time at all even in the struggle against it. But thanks to that 'insertion of a fighting presence' called thinking, the very shape of things alters away from the linear.[4] Perhaps poems would be better understood if they were called insertions into life. This third state, holding-ground, zone of immanence—whatever the term for the extra human room that the literary work helps re-insert in the individual or group—is the site for the otherwise invisible and elusive contemplation that too often is missed or missing in a life. Reading exists to re-create it in place of what the world will not otherwise yield.

In his preference for process over the end-product itself, William Stafford always said that he set the initial standard for his writing quite low—and that not because of lack of confidence or ambition, but in the desire to start it every morning and be able always to re-enter the poetic place of thinking without a too steep threshold. It is not the great finished accomplishment of a few people that Stafford saw as 'art': rather it was the participation of as many as possible in the process, in the feel, in the sense of immersion for which poetry was no more and no less than a prompt and stimulus. It was getting inside the making-process—even if as a writer you did not always do it well enough yourself, even if as a reader you didn't ever create it at all—still, that was art. The untidy resonant matter in a poem, the incomplete suggestion, the half-said thought, the autobiographical by-product—all these are, like bequests, the rawer unspoken material that still surrounds the apparently finished thing on the page. The writer's loose ends of life and thought get woven into the apparently finished poem that isn't really finished but becomes the reader's own loose ends instead. 'The comings and goings from miles away/ that hold the stillness exactly before us.'

Stafford's refusal of 'finish' in poetry is somewhat like Ruskin's in relation to painting—in particular to the practice of Turner in comparison with supposedly more composed realists. If a landscape painting was too finished, said Ruskin, it looked like no more than a varnished imitation. Art then became like a mere window on the external world, falsely seeming finished as though it were a complete end in itself. But then the baulked imagination of a Ruskin, viewing the depicted scene, says in frustration, 'I knew all that before … Stand aside from between that nature and me'.[5] I may as well have nature direct. But the greater work is achieved when one such as Ruskin is enabled actually to see, through the brushstrokes of suggestion, how far the imagination of a Turner lies beyond his own powers of execution, how far his vision—the human seemingly called out by nature to make more of nature itself—is expressed even through the imperfection of its means. Imperfection is the law of life and of vitally unfinished proliferation, says Ruskin. Never 'prefer the perfectness of the lower nature to the imperfection of the higher': no great artist 'ever stops working till he has reached his point of failure'.[6] The readers who rediscover the unfinished business of deep inner thinking, through the act of reading a poem, know that art is made of what Proust, reading Ruskin, called not 'conclusions' but 'incitements'.[7]

In the same spirit, it is important that research into 'the benefits' of reading is not just about simple ends and neat outcomes, measurable targets, or wherever it is that the story finishes up. Not when it involves people whose own lives, if viewed from the simple perspective of 'results', might look like no more than failures or dead-ends, especially to themselves. But patterns in a life are more complex than ideas of linear progression, and realizing that is part of the experience of reading literature. Out of that experience, it is important to understand a different dimensional framework in which people who cannot be cured of life and simply move on, or change or grow, who are unable to achieve steadily incremental improvement without lapses, or be simply rewarded with lasting success—most of us, that is— nonetheless can still recognize and value what may often seem later to have been no more than temporary or episodic, superseded or even spoilt by subsequent events.

In the psychosis day-centre, Jud reads Arnold's 'The Buried Life':

> But often, in the world's most crowded streets,
> But often, in the din of strife,

> There rises an unspeakable desire
> After the knowledge of our buried life;
> A thirst to spend our life and restless force
> In tracking out our true original course...

'To know/ Whence our lives come and where they go.' A staff member helping to run the group dares to ask Jud, in the silence that follows: 'Do you think *you* have any original buried plan?' He answers, quite carefully:

> **Um yes, possibly but it seems far removed from the reality I am in now [*smiles ruefully*]. ... Yes, it seems to be quite a distance between the person you once were—hoping to be, and the person you have become, so ... er ...**

We who watch the film of this are always interested in the moments when people pause in the midst of formulation—as here when Jud says 'the person you once were' and hesitates and then goes on, 'the person you once were—hoping to be' in a formulation that goes beyond a simple forward line of time. And we are interested in places where people stop and cannot go on, often because as people whose outcomes are poor, they cannot yet see a future for their thought. This is Jud who in the present looks back to a past which now seems to have lost the future it once had. That he could think and say that, in part due to Arnold's poem, and without solution or cure, is what the Wordsworth of *Lyrical Ballads* would think to be a sort of real-life poetry itself.

*

People need some sense of that hold on the river of their life, in a place of resonant silence such as 'Ask Me' temporarily provides. Stafford himself wrote of what an increasing struggle he found it, to be simply immersed in living, as he aged. In his relationships he felt he was relying more and more on the cautious strategy of 'making sure events pass without upsetting a participant'. He wrote to himself that instead of progress through time, 'Now becomes only anticipated history' (*Early Morning*, p. 249).

Using a very different figure of speech for holding onto one's existence Thomas Hardy writes, 'Persons with any weight of character carry, like planets, their atmospheres along with them in their orbits' (*The Return of the Native*, 1878, chapter 3). But we don't all have or can keep that dynamic personal aura, carrying around with us the emotion of what matters in and about a life. Feeling they lack such force and weight, people too often feel anonymous or vulnerable, and shrink into something apparently routine and banal.

That is when poems may restore atmosphere.

Here is a poem about nothing more, it seems, than the daily act of boiling an egg. 'A Quiet Life' is by the American poet, Baron Wormser (born 1948), on behalf of small and simple things and the underlying processes behind them. He writes me: 'People sometimes say to me, "Did you write the egg poem?" It's a funny way to be known to people but I'm good with it. I wrote the poem all in a flash one night decades ago when I was sitting late at night in the rocking chair by the wood stove in our house in the Maine woods. I have no idea where it came from. Totally out of the blue and onto the page':

> What a person desires in life
>   is a properly boiled egg.
> This isn't as easy as it seems.
> There must be gas and a stove,
>   the gas requires pipelines, mastodon drills,
>   banks that dispense the lozenge of capital.
> There must be a pot, the product of mines
>   and furnaces and factories,
>   of dim early mornings and night-owl shifts,
>   of women in kerchiefs and men with
>   sweat-soaked hair.
> Then water, the stuff of clouds and skies
>   and God knows what causes it to happen.
> There seems always too much or too little
>   of it and more pipelines, meters, pumping
>   stations, towers, tanks.
> And salt—a miracle of the first order,
>   the ace in any argument for God.
>   Only God could have imagined from
>   nothingness the pang of salt.
> Political peace too. It should be quiet
>   when one eats an egg. No political hoodlums
>   knocking down doors, no lieutenants who are
>   ticked off at their scheming girlfriends and
>   take it out on you, no dictators
>   posing as tribunes.
> It should be quiet, so quiet you can hear
>   the chicken, a creature usually mocked as a type
>   of fool, a cluck chained to the chore of her body.
> Listen, she is there, pecking at a bit of grain
>   that came from nowhere.

The reader of this poem is Laura. She remembers it from the first time she came to a reading group in a Recovery College. She summarizes: 'There must be this, there must be that. And then something else too. I know that everything needs something else and something else again to make it. You can't get just one thing, because it needs more, just to become that one thing.'

All her life she has tried to be a help to others, working in schools for disadvantaged teenagers with special needs, fostering, and volunteering, because, beneath that, in her own early life no one in her family was a help to her and she had a bad first marriage. It was like running on adrenaline, she said, always suffering from psychological problems but hiding them. Then she met the man who became her second husband and suddenly, just when she had stopped running and had someone with whom to share her life, she relaxed, let go, 'And my body said, "Oh my God", and fell apart'. Nothing now worked automatically; everything in the unknown infrastructure that lay behind her ability to perform the simplest practical actions seemed to have broken down and come apart.

She suffered and continues to suffer from depression and anxious intrusive thoughts, physically also from diabetes, fibromyalgia, and rheumatoid arthritis, and resulting problems of weight and mobility. In the Recovery College after her breakdown, the courses on offer were meant as 'stepping stones' to better mental health—'All medical, goal-oriented, about your issues, I just burst out crying because I thought I can't do any of that'. But then right in the middle of the programme-brochure was the reading group, and this she could do because she remembered 'sitting against a tree when I was about nine, with a yellow gingham dress and socks up to my knees, just leaning against a tree and simply, quietly reading a book'. They read the poem about boiling the egg, when she could not even do that normal thing for herself now. 'I just wanted what the poem said, a quiet life.'

And what she also thought was metaphorical: 'Oh my God, for me to be like a little efficiently boiled egg, I've got to go and dig all of this up.' To function simply and efficiently again, 'I've got to go miles and miles back, digging up the past'. Metaphor hidden within literal description was a way of thinking that suited her: 'I am what is called a kinesthetic learner,' she told us, 'I am used to learning through one sense—like physically seeing or touching—in order to reach another more mental level.'

> I was sat reading this poem and I imagined myself sat at a table with a little boiled egg and behind me was this massive, massive refinery … in my head. A little boiled egg is … so little. And all you have to do is put it in water. But to put it in water you've got to have those pipes to get the water, and everything goes from that little thing to massive really quickly. It feels like I am carrying a refinery in the back of my head.

The poem says:

> This isn't as easy as it seems.
> There must be gas and a stove,
>   the gas requires pipelines, mastodon drills,
>   banks that dispense the lozenge of capital.
> There must be a pot, the product of mines
>   and furnaces and factories …

Laura re-read, 'And more pipelines, meters, pumping/ stations, towers, tanks', and then began to talk at length to her interviewer, as follows in her own voice.

> For me, all that stuff: it was still not enough to work, and yet too much to cope with. My head was full of rubbish. My head felt massive and full of things that I couldn't sort out, all those things that are going on to make my little life as it is. And I was trying to compare my life with all the pipes and the mastodon drills and everything going at me, behind me, just to make me how I was.

'Mastodon drills?' asked the interviewer. Laura replied:

> They are those massive ones that go right down, because you've got to go deep down into the ground to get these pipes working. Digging into my life: these mastodon drills, they were trying to make my life into this quiet boiled egg. That is what I face when eventually I get the counselling from IAPT services; I've been waiting three years now.[8]

In her quiet moments in the meantime, she returns to the literal: the egg can be a coffee instead, ten steadying minutes at the start of the day, or sitting down in a café when she is out and about, and getting agitated. Then little words and thoughts from the poem come to her and 'get mixed up with life'. Or she'll read a quiet poem, with nobody to look after for a while, in what she calls 'my time and my space'.

> the chicken, a creature usually mocked as a type
> of fool, a cluck chained to the chore of her body.

'That's me, a fool, with feelings that really hold me. When all the digging's been done, I'm going to feel … free.' She talks about her grandmother keeping chickens, going outside to kill one, useful but expendable creatures. Which is how she felt until she met her second husband.

The interviewer then asked Laura what was her favourite line in this poem, and her voice breaks when she says it is the last one and reads it again:

It should be quiet, so quiet you can hear
   the chicken, a creature usually mocked as a type
   of fool, a cluck chained to the chore of her body.
Listen, she is there, pecking at a bit of grain
   that came from nowhere.

It's so big, as big as the first line 'What a person desires in life' before it shrinks again for the next few lines. Then: 'That came from nowhere.' Something you can't always see for sure but can make out by quiet hearing. 'Listen she is there', hear the pecking. A tiny bit like God imagining something 'from/ nothingness'. She is pecking at the grain, she's picking up just little bits of life, like I am. They come 'from nowhere' like the salt comes 'from nothingness'. And that's when you go back to the beginning of the poem. It's like the egg, it is a kind of simple gift. The chicken and the egg, before all the machinery that followed. She is ready to give, after all that's happened, she is ready to give again.

Laura talks about how being able to go back to reading has widened her vocabulary, widened her brain, widened everything.

Then water, the stuff of clouds and skies
   and God knows what causes it to happen

She sort of believes in God, which makes the cliché 'God knows' rather different, and she thinks of some time after her long-awaited counselling when—her own speech changed by the feel of the poem—'the freshness of the water will be washing me out'.

For Laura, the poem and the group have made what she calls a little 'chink' for her in terms of possibility, or, to put it another way, 'a foot on the ladder' when she could have fallen flat on the floor.

She has done a few things to try to keep the reading real, to try to retain and use it as a part of her actual life. Like regularly sitting down in the kitchen to that boiled egg, which gives her a grin. She loves funny and feisty little acts, buying a toy parrot during the course of her first marriage and making it say cheeky things whenever her horrible first husband went by. Another act was taking this photograph (Figure 12). Coincidentally she lives in Crewe, near Winsford, the salt-mining centre of Cheshire, and went to photograph the refinery. 'It was because of this poem. The refinery is huge. I did it at night time with the lights and the fire blazes, and everything amazing.'

She got some training and is now running a reading group of her own, an ambition of hers. She is still helping people, though in a way that also helps her, through the sharing of the literature.

Figure 12. Oil refinery. © Laura Prime.

Yet it is not quite sufficient. Though the reading works wonders, particularly for the time it lasts, it is also, she says, only masking long-underlying problems that remain and threaten. Reading is not like a medical remedy; it is more like part of experience than an intervention. But it is a part of experience that, she hopes, may further the capacity for experience, for thinking about experiences in the meditative space that a poem such as 'A Quiet Life' or 'Ask Me' also allows. Perhaps, she sometimes thinks, it should not be called 'reading' which seems such a restricted and studious activity, but something you do with books that you feel you should be able to do without them. Even so, she cannot always occupy for long enough the richer space that reading gives her and cannot make it become more present in her daily life. The main issue is the gap she feels between what she calls 'book-time', where she loves to live, and 'normal-time' in which her struggles continue. It makes things worse sometimes that the book-time can be so much warmer and richer. But, though it is not the books' fault, and though literature itself does not seem much concerned about boundaries, she still cannot wholly carry over the one into the other—book-time into normal-time—or consolidate who she is.

Always wary of a further breakdown, Laura still awaits the counselling that she hopes will be a talking cure. She has to hope that counselling will make 'a bridge' if literature is not to leave her half-stranded. In the little last words that most moved her in the whole poem, that minor miracle would be something

> that came from nowhere

where 'nowhere' was where gifts come out of, and not just what lives needed to be rescued from.

*

Evanna remembers a poem that quite out of the blue did have an effect on her life. Or actually, she doesn't wholly recall it. 'I can't remember exactly which one, but at the end of the poem I said to myself: "Evanna, you need to make this decision and start looking for work"'. It had made her address herself:

> The poem was that this person was out in the desert and wanting to reach out to a greater force, wanting to reach out to the universe—and found it very difficult. He talked about his dark place, about being trapped and he can't escape. For him it looks like it is too late; he is held by his own indecisiveness. And I thought to myself, 'Sometimes this fear is why we are indecisive, because we feel trapped in our own fear. This is something for me to think about. I'm not going to be trapped in this situation because you've got to try ... ' The poem was talking about you've got to try.

He, I, myself, we, me, I, you: this is the sort of rapid pronoun shift that takes place once the mobility of literary thinking is released.[9]

But this is not a person to whom freedom of thought or movement has come easily. Born in Croydon, Evanna, now in her mid forties, lived most of her early life in Jamaica to which her parents had returned when she was just a baby. Her mother then had a breakdown after her next baby died suddenly, and thereafter lived apart from her husband. Evanna's education was interrupted as a result and she was never much of a reader, not academic. When she eventually got to secondary school, she concentrated on practical skills, especially cookery. After her mother had collapsed, she had had to go to live with her aunt who never wanted her to leave or take work, but as Evanna got older she began to feel trapped. She ran away to the big city, to Kingston where she survived by babysitting, but then had to come back when she couldn't really manage.

The plan originally laid by her father was for her to return to England for work and further training, and she finally did so when she was twenty-one, first of all staying with a cousin. She had had plans for going to college, for entering the army or nursing, but instead she had a series of temporary jobs, cleaning or care work or working in shops, each one of which she left whenever she felt she was getting too comfortable in a low-level occupation. She initially concentrated on earning money so as to be independent for the first time and had half forgotten about college, but was worried by her lack of qualifications especially when applications to upgrade herself got nowhere.

By her early twenties, a brief marriage of less than two years had failed, leaving her depressed because she had found value only in her more experienced and articulate husband. She felt she had not been brought up to understand her own emotions or to communicate them, and eventually went for counselling. She began buying books, but not reading them, just putting them on her shelf. Later she joined a shared reading group advertised at her doctor's. That is when, a few years ago, she came across the desert poem, a place of emptiness, she says, or a low place like a valley or a pit.

Our interviewer asked her what it felt like when she read the poem and suddenly felt so connected to it. Evanna characteristically speaks slowly, carefully, but what she describes within that is neither slow nor cautious, 'a quick thing that happened within my thought'.

> *Evanna:* I had an epiphany of the many years that I've spent being fearful. It speaks home. I think I must take a hold of the moment. You have a moment and you have a space. And you know that something just happened in that space: what was *that?* And you have to realize what it was. I've got this space.
>
> *Interviewer:* Space? Why not something like … idea?
>
> *Evanna:* Because space was the moment I had the epiphany in. It just dropped into my whole being, erupting, so you can't stay the same in normal time. That space where you kind of breathe and you think, 'Wow, I've got to grab this before I lose it.' Whatever has just transpired to me, through that message of that poem or short story I've read, I've got to quickly connect with that space. So I don't lose that space. So that I don't lose that moment.

Evanna pauses here:

> It was the *space between time*—the time that I have lost and the time that I'm catching up with. Does that make sense? Maybe say I've lost about ten years of my life you know, being afraid, being fearful.
>
> *Interviewer:* About this in-between time in the poem: what is that other time you are catching up with?
>
> *Evanna:* It is on the other side. A possible future way forward, for a moment. You've lost so much, lost that precious thing that you could have done something with, you've left it at that place where you first met it; but you can gain some of it back and pick up what is necessary for this particular time. It's almost like you are re-living it all. It's a space where you feel: I have lived this life where I did not believe in myself; but now to make that step further, to go beyond, and come out from the dark place and cross over … into the unknown.

It doesn't last very long, that's why you have to kind of quick deal with it and reconnect yourself to it all the time. You feel very motivated. If there was something that was asleep inside of you, it awakens that idea. For you to do something about it.

Evanna is a practical person who, in a most unusual combination of no-nonsense and yet profundity, wants her thoughts to be translated into something tangible and active. Afraid the moment would disappear and that week after week might pass and she would forget, what she did on reading her mystery poem was almost straight-away go to the computer and start applying for the job she had been hesitating over. But she says she would not have taken this practical initiative through the influence of practical self-help books:

> With a self-help book it's giving you instructions, always positive. But it's almost like the human being is speaking to you with a poem. A poem does not advise you. It talks poetically to you.

It makes a similar difference in energy, she says, if she simply tries to tell her story in a counselling session or if instead she suddenly finds it involuntarily coming back to her when reading. She speaks of sheer simple fear in the story of her life, but this time, stimulated by the poetry, she managed to use that fear against itself: 'I was fearful of *not* stepping out of my comfort zone.'

It is this inventive adaptation of the apparently or initially negative that applies also to her response to the poem she can best remember. It is 'First Lesson' by a third minor American poet—each of them broadly in the tradition of Robert Frost or Thomas Hardy, half-hiding their depths within apparently conventional forms and approachable surfaces. Philip Booth (1925–2007) was a man who in particular loved the sea. This is 'First Lesson':

> Lie back daughter, let your head
> be tipped back in the cup of my hand.
> Gently, and I will hold you. Spread
> your arms wide, lie out on the stream
> and look high at the gulls. A dead-
> man's float is face down. You will dive
> and swim soon enough where this tidewater
> ebbs to the sea. Daughter, believe
> me, when you tire on the long thrash
> to your island, lie up, and survive.
> As you float now, where I held you
> and let go, remember when fear

> cramps your heart what I told you:
> lie gently and wide to the light-year
> stars, lie back, and the sea will hold you.

Evanna: It is someone who is learning to swim—that's in the literal sense, and she is out at sea and she has not yet got the skills to be a good swimmer on her own. And she must have to think 'Am I gonna drown?' But there was this father-figure who was encouraging the girl to swim, regardless of how she may feel, who was literally supporting her. You may feel fearful but be courageous—dive, take the plunge. She herself had ever been fearful:

> remember when fear
> cramps your heart what I told you:
> lie gently and wide to the light-year
> stars

She first read this, says Evanna, when going through a transitional time, when she was considering whether to help with the local Sunday School and try to learn something new in the process. The interviewer asks what specific line stands out for her. She replies it is that repeated soothing sense of 'Lie back … and I will hold you'—till finally 'lie back, and the sea will hold you'. But most of all it is

> Daughter, believe
> me, when you tire on the long thrash
> to your island, lie up, and survive.

Evanna then notes: It is 'lie up'—like rest up or like holding up—instead of 'lie back' now. Up: not being down and depressed and subdued, or trying too hard to get wherever too fast. Instead: survive, relax a bit, and trust you have something to float upon. When I first read it, this spoke about me being in a low place, and hopeless. It was with a sense of loss and loneliness: my parents are not part of my life, both deceased now, and before that I did not have a mother or father to run to in those times. Maybe there should be God instead, maybe now only this poem for support.

What the poem offers and inserts is what she did not have, as with Dan in chapter 7. And so it is with Evanna too: the fact that she never had that love and support is not, in this context, a matter of envy or self-pity or angry bitterness, but imagination momentarily in place of saddened autobiography. It is the creative appreciation of a value she feels precisely through not experiencing it. That there would be somebody in the world, something finally supportive in the universe, that would stop you falling or sinking. It is what William James in *The Varieties of Religious Experience* writes of as a basis of religion, against the fear of a great pit of insecurity beneath the surface of life. In lecture 5 James tells of a revivalist preacher who would often tell of a man who found himself at night slipping down the side of a precipice. He caught at a branch to halt his fall, and clung on in misery for dark hours, until finally he had to let go. He fell just six inches. If only he had given up the struggle earlier, said the preacher, had let go and trusted.[10] But James, often a depressive, is unsure he himself could have done that, and makes us think of blind Gloucester in *King Lear* who thought he fell from a Dover cliff but, for once in that terrifying play, is saved, albeit by a pratfall. Still it is not the one particular outcome, it is the fact that there are always the potential falls that matters:

> The fact that we *can* die, that we *can* be ill at all, is what perplexes us; the fact that we now for a moment live and are well is irrelevant to that perplexity. We need a life not correlated with death, a health not liable to illness, a kind of good that will not perish, a good in fact that flies beyond the Goods of nature.
>
> *Varieties*, p. 140, lecture 6

We 'can' in natural liability; we 'need', equally, from our very nature: William James knows the stress of those words, psychologically.

We know of another reader of this poem 'First Lesson', a younger woman who has a lifetime injunction taken out against her alcoholic mother for years of physical abuse against her and her sibling. She told us one of the rawest and most traumatic things a poem such as 'First Lesson' could ever secretly contain for a reader. Her mother, she said, used to hold the children under the water until they passed out. 'A dead-/man's float is face down.' The father wasn't interested in what was going on, but was like a ghost in the family. But here in this poem, she said, I imagine someone is holding my hand and they are not going to let me go, unless they think I'm ok. It should have been my mum. But I think my mum would be a dead man's floating face-down. She'd be the one that keeps me down.

Like Evanna she loves the poem *though* she has never had anything like supportive parents, and *because* she had never had supportive parents. *Though* and *because*, together, may be a crucial language of literature. This means it is not fantasy or wish-fulfilment here: these two women who do not know each other, know very well that this trust and support are not something they had as children, and in their different ways they still suffer in the struggle to stay afloat in life. But the deprivation and the damage and the suffering are here *used* for good, and for belief in good still. And neither the poem nor the poet of course ever knows how many people found something of themselves supported in the words. Just two of us, officially in a formal research unit, have a brief and tiny glimpse of that.

There are family secrets that are kept for years, as though that were the most important thing the child can help do. And—she goes on—the keeping of them is so rigid and closed, so demanding and exhausting that it prevents anything else good getting into the thinking. But when the younger woman describes what 'First Lesson' first felt like, the experience is surprisingly easy. She talks of the flow of the reading, such that 'without realizing it', before she realized it, she found the poem 'taking the pain' of what she had been through. But 'taking' is what she says, not taking away. She has had thoughts of jumping from a motorway bridge or station platform, which is what 'tiring of the long thrash' means to her. But she says when she first heard someone quietly reading aloud the poem to her, it was 'almost her childhood', all that she missed in never being read to. The reading carries her, she says, it gently holds her, it makes her elevate from the world for the while, till she can float back down again and feel physically relaxed and not heavy. The words she uses here all seem taken from the poem itself.

If her own bad childhood experience makes her feel almost physically the good in the poem and hold onto it, she wants to turn good out of bad in one further way, beyond the books. If possible, she says, she would like to adopt a child of her own some time in the next few years, to stop the cycle of harm and make for a better generation in all she did not have but knows is needed. 'As you float now, where I held you/ and let go ...

'Any reasonable person who looks at water, and passes a hand through it, can see that it would not hold a person up ... But swimmers know that if they relax on the water it will prove to be miraculously buoyant,' says William Stafford. 'Swimmers are (and from teaching a child I know how hard it is to persuade a reasonable person of this)—swimmers are persons who relax in the water, let their heads go down, and reach out with ease and confidence.' So it should be with writers and with readers, he says:

> It is strange to me that we can come to accept the idea that language is primarily learned as speech, is soaked up by osmosis from society by children—but that we then assume the writing down of this flexible language requires a system ... '[11]

The childhood acquisition and use of language through speech is an equivalent to that 'miraculous' buoyancy of water and the relaxing power of 'confidence' within it. Then something bad happens, Stafford says, in the way of inhibition, partly through poor education. But literature as written-speaking remains for Stafford like speech, essentially not so very separate or specialist. For all the inner complexities, and the confrontation with adult difficulties no longer easily spoken of, Stafford wants writing and reading to remain in the human mind as still radically simple and natural in origin and purpose, an extension of conversation into an alternative form. That is why literature works so well when spoken again out loud.

But still, even in an apparently natural simplicity, there remains something big within the little. The maximum of what is at stake in the little poem by Philip Booth, hinges upon

> Daughter, believe
> me, when you tire …

and is expressed at its fullest in the great end of the first part of John Bunyan's *The Pilgrim's Progress* (1678), which is like turning from problems of modern confidence back to the ancient issues of faith that lodge hidden within them.

To reach the heavenly city the two pilgrims, Christian and Hopeful, are tested by the waters of the river of death in which they are told 'you shall find it deeper or shallower, as you believe in the King of the place'. Almost at once on hearing that, Christian finds his heart sink and feels himself sinking, and the deeper he sinks the more in his drowning panic he supposes himself a man without sufficient belief to be saved at the very final end. It is the perhaps most terrible account of the vicious circle of despair in all English literature. He is almost no longer Christian but, in the allegory, is become Fearing instead. Yet Hopeful, who can feel the river bottom, can see men standing at the gate on the far side, on shore, waiting to receive them both, has much ado to keep his brother's head above water.

> But Christian would answer, ''Tis you, 'tis you they wait for, you have been Hopeful ever since I knew you.' 'And so have you,' said he to Christian. 'Ah brother,' said he, 'surely if I was right, he would now arise to help me, but for my sins he hath brought me into the snare and hath left me.'

What Christian hears from his companion serves only to realize Hopeful's name, not his own rescue. But Hopeful has another text which he does not leave flat on the page of the Bible but brings to life again in his own voice, in saying of the wicked that is they who 'are not troubled as other men, neither are they plagued like other men' (Psalms 73:5). You, Christian, he says, are not the wicked but those other men, less assured; and to get through you have to remember again deep inside who you are and what you have been through:

> These troubles and distresses that you go through in these waters are no sign that God hath forsaken you, but are sent to try you whether you will call to mind that which heretofore you have received of his goodness, and live upon him in your distresses.

It is not that God gives you assured faith, but that your doubtful faith—like the two-part cry 'Lord I believe; help thou mine unbelief' (Mark 9:24)—gives you God.

> And with that, Christian brake out with a loud voice, 'Oh I see him again! And he tells me, *When thou passest through the waters, I will be with thee, and through the rivers, they shall not overflow thee.*'

It is Isaiah 43:2, but again as voice and not just text.

It was for the equivalent of this comparison between 'First Lesson' and *The Pilgrim's Progress* that William James wrote *The Varieties of Religious Experience*: to show the psychological continuity in humans across the ages when the real core of the religious problem lies in one repeated cry, 'Help! Help!' (*Varieties*, p. 162, lecture 7). No prophet, adds James, can claim to bring a final message unless what he says has a sound of reality in the ears of those who feel that helplessness: 'I will be with thee.'

At the end of the second half of *The Pilgrim's Progress*, Mr Despondency leaves his fear and despond behind on the shore as he enters the water, hoping in his will that those feelings will never be picked up again by those who live afterwards. For Mr Fearing, next up, the waters were made lower than at any time ever before.

But for these readers we are thinking of, even when they seek the help of belief, there is no clear culminating end in the modern world as there was for Bunyan's pilgrim, no text that can make promises, however hard, as the Bible has seemed to do. They wait for medical help, counselling, a better job or a happier marriage, some lift of the spirits or a manageable goal.

One reader who ran reading groups in difficult settings let me read this piece of his. 'I am writing this on a train. The significance of this will be clear in a moment.' He had always believed that reading was 'safe' such that 'the writing can go to the unsafe places we need to go. Safe writing would mean stuff that doesn't work—stuff that avoids, smoothes over, obscures'. To that effect he had undertaken with a friend a long, intent reading together of T. S. Eliot's *Four Quartets* over several weeks, to take on something difficult and in it to find something that was hard to put into language. 'So here I am, in the middle way, having had twenty years—/ Twenty years largely wasted … ':

Trying to use words, and every attempt
Is a wholly new start, and a different kind of failure
Because one has only learnt to get the better of words
For the thing one no longer has to say, or the way in which
One is no longer disposed to say it.

'It rang a bell, and at first the strongest resonance was its relation to what I was trying to do professionally with reading groups, in getting beneath the facile to the inarticulate. Even the words describing their own inadequacy seemed so adequate. But then when I read it again, for myself, *I* was the beaten bell. There was no containment. It was Failure.' But still, even with damaged, inadequate, and shabby equipment, 'there is only the trying', the poem said, 'The rest is not our business'. So he continued running his reading groups, even at the same time as he found himself becoming increasingly depressed, taking medication, undertaking counselling, barely able to read alone, and only in preparation for his group. Then even as he was struggling to carry on, getting through the difficult down-time between reading-groups, he was reading this with his friend, again from 'East Coker', concerning the moment—

... when an underground train, in the tube, stops too long between stations
And the conversation rises and slowly fades into silence
And you see behind every face the mental emptiness deepen
Leaving only the growing terror of nothing to think about;

'It is this roar of silence, the dark space between groups, that was my biggest difficulty. Eliot's words about the train paused "*too* long" helped me conceptualize the terror I felt when staring at the computer screen, or not preparing for a group which would come alive anyway when we start moving again.' It was the sudden opening of an in-betweenness that made a nonsense of the normal idea of any destination, of really getting anywhere. The medication only served to take some of the terror off, waiting in the tunnel.

But more specifically it seemed to lead to, or rather become connected with, a moment of hidden crisis a little later. He was at a London station and it had been a hard, busy day. His own personal session with a counsellor earlier in the day had gone badly. Immediately after he had felt panicky but had still run his group, only in a blur, feeling he was no longer a safe guide, though the session itself seemed somehow to have gone well enough. He was then due to catch the train for a team-meeting, but had a second panic-attack and was suddenly taken with the idea of throwing himself from the platform in front of an engine. This feeling was repeated every time on that journey he had to change trains. It passed and nothing happened as such: he knew the suicidal impulse could not simply be caused by the poem, was not a poem's fault—he was truly unwell and vulnerable, there were long-established problems from the past. But it was reading, just as much as it was when claiming good; it was intensely serious; and he never again felt quite so secure in the conviction that reading was always safe or healing. Eventually he and his friend did finish their joint venture with *Four Quartets*, and he was glad he had survived it, 'felt like a veteran of it', believed he would still somewhere carry it with him as something important. But he had had a nice copy of the poem: 'Then I managed to leave it in the train. That seemed like the right place for it to be left.'

Others carry on. It is a good sign whenever a reader in a dementia care home, or a drug rehabilitation centre, or a prison, does not leave the poem or the story behind after the session but takes it back to their room or their house or a relative, sending it on by letter, pinning it to a wall.

And still, across this spectrum of responses, a reader such as Evanna Goodwin or Laura Prime sometimes feels in the midst of a book or poem, 'Something just happened, what was *that*?' 'This space,' Evanna says, 'You get a moment.' It doesn't last very long, it may not have a sustainable future, it can seem frightening, but it

Figure 13. 'Reading Hands'. © Joe Magee, www.periphery.co.uk.

also seems to offer a present-busting potential, a lyric energy of emotional message left behind, like memory not looking back but coming forward. 'So here I am, in the middle way', hardly knowing which way to turn, which way it might go. You want to do something with it, says Evanna, before you lose it. But sometimes the words just have to come first and be got right there, ahead or instead of lives knowing what to do with them.

People customarily speak of the so-called 'inadequacy' of words in the face of experience, and, granted, verbal proficiency is not sufficient in itself for a life. But a powerful literature ensures that it is not the *words* that the readers in this chapter find inadequate. Language is considerably more adequate than most other things in human existence.

CHAPTER 9

THE NOVEL EXPERIMENTER

There is a man working late at night in the Manhattan office of the law firm in which he is successful partner, wholly absorbed in his writing. After 10 at night, the motion sensors take over to save costs, and he is so concentrated on his work, moving so little, that the lights go out on him. When he realizes it, he is doubly amazed—startled at how totally immersed he has been, and then, waving his hands to bring back on the lighting, surprised at what feels like re-entry into the physical world: 'Himself as something more than mind thinking.' All this, the man realizes, was a kind of sheer happiness.

Years later, after much physical illness and consequent demotion within the firm, this near-ruined man, called Tim Farnsworth, can still become engrossed in carefully writing a motion for summary judgment, while even so all his life is going to hell. In his work he seems, incongruously, to have quite forgotten his own surrounding story. Though the document has a genuine legal context and purpose, it is for the time a pure act regardless, an act of concentrated writing, of thoughtful precision on the page before him:

> To be lost in the writing was to be absorbed, and to be absorbed was to lose awareness of everything—the shitty view and the third-class furniture, but also, and here was the paradox, even the contentment. To be lost in the writing was to be happy, but it required giving up any awareness of that happiness, of any awareness whatsoever, and so he was blissfully unaware … He kept his head down and slowly worked himself, word by word, back into communion with the other hours, days, years—there was in fact no name for this particular unit of time—that together formed a continuum of unawareness that was as close to transcendence as he would come. He was working himself, as if with a spade in a tunnel that finally yields to light, out of the physical world.[1]

It is the ironic paradox that an almost pre-lapsarian unawareness is lost in the moment of realizing it: the temporary happiness and transcendence depend upon his not consciously experiencing them as such until after they have ceased, as if the consciousness of them might even have caused their cessation.

These two pure, peaceful moments of what seems almost primary *being*—of not knowing where you are, and not needing to—come from a novel published in 2010, *The Unnamed* by Joshua Ferris. But they are surrounded by a life and a story that will not let them be. Tim Farnsworth is a man with an inexplicable but recurrent illness that involves him in compulsive and involuntary walking—out of the office, out of the house and family, out of the comfortable world that can be taken for granted—on and on, unstopping, into God-knows-what-or-where, until he drops. This is no *Pilgrim's Progress* but its modern counterpart: an apparently purposeless journey to nowhere.

I say illness but no one knows if Farnsworth's compulsion is primarily a physical, a psychological, or a spiritual condition—as though all those categories were up for grabs or under threat, as the man walks clean out of the explicable norms of existence. This is what this novel, and often The Novel itself, exists for: when forms and categories either break down or become over rigid, to be a holding ground for whatever does not easily fit in the world. 'It's back' is all the man can say, in the bare last words of the first chapter (p. 6). The unnamed.

Without a diagnosis, Tim feels he has become 'the frightened soul inside the runaway train of mindless matter, peering out from the conductor's car in horror' (*Unnamed*, p. 24). That train without brakes is, he feels, a disease of his body, not the mind which, unable to get out of it, is carried along step by step. 'He looked down at his legs. It was like watching footage of legs walking from the point of view of the walker' (*Unnamed*, p. 33). Tim consults all manner of doctors to exonerate him from the charge of mental illness. His psychologists think, however, that there must be something somewhere in him that wants out of job, family, home, civilization itself. What does his body know that he won't admit? Yet all that's known is that 'it' keeps coming back, regardless of explanation and without remedy.

Joshua Ferris himself worked hard against the impulse for explanation, to keep his novel full enough of compelling complications to remain unresolved. In an interview with *The New Statesman* at the beginning of March 2010, he said: 'I certainly didn't want to give any more than I gave. Or withhold more than I withheld. Again, it was walking a tightrope.' The strands of potential explanation en route 'stop and start in the same way as Tim's disease stops and starts'.

In the first draft the novel began simply with the disease's first appearance, but the final published version begins with its third manifestation. It comes four years after the first attack, which had lasted four months and then disappeared as if nothing had happened—but only to occur a second time for a further thirteen months. Repeatedly, Tim's wife Jane has to find out his whereabouts, come and get him by car, trying to bring him home and keep him there. 'I'm not in control, Jane' is his persistent cry (*Unnamed*, p. 24), in a world that seems to expect that 'control' is always possible.

The third episode goes on for twenty-seven months. Then four years later, after the marriage had seemed beautifully re-created, it comes a fourth time, 'It's back'. He was fighting again 'on a playing field that most people never realize exists until the final days and moments of their lives' (*Unnamed*, p. 109). The novel's readers are probably 'most people'.

During the years of journeyings Tim loses fingers and toes in the cold, health both mental and physical, and undergoes protracted hospital stays faraway from home. And still the body drives him on, and he drives it on, to try to drive it with him into the ground. What he calls 'the chain of command' keeps changing from mind to body, from body to mind, back and forth at the crucial blood–brain barrier: 'That is the real frontline in the battle between the two' (*Unnamed*, p. 230). Sometimes in his sickness, amidst hallucinations, Tim feels, like Job, that his very self is God's own battleground for a final struggle between soul and body, on either side.

I have with me the reader who first introduced me to this novel. Georgina, who has been talking about her reading with me, and sending me her notes, seems to know this novel more inwardly than I do. The quotations throughout this chapter are for the most part those she herself highlighted in her reading diary, saying how she felt about each of them. For my part, I appear to know this novel, initially at least, more from the outside—via the response of the wife Jane, after she had nursed her husband not once but twice, and then finds 'It' hitting the family a third time, and then a fourth. In relief, Tim had simply gone back to work after the second occurrence, but for her, even by then, it was never again going to be so easy:

> He treated his first day back like any other day, while she was left wondering just what day is it? What cycle of their marriage had they left off on? How did she resume ordinary life ... He was fine again, as if nothing had ever happened, but she wasn't unchanged. She was suddenly bereft of a purpose.
>
> *Unnamed*, p. 21

This is where I start: from the normal, albeit barely able to get back to normal after the ordeal. It may be almost tolerable whilst you are in the midst of crisis, helping your partner, provided it does not last too long, if only it does not keep recurring. But once you are out of its temporary absorption—the sense of let-me-just-get-through-this—then it is like the lights coming back on again in Tim's midnight office, but in a different sense. You have to take up your life again, left both exhausted and newly uncertain, without the emergency sense of purpose. The realist novel is good on that austere demand, as if the challenge was also in the anti-climactic, the post-dramatic, the shaky return to ordinary time. But then 'it'—the traumatic occurrence—comes back again, and it makes a difference in the form of things that this has happened twice before, and is no temporary crisis but an unpredictably recurrent one. Hence she asks herself: 'Was she really up for a third time?' She would give up her job to help him again: 'But what would happen when it was over? When it was over, if she quit and took care of him for however long, what life would she have to return to?' (*Unnamed*, p. 21). I need the wife, Jane, to measure for me the angle of almost unbearable deflection from the norms to which those of us who want to remain secure so dependently cling.

From childhood onwards Georgina has had a life at times near chaos, though she has never told me the actual facts of her story, save indirectly through what she says about her reading. So much that happened had physical effects, illnesses or drives not really known to her, not under her control. She says she has learnt how to become more normal, so to speak, to be a partner and mother with a family of her own, whereas I, she knows, started from much firmer foundations and more secure back-ups—perhaps, after all, one of those people who hardly know such extremities exist 'until the final days and moments of their lives'. But one of the books that obsesses her, as much as *The Unnamed*, is Conrad's *Lord Jim* (1900). In it Conrad's Marlow, the aged observing narrator, can never fully understand the younger sailor, Jim, who in a moment of panic abandoned a sinking ship and is for ever disgraced. Jim had always thought that in a crisis he would act like a hero: he had not, he had jumped ship, and then the ship had not even sunk. It was a curious experience of negation, an anti-climax and a non-event; yet for the sake of that moment the whole of Jim's subsequent life was ruined. Georgina is very concerned with the experience of shame, especially when it is not wholly deserved ... and yet without a claim for complete innocence either.

At his tribunal, Jim is questioned closely as to the facts of the case in order that the court of inquiry might ascertain the so-called truth of what happened: 'Facts! They demanded facts from him, as if facts could explain anything' (chapter 4).[2] But Jim must try to provide the facts, offering his evidence in a cold hard courtroom of unfeeling judgement, where even mitigation feels like admission of guilt:

> and while his utterance was deliberate, his mind positively flew round and round the serried circle of facts that had surged up all about him to cut him off from the rest of his kind: it was like a creature that, finding itself imprisoned within an enclosure of high stakes, dashes round and round, distracted in the night, trying to find a weak spot, a crevice, a place to scale, some opening through which it might squeeze itself and escape.
>
> *Lord Jim*, chapter 4, p. 65

He is close confined in one place, physically, under scrutiny from all around him. At the same time, his mind is working unsynchronized, at a different pace, seeking another place as a way out. That terrifying discrepancy in the rent of reality—with a whole life of threatened discrepancy thereafter—is what Georgina is pointing to. 'The creature finding itself imprisoned.' If Conrad could have been sanely content with the world of the law courts as the right place for human trial, then there would have been no novels. But when alternatively the courtroom is taken into the perspective of the novel, readers must begin to witness in Jim, as he stands in the dock, 'the true horror behind the appalling face of things' (Lord Jim, chapter 4, p. 65).

'The true horror' behind the face. Georgina is at once sceptical of, and frightened by, the idea of 'the truth'. She is sceptical as to whether a relative, friend, or witness, like Tim's Jane or Jim's Marlow or just myself, could ever presume to know the truth of another person. But she is also fearful whether that other person, alone in herself, could ever avoid the reach and effect of truth below the level of consciousness, denial, and control. She loves the sensors passage with which I opened this chapter, and it was her first choice because it would be lovely just to be, when actually, because of the past, she feels she has to be almost continuously wary, on conscious alert for threats. She is nonetheless a phenomenally strong raw thinker, though, or because, she can sometimes hardly bear to think. That is why she is so interested in the force of the *involuntary* in *The Unnamed*, of all the man is forced to do and think and be, it seems, despite himself.

'I'm not in control, Jane': 'So much of what he was was involuntary' (*Unnamed*, p. 243). That immediate double 'was' there, like a little moment of poetry in the midst of the prose, says of identity that it won't *stay* under control. There is some terrifyingly bigger story being somehow physically played out in Tim, without his being able to tell it, only be it. It is like an ancient story that has come out of Job and the experiments of God, or out of *King Lear* with the mad king in the stormy wilderness, to take over this otherwise small, modern, middle-class human life. Georgina knows other extreme stories, rooted in ancient trials: in addition to *Lord Jim* she thinks of Michael Henchard in Thomas Hardy's *Mayor of Casterbridge*, of John Marcher in Henry James's novella 'The Beast in the Jungle', and of Jack Broughton in Marilynne Robinson's *Home*. Each in a different way is 'like a creature that, finding itself imprisoned, dashes round and round, trying to find a weak spot, a crevice through which it might squeeze itself and escape'.

They are what she calls 'full-on' stories of what, at base, is almost impossible for human creatures to bear or live with, compared to what normal contemporary life is meant to be like. 'When I took *Lord Jim* into hospital, in the waiting room I got it out with a sort of "Ok, come on, show me something then". And in reply the places that first got me were about seeing things on the characters' faces, Marlow reading there what he thinks must be going on in their minds. I suppose that is about always wanting to know *what's going on, what's really, really going on*. Maybe you don't get that in real life itself (thank God).'

Georgina goes on to say that she doesn't think about books in the living of her life:

> When I try and look back, and think—'What did reading x, y, z do for me? What did I get from it?'—I draw a blank, no way of knowing. It is not that way round for me. Instead I think of life suddenly in the midst of reading books, in regard to what I am reading now—a *now* in the middle of it, a *live* thing, connected to the fact that when you are reading you can't be doing anything else. (Especially I'm finding that with Conrad's big long winding sentences.) You've got to be *there*, in it. I'm not talking about escapism—I don't think. More like a parallel.

In *The Unnamed* Georgina follows Tim into the world of the human creature taking with him the imprisonment he is also trying to escape. Eventually, it has to be the troubled daughter, Becka, who replaces her exhausted mother in the search for Tim that takes her too beyond the usual conventions of life. She drives her car onwards, looking from one side to another, never knowing if she is even going in the right direction:

> He was nowhere. Or he was standing right at the point she had just turned away from an instant earlier. She felt the deep deficit of not being omniscient and the insecurity of human limitations that a time of crisis lays bare.
>
> p. 203

Right at the point she had *just* turned away from ... As if to say: Where *are* you while I don't know whether to carry on or go back—or even where and when to make that decision? Without my knowing it, you are someplace or your death has happened. It is like chasing reality or truth: you know it must be somewhere there, at the very same time as you are also unable to find it. It is like the moment when Conrad's Jim goes back to the place where he jumped ship, only to see on the water nothing there at all, no physical mark of a reality he nonetheless cannot escape.

'She felt the deep deficit of not being omniscient.' This speaks of what is missing in this novel that, in place of the lost God, many other novels traditionally have provided: the implicit frame of a narrative omniscience and a linguistic certainty that we cannot be secure of in the experience of life itself. It is the reassurance Georgina never really has anywhere. She feels close to *The Unnamed* and to *Lord Jim* because of that terrible core-terror in Conrad that Bertrand Russell described:

> He thought of civilized and morally tolerable human life as a dangerous walk on a thin crust of barely cooled lava which at any moment might break and let the unwary sink into fiery depths.[3]

It destroys confidence in the firmness of the surface. In *The Unnamed* the mysteriously relentless walking had 'hijacked his body and led him into the wilderness':

> (for everywhere was a wilderness to him who had known only the interiors of homes and offices and school buildings and restaurants and courtyards and hotels)
>
> *Unnamed*, p. 247

The wildness and the wilderness, and the possible plunge into depths below the thin crust she walks upon, are almost always present to Georgina, unless she can stop thinking, or stop what thinking becomes inside her body.

That almost constant uncertainty is why there is a part of me that is almost relieved to hear at the beginning of the novel's fourth and final movement, sixty pages from the end, the firm anonymous voice, usually missing from life, that states with authorial certitude: 'His condition never went into remission again, the walking never ceased' (p. 247). That 'never' is, in its retrospective rescue from the perilously contingent, at least definite and final. It is like the answer that can never be given to Jane, when she cries near the beginning of the novel: What cycle of life are we now upon? But Georgina asks: Is that what literature is for, to tell you what you don't know and cannot know in life itself? Georgina tells me frankly, against the pieties, that she sometimes thinks that literature is a form of cheating, of false and fictive security. And sometimes she hates reading, and won't read for months, because it seems so unphysical, a second-hand, sickeningly artificial way of mentally not living.

But after an interval that she sometimes thinks must be final, she keeps coming back to books, again almost involuntarily. When she forgets it is just a book, she says, the literature strikes her with what she otherwise cannot bear to choose seeing or hearing.

> The words have to be hard: if they were less challenging to translate, if the sentence-structures were simpler, they would not make me have to go deeper to understand.

And then, she says, 'I keep moving, backwards and forwards, between the hard text and the memories it has for me, not knowing where I am, except that this is the stuff I need to know more about, if I can stand it.'[4] This contributes to what she half-jokingly calls her evolution. Not that she believes that thinking can solve the problems or cure the conditions. Much of the popular pious vocabulary of growth and change irritates her. But something of the original purpose to thought, a commitment to trying to think about her life, stays with her, even when she is ambivalent about it.

She singles out one devastating moment, one sentence in particular. Late in the book his own body seems to say to Tim, as he tries to drive himself into the ground and it with him:

'You didn't really think I would let you kill us, did you?'

Unnamed, p. 222

Georgina writes in her notes: I find it hard to cope with that sentence—'really', 'let you', 'us'. That secret inner voice saying to its supposed owner, You know I won't let you kill us, I will make you eat and rest.

> It is as though everything good and right, the principle of self-preservation and self-care, is turned on its head here, made bad and cruel in its denial of any end to the suffering. In still fighting for life, in the body howling 'Food, food, food', it is as though the right thing is in a wrong place, confused within a distorted form, the right pattern in the wrong context.

And that is how Georgina sometimes feels herself, ill-put together, fucked up. And yet she says she also cannot help admiring that 'I won't let you kill us' survival voice from the resented body—in whatever way it has to come out. She can't help feeling a sort of re-surprised admiration in relation to anything that will fight, for itself and despite itself, and in half-deceived defiance of all that it knows could be said against the effort. Just that it will fight, involuntarily or even discreditably, by means of delusion or will. That it will go on stupidly, stubbornly, rebelliously, whatever it is or whatever its name is. The unnamed.

Here is another of those out-of-place places she highlights. Tim, nearly broken on the road, his mobile dead, finds a pay-phone and a few bits of loose change to ring Jane. The body had cried for food, food, food, and he had fed it. 'I've fed the son of a bitch,' he tells her, 'and now we're standing outside the mini-mart.' Which mini-mart? she asks, Tell me where you are and I'll pick you up. Come home, you need to come home. 'We're feeling better,' he merely replies. And she, not understanding, has to ask, 'Are you with someone?' We are fine, is all he says—but he is running out of change.

'Tim!'
'Don't worry about us,' he said.
He supposed that decided it: he wasn't going to be picked up.

Unnamed, p. 201

That is how a decision gets made now, seemingly the wrong round, back-to-front. Not 'he had decided it', but rather that the following along of a certain way has suddenly become decisive, too late for anything else. At some level this almost perverse act seems right to Georgina, as a form of life, compared to the ponderous two-stage model of the rational plan in advance followed by its deliberate and careful execution. What the hell. But at another level it is also of course just letting it happen heedlessly or recklessly, the irresponsibility that comes like a devil out of the patterns of despair. It is like doing something, says Georgina in her notes, ahead of knowing what you are doing, or have done, and only then realizing it almost immediately afterwards. It is like *finding yourself* doing something, before any thought of it. I keep writing 'like' and I will tell you why, she says: it is because I can only tell what things may be like, can guess or fear, but not what they really are.

I know this sounds morally terrible, she writes, but I can't quite tell the difference between this 'decision' being life and this 'decision' being mad—though I do know the outcome of its having been one rather than other can turn out afterwards to be devastatingly clear. And then there comes that moment when you realize, probably too late, that I've been doing it all wrong, and thinking it all wrong as well. And instead of the thinking being to some extent an alternative to the way my life has been going, perhaps unconsciously it has been entirely conditioned by it, perhaps it has not even consciously tried to be much different from it.

And then that whole impossible realization will go away again, so you can go back to being yourself, until something like this book reminds you of what you fear to see *and* are afraid not to see.

In just that sort of mess Tim thinks it is an act of selflessness—cruel only to be kind—to refuse Jane's help and let her go. It would be to save her from him by throwing himself away, as though now in this twisted tangle of instincts in predicament the fight has to be, not to win, but to lose. Jane comes to him in a dingy café, and says to him to tell her honestly if, in this extremity, this is now the best or only way he has left to live. Tell her if he has to go it alone, tell her that he does not want her, and if so 'I'll go away,' 'I will leave you alone'.

He sat very still like a sullen boy whose stunted brain lacked the resources to admit error and forsake the lost days for a better way. ... He sat silent and unmoving. Her chin was against his shoulder. He felt her hot tears.

She felt his reply in the vibrations of his body.

'I don't want you,' he said.

p. 244

It is another 'decision'. But this self-sacrifice is also self-destruction, a despair of himself that is by cruel irony hurtful to the love she still deeply wants to offer him. When he says to her 'Be happy. Remarry.', 'I can't believe you'd say that' is her reply (*Unnamed*, p. 253). We think there are limits, but there is no limit to how far this can now go. And part of Georgina rather terribly loves that release, even when it seems childish, like a sullen boy. Throwing it all up but without admitting it; kicking off against the rules by going destructively AWOL: what does it all matter, could not care less, nothing to stop me, no more compromises, no safe-illusory middle-class life, nothing or everything left to lose. 'Be happy. Remarry. And I will go on. And keep going on and on.'

When the good thing becomes bad, she writes, or the bad thing has good in it, then in that mess I can't properly make out the crucial differences any more. That is what it feels like a lot of the time to me, that the key elements of life have mutated into some horribly twisted compound that I have become, like the walker caught between mind and body and still going on and on and on, without a goal. But I also kinda admire that in him too: the stubborn, raw, involuntary force of it, and again I wonder if it isn't related to some lost but better version, the belief in going on forward, not just stoically or with the promise of reward, but full on without the assurance of where to or what for. I have done bad stuff with the same vitality as if it were good, to get the dopamine fix in feeling alive. I suppose that comes out of the mix-up of what they call 'value-systems', that a bad thing in one perspective has signs of what is good from another, and sometimes that exhilarates and sometimes it scares me.

This is when immanence—that state fluctuating between chaos and order discussed in the previous chapter—veers more towards chaos, chaos experimentally pushing at order to see how much more it can take, in a person, than is conventionally allowed. Conrad knows this unstable equilibrium when he writes of those exiles and outcasts, 'without a fireside or an affection they may call their own', who want to return home, bearing a clear conscience to go home with. 'I don't know how much Jim understood; but I know he felt, he felt confusedly but powerfully, the demand of some such truth or some such illusion—I don't care how you call it, there is so little difference, and the difference means so little' (*Lord Jim*, chapter 21, pp. 206–7). Georgina is interested when there seems so little difference between need and fantasy, so much confusion of one in another, in the struggle to have a life. But then, in the upshot of blind impulse, she believes a slight difference, one degree or another, can after all turn out to mean so much.

Ferris's novel tries to tilt itself again, and turn its compass-needle towards order. When Tim learns Jane is dying of cancer, he almost heroically manages to force his way back to her, walking back against his walk's direction, circling round bit by bit, day by day. This is, for him, to 'be more than the sum of his urges', it is to recover human love as lending purpose to a life (*Unnamed*, p. 264), and it is the old, straight direction for good we feel glad to admire. And yet when, against all odds, she recovers, it is then that 'the urgency to return, the motivation to get back to her, began to wane' (*Unnamed*, p. 296): the rush of effort subsides when it is no longer a matter of life and death but just life again. Then you go back to your walks, or whatever have become your own fixes, resuming your own bits of chaos or habit. Reading of these possibilities in books, reading of when they are lost or squandered again, these are the moments that kill you, where you die a bit again, writes Georgina, quoting:

> and a wave of death washed over him. Not biological death, which brought relief, but the death that harrows the living by giving them a glimpse of the life they're being denied.
>
> *Unnamed*, p. 254

*

I can't clearly make out what I know should be the crucial differences, Georgina repeats. This helps explain why Marlow witnessing the ruined young mess that is Jim, and trying to make him out, is so compelling to her. Disaster, failure, scandal, truth and fear of the truth, irrevocable shame: never to get over it or away with it or from it, but to have to try to live on after it nonetheless—these are the nominal terms of life for the young man as he goes into exile, in search of a second life. 'He was running,' writes Conrad, and adds, 'Absolutely running, with nowhere to go' (*Lord Jim*, chapter 13, p. 157). And it is in the long-running aftermath that, crucially for Georgina, Marlow himself cannot make out what ought to be a vital difference in Jim between defiance and denial, fight or flight, in the act of attempted forgetting or overcoming: 'Firmness of courage or effort of fear? What do you think?' (chapter 10, p. 133). Marlow's own confidence is shaken by his failure to provide an answer:

> I strained my mental eyesight only to discover that, as with the complexion of all our actions, the shade of difference was so delicate that it was impossible to say.
>
> Chapter 19, p. 187

It was not a lie—but it wasn't truth all the same. It was something … There was not the thickness of a sheet of paper between the right and wrong of this affair.

Chapter 11, p. 138

Marlow says to an experienced old colleague that the young sailor's facing up to the charges, instead of running away, is a sort of courage, after all. Captain Brierly replies that he would sooner Jim had run away: the only courage worth having, he says, is if it keeps a man straight (chapter 6, p. 92).

Whatever Jim did or did not do, was or wasn't, seems in its obscure truth to Marlow 'momentous enough to affect mankind's conception of itself' (chapter 8, p. 112). How was I to save everyone? Jim asks Marlow, in direct challenge of his preconceptions. Jim says in mitigation of himself:

> 'Hang it—to do a thing like that you must believe there is a chance, one in a thousand, at least, some ghost of a chance; and you would not have believed. Nobody would have believed. You think me a cur for standing there, but what would you have done? What! You can't tell—nobody can tell … '
>
> He drew quick breaths at every few words and shot quick glances at my face, as though in his anguish he were watchful of the effect. He was not speaking to me, he was only speaking before me, in a dispute with an invisible personality, an antagonistic and inseparable partner of his existence—another possessor of his soul. These were issues beyond the competency of a court of inquiry: it was a subtle and momentous quarrel as to the true essence of life.
>
> Chapter 8, p. 111

Without hope of or belief in success, what would *you* have done? But Marlow does not feel unequivocally kind or conventionally helpful towards the unfortunate young man, when he offers a challenge which is at once both self-interested and justifiable. Marlow responds, inside, with something tougher and less automatic than dutifully decent second-order feelings:

> I felt the risk I ran of being circumvented, blinded, decoyed, bullied, perhaps, into taking a definite part in a dispute impossible of decision … I can't explain to you who haven't seen him and who hear his words only at second hand the mixed nature of my feelings. It seemed to me I was being made to comprehend the Inconceivable—and I know of nothing to compare with the discomfort of such a sensation. I was made to look at the convention that lurks in all truth and on the essential sincerity of falsehood.
>
> Chapter 8, p. 111

There is part of Marlow that understands full well how Jim must try to let himself off the hook, shielding himself from the unbearable, and there is also part of him that cannot bear to see Jim try to do it. That is what he means by the falsehood inextricable from the sincerity in Jim's question—as if it made a difference whether Marlow would have done just the same! The sincerity and the falsehood go on in Jim at different levels—the chain of command, as Joshua Ferris called it, changing from moment to moment. 'I had no intention for the sake of barren truth,' says Marlow, 'to rob him of the smallest particle of any saving grace that would come his way' (chapter 7, p. 102). Indeed, he isn't even sure how much Jim is in control of the shifts he is trying to make: 'and I suspect he did not know either; for it is my belief no man understands quite his own artful dodges to escape from the grim shadow of self-knowledge' (chapter 7, p. 102).

Georgina asks, why is it *barren* truth, in 'I had no intention for the sake of barren truth to rob him of the smallest particle of any saving grace ...' And she writes: 'Like, you can't *make* anything out of it. So it becomes wholly negative, pointlessly destructive.' She likes the detailed phrasing in that 'no man understands quite his own artful dodges'—the 'quite' that means you understand enough for it to be painful, to be avoided as much as you can. But a moment later Jim is involuntarily fantasizing out-loud about what it would have been like had he actually taken that moment on ship to be what he had always romantically wanted to be—heroic. '"My God! What a chance missed!", he blazed out, but the ring of the last "missed" resembled a cry wrung out by pain' (chapter 7, p. 104). 'He was very far away from me who watched him across three feet of space': as if, again, he was speaking not 'to me' so much as 'before me': that is what the metaphysical means in these novels, when the physical won't bear or explain it.

And still Marlow has to overhear there what should never be said aloud, without saving grace. Jim keeps giving away these terrible glimpses through the masks, the conventions, the rents in the thick fog. This is a young man in a disgrace yet here he is visibly thinking again about what he might have done. 'Ah, he was an imaginative beggar! He would give himself away ... I could see in his glance darted into the night all his inner being':

> He had no leisure to regret what he had lost, he was so wholly and naturally concerned for what he had failed to obtain. ... With every instant he was penetrating deeper into the impossible world of romantic achievements. He got to the heart of it at last! A strange look of beatitude overspread his features, his eyes sparkled in the light of the candle burning between us; he positively smiled ...
>
> Chapter 7, p. 104

'My God, what a chance missed!' he blurts out again in that out-of-place ecstasy. To which unbearable cry of the ego Marlow cannot help replying, mercilessly, 'If you had stuck to the ship you mean!' (chapter 7, p. 105). It is like the moment of Jim's fall happening again, one of those little moments of non-biological death described in *The Unnamed* when the reality principle kicks in hard.

> He turned to me, his eyes suddenly amazed and full of pain, with a bewildered, startled, suffering face, as though he had tumbled down from a star. Neither you nor I will ever look like this on any man.
>
> Chapter 7, p. 105

We perhaps know better how to hide. But Marlow's 'if you had stuck to the ship' is a puncturing reply that makes barren

> those struggles of the individual trying to save from the fire the idea of what his moral identity should be, this precious notion of a convention, only one of the rules of the game, nothing more ...
>
> Chapter 7, p. 103

Again, Marlow hates seeing through the clumsy salve of self-extenuation, 'the convention that lurks in all truth'. It makes 'the blight of futility' fall upon Marlow's spirits and upon all the talk between the two men (chapter 13, p. 152). Georgina feels the whole protective artifice being taken apart: It is only an '*idea*' of moral identity; worse, it is only an idea of what it '*should be*': and worse still, less an idea than a precious '*convention*'. 'But all the same', adds Marlow and Conrad, 'so terribly effective in its assumption'—for as Georgina rawly puts it, 'It's got you anyway, no matter if you even dared know it is a rubbishy cover-up; you have to try to have that sincere lie, in order to have something by which to keep going. Truth or illusion, it's survival.'

I know these safeguards, writes Georgina in her reading notes, and the damage they do even in the damage-control. You have to try to hang onto *some* of the bad thing, because if the thought of it is still partly there, then you mustn't forget it so much that you can be ambushed by suddenly having to remember it totally. If you always know the bad thing and keep it a bit close, near-ish, like an injection of cowpox against the infection of smallpox, then the bad does not come back so hard—and also it keeps the good stuff safely away. And you need to do that, to cut the risk of greater pain, because you can't ever have the good stuff again, anyway, not totally. But then sometimes I do make some effort over a small thing, an effort that stands for more than the thing itself perhaps, and then I find myself thinking, it is only like taking the piss out of trying for something bigger. Which makes me then want to do what Conrad calls 'flinging away your daily bread' (chapter 19, p. 187).

Georgina reminds me of something from another of her extreme books, *Home* by Marilynne Robinson. It concerns Jack Broughton, the black sheep of the religious family, the figure of shame, who returns home after twenty years' absence to try to make some kind of peace with his dying reverend father. He has done some terrible things, he knows, and his sister Glory still tries to mitigate his guilt:

> 'That was all so long ago. You were young.'
>
> 'No. I wasn't young. I don't believe I ever was young'. Then he said, 'Excuses scare me, Glory. They make me feel like I'm losing hold. I can't explain it. But please don't try to make excuses for me. I might start believing them sometimes.'[5]

Jack *needs* his guilt now without excuse or absolution, says Georgina. Even as ruined integrity, it is the only thing holding him together: to lose it would be like 'losing hold'. But it is important that he 'can't explain it': as if his life-impulse now depends on hanging on to something that in some horribly tangled way also seems to condemn his life. Someone, Georgina says, once said to me that guilt is worse than shame. But it isn't to me because guilt is specific—located in a particular deed—and internal. You don't have that localized place with shame, it goes every-where. Jack knows he never belonged in that conventionally good and pious family. His shame began before he did much he could be judged for.

We talk about what it might be like to be more than 'let off'. But there is nothing here that will do what is miraculously done at the end of *The Pilgrim's Progress* when the pilgrims cast off their fears on the bank of the river of death, or at the close of *The Winter's Tale* when Perdita calls upon Hermione to 'be stone no more':

> Come,
> I'll fill your grave up: stir, nay, come away,
> Bequeath to death your numbness, for from him
> Dear life redeems you.
>
> *The Winter's Tale*, 5.3 100–3

Most commentators say that Perdita is offering (metaphorically) to backfill the grave with earth, because it is no longer needed. But Georgina thinks the casting-off has to be more earned than that, that Paulina herself, an old woman, is offering her aged life for Hermione's in a kind of sacrifice and transfusion, like bequeathing to death your numbness a line later. To shed a past life, to be able to leave it behind, where something or someone goes back, so as to enable you to go forward: that is the lost alternative to desperately driving on and using up a life, like Macbeth so far gone in the middle of the river 'that should I wade no more/ Returning were as tedious as go o'er' (*Macbeth*, 3.4 137–8).[6] He cannot stop, for what might overtake him.

And Jack's sister Glory cannot stop trying to give Jack a home, some peace. She is unlike Marlow because, in her goodness and her closeness, she needs to try to help and console. Instead, across a tough distance, without the veil of excuses, what Marlow can see in his mind's eye is the invisible hiding place in the man he witnesses:

> It is when we try to grapple with another man's intimate need that we perceive how incomprehensible, wavering, and misty are the beings that share with us the sight of the stars and the warmth of the sun. It is as if loneliness were a hard and absolute condition of existence; the envelope of flesh and blood on which our eyes are fixed melts before the outstretched hand, and there remains only the capricious, unconsolable, and elusive spirit which no eye can follow, no hand can grasp.
>
> *Lord Jim*, chapter 16, p. 175

I say to Georgina this is the sort of lengthy passage some readers of Conrad find almost deliberately difficult, portentously abstract, and on the verge of the incomprehensible. But though she somewhat agrees, she says some of these sentences have made her think as if for days. This passage is a vision because it is about what cannot be seen, she says; it has to be written because it is about all that can't be said to someone else; the language is hard in both senses of the word because the invisible and unsayable and unbearable thing is even harder to grasp and needs to be felt as being so. 'As if loneliness were a *hard* and absolute condition of existence.' That's why 'the envelope of flesh and blood *melts*', and wants to melt, but only to give way to the hard thing it encloses. And so what it is about for me, says Georgina finally, is that less-outward reality I may be ignoring, and even at the same time mis-inhabiting, as I go on going wrong. The word that kills me is not that the spirit within the flesh and blood is 'capricious' or 'elusive': it is the word in between the two, 'unconsolable'.

It is weird, she writes, that I do not find that depressing, because the book is about the massive futility of trying to help, the terrible negative of the absolute loneliness—while we pretend we are here together sharing 'the sight of the stars and the warmth of the sun'. I can't say why, but after reading *Lord Jim* I believe *more* in the point of it all, not less, because of Marlow not trying to arrange consolation or uplift. I do not like deliberately 'positive' messages, the unconvincing will in them. But to me the negative is not nihilism: it means first of all *not* being able to make something up to cheer or cure all too easily. It is a sort of respect for the real as resistant: the inconceivable, invisible, unconsolable, incomprehensible. 'In the destructive element immerse' says this novel (chapter 19, p. 200); immerse in the *Unnamed*, says that other book. There is a sort of remainder—the metaphysical power of the language, the awe of the terrible realization—above and beyond the concept of it all being meaningless and futile. The literature has a sort of rightly suppressed yearning in what it is stopped from directly saying or wanting; wins a power in the unwelcome prohibition from being positive, when the positive has to go into the negative and somehow survive within it.

Can you give a final example of this? I ask. This passage about Jim's effect on Marlow, she replies, and points me to the quotation in her reading notes:

> It had the power to drive me out of my conception of existence, out of that shelter each of us makes for himself to creep under in moments of danger, as a tortoise withdraws within its shell. For a moment I had a view of a world that seemed to wear a vast and dismal aspect of disorder … But still—it was only a moment: I went back into my shell directly. One *must*—don't you know?—though I seemed to have lost all my words in the chaos of dark thoughts I had contemplated for a second or two beyond the pale. These came back, too, very soon, for words also belong to the sheltering conception of light and order which is our refuge.
>
> Chapter 33, p. 274

Joshua Ferris's man walked right out of that refuge and shelter to the place where humans don't know where they are. Which he says, many people perhaps may only find in the final days and moments of their lives, as if we put it off but also can't quite. Hence that second or two outside the shell, or beyond the pale: 'momentous enough to affect mankind's conception of itself', with 'the power to drive me out of my conception of existence'. 'Words also belong to the sheltering' but these words are, for a second, not like that, they let in the freezing cold.

Of course it is impossible to get to and stay in these places of maximum realization voluntarily or for long, even though the evasive suspicion of their always being there remains, like insecurity, and comes back to extreme consciousness occasionally to crack the shell. Above all, Georgina herself keeps coming back to the sentence in *The Unnamed*: 'So much of what he was was involuntary'. She believes that in its false attempts at integration the world is not set up—in 'mankind's conception of itself'—to understand that. But literature *is* set up, she says, to work both ways ('was was') on the edge between the voluntary and involuntary, able deliberately to create a non-deliberate situation that makes the unnamed, and all that does not easily fit into the world, yield its hard voice. She is herself, not always willingly or carefully or happily, an experimenter.

CHAPTER 10

THE ANTHOLOGIST

Some things that seem otherwise impossible, poetry can do. The poem is 'The Salutation' by Thomas Traherne (1637–4), which lay unpublished until 1903:

> These little limbs,
> These eyes and hands which here I find,
> These rosy cheeks wherewith my life begins,
> Where have ye been? behind
> What curtain were ye from me hid so long?
> Where was, in what abyss, my speaking tongue?
>
> When silent I
> So many thousand, thousand years
> Beneath the dust did in a chaos lie,
> How could I smiles or tears,
> Or lips or hands or eyes or ears perceive?
> Welcome ye treasures which I now receive.
>
> I that so long
> Was nothing from eternity,
> Did little think such joys as ear or tongue
> To celebrate or see:
> Such sounds to hear, such hands to feel, such feet,
> Beneath the skies on such a ground to meet.
>
> New burnished joys,
> Which yellow gold and pearls excel!
> Such sacred treasures are the limbs in boys,
> In which a soul doth dwell;
> Their organizèd joints and azure veins
> More wealth include than all the world contains.
>
> From dust I rise,
> And out of nothing now awake;
> These brighter regions which salute mine eyes,
> A gift from God I take.
> The earth, the seas, the light, the day, the skies,
> The sun and stars are mine if those I prize.

Long time before
I in my mother's womb was born,
A God, preparing, did this glorious store,
The world, for me adorn.
Into this Eden so divine and fair,
So wide and bright, I come His son and heir.

A stranger here
Strange things doth meet, strange glories see;
Strange treasures lodged in this fair world appear,
Strange all and new to me;
But that they mine should be, who nothing was,
That strangest is of all, yet brought to pass.

'Reading should not be only about people in trouble, or all about human misery,' she told me—neither in the poems themselves nor in the readers of them. 'And this poem by Traherne goes back to something much earlier and purer than that.' This is Angela Macmillan who since 2010 has become a notable complier of anthologies of poetry. She edits a series entitled *A Little Aloud* published by Chatto & Windus, and has been praised in reviews as 'a natural anthologist'. It is an apt description because this editorial work which has taken place in later life, has been a natural extension of being a serious reader, bringing together what Iris Murdoch called a collection of resources: 'refuges, lights, visions, deep sources, protections, strongholds, footholds, icons, starting points, sacraments, pearls of great price'.[1] They are, said Murdoch, in the spirit of Philippians 4:e8:

> whatsoever things are true, whatsoever things are honest, whatsoever things are just, whatsoever things are pure, whatsoever things are lovely, whatsoever things are of good report; if there be any virtue, and if there be any praise, think on these things

Though not a formally religious person, Angie says that now, in her early seventies, if she had to choose just one poem, it would be Traherne's 'The Salutation'—a thing to 'think on' for the greeting of life found in all those verbs it uses in delight: to 'welcome', 'celebrate', 'meet', 'salute', and 'prize'. If there be any virtue, any praise whatsoever, it is to be found in the sense of plenitude released and valued because of verses of good report like these.

'The Salutation' she says to me, makes possible two things at once—a *baby*, yet with an innocently *adult* consciousness inside it, in wonder at 'the gift' of its own life. Impossibly, the newborn child is given a voice to say '*these*': looking at 'these' limbs, 'these' eyes and hands which are its own, even 'these' rosy cheeks. It is, Angie says, in marked contrast to a murderous Macbeth, seeing on himself the blood he has shed, 'How is't with me ... ?/ What hands are here? Ha! they pluck out mine eyes' (2.2 56–7); or to a Lear barely recovering from his collapse into madness, 'I know not what to say/ I will not swear these are my hands.' (4.6 55–6). 'These' in Traherne is to do with the pristine now-ness of the poem, the spirit inside the baby coming into present awareness of its own bodily life. 'Welcome ye treasures which I *now* receive' says the second stanza, and 'And out of nothing *now* awake' says the fifth. It is a voice of now, of new wonder, as if for the first time in the world.

And later in the poem, in stanzas 3 and 4, 'these' becomes another even finer word of implicit valuing of quality, 'such': '*Such* sounds to hear, *such* hands to feel, *such* feet/ Beneath the skies on *such* a ground to meet', '*Such* sacred treasures are the limbs in boys'. Angie loves even that little word 'in'—not merely 'the limbs of boys' but 'the limbs *in* boys' as if like 'organizèd joints' two lines later, they bespeak something not added or owned but intrinsic to the very quick of life forming itself. It is an x-ray vision through which you can feel the elasticity of muscle within the flesh, and imagine a creative principle working within the underlying structure of the children. Angie loves it when she sees the people with whom she reads spot such minute details, or does it herself: there is a delight in the subtle life of the text itself; there is a joy in the sheer care of someone noticing and detecting it.

Normally we value what we have previously taken for granted too late, after loss or nearer life's end. And that must be because in life a happening and the articulated consciousness of it are never so synchronized as Traherne's poetry here makes them. 'It is ironic, it seems a humanly fallen thing, that we cannot know life even as we have it, that there is always a time-lag as of a creature no longer instinctively whole in all its times and capacities': Angie recalls T. S. Eliot in 'The Dry Salvages in *Four Quartets*, 'We had the experience but missed the meaning'. Only in 'The Salutation', the experience and its meaning are for once made coincident.

And yet even so the wonder at this new life also immediately turns backwards. All these bodily things now around me: 'Where have ye *been*?' (She emphasizes that last word, it marks the openly wondering voice she values and wants.) And in the poem's shorthand, the answer is already half-given at the line-ending, 'behind':

> Where have ye been? behind
> What curtain were ye from me hid so long?

'Behind', she says, is mind-blowing: a word opening up a whole new dimension in perspective. And the poem is full of these little messages, especially in the short lines that begin the stanzas: 'When silent I', 'I that so long', 'Long time before'. They have an effect even *before* the completion of the sentence that makes full sense of them. And as we talk about this, I try to say that the poem is about such initial half-uttered things, infant inklings of the spirit, that—like inchoate nerve impulses—come just ahead of their physical fulfilment in mundane sense, but seek it and spark it.

We also talk about a video recording I had asked Angie to watch in advance of our conversation, a *Reader* group also thinking about 'The Salutation'.

Some of the group talk as mothers, knowing what babies give them, feeling themselves speak lovingly on the baby's behalf. But Angie, though a mother herself, says it is herself she thinks of most when reading the poem. And in the recording the person who most interests her is one of the early members and founders of *The Reader*, along with Angie herself, Kate McDonnell.

Kate now in her sixties has been largely confined to a wheelchair since her twenties, with chronic arthritis. We watch her reading these moments:

> These little limbs,
> These eyes and hands which here I find,
> These rosy cheeks wherewith my life begins ...
>
> When silent I
> So many thousand, thousand years
> Beneath the dust did in a chaos lie,
> How could I smiles or tears,
> Or lips or hands or eyes or ears perceive?
> Welcome ye treasures which I now receive.
>
> Such sounds to hear, such hands to feel, such feet,
> Beneath the skies on such a ground to meet.
>
> Such sacred treasures are the limbs in boys,
> In which a soul doth dwell;
> Their organizèd joints and azure veins
> More wealth include than all the world contains.

Kate barely ever mentions her disability, though she is often in pain. But this time suddenly but quietly, she says:

> That kind of delighted physical sense ... you take it for granted, those 'limbs' and so on. Maybe you get to a certain age when you do appreciate it. But I don't know whether when you are a boy or girl you do ... though you have fleeting moments, don't you. Maybe because I lost it early, it was different; whereas I think for most people it goes gradually. For me it was quite sudden: in my twenties I had that 'welcome these treasures which I now receive', but I had it after they had *gone*. I suppose anyone getting older feels more like that. But perhaps I had such a very, very strong sense of that. I suppose I am wondering whether ... I look at a photograph from before and I think 'Is that *me*? Why didn't I go up a mountain more while I had the body to do it in?'

She wasn't to know of course what lay ahead.

Kate makes this long statement gently and tentatively—'maybe', 'perhaps', 'I suppose'—thinking back without pain or bitterness but willing to be overheard in doing so. When we showed Kate herself the video afterwards, just as she had once shown herself the photograph of her healthier youth, we asked whether she had meant to say something of her illness in that session. 'No,' she replied, 'I don't talk about my illness very much.' It had happened spontaneously, involuntarily:

> It was amazing how it gets you back in *touch* again. It took me back to being a teenager so completely, and then feeling that kind of frustration and shock of having health taken away very suddenly. And that feeling was back in the room, it was back in me, and I had to get it out in the room or it just came out, it didn't feel like a choice. You have no idea it's coming—the thought of it, the saying it. And there you are with this feeling coming up inside you, and before you know it, it is coming out of your mouth, unstoppable. It was a kind of benign ambush.

This comes from somewhere before consciousness. It is a physical mentality, driving thoughts up from below, prior to mental volition, and as such is characteristic of literary reading as reading in action. As a consequence the poem can say to the sad norms of consciousness: Imagine if experience did not realize only belatedly what now is gone and, before, was taken for granted. Imagine instead an innocent consciousness expressed within a tone of wonder for the unbelievably good thing of life felt at the very time of its happening and being.

After the video Angie and I talk more about the poem, together. What she loves is *connection* whether it is in large or small—that is, across different whole works, or between different little words in the same small work. It is not simple connection, like easy replication or synonym, but what Wordsworth in the 'Preface to *Lyrical Ballads*' calls similitude found in dissimilitude with that sudden electric charge of subtle recognition, identity, and kinship which, for him, is the language of creation as well as poetry. 'The same but not the same is what interests me,' she says, 'The same but slightly different, where the "slightly" is also vital.' And often the connection is found only retrospectively, as if for all the fallenness of not being able to live fully in time with time, that is now how the mind *should* work—not in controlled forward planning but in finding back-to-front what it has been involved in doing. 'It all gets made up behind you, things come together in later consciousness. I am not an abstract thinker who can start from the beginning, from some first principle,' Angie concludes, 'I need reading to help make me think.' Thinking for her is like finding the connection suddenly registered between the end of the first stanza

> Where was, in what abyss, my *speaking* tongue?

and the beginning of the stanza following—which remarkably goes not forwards as norms might suggest, but further backwards into pre-existence:

> When *silent* I
> So many thousand, thousand, years ...

'Silent' before 'speaking' comes after it in the next stanza. I think this is partly what the poem is about: the birth of speaking, of being able to articulate and explore what before was silent. And again in terms of slight but vital differences, Angie points to stanza 3:

> I that so long
> Was nothing from eternity,
> Did little think such joys as ear or tongue
> To celebrate or see

The quiet subliminal difference between that long *'nothing'* in the second line and the sudden *'little'* think in the third is greater and more essential—as the difference between nothing and something—than the cumulative difference that exists more simply between there being 'a little' and there being 'a lot'. There is a preconscious 'long-ing' also in all that, a longing to become something, a human creature made flesh. But what really interests Angie is another intricate difference in the first stanza still:

> These eyes and hands which here I find,
> These rosy cheeks wherewith my life begins,
> Where have ye been? behind
> What curtain were ye from me hid so long?

It makes a little but significant difference that 'I find' is not in charge at the head of line 1, or that it is not more lineally and casually 'which I find here': 'here I find'. Just as it makes a difference that it isn't phrased as 'behind what curtain were ye hid from me so long?' but rather 'behind what curtain were *ye from me* hid so long?'. What Angie is interested in here, in the delay of the verb 'hid', is the close relation of 'ye from me' which, she says, are 'in rhyming contrast' and then their relation to that earlier 'I'. We have been jumping excitedly around the poem's connections, like synapses in its newly working brain. 'The connections, that's what is alive in the poem,' she says. But we pause for a minute when I read her something very different that occurs to me, from a recent non-fictional work by the novelist Tim Parks on brain and consciousness.

Parks reports on how he sees scores of things on first awakening in the morning, but then thinks how they get turned into conventional language-report:

> I see bits of lots of things … and now I realise that there are no gaps between these parts. I mean there are probably scores of things I see (part of) if I bothered to list them—switch lampshade picture sock (one) tissues (many) carpet floor book wrist-watch hinge of wardrobe door—but although I perceive these things as separate there are no spaces between them the way there are spaces between the words that designate them, even when I don't put commas in the list ….
>
> Experience is more continuous and more happening at once, as it were, than words where only one thing can be said at a time. Words are linear. They sort things out, pull them out of the mix.[2]

It is no good if the words are automatically linear, just going on left to right for the easy processing of reality, piece by piece, comma by comma, in a medium quite foreign to it. But the great linguistic moment in literature is when as the poet Yeats put it, the poem goes 'click': words that had seemed separate units at once inter-connect and lock together, and all those distinct grammatical 'now's suddenly link—previously separate bits and items melting and flowing into each other without a gap. Those are the connections, when the seams disappear, that Angie relishes: 'behind/ What curtain were ye from me hid so long?' Those nascent particles of thought—'behind-what', 'ye-me', 'hid-so-long'—are what the grammar must adapt itself to, working in the spaces that the first-mind (as it were) leaves and finds for it. Then in the second place everything enters the sense of the world.

Even in that larger, wider world what Angie values are connections, lest otherwise her life should have been only an unthinking sequence of 'and then … and then … and then': for otherwise, as she puts it, it is all 'blur and bleurgh'. She points to what George Eliot says in *Middlemarch*: 'Has it not by this time ceased to be remarkable—is it not rather that we expect in men, that they should have numerous strands of experience lying side by side and never compare them with each other?' (chapter 63). She does want to compare the many strands, one with another. Serious reading began for her in mid-life, she tells me, as a result of a simple tool: the use of a pencil to mark in the margin certain passages that moved, interested, baffled, or upset her, without her first knowing why completely: 'When you look back at those instinctive marks, you discover in their subliminal relations what you were thinking but didn't know you were thinking. Putting it together—the poem, the novel, your marked places, bits of your own life too. Before I joined a shared reading group in my forties, before I used a pencil to mark the places, I would want to be reading all the time— but without knowing what I was reading *for*.'

The first time she went to a reading group over thirty years ago, the poem was Tennyson's 'Tithonus':

> The woods decay, the woods decay and fall,
> The vapours weep their burthen to the ground,
> Man comes and tills the field and lies beneath,
> And after many a summer dies the swan.

She still recalls and feels the quality of the after-pause and silence in the group when the *Reader* leader finished saying those opening lines aloud. She thinks now that much of the effect was caused through those repeated 'and's in lines 3 and 4: it makes a difference to *us*, emotionally and individually in the cycle, but it makes no difference to the system we live within and die by: man comes, and tills the field — *and* lies beneath it. That second 'and' feels so different from the first, but nothing in it admits that.

'I am interested in "nothing",' she goes on, wryly, re-quoting Traherne:

> I that so long
> Was nothing from eternity
>
> From dust I rise,
> And out of nothing now awake
>
> Strange treasures lodged in this fair world appear,
> Strange all and new to me;
> But that they mine should be, who nothing was,
> That strangest is of all, yet brought to pass.

'The idea of nothing and the idea of not existing any more are suddenly interesting to me at the moment.' She is referring quietly to her age and significant current health problems of her own.

But now she points me to two prose passages she has noted in advance of this interview in relation to 'The Salutation' and to coping with the very idea of not being. One is just a single sentence from Samuel Beckett and his *Textes pour rien*:

> Oh, I know I too shall cease and be as when I was not yet, only all over instead of in store.

The other is from the very beginning of Vladimir Nabokov's autobiography *Speak, Memory*:

> The cradle rocks above an abyss, and common sense tells us that our existence is but a brief crack of light between two eternities of darkness. Although the two are identical twins, man, as a rule, views the prenatal abyss with more calm than the one he is heading for (at some forty-five hundred heartbeats an hour). I know, however, of a young chronophobiac who experienced something like panic when looking for the first time at homemade movies that had been taken a few weeks before his birth. He saw a world that was practically unchanged—the same house, the same people— and then realized that he did not exist there at all and that nobody mourned his absence. He caught a glimpse of his mother waving from an upstairs window, and that unfamiliar gesture disturbed him, as if it were some mysterious farewell. But what particularly frightened him was the sight of a brand-new baby carriage standing there on the porch, with the smug, encroaching air of a coffin; even that was empty, as if, in the reverse course of events, his very bones had disintegrated.[3]

The young chronophobiac was of course himself, so much disturbed by time's lines and loops. But I mention to her Boswell's reporting to Samuel Johnson that the philosopher David Hume in his logical equanimity had claimed to have no terror of death. Hume, said Boswell, was no more uneasy to think he should *not be* after this life, than that he *had not been* before he began to exist. To which Johnson, rooted in both a strong sense of experience and a great fear of dissolution, retorted that the difference was that in dying the man 'gives up all he has'. If Hume really was unafraid of death, then, Johnson declared emphatically, Hume was mad. 'Give us no more of this,' shouted Johnson, his nerves jangled.[4] But Angie still says: These are ways of thinking about nothing, about imagining existence going on after your death.

It is an austere vision, she says: I am no longer thinking about the brevity of life. That feeling of impermanence came to me most powerfully in my earlier reading in middle life, with Tennyson's lyric 'Tears, Idle Tears', and the constant varied refrain at the end of each of the four stanzas: 'the days that are no more'. The words 'no more' often had that shock for me, as though unimaginable. 'And thinking of the days that are no more', 'So sad, so fresh, the days that are no more':

> Ah, sad and strange as in dark summer dawns
> The earliest pipe of half-awaken'd birds
> To dying ears, when unto dying eyes
> The casement slowly grows a glimmering square;
> So sad, so strange, the days that are no more.

'O Death in Life, the days that are no more!' That death-bed scene, the darkening window, what the ears can make out when the eyes can hardly do so: these have been related in me with the first four lines of 'Tithonus', and partly why I wanted as a mature student to do a PhD connected with Tennyson. In particular trying to go on from *In Memoriam* 56 where Nature is given a voice to say she cares for nothing, all shall go, she knows no more: then, says Tennyson, 'Shall he, Man', nature's last work –

> Who trusted God was love indeed
> And love Creation's final law—
> Tho' Nature, red in tooth and claw
> With ravine, shriek'd against his creed—
>
> Who loved, who suffer'd countless ills,
> Who battled for the True, the Just,
> Be blown about the desert dust,
> Or seal'd within the iron hills?
>
> No more? …

That terrible driven move across the line, across the stanza, to those two blank words of his, ending in a question mark. Angie says: I'm interested in the sense that its not possible simply to 'get over' loss by keeping on going forward—because the absence will always be present. I am more involved in the effort to come to a point from which it's possible to think back, not simply to remember, but as if to recall something anterior to it all, behind it all. And now I realize that the sense of something before or behind or earlier is in a lot of my poetry choices, as though what or where we come from, is more important to me now than to where it is all going or leading.

Compared to when I started work on Tennyson, I am consciously nearer the end. Can't help that now. So at this stage I am looking for something less personally emotional in a way, something more steadying and austere—to do with the laws of not-being both before and after you are a person here. So, Nabokov's sense of passing between two eternities of darkness on either side, is something which a poem might temporarily hold in the place of 'now', just as 'The Salutation' does. Or Beckett's time when 'I too shall cease and be as when I was not yet': cease *and* be— meaning, really: not be, a future where there won't be future. I almost hear it as: 'I shall … be/ as I was/ when I was not yet', but that second 'I' has gone, and the very word 'I', used ever so slightly differently in each case, has to cope with the unspeakable and almost unimaginable. To imagine that that 'I', which we are forced to use grammatically in order to make sense, will not think or feel or exist at all. It is for me, as I am, to imagine in future no 'I' or 'me', even *now* from within myself. I am interested in what goes beyond the limits of our understanding and our expression—and that we know it does. 'I know I too will cease ... ' 'I know no more'.

She has brought another poem to go with this thought of nothing. It is Wendell Berry's 'The Slip' on an erosion which is also a reclamation of the earth:

> The river takes the land, and leaves nothing.
> Where the great slip gave way in the bank
> and an acre disappeared, all human plans
> dissolve. An awful clarification occurs
> where a place was. Its memory breaks
> from what is known now, begins to drift.
> Where cattle grazed and trees stood, emptiness
> widens the air for birdflight, wind, and rain.
> As before the beginning, nothing is there.
> Human wrong is in the cause, human
> ruin in the effect—but no matter;
> all will be lost, no matter the reason.
> Nothing, having arrived, will stay.
> The earth, even, is like a flower, so soon
> passeth it away. And yet this nothing
> is the seed of all—the clear eye
> of Heaven, where all the worlds appear.
> Where the imperfect has departed, the perfect
> begins its struggle to return. The good gift
> begins again its descent. The maker moves
> in the unmade, stirring the water until
> it clouds, dark beneath the surface,
> stirring and darkening the soul until pain
> perceives new possibility. There is nothing
> to do but learn and wait, return to work
> on what remains. Seed will sprout in the scar.
> Though death is in the healing, it will heal.

And here are her pencil-marks: 'The river takes the land, and leaves nothing', 'An awful clarification occurs/ where a place was', 'its memory breaks', 'emptiness', and especially:

> As before the beginning, nothing is there

'Nothing *is* there': another mind-blowing piece of grammar, like Beckett's 'I too shall cease and be as when I was not yet'. And again the poem works imaginatively backwards, as though the act of taking away is a more revelatory process than that of adding: 'And yet this nothing/ is the seed of all'; 'The maker moves/ in the *un*made'—far more than in the 'made'. This is how, crucially for her, an apparent negative, a non-human, a pre-human feeling becomes part of the human: 'There is nothing/ to do but learn and wait' (important, she says, that the line ending comes at 'nothing', before ever you know what then to do), followed by those 're'-words: '*re*turn to work on what *re*mains'. No wonder Angie has also on her list of favoured texts, T. S. Eliot's words from 'East Coker', another of the *Four Quartets*:

> I said to my soul, be still, and wait without hope
> For hope would be hope for the wrong thing; wait without love
> For love would be love of the wrong thing; there is yet faith
> But the faith and the love and the hope are all in the waiting.

What she has marked in that is the word 'without' (instead of going *with* 'the wrong thing'); and then 'yet' signalling the turn of the penultimate line into what the little word 'in' does in the last line by shifting all those fixated nouns into a gerund ('the waiting'). 'There is nothing/to do but ... '

'Nothing' is a more important word than 'all', she says—and when I ask her why she thinks that, she replies: Because 'nothing' is connected with what is terrifying, unthinkable, but in these various verses is a place safely to look at the worst. A caring negation means *not* being able to make something up to cheer or to cure, too easily.

She takes me back to the movement from the penultimate into the last stanza in the Traherne verses. When long before, the speaker lay in his mother's womb:

> A God, preparing, did this glorious store,
> > The world, for me adorn.
> Into this Eden so divine and fair,
> So wide and bright, I come His son and heir.
>
> > A stranger here
> Strange things doth meet, strange glories see;
> Strange treasures lodged in this fair world appear,
> > Strange all and new to me;
> But that they mine should be, who nothing was,
> That strangest is of all, yet brought to pass.

What strikes her is that passage across, from inheriting the earth like God's son and heir, to the abrupt arrival of being also 'A stranger here' when first incarnate. And how that repeated word 'strange' can be turned around, like fear and insecurity made into awe and wonder. It is almost like the opposite, she suddenly thinks, of

Tennyson in *In Memoriam*, where he is made a stranger on the earth not by birth but by bereavement. Yet he too can turn around the word 'strange'. What if from the ship bringing home the body of his dead friend, Arthur Hallam himself walked off alive and well after all:

> And I perceived no touch of change,
>   No hint of death in all his frame,
>   But found him all in all the same,
> I should not feel it to be strange.
> *In Memoriam*, 14

The tonal implication is how strange 'not' to feel it to be strange. Or when looking over dead Hallam's letters, Tennyson suddenly seems to hear his friend's own voice come to life again in the reading of them:

> And strangely on the silence broke
>   The silent-speaking words, and strange
>   Was love's dumb cry defying change
> To test his worth; and strangely spoke
>
> The faith, the vigour, bold to dwell
>   On doubts that drive the coward back
> *In Memoriam*, 95

This strangeness—even about what writing and reading do to the senses—is 'on the very edge of something, the very limit of what you can understand or believe or think is possible'. Angie's PhD thesis was on wavering agnosticism, as compared to downright atheism on the one hand and dogmatic belief on the other, but always pitched just a shade more to the side of believing. 'I wanted to investigate the meaning of agnosticism not as Thomas Huxley, who coined the word, defined it in the name of science and secularization, but as a finely balanced religious position which could be consistent with belief in God.' It included thinking about an old religious text, Bishop Butler's *Analogy of Religion* (1736) which saw a *consistent* pattern of failure, inadequacy, and deficiency in the fallen mortal world, as though that in itself were a structure—not so much accidental or malevolent, but left purposively incomplete. And here Butler offered a tentative imagination at the very limits of our understanding: what if that incompleteness were a systematic pattern because it mirrored everything on this side that would be completed and put right on the other, in the world hereafter. It is something like what Ludwig Wittgenstein said in a letter about his work consisting in two parts—only one of which was written. The other would sound like too easy a get-out if spoken in human terms. But it is precisely the second part, the unwritten and unspoken part, that is the important one, resonant on the other side of the first part because created out of its silent implications, beyond the dared boundaries of human sense.[5] Poetry is that otherwise unwritten part: so in Traherne, eternity is what is 'behind', while in Tennyson the same word—'Behind the veil, behind the veil' (*In Memoriam*, 56)—means 'beyond' imagined from a different direction. And like 'behind', the word 'strange' is also on a borderline, because simultaneously encased here in the world, and finding within it what almost bursts its very own framework:

> Strange treasures lodged in this fair world appear,
> Strange all and new to me;
> But that they mine should be, who nothing was,
> That strangest is of all, yet brought to pass.

'It makes me cry almost every time I read it, and whenever I hear it sung by Wilfred Brown in Gerald Finzi's musical version if it; but cry not out of sorrow.' What she loves in the intricate secrecy of the formulation is that the last two lines are each composed of half lines that work together in complex fashion. The poem gets to them by strange, strange, strange, strange, and then, through the memory of 'nothing', 'strangest'. Or again through 'But that' and 'That': the varied uses of that enabling word. And then 'they mine' in that penultimate line is like 'ye from me' earlier in stanza 1. But above all, she points again to the mid-line break between the two halves: 'they mine should be || who nothing was', 'strangest is of all || yet brought to pass'. There held in line by that caesura, she says, is a release that feels something like what the experience of God must feel like.

Or like what Herbert feels in 'The Flower' when suddenly his depression is lifted:

> It cannot be
> That I am he
> On whom thy tempests fell all night

Pitched in between two eternities for their duration, these poems are indeed written in lines, but what is worked along and down them is non-linear—making connections, links, and ligatures in a counter-linear form that is an alternative way of seeing and thinking. In this, she loves the negatives that are not simply negative—cannot, nothing; she loves the magnetism of pronouns across different times—I am he, they mine should; she loves the word-tools you never look up in a dictionary but which make for the structural possibilities of utterance—that, who, this. She has this strong image of Herbert the poet, bending over his careful small work, as if everything was vital. But what she loves most of all is what is achieved in these poems against all possible odds: —'It cannot be/ That I am he', 'But that they mine should be, who nothing was'.

I ask her: *Are* you religious? And she says she is not, not formally: 'But I find all the reading I most like to do turns out to be religious.' Or doing something for the spirit, in keeping up my spirits. I have told you, and myself, that I don't want life to be made of problems. I don't want the sense of problems to cause what Newman calls 'the temporary obscuration of some master vision'—the thing we lose or forget 'when nothing seems true, or good, or right, or profitable'.[6] I know master vision will seem a bit grand for most of us but keeping an unoccluded sight of something that is not your problems, that is prior to problems, even though disturbed by them and not pretending to ignore them—that is what I am about.

It need not seem big; it can be in a little reminding poem like 'A Scattering' by Christopher Reid. He remembers footage of elephants finding the bones of one of their kind—without hands, as we have, to do anything carefully reverential about it. All they can do is hook up the bones with their trunks, and cast them about here and there, in a great awkward scattering of heavy woe—while (writes the poet) 'the play of their trunks/ lends sprezzatura'. It is that sprezzatura I value—a sort of elegant gifted nonchalance—that is beautifully other than the grief, even in being part of it. Or she thinks of a Norman Nicholson poem, 'Old Man at a Cricket Match', which I think reminds her of her own father, where the poet is struck by a single dialect remark about the doubtful weather: 'It's mending worse'. The sense of mending is still there, as the old man watches: 'Life and the weather mending worse,/ Or worsening better.' Comedy tonally mixed with that gentle sadness is for her the elephant's trunk.

I ask my friend whether she thinks the feeling she has for 'The Salutation' could help her when she does face nothing, when as in *In Memoriam* a Tennyson might pray, 'Be near me when my light is low ... Be near me when I fade away/ To point the term of human strife' (50). She says it is probably not permanent like that, poems don't work deliberately to solve, cure, or resolve. But if not permanent, it is recoverable, she says, repeatable -'it always affects me'—and it just might remain part of her without the poem, she won't know. T. S. Eliot again, famously, from *The Waste Land*, 'These fragments I have shored against my ruins'.

*

I have thought to myself, Angie says in the second part of our conversation, that this piece, which I have brought from George Eliot's *Daniel Deronda*, is the opposite of my Traherne. And by that I mean that in my head it is the attitude that 'The

Salutation' exists to oppose in the human world. The beautiful young woman, Gwendolen, spoilt but despairing in her marital trouble, is telling her mentor why life does not seem wonderful to her:

> 'But you were right—I am selfish. I have never thought much of any one's feelings, except my mother's. I have not been fond of people. But what can I do?' she went on, more quickly. 'I must get up in the morning and do what every one else does. It is all like a dance set beforehand. I seem to see all that can be—and I am tired and sick of it. And the world is all confusion to me'—she made a gesture of disgust. 'You say I am ignorant. But what is the good of trying to know more, unless life were worth more?'
>
> *Daniel Deronda*, chapter 36

What is the good of it? It is all predetermined, before me. I can't even make an effort, unless I know in advance that it is worth trying. Gwendolen says 'What can I do?', Angie notes, but it is more exclamation mark than question mark, and then Gwendolen hurries away from her own question. Angie recalls the words of that other beautiful woman, Rosamond in *Middlemarch*, when her doctor husband, Tertius Lydgate, tells her that through domestic extravagance they have got themselves into financial difficulties:

> 'What can *I* do, Tertius?' said Rosamond, turning her eyes on him again. That little speech of four words, like so many others in all languages, is capable by varied vocal inflections of expressing all states of mind from helpless dimness to exhaustive argumentative perception, from the completest self-devoting fellowship to the most neutral aloofness. Rosamond's thin utterance threw into the words 'What can *I* do?' as much neutrality as they could hold. They fell like a mortal chill on Lydgate's roused tenderness.
>
> *Middlemarch*, chapter 58

Those differences in the tone and emphasis of utterance are precisely the slight differences that Angie cares about the most, sensitive to the difference that such things can make between life and death in a marriage. What can *I* do? says Gwendolen and does not pause for an answer. But when in 1988 Angie was taking her Masters degree on the part-time course for mature students I ran on Victorian literature, the key moment for her came when she found herself asking, in relation to what her final dissertation should be about, 'What shall I do?' It was not merely what should she do about the dissertation, but at the deeper level which both Rosamund and Gwendolen avoided, the life-question: what should I do?, as itself the subject of her work. She had been reading Bunyan's *Pilgrim's Progress* and thinking about its continuing influence on Victorians who were nonetheless agnostic. From the beginning Bunyan dreamt of the Man who become Christian: 'Now I saw upon a time, when he was walking in the fields, that he was (as he was wont) reading in his book, and greatly distressed in his mind; and as he read, he burst out, as he had done before, crying, *What shall I do to be saved?*

For Angie, that question as it arose out of her reading included within it two others: What makes life worth living? and How can I live with *myself?* That last, expressed even in her later concern over the little pronouns in 'The Salutation' or in Beckett, was all the more pressing after the loss of her parents and her divorce, with her children quite grown-up, when as she puts it 'I was finding myself *by* myself'. Hence the power for her of Bunyan, of Gwendolen, or of young Pip leaving home at the end of the first stage of *Great Expectations*: 'It was now too late and too far to go back, and I went on' (chapter 19). But especially for her, it was Tennyson in *In Memoriam* situated at the end of something when life had still to go on, past it.

She has always been a private person, but her distaste for personal moaning and confession is also part of her need for something more than personal, if something more than that exists. 'How if you don't believe in God, do you get to something that isn't just me?' she asks, 'that is bigger than just me?' What asks that question is for her not just a self but, as it were, a soul. 'Such sacred treasures are the limbs in boys/ In which a soul doth dwell.' A soul not perhaps ever, for her, detachable from what it lives within, but more like the voice inside the poem, something that poetry helps her to get to in herself. She remains utterly interested in the psychological realm but mainly or finally in this respect: that 'There is something going on in my mind'. She means something more than psychological, though found through psychological investigation. She says of her own mental processes: 'There are fragments there that I cannot get to, that only come out because I am reading. And in retrospect I can begin to make or see connections between them. But if I cannot help bring them together, if I am not at peace with myself in being able to do that, life is worth less.'

In this second part of the interview we talk of her interest in novels. It is to do, she says, with 'slow unfolding'. And particularly when the novel works within new and unclear stages of life that do not announce themselves formally. Young Dorothea in the first months of her mistaken marriage to the failed old scholar, Casaubon:

> She was as blind to his inward troubles as he to hers: she had not yet learned those hidden conflicts in her husband which claim our pity. She had not yet listened patiently to his heartbeats, but only felt that her own was beating violently.
>
> *Middlemarch*, chapter 20

She has to go on living with—within—the mistake she has made in her own naive choice of marrying such a man. And it is the repeated 'not yet' that Angie seizes upon. Dorothea had early begin to emerge from egoistic stupidity but she had 'not yet' been able 'to conceive with that distinctness which is no longer reflection but feeling' that her husband 'had an equivalent centre of self' (chapter 21). Dorothea is in transition: unlike the voice in 'The Salutation' she does not know what she is feeling or thinking at the time she is undergoing these things. And it may be impossible for a human creature fully to know or say what is happening to her, even afterwards, were it not for the presence of something like George Eliot here. Otherwise everything is—and Angie chooses two adjectives carefully—'lonely and silent'. That is why 'I think George Eliot's is a voice not to moralize, as people say it is, but to save'. Reading with George Eliot is a bit like reading in a group: she reads the texts with you, she helps you put the book down, as it were, and stop and think.

To think, and in that dimension to save life from transience is the aim: doing so especially when life is hidden in the ordinary, like Traherne's 'strange' too often hidden within the familiar, or the emotionally great obscured within the small, the invisible, or the gradual. 'It is in these acts *called* trivialities that the seeds of joy are forever wasted,' she quotes from chapter 42 of *Middlemarch*. One of the lovely moves in her anthology *A Little Aloud with Love* was to put a chapter (76) from *Middlemarch* on what had seemed previously a negligible character, Mrs Bulstrode loyally living with her husband's disgrace, alongside George Herbert's 'Love III' on God's forgiveness. That is the spectrum she likes to think across.

But now she chooses this younger moment from George Eliot's *The Mill on the Floss*, when after the collapse of her broken father, the adolescent Maggie is left vulnerable in the midst of life. 'I am always drawn to literature that finds itself privately, personally, in the midst of something, inside the living of time':

> Their mother came in now, and Maggie rushed away, that her burst of tears, which she felt must come, might not happen till she was safe upstairs. They were very bitter tears; everybody in the world seemed so hard and unkind to Maggie; there was no indulgence, no fondness, such as she imagined when she fashioned the world afresh in her own thoughts. In books there were people who were always agreeable or tender, and delighted to do things that made one happy, and who did not show their kindness by finding fault. The world outside the books was not a happy one, Maggie felt; it seemed to be a world where people behaved the best to those they did not pretend to love, and that did not belong to them. And if life had no love in it, what else was there for Maggie? Nothing but poverty and the companionship of her mother's narrow griefs, perhaps of her father's heart-cutting childish dependence. There is no hopelessness so sad as that of early youth, when the soul is made up of wants, and has no long memories, no superadded life in the life of others; though we who look on think lightly of such premature despair, as if our vision of the future lightened the blind sufferer's present.

Maggie, in her brown frock, with her eyes reddened and her heavy hair pushed back, looking from the bed where her father lay to the dull walls of this sad chamber which was the centre of her world, was a creature full of eager, passionate longings for all that was beautiful and glad; thirsty for all knowledge; with an ear straining after dreamy music that died away and would not come near to her; with a blind, unconscious yearning for something that would link together the wonderful impressions of this mysterious life, and give her soul a sense of home in it.

No wonder, when there is this contrast between the outward and the inward, that painful collisions come of it.

The Mill on Floss, book 3, chapter 5

Again it is the Victorian version of the religious question set in an ordinary world: What can she do? 'If life had no love in it what else was there for Maggie?' This is what is known technically as free indirect discourse: it is not George Eliot writing Maggie's direct cry in the first person, in exposure, 'What is there for me if life has no love in it?'; nor is it narratorially framed from a distance, as 'Maggie thought that if life had no love in it, there was nothing else there for her'; but in between those two the author and the character are suddenly blended in a private cry of lonely hurt that otherwise has no place in the world. Angie writes in some notes made in the aftermath of our talk:

> This is George Eliot writing in place of those *unreal* novels of Maggie's which, unlike George Eliot's own, pretend the world is easy and happy. George Eliot's is writing in place of total subjection to the outside world, though the outside world still has its surrounding force of inertia—which is registered far more in the novel that it is in a poem. But this is writing also in place of those adults who blithely dismiss youthful emotion as immature, as too dramatic and too absolute to be worthy of being taken seriously. And so too it's writing in place of a dying father and an ineffectual mother, for the parent-figures we no longer have.

The novelist's use of free indirect discourse is for Angie the equivalent of that 'impossible' voice released in 'The Salutation'. Simultaneously it is and it is not a sort of literary magic, because though it is there inside the novel to do rescue-work with Maggie, inside the novel's reality Maggie herself cannot of course know of George Eliot's support. It is the equivalent of what in film or television we might now think of as a split-screen vision, the reader turning quickly from one parallel reality to another. That is like a clue to what the literature that I most value is trying to do, she concludes. It is not just contenting itself within the world of books but trying within the world of books to forge a new link between that world and the world itself.

And what it speaks on behalf of here is the girl who, like Angie herself more consciously years later, needed to make connections. 'A blind, unconscious yearning for *something that would link together* the wonderful impressions of this mysterious life, and give her soul a sense of home in it.' It is the word 'something', here and in Tennyson and in Wordsworth, that Angie characteristically seizes upon as most valuably agnostic. In the midst of what is not at all clear in the stages of life, Maggie is looking for 'something' beyond and other than herself that is perhaps not there, except through whatever George Eliot can stand for; something which would make connections and meanings, and meet serious human needs, without the painful division between the outward and inward life.

Maggie is desperately, youthfully impatient. The links do not forge themselves as immediately as she wants them to. She wants as it were a first gift, early revelation, but Angie Macmillan is more interested in a later or even last one. She is grateful for what she has also worked hard over the years to attain: that which George Eliot calls, alongside her own younger self in Maggie, 'long memories ... superadded life in the life of others'. She talks again about the slow unfolding of development in the realist novel. In a long immersive novel by Trollope or Mrs Gaskell, and all the more without the intervening voice of George Eliot, you keep coming back to the same lives again and again in time, with minute changes of perspective, with slightly different emphases amidst gradually altering relationships. It is like the subtly wonderful process that she finds in a great passage she now reads me from John Henry Newman's *University Sermons*, from a sermon of 1841 'Wisdom, as contrasted with Faith and with Bigotry':

> We feel ourselves to be ranging freely, when we not only learn something, but when we also refer it to what we knew before. It is not the mere addition to our knowledge which is the enlargement, but the change of place, the movement onwards, of that moral centre, to which what we know and what we have been acquiring, the whole mass of our knowledge, as it were, gravitates. And therefore a philosophical cast of thought, or a comprehensive mind, or wisdom in conduct or policy, implies a connected view of the old with the new; an insight into the bearing and influence of each part upon every other; without which there is no whole, and could be no centre. It is the knowledge, not only of things, but of their mutual relations. It is organized, and therefore living knowledge.
>
> *University Sermons*, sermon 14, p. 287

If you think in Newman's way, and not the way of simple knowledge-addition, it is not just a different way of thinking—it feels, says Angie, like a wholly different world-view, the taking on of which makes you a different and deeper kind of human being. It is completely apart from the world of mental accountancy, totting up the separate pluses and minuses of life. Because it is not the 'mere addition' of a new fact or idea that counts, but the 'change of place' within the mind's organization that may begin to result from it. What Newman describes, she goes on, is a way of coming to *expand* what you know about life. And this not in a simply 'knowledgeable' way—by simply accruing new bits of extra conceptual information; but in ideas coming to life in your mind that relate back to what you find you had already begun to know. It is what Newman calls *wisdom* (not just knowledge) that feels so structurally organic here, invisibly gradual, cumulatively achieved over a life—without perhaps anyone being able to point to a single recallable moment of definitive change. It won't then do to paraphrase this as merely connection and organization: the language is closer to what all that means in origin. That delayed verb—'as it were, gravitates'—is the phrase she most loves: mutual relations, not just immediately put in order but slowly becoming organized, like 'organizèd joints' in a growing living creature.

This way of inter-massed thinking makes 'what shall I *do?*' a question that for her can have, of course, no single, simple, permanent answer in time. There are, instead, moments of sometimes painful clarity when what comes through is more like what in retrospect I *should have* done, or done better. Thinking of George Eliot standing in lieu of father and mother for Maggie, Angie remembered also the death of Adam's drunkard father, Thias, near the beginning of *Adam Bede*. Adam had almost despised his father in his latter years when the old man himself could see in the eyes of his own two sons reflections of his decay and humiliation. But at the very end of chapter 4 there is a single devastating sentence that arises out of Adam's feelings. Too late (since this is realism, not 'The Salutation'), his mind 'rushed back over the past' and out of that guilty pain there comes this general thought:

> When death, the great Reconciler, has come, it is never our tenderness that we repent of, but our severity.

Though a faithful daughter to people far more solid and decent than Thias Bede, she knows from the loss of her own parents this thought of things ill-managed or mis-said. But even here what she uses the pain and sadness *for* is not a continual harping on guilt but rather has most to do with the word 'tenderness' itself. 'It is never our tenderness that we repent of, but our severity.' She writes me in after-thought:

> The word 'tenderness' implies gentleness, loving kindness but also a sensitivity to pain. I find it in much of nineteenth-century fiction—where it is too easily dismissed as sentimentalism. But it is *mixed* emotions like tenderness that most give me the sense of all that goes into life.

She then gave me finally three examples of this saturated tenderness, all from Victorian novels.

One was from chapter 4 of *David Copperfield* where the boy is locked in his room by his unkind stepfather, and his beloved old nurse can only speak to him through the keyhole in hurried comic gasps. 'Then Peggotty fitted her mouth close to the keyhole, and delivered these words through it with as much feeling and earnestness as a keyhole has ever been the medium of communicating, I will venture to assert: shooting in each broken little sentence in a convulsive little burst of its own.' It goes on like this:

> 'Davy, dear. If I ain't been azackly as intimate with you. Lately, as I used to be. It ain't because I don't love you. Just as well and more, my pretty poppet … What I want to say, is. That you must never forget me. For I'll never forget you. And I'll take as much care of your mama, Davy. As ever I took of you. And I won't leave her.'

It is ludicrous: 'Peggotty fell to kissing the keyhole, as she couldn't kiss me.' But at another level it also protects what is being said, when the common prose is cut up into vital messages, suddenly as emotionally transcendent as words and lines of formal poetry: 'It ain't because I don't love you/ Just as well'; What I want to say, is/ That you must never forget me/ For I'll never forget you.' Through and against the 'nots' and the 'nevers', Peggotty must get her message across to him. For it means more to Peggotty that David is going to lose her than that she is going to lose him. That is why she wants to make it so that every time he does not forget but remembers her, he should think of her not forgetting but remembering him at the self-same time. It is that Dickensian thing of laughing and crying, of hurting and loving almost simultaneously, and Angie says: 'Somehow it is using all of you between those two extremes put together, a version of all your feeling and thinking.'

That is what she means by the power of mixed feelings. She is not saying that in response to The Question, 'What can I do?', there is The Answer, such as 'Show more tenderness now, rather than too late.' It is not about a definite solution, but more about an actual emotional site or place. What the tenderness does in her other two examples is to hold together an area of feeling so dense that it is only *there* that she feels that thinking about what may be done in life can ever be real. And that, far ahead of whether on any occasion that thinking can actually result in successful practical outcome or answer. Like others in this book, Angie is not in the slightest convinced by so-called Novel Cures or Poetry Pharmacies: proposed literary 'remedies' for human 'problems', however well-meaning, seem to her too like Newman's add-ons, cheapening both literature and life.

The area she wants to think within is something like this which she cites from Trollope's *The Duke's Children* where the Duke, formerly Liberal Chancellor of the

Exchequer and Prime Minister, is left out of power, newly made a widower with three more-or-less grown-up children. A deeply reticent man committed to public service, he gradually finds now how much he has depended upon his late wife, for all her waywardness, in private and emotional matters. In chapter 26 he dines for once with his son and heir Lord Silverbridge in the young man's club. The talk turns to marriage, and the buttoned-up old man finds a different tone:

> 'I should be glad to see you marry early,' said the Duke, speaking in a low voice, almost solemnly, but in his quietest, sweetest tone of voice. 'You are peculiarly situated. Though as yet you are only the heir to the property and honours of our family, still, were you married, almost everything would be at your disposal. There is so much which I should only be too ready to give up to you!'
> 'I can't bear to hear you talking of giving up anything,' said Silverbridge energetically.
> Then the father looked round the room furtively, and seeing that the door was shut, and that they were assuredly alone, he put out his hand and gently stroked the young man's hair. It was almost a caress,—as though he would have said to himself, 'Were he my daughter, I would kiss him.'

She writes: 'This is a moment, *almost* a non-moment, that contains all the love, all the aspirations, a lifetime of things unsaid and caresses withheld. That is what meaning is—that connection across characters, across times, the more poignant despite conventional manners and stereotypes of gender.' It *relates*—and does so not only between father and son but inside the very father himself. In him this brief under-stated lived experience in the club for once comes out of and blends into the whole background of the individual's life, reconfigured into an emotional system of inter-related tones and resonances.[7] It would be less powerful were it less restrained.

In that private anthology of hers that lies behind her published work, Angie puts alongside this another father and son, the taciturn Squire, one more old man who has recently lost his wife, sitting with his second son Roger in *Wives and Daughters*, chapter 23. Roger knows he remains only second-best to the spoiled first-born favourite Osborne, despite all the trouble Osborne has caused the mother and father. Perhaps no one knows that in the long run Roger is the better man. But here, still underrated, he takes his late mother's place in the ritual filling of the Squire's pipe, across gender and age, to offset his father's self-absorbed moaning:

> 'It's thinking of how Osborne grieved *her* at last that makes me so bitter with him. And yet there's a deal of good in him! and he's so quick and clever, if only he'd give his mind to things. Now, you were always slow, Roger—all your masters used to say so.'
> Roger laughed a little—
> 'Yes; I'd many a nickname at school for my slowness,' said he .... .

The Squire sat and gazed into the embers, still holding his useless pipe-stem. At last he said, in a low voice, as if scarcely aware he had got a listener,—'I used to write to her when she was away in London, and tell her the home news. But no letter will reach her now! Nothing reaches her!'

Roger started up.

'Where's the tobacco-box, father? Let me fill you another pipe!' and when he had done so, he stooped over his father and stroked his cheek. The Squire shook his head . . . .

'Osborne was once a little boy, and she was once alive—and I was once a good master—a good master—yes! It's all past now."

He took up his pipe, and began to smoke afresh, and Roger, after a silence of some minutes, began a long story about some Cambridge man's misadventure on the hunting-field, telling it with such humour that the Squire was beguiled into hearty laughing. When they rose to go to bed his father said to Roger,—

'Well, we've had a pleasant evening—at least, I have. But perhaps you haven't; for I'm but poor company now, I know.'

'I don't know when I've passed a happier evening, father,' said Roger. And he spoke truly, though he did not trouble himself to find out the cause of his happiness.

This is the full, mixed area of feeling, of little touches—the Duke almost kissing his son, the son stroking his father's cheek—in which Angie believes thinking about life best goes on for her. It is not without pain, it is not largely demonstrative or decisive, but it contains hidden matter that inextricably relates human troubles to what within them also struggles to keep up human spirits: a tenderness that holds it place before—as it says elsewhere in *Wives and Daughters*—such moments once again become 'merged in the general familiarity of the household life' (chapter 10).

CHAPTER 11

THE NOVELIST

Salley Vickers had not long finished writing her novel *The Librarian* about a young children's librarian, Sylvia Blackwell, newly employed in a small provincial town in the late 1950s. She was missing it. It had been connected, she told me, to her own childhood reading under the guidance of the local librarian in Chiswick whose name was Miss Blackwell, her first name never known. Writing the book, published in 2018, was a kind of therapy after the painful family story *Cousins* (2016). It began from her re-reading, for sheer enjoyment and nostalgia, a lot of the children's books she had read as a child. But—she corrected herself—it became more than nostalgia. She saw in those children's books the roots of her adult novels.

Tove Jansson's Moomins had offered her an extremely eccentric but unquestionably contented family, led by a very strong matriarchal figure who wants everyone to be happy and safe, with a variety of comforts always ready to hand within her capacious bag. These books represented something that her own family did not have. That was the therapeutic aspect. Her own mother Winifred, known as Freddie, a staunch Communist, lost her legs below the knees in a German bombing raid in 1942, trapped in the burning wreckage of a house, not her own, in Cambridge:

> Repeated efforts to free her seemed to be doomed. Believing she was about to die, she addressed her frustrated rescuers with what she must have believed was her final speech (she was an acclaimed speaker at rallies): 'My feet, it's burning my feet, it's no good, I'm done for. Long live the party! Long live Stalin! Goodbye, boys.'[1]

But she was saved. Uninformed of what had happened, Salley Vickers's father, Jon, then escaped a German prisoner-of-war camp and returned home, only to find his formerly athletic wife fitted with artificial legs. They had met through their mutual involvement in the student Communist Party, but the resulting marriage was tense. The man whom the mother had really loved died in that bombed house she was sharing with him in Cambridge. Theirs had been a liaison during her husband's absence which would have probably have become permanent had the man lived. These events appear in transmuted form in the background of *Cousins*.

Against medical advice regarding her damaged pelvis, the strong-willed woman managed to give birth to two children, the first being Salley in 1948. But Freddie was no Moominmamma; she powerfully sought the limelight both on her own account and by proxy. 'I had the limbs she had lost and began to show talent in territories that had once been hers.' The daughter developed an early talent for dancing and was considered for the Royal Ballet School; 'but while my mother was always ambitious for my success, I instinctively knew that to keep her affection this was a path I could not afford to go down':

> She felt she 'owned' my legs but, understandably, resented them—as in a larger way she must have felt she owned and yet resented me. As a child, I learned to track her moods in order to pre-empt them. Only in adolescence was my will any match for hers. At sixteen, in a bid for autonomy, I bolted. I ran away to live with my much older boyfriend. I had just found a job at the cosmetics counter at Selfridges when I heard that my mother had lost the ability to walk. Heart in mouth, I hurried home to be greeted by a gaunt figure in a wheelchair. With impeccable dramatic skill, she had known how to bring me to heel.
>
> *The Guardian*

In a later interview, the novelist she was to become speaks of how she turned this also into her family chronicle, *Cousins*: 'Trauma passed down from generation to generation is kind of haunting', its memory persisting beyond a single individual life.[2]

> I jettisoned the boyfriend, and the job and obediently won scholarships to Oxford and Cambridge, where in my mother's script I was billed to embark on a high-flying career in academia. Perversely—or inevitably?—I chose to go to Cambridge where the long shadow of that bomb still loomed; and where I suffered a well-concealed, but necessary, breakdown. My former academic fluency dried up along with my always fragile confidence. In thrall to a nameless dread, I was incapable even of entering the university library.
>
> *The Guardian*

It had never been like that before. Years earlier as an enthusiastically bookish child in Miss Blackwell's local library, she had relished the novels of Rosemary Sutcliff, which in contrast to the Moomintroll family offered a dramatic version of something closer to home. Sutcliff had suffered from Still's disease, childhood rheumatoid arthritis. Confined to a wheelchair as an adult she wrote novels for children which often included characters who suffered emotional or physical disabilities. At some level the young reader was aware of that emphasis. A favourite was *Warrior Scarlet* (1958), a Bronze Age tale of a young boy who despite his having been born with a withered arm, has to try to face his tribe's test of heroic manhood by wrestling a wolf.

Jansson and Sutcliff offered two different uses of literature: the first to do with possibilities that were not available to you in your lived life; the second providing company for the problems that you were actually enduring. 'Warrior Scarlet was like an objective correlative of my fighting mother and her disability; the Moomins offered the imagination of a warm emotional counter to that.'

I asked whether those two different ways of helping could be available within the same book. She replied that the two were more likely to be separate in children's books: probably one or the other, to deal with what you have, or to imagine what you haven't; but they could be intermingled in adult writing, including her own.

I thought of my favourite among Salley Vickers's novels, The Other Side of You, her fictional account of what she herself had been—a psychoanalyst, here David McBride—thus blending her two professions:

> It was left to my younger brother to fulfil our mother's academic aspirations, while I found another métier for the gifts she had unwittingly bestowed: the fine-tuned radar, a fascination with secrets, a deep understanding of how the past never really goes away. In time, I became a psychoanalyst, a profession that by definition abjures the limelight, and managed a judicious balance between doing well enough to please her and not too well to threaten.
>
> Towards the end of her life, my mother developed Alzheimer's. It was only then, when she was no longer able to peer over my shoulder and judge what I was doing, that I began to write. While I regret that she was never conscious of how her ambition for me found its proper end, I know I couldn't have done otherwise.
>
> I owe her so much of what has been invaluable in both professions. And for all her manipulative and insouciant trickiness, I miss her. But of course she has never really gone. She wouldn't.
>
> The Guardian

The legacies and the consequences are not wholly predictable. In The Other Side of You the title, taken from T. S. Eliot's The Waste Land, refers to the elder brother who died in a childhood accident trying to help David across the road. It still leaves David feeling responsible, with something always missing in him on this side. But the title is also related to another of the book's concerns—the capacity of painters and writers to know the other side of themselves better than whatever side they are in at the time.[3] So Caravaggio painted his David by putting his own sin and ugliness into the face of Goliath precisely in order to be able to create the fairness of David in contrast. One of the characters in the novel quotes Thornton Wilder on this, from the preface to The Angel That Troubled The Waters (1928):

> An artist is one who knows he is failing in living and feeds his remorse by making
> something fair, and a layman is one who suspects he is failing in living but is consoled
> by his successes in golf, or in love, or in business.

Or of course the layman may have no such successes that compensate; but still the
artist, different in degree not kind, only seeks compensation in a harder, higher
form. And doing so, it is perhaps also for the sake, or benefit, of those others who
cannot compensate or redeem at all. At any rate, you don't paint as you are, the
novel says, you paint as you're not. But—and crucially—you only know what you're
not through knowing what you are (TOSOY, p. 164). It is, says the novelist, the adult
version of going through a door or a mirror, in the magic of children's fiction. That
is the movement from Caravaggio's Goliath to Caravaggio's David.

I re-read the work before our conversation. It is a novel I have found full of
somehow personally resonant thoughts for me, as a reader, that I haven't always
known quite how to use yet. For example, the most unorthodox psychologist in the
novel says, in reply to the cliché that love takes many different forms, that love is
basically always the same. 'It simply moulds itself to the person,' says Gus Galen, '—
obviously you don't show love to a babe in arms the way you do to your mistress.
But in essence it's the same' (TOSOY, p. 236). There are many other powerful places
like this one, when her books say that human beings find it dismayingly *hard* to be
happy, or to simplify and be simple; hard, to take the risk of being seen even while
they know they need to be; difficult, to try to think of all one's experiences as if they
were somehow necessary, or to realize that we are punished not *for* our sins but *by*
them. The spirit of these thoughts in their context feels freeing and cleansing,
blowing away some artificial boundaries, and I feel I am looking for the right
context in which to re-call them, at some level, outside the books.

We talk a little more about the psychiatrist David McBride. How he often drove
without a seat-belt, or secretly hoped for some fatal illness to release him guiltlessly
from the demands and responsibilities of life. How in the meantime he worked so
hard for other people's lives, giving up his will to live to his patients, to lend
existence some point and purpose (TOSOY, pp. 196–7). She sometimes feels that
there are rescuers and rescuees in life, and cites Joseph Conrad's little-read novel *The
Rescue* in this respect—adding that there is always of course something askew
with people in either category. But for those who have a lack of will to live—to
whom she feels close—there is, even in David's own risky need to be a rescuer, a
sort of weakened laziness, she feels. Perhaps because of some dramatic catastrophe
and trauma that leaves a broken spirit. Or 'maybe a vital *source* not fed from an
early age'.

It interests her, this vital difference between people with an utter will to live, hanging on however desperately, and those who find it hard to endure and want to let go. In her fiction she says, she does not *know* in advance which one of the two, or any other number of possibilities, her characters might become: 'They tell you whether they can live with this, they tell you if they can live "capable of their own distress" as *Hamlet's* Ophelia in her madness was not.' It is not that she believes in simple opposing categories, people being either this or that, save as an initial prompt for further thinking in subtler fractions:

> Like is drawn to like. Alter the biographical circumstances a *fraction* and my colleague who worked with psychopaths would make an expert serial killer.
>
> TOSOY, p. 4, my italics

David thinks of a smart comment made by a character in Harold Pinter: 'Apart from the known and the unknown, what is there?' But then the psychoanalyst in David answers that the serious matter always exists somewhere *between* the known and the unknown (TOSOY, p. 172) At the very beginning of the novel, he says moreover that his own preoccupation is with those who exist perilously between life and death, 'the denizens of that hinterland where life and death are sister and brother' (TOSOY, p. 4).

We talk about the complicated connections made through acts of writing and of reading in the subtle area between books and lives. I mention the example of a reader reading, as it were from the other side of himself—to do not with the life he has lived but, as Salley Vickers calls it, the life unlived. It is the reader I called Dan in chapter 7: how he valued a Renaissance love lyric by Herrick because it spoke of all he had *not* had; how this seemed an example of what we might call imagination, in place of what so easily could have been reduced to personal resentment or mourning; and how this was like Arthur Clennam in *Little Dorrit* who, both despite and because of his own experience, was still able to have belief 'in all the gentle and good things his life had been *without*'.

She likes this. It takes her back to a great children's book that, she says, does its work in these dense in-between areas to blend both lived and unlived lives, problems and imaginations across time, in the mingling of human consciousness. It is *Tom's Midnight Garden* (1958) by Philippa Pearce, which takes its beginning from a child's loneliness.

Tom Long is sent away from home to live with his aunt and uncle for a while, in order not to contract his younger brother's measles. But because he may be infectious he is not allowed to play out with others. The aunt and uncle lived in an apartment within a large converted Victorian house. Above them lives their reclusive aged landlady, Mrs Bartholomew. There is no garden for Tom to play in, only a small backyard.

Then one night, lying awake lonely and bored, Tom hears the hall clock strangely strike thirteen. Getting out of bed to investigate, he goes out through the back door to find instead of the backyard, suddenly, a garden and in it another lonely child, Hatty. Every night from then on he visits her in her garden, in what gradually becomes clear to the reader is the Victorian past. Time is no longer linear:

> He did not always go back to exactly the same Time; nor did he take Time in its usual order. He had seen Hatty as a girl of his own age, then as a much younger one, and recently as a girl who—although Tom would not yet fully admit it—was outgrowing him altogether. In flashes, Tom had seen Hatty's Time—the garden's Time—covering what must be about ten years, while his own Time achieved only the weeks of a summer holiday.[4]

At one point he has even found himself having travelled backwards to a Hatty younger than he has known before, an orphan dressed all in black, newly arrived at her aunt's house, and treated as 'a charity child, a thankless pauper'. 'Tom had never seen a grief like this...for some reason, he could not say this was none of his business' (TMG, pp. 94–5). It is the first time he finds his voice there in her world, to speak to her. On a later occasion he visits her in her sickness, in her bedroom—which in its modern alterations has become his own bedroom years after, without the garden and river view, but with a partition for a separate bathroom. Silently caught between two worlds he feels the difference:

> Hatty looked at him puzzled: she could not understand the connexion of his thoughts, nor understand a sadness that seemed to have come over him. 'Tom, there's nothing to be sad about.'
> Tom was thinking about the Past, that Time made so far away. Time had taken this Present of Hatty's, and turned it into his Past. Yet even so, here and now, for a little while, this was somehow made *his* Present too—his and Hatty's.
>
> TMG, p. 146

It is like what another of Salley Vickers's favourite authors, George MacDonald, says of the creation of a fantasy world—that even in an imaginary universe there must still be laws.[5] Tom's sadness is a tacit acknowledge of those laws in that mind-turning blend of past and future, imaginative time-travel, and continuing human realism. In the law of his own growth Tom himself eventually—but suddenly as if for the first time—sees this from the other side, from a reversed imagination of Hatty's point of view: 'she might step forward into my Time, which would seem the Future to her, although to me it seems the Present' (TMG, p. 170).

For Salley Vickers this is thinking like a novelist might, working between worlds: 'He lived his real and interesting life at night-time, when he went into the garden; in the day-time he wanted only peace—to think back and to think forwards . . . He liked the cinema best, because he was in the dark, and so he could sit with his eyes shut and think his own thoughts' (TMG, pp. 99–100).

The garden is and is not there. And a novel is like that equivocal garden-place when she is working on it. Not at the beginning but in the middle of writing a fiction, sitting at her desk still in her nightclothes but not really knowing where she quite is, the novelist forgets that what she is doing is just called 'Writing a Book'. This is what this novelist means by the children's books, and especially *Tom's Midnight Garden* through its medium of dream, being the roots of her adult writing. As between Tom and Hatty, her works are responses to the emotional need to find, to recreate, to meet and connect with others. 'The writing can be more real to me than everyday life. Now, amid everything else, I am still grieving the finish of my last book. I miss the people in *The Librarian*, especially the troubled child Sam and the old woman Miss Crake.'

In the house of *Tom's Midnight Garden*, above all, there is the aged Mrs Harriet Bartholomew, dreaming of the past. Then she was a girl called Hatty, living on sufferance in the house she later comes to inherit. It is this old woman dreaming that allows the boy Tom, living just beneath her in the modernized apartment, entry into her childhood. That is why, Tom realizes, the times he had entered through the back door had been so apparently random:

> It had all depended upon what old Mrs Bartholomew had chosen to remember in her dreams.
>
> TMG, p. 222

Yet it was not wholly dependent on her. For never before this summer has she dreamed of the garden so often and intensely that 'it had *felt*' like being the little Hatty again, longing for someone to play with. And Tom had had exactly that longing too:

> and that great longing, beating about unhappily in the big house, must have made its entry into Mrs Bartholomew's dreaming mind and brought back to her the little Hatty of long ago.
>
> TMG, p. 223

'Oh, Tom,' she cries near the end of the book, 'don't you understand? You called me: I'm Hatty' (TMG, p. 215). It is Tom the boy who summons her dreams, as much as her recollecting what by a strange loop of time has now become their past. Childhood reading and adult writing are like a part of that encounter for Salley Vickers.

In *The Librarian* the unconventional old wise woman Miss Crake, who worked at University College London with the geneticist J. B. S. Haldane in her youth, talks about the ninety-eight per cent of DNA that Francis Crick dismissed as mere junk, because not used for coding. The Haldane team had a different hypothesis: for them the apparently unused ninety-eight per cent of memory was a huge biological database of all the experiences and emotions of our lives. And bizarre as it may sound, between those in whom there is a high correspondence of that apparently useless DNA, there may be formed a connection. A code of sonic vibrations may be like a form of language between such people across time and space, creating a hyper-communication of information conveyed beyond the individual's own knowledge base. We experience this tuning-in as a strange sense of psychic affinity, felt as intuition or inspiration. As Miss Crake puts it, in the voice of Salley Vickers herself:

> 'In Philippa Pearce's ingenious book I detect just such an affinity between the DNA of old Mrs Bartholomew and Tom, which is why when she dreams of her youth as the child Hatty, he can enter her past and become her playmate before he is even born.'[6]

This is at the very least, says the novelist, a great metaphor for what literature is so very good at: creating a DNA of vicariousness, that tuning-in across time which she does not want to normalize as just 'identification' or 'empathy'. Instead she redefines it as the reader co-habiting a mental space with, say, Jane Austen's Emma or George Eliot's Hetty Sorrel, through a kind of dream, a sort of back door, without ever occupying the same physical place as the characters imaginably do. That is how reading creates a place in which to overcome the paradox of our needing both not to be exposed and known, and yet nonetheless to be recognized and accepted.

When writing *Cousins*, the painful account of family life she had long deferred, what had helped her to come back to the story was a phrase about strange meetings and reunions that Joseph Conrad used in the Author's Note to *The Rescue*, a novel he had begun in 1898 to return to only in 1918:

> As I moved slowly towards the abandoned body of the tale it loomed up big amongst the glittering shadows of the coast, lonely but not forbidding. There was nothing about

it of a grim derelict. It had an air of expectant life. One after another I made out the familiar faces watching my approach with faint smiles of amused recognition. They had known well enough that I was bound to come back to them.

The phrase she kept in mind was the 'faint smiles of amused recognition' from the awaiting characters, as though saying 'You're back'.

So much for her is like the meetings that happen across differences inside *Tom's Midnight Garden*. The best is at the great emotional ending, as reported through Tom's aunt. Back in present time and space, the little boy and the old woman part in a farewell embrace of mutual recognition, despite the different physical shapes and ages they appear to occupy:

> He ran up to her, and they hugged each other as if they had known each other for years and years, instead of only having met for the first time this morning. There was something else, too...it sounds even more absurd...Of course Mrs Bartholomew's such a shrunken old woman, she's hardly bigger than Tom, anyway; but you know, he put his arms right round her and he hugged her good-bye as if she were a little girl.
>
> TMG, p. 226

It is a great Wordsworth-like moment, that the little girl is still alive there inside the seemingly unrecognizable old woman; that Tom can reach her there, and like an adult comfort both the little girl and the old woman at once; that an old love may reach through the incongruity of their ostensible appearances, back and forth across the bands of years. *Tom's Midnight Garden* is Salley Vickers's great childhood image of what it feels like to write and to read.

She then says something particularly surprising. That she thinks that though they are simply called 'books' and having to do with them is called 'reading', it is really all so much odder than that. On the boundary between the material and the immaterial, with all those printed pages and words and the thoughts and feelings connected with them, 'What are they—what *are* they—books?'

Listening to my recording of this interview, this makes me think later of something that David McBride thought when he was talking to one of his patients, Hassid, a student of quantum physics, about the crazy existence of electrons as 'potential'. Electrons, Hassid says, occupy no physical space in the material world until called into being by human beings taking measurements to determine their location, and David thinks later:

> I've always thought it remarkable that, while our bodies stand in the visible world, we ourselves are not in the world of three dimensions, and our inner life has no position in

space. And, equally, how little of another person's reality is visible to us. We see their form, their features, their shifts of expression, but all that constitutes that sense of self remains unseen...

TOSOY, pp. 53–4

The electron, the student goes on, 'is like a thought before one performs an action. The electron is no place, and then...presto! Suddenly it is here, coming into existence out of seeming nothingness...' (TOSTOY, p. 54).

Sally Vickers often appears at first sight like a conventional realist novelist but within that visible form she becomes strikingly unconventional—and that, solely to let in more life, the 'more' that does not always simply fit. I think she likes that realist novelist's hiddenness, miming what goes on beneath the norms of appearance in visible reality itself. It is about creating within one system, without quitting it, the capacities of a second and different other; a second language—a literary language—working within our normal language. It is about people being at their best *in* the world, in the institution, or even in the book, by not being wholly *of* it. Or to do with something that transcends the medium in which it operates, but only by being made operative within it. So in *Cousins*, the grandmother says, 'Love is stronger than morality, thank heavens.'[7]

The novelist talks more to me about the strangely mixed power of connection and vicariousness through books, and about the second life the reader gets from reading. And this time she offers a famous example from Jane Austen's *Emma* which she has to hand on her Kindle. It is that moment at the party on Box Hill when the egoistic young Emma, wholly self-possessed, playfully directs the company to offer in conversation either: one thing very clever, or: two things moderately clever, or three things very dull indeed. And the decent but boring old spinster Miss Bates says, with relief, that she had better volunteer for the three dull things:

> Emma could not resist.
>
> 'Ah! ma'am, but there may be a difficulty. Pardon me, but you will be limited as to number—only three at once.'
>
> Miss Bates, deceived by the mock ceremony of her manner, did not immediately catch her meaning; but when it burst on her, it could not anger, though a slight blush showed that it could pain her.
>
> *Emma*, chapter 43

It 'burst' upon her, all the more for being in minutely delayed realization of meaning. Salley Vickers then says: you know, and Emma knows, at the moment of that absolutely *felt* blush that she has done something truly terrible—even though it looks quite trivial and is the kind of thing people say all the time.

Emma tries later to defend herself against Mr Knightley's rebuke by claiming that though she knows there is no better creature in the world than Miss Bates, 'you must allow that what is good and what is ridiculous are most unfortunately blended in her'. To which Knightley retorts, to her mortification, 'How could you be so unfeeling to Miss Bates?'

> 'She is poor; she has sunk from the comforts she was born to; and if she live to old age must probably sink more. Her situation should secure your compassion. It was badly done, indeed! You, whom she has known from an infant, whom she has seen grow up from a period when her notice was an honour—to have you now in thoughtless spirits, and the pride of the moment, laugh at her, humble her—and before her niece, too—and before others . . .'
>
> *Emma*, chapter 43

One thing inside another: the terrible within the trivial. And many things all together: Miss Bates's shame, Knightley's protest, Emma's mortification—the reader is asked to feel all these, vicariously and almost simultaneously. The novelist relishes it that this is the first moment in a life, in Emma's life, when the self, experienced as the centre of the world, suddenly feels it might be otherwise; when feeling first turns back round upon itself in a sort of revolution, realizing in others an equivalent reality and a better truth than for the moment one has left in oneself.[8] It is no conventional liberalism or acceptance, effortless empathy, or altruism—to use the normal names and descriptions of which Salley Vickers is dismissive because they are so 'belittling'. Instead in Jane Austen's language: 'She was forcibly struck. The truth of his representation there was no denying. She felt it at her heart. How could she have . . .' (chapter 43). Flushing, shocked, and near tears, Emma, through Mr Knightley, suddenly knows what it feels like to be Miss Bates: for a moment, says Salley Vickers with another of her exciting emphases, she has *become* Miss Bates. For both of them have been 'struck'. What I am interested in—she goes on—is the moment when she loses that self-centredness; and that it is a moment which, even though felt as pain, is liberation—the liberation and the pain simultaneous even while Emma is more aware of the pain. Her own conduct stood there before her, Jane Austen says, in new and terrible self-reflection.

The novelist points to a few scenes later, from her Kindle. In chapter 49, Knightley comes to speak to her again, and Emma, fearing he is going to tell her that he is going to marry Harriet, immediately cries, 'Don't speak it, don't speak it'. But then seeing Knightley's own downcast mortification, and realizing that she has given him a blow of rejection, she changes her mind. Saying instead 'I will hear whatever you like', she lets him speak to her in what she supposes will be a painful confidence for her to bear as a friend only. Though what he says actually turns out to be his love for her, what interests Salley Vickers before that is that Emma can bear to tell him to 'Say It, Say it', despite herself—and this because of that painful experience on Box Hill.

Again transcribing the recording at a later date, I think that it is this remorseful depth of reality that is compelling to David McBride. He speaks to his mentor, Gus Galen, about the terrible sight of 'a difficult repentance' when he finds his patient doubled-over with grief for losing her lover. Elizabeth Cruikshank never believed in herself sufficiently to make fully possible Thomas's love, and now he is dead and she hopelessly penitent:

> But when I spoke of this to Gus Galen, he told me that what we translate as 'repentance' means more accurately, in the original Greek, a turnaround, or change of mind. Metanoia. I would rather say a change of heart.
>
> TOSOY, p. 176

It is these mental 'turnarounds', in the *second* place, that Salley Vickers finds extra-ordinary in human beings: the change of heart an achievement as well as a loss, achieved through the midst of loss.

I ask her if she thinks the pain of such figures as Emma is in some sense the *cause* of their new development. And going back to the example of my reader Dan on Herrick's love poem, I try to say that the love he has not got is, however surprisingly, the *cause* of his appreciation of the love he reads of. She rightly notes that this is a strange use of 'cause'. After all, reading about what he did not have might have more likely caused bitter envy or protective cynicism, rather than celebration. And she adds: I wonder why it is more likely to be the case that it *is* celebration when it is something we are reading, rather than thinking about. 'Why *is* that?'

It is another of her questions, asked in the same tone as 'What *are* books?'. Alongside extreme suffering, she continues, comes something that isn't what it so easily could have been—such as bitter hurt. Listening to the recording, I hear myself replying that that is why I had wanted to try out the idea of 'cause'—to accentuate the odd sense of both connection and separation here. That is to say: the cathartic connection between having an unhappy love-life and being glad of a beautiful love poem is registered experientially in the emotions being quite separate. She says: It does seem, indeed, that it is the bad experience that sharpens consciousness and liberates an appreciation of the good. And then she adds: It *is* more magical if in that way a cause ceases at the next moment to be a cause. Or becomes somehow transmuted into the cause of something quite different.

In her commitment to complex psychology and to the novel, it is part of her unconventionality to dislike the idea of reductively simple causation: that is the force of her interest in strange physics and the ideas of potential—when suddenly an electron appears like something coming out of nothing, or when the inchoate thought behind an action seems created only afterwards by the act's completion. She explicitly reminds me at this point of what Miss Crake says to the young librarian who had dared to ask her whether she regretted the failure of her past affair with Haldane, as a married man:

> 'Sometimes I do. Very much. Sometimes I am relieved. One isn't consistent.... People are not consistent. That is a modern delusion No one in the ancient world made such an absurd assumption. The Persians debated all important matters twice: once drunk and once sober.'
>
> *The Librarian*, p. 300

It may be that whatever in her became the psychotherapist is what is so against consistency and causation. She certainly wonders if the expectation of human consistency is not another by-product of the Industrial Revolution, another form of mechanization. But despite (or because) of having been a psychotherapist, she is also opposed to an over-ready use of explanatory terms of sub-conscious motivation such as 'denial' or 'masochism' to iron things out. And she especially resents these diagnoses when they are used to explain away these episodes when ego is wonderfully surrendered. Not that these sceptical interpretations of selflessness cannot sometimes be true, but rather that they are not always true. There is 'a genuine stretch', she insists, of which human beings are capable.

I tell her I still feel uneasy about the value of pain or suffering, and about the loss of self in selflessness, and she is wryly sympathetic. 'It is part of what you signed up for—in "the rash act of being born"—as Enid Welsford put it in her book *The Fool*.' So I ask, what if Emma had not been rewarded with Mr Knightley? I am thinking of her left suffering, but morally improved: 'Left only to recognize more clearly what you cannot have or have failed to be: is that an achievement? If so,' I go on, 'then to point me towards something as an achievement, which marks exactly what I cannot be: well, that, however admirable, has to be what Thomas Hardy called one of life's bitter little ironies.' She thinks, on the contrary, that it is what we call grown-up: to be aware of painful limitation in oneself *and* to have an expanded awareness of what lies beyond it. Her wise psychologist Gus Galen says to David of his despairingly depressed patients, that the question is not 'how to cure or be cured, but how to live':

> The people we were treating were not so much looking for a remedy for anxiety or depression, they were looking for a reason to be alive. For the most part, the human race takes for granted that life if not a blessing is at least desirable enough to cling to. But for those for whom the business of being alive is a much more vexed question, the illness is the question, or, to put it another way, the illness is how the question may be posed.
>
> TOSOY, p. 18

She quotes for shorthand Gus's clinching sentence, 'There's no cure for being alive' (TOSOY, p. 19). He's good on that, she says.

But she takes me back to a literary example, instead of more arguing. She has been re-reading Henry James's rather neglected novel *The Awkward Age* (1899). It is about Nanda, an innocent eighteen-year-old girl in a sophisticated but corrupt milieu created around her beautiful but ageing mother. In it there is a decent old man Mr Longdon who was once hopelessly in love with Nanda's grandmother whom Nanda resembles, and who now cares for Nanda herself in a wholly honourable fashion. Nanda is in love with Vanderbank, a young civil servant with little money, but her own mother very much depends upon her own ambiguous relationship with 'Van'. Mr Longdon, seeking to rescue the young woman, even offers Van a considerable dowry to marry Nanda and make her happy. But after long hesitation, concerned as to what damage her upbringing has done to Nanda, Van cannot rise up against his condition and boldly accept the offer. Instead, amidst the mess of it all, Nanda finds herself having to urge *him* to find his way towards remaining a supportive friend to her mother. Mr Longdon is left to talk it over with Nanda in the novel's final chapter, which she now reads to me:

> 'It would be good for me—by which I mean it would be easier for me—if you didn't quite so immensely care for him.'
>
> 'Oh!' came from Nanda with an accent of attenuation at once so precipitate and so vague that it only made her attitude at first rather awkward. 'Oh!' she immediately repeated, but with an increase of the same effect. After which, conscious, she made, as if to save herself, a quick addition. 'Dear Mr. Longdon, isn't it rather yourself most—?'
>
> 'It would be easier for me,' he went on, heedless, 'if you didn't, my poor child, so wonderfully love him.'
>
> 'Ah but I don't—please believe me when I assure you I *don't*!' she broke out. It burst from her, flaring up, in a queer quaver that ended in something queerer still—in her abrupt collapse, on the spot, into the nearest chair, where she choked with a torrent of tears. Her buried face could only after a moment give way to the flood, and she

sobbed in a passion as sharp and brief as the flurry of a wild thing for an instant uncaged; her old friend meantime keeping his place in the silence broken by her sound and distantly—across the room—closing his eyes to his helplessness and her shame.

The Awkward Age, chapter 38

That it should be that repeated 'oh' which matters most in this otherwise supremely articulate novelist of consciousness is extraordinary. But something happens between those two 'oh's, of which Nanda seems to be on the receiving end, as if something was coming home to her. Salley Vickers is vehement about that: Something happens there which is *instead of* the diagnoses of masochism or fear or denial, which is not at all to be reduced to calling her a wimpish victim or thinking she is merely masking her pain or offering a false acceptance—all those normative names that could turn what happens here into something one cannot really believe in. Nanda does love the man she calls Mr Van but, equally, she is not lying: 'Nanda is incapable of not telling the truth'. There is a second repetition when Nanda replies to her patron's sorrow at how much she loves Van: 'Ah but I don't—please believe me when I assure you I *don't*!' It means she does love Van, insists Salley Vickers, but no longer in the way her aged friend Mr Longdon believes; and all the tears afterwards are in residual memory of that lost love. She has gone beyond simple passion for Mr Van into a larger form of love—even for a mother who does not really love or even like her and whom she herself does not really like. But it is only because she is so hurt and wounded, her wings so clipped, that something in her painfully *expands* into a second life—in which we will never know what happens. But this is happening now, 'Oh! . . .' and a second life begins out of that second 'Oh! . . .', and it makes you know that *it's possible*, this is possible, in the world. It is not just about vague 'possibilities' different from the life you have been living, but a potential suddenly realized in an unexpected form. It is about something that plausibly *could* be viewed with scepticism or belittled with dismissiveness, nonetheless existing and holding its place in the world. And it is more austere to say that it is *not* just suffering, though created through it, than to say what actually it should be called. What I am trying to do in my books, she concludes, is to say that *What is happening is interesting*—whatever 'it' is. Whereas the natural reactions about it, such as regret or guilt or excuse or complaint or secondary explanation, are not interesting but comparatively pale and bloodless. It is what James sees here as 'the wild thing for an instant uncaged'. That is why it is often better to read a book than go to a psychotherapist: literature makes it more persuasive that *this*—whatever it is—happened, could happen, and is a possible.

The Greeks were good on this when the Oracle says: This is how it is. And this means that without moaning, one must meet the fate that one has provided for oneself and whatever remains of the possible within that. 'Oh!...Oh!'

'Interesting' is not here a painless, neutral, or merely distancing stance: it involves acceptance but something also more active than acceptance. It says: if writers can use their experience whatever it is, in their writing, then readers should also be able to do that in their reading, and not just for aesthetic reasons. *People* should be able to do that: to turn an artistic capability back over into a human one again; be able to look at oneself as an 'I' *and* at the same time as a 'he' or 'she'; make whatever happened to them part of a life, a matter not for repression or vain disappointment but for wholehearted witness and committed thought.

This talk of the oracle makes me think afterwards of one my favourite moments in reading *The Other Side of You* when Thomas, her lover, had insistently yelled out this, to the faltering Elizabeth Cruickshank, in reply to her 'I'm sorry. I don't mean to be feeble':

> 'YOU ARE NOT FEEBLE...That's the trouble. You're FORMIDABLY STRONG! . .
> I know what I am and how I seem!—but the truth is, I am much, much feebler than
> you. I just go on like this to keep my end up.'
>
> TOSOY, pp. 126–7

But Elizabeth still cannot accept that. And it can only become true if she believes that what he sees in her *is* true because his seeing it helps to make it so. But as Thomas writes in the diary with which he leaves her after his death: 'It's funny how you imagine loving someone is enough to make them believe you love them. Love needs belief, not to exist but to work' (TOSOY, p. 177). People write to the novelist especially about Elizabeth Cruikshank, she has told me, telling her they had never thought that anyone would know how they felt. It is one of the best things a novelist can achieve. But I myself also wish Mr Longdon could have been able to make that cry to Nanda, 'You are not feeble.'

At the time I can only say: If you think that this from *The Awkward Age* is even in its pain an achievement, do you at least think Nanda herself can feel this to be so?

And she replies: To go back to Herodotus, I don't think anything is consistent. We get little flashes when what in the 'Immortality Ode' Wordsworth calls 'the shades of the prison house' seem to have disappeared—and then in the twinkling of an eye, the shades are back again more oppressive than before. There are these moments of expanded consciousness when everything falls into place and one's little wounded ego seems not to matter—and then at another moment one is furious, angry, hurt again. Henry James does not say this is a turning point. The value of it is that it happens; not whether you, she, can remember it or re-create it, or know it and benefit from it. I think we just have to put up with the fact that the good is in that flash. Our delusion is to think we can do something about it all: to manage, control, or to keep hold. There is no cure for being alive. But without being a cure, literature is good at representing, vicariously for a reader, the possibilities we miss or cannot see in life itself. And even in life I *am* inclined to think these good things do go in or go on somewhere, as they do with children. And that is why I have been thinking of Wordsworth while we have been talking: that moments go, but there is a faith that they *amount* to something.

I should have asked her which Wordsworth, though I know she had brought 'Resolution and Independence' and 'The Immortality Ode' with her. The first is for perseverance, 'a man from some far region sent,/ To give me human strength, by apt admonishment'. The second is for loss, 'O joy! that in our embers/ Is something that doth live'. And also the lines from 'Animal Tranquillity and Decay' on the old man stoically travelling on, as 'one by whom/ All effort seems forgotten':

> one to whom
> Long patience has such mild composure given,
> That patience now doth seem a thing of which
> He hath no need.

In those long lines turning across a winding sentence, that is the sort of transmutation that is so crucial to this novelist: the shift of 'a thing' like patience from causal importance to unthinking acceptance. It is Tranquillity *and* Decay. It is the creature, the animal 'by nature led/ To peace so perfect, that the young behold/ With envy, what the old man hardly feels': that is what it is, both perfect peace and mental decline, loss and gain, 'envy' felt by the young against what is 'hardly' felt by the aged.

Later, I also think of the youthful Wordsworth chastened to find that he has crossed the Alps without knowing the exact moment he had done so. The congratulatory climax he had been hoping for never happened. 'I was lost, as in a cloud ...' Out of the disappointment of the ego when something is lost or not realized in the world, he is led to find instead at a another level something less material, more austere, and seemingly arising out of nothing—which 'through sad incompetence of human speech', he has to call 'Imagination':

in such strength
Of usurpation, in such visitings,
Of awful promise, when the light of sense
Goes out, in flashes that have shown to us
The invisible world, doth greatness make abode,
There harbours, whether we be young or old.
Our destiny, our nature, and our home
Is with infinitude, and only there;
With hope it is, hope that can never die,
Effort, and expectation, and desire,
And something evermore about to be.

The Prelude, 1805, book 6, lines 532–42

That last line is not in the least ironic for this poet—as if it meant jam only ever tomorrow—nor is it so for the novelist who admires him for working at the very verges of thought and hope.

'In flashes that have shown to us/ The invisible world.' The novelist has a vision, an implicit world-view, that has seemed to me at times close to what might be paraphrased as self-sacrifice, but that I can see arises out of something more strangely excited and alive than that, most especially when I read and re-read the actual texts—hers and others—that speak to and for her. It is less voluntary and much braver than I thought: that the trouble, and even the emotions accompanying it, are less important than where it takes you, if you can bear it, and even when you can't. But through a book you can.

The books let loose other parts of Salley Vickers, her own characters release other sides of her. It makes me think of the climax to *Cousins* when the grandmother, another of those old wise unconventional figures, takes the prison rap for the assisted death of Will, the young man who no longer wants to live because, as a result of a reckless fall when night-climbing, he can communicate only by blinking. The mercy killer is actually Will's young cousin, Cele, who has what would be called an incestuous relationship with him were the book more conventional. 'Basically love is always the same...' But the grandmother has always said, 'I'd rather be hanged for a crime I hadn't committed than for one I had' (*Cousins*, p. 143). She writes to Cele:

I am an old woman. If I plead guilty the sentence will be very much lighter than any sentence likely to be laid on you...

And, it is important that you understand this, it will help me to set things a bit right. Or a bit righter, at least. You must take my word, and I have never lied to you, that it will be a comfort foe me to do this and not a sacrifice.

Cousins, p. 386

She was grateful that love was stronger than morality.

There is a moment towards the end of our talk together when we discuss something mysterious she really loves in the act of novel-writing that is to do with the strangeness of literature. And to do with her own passionate desire to escape what she calls 'the prison of self-regard', especially through being a writer. She talks about something that happens when deep interior thoughts come out between the character and the novelist, unspoken and sub-conscious matter thrown up, which the novelist picks up and relays. Often her copy-editors, she says, irritatingly query such moments of abrupt shift of mode in the discourse, the sudden interpolated leaps that mark a change in the mode of reality—because they want to insist on consistency, a smooth linear tidiness. But often the shift and leap arise in the form of a question—and not recalling a specific instance from her own work, she offers a simplification to show the basic thing raw in action: 'But did she care after all? What on earth was this word love about anyway?' Or: 'She felt she scarcely knew her. Did she despise her mother?' Then, she says, *I don't know which consciousness that is coming from, if that is me or the character. But I do know I am moving in and out of the character's consciousness, and that the consciousnesses are blending and intermingling. And again that is why* Tom's Midnight Garden *is so important to me.*

She ends: It is a mystical area. We don't know where thoughts come from. But as soon as a thought becomes possible, it must not be lost: someone or something somewhere has to have it and try to use it. To set things 'a bit righter'.

When a thing was true it went on returning in different likenesses, borrowing from what went before, finding new ways to declare itself. [9]

AFTERWORD

I was against it because it seemed reductive summary, a wholly unliterary kind of labelling. The proposal was that participants in the various groups were asked to write down two words or a phrase that expressed their experience of each session directly after it. This was a research project in which one local-community group of six participants undertook the shared reading of literature for six weeks; while the other, also of six people, concentrated on the environment, creatively planning the renovation of *The Reader*'s great house and its relation to Calderstones Park, Liverpool, in which it is sited. Then, in a crossover design for the sake of comparison, the two groups swapped activities for the following six weeks.

Of course there were the normal conclusions, 'interesting' and enjoyable', conventional adjectives employed blandly across both activities. But often, to my surprise, the words chosen were more immediate and specific, the parts of speech almost as varied as in functional shift. For Shared Reading these terms included versions of: 'Moved', 'Warmth', 'Animated', 'Reflective'; while for the Built Environment, in contrast, there was: 'Knotty', 'Positive', 'Developing', 'Progress'. Where Shared Reading prompted 'Memory' and 'Open', for example, the Built Environment seemed to have more to do with 'Anticipating' and 'Focused'. The researchers put these words—200 of them—into two broad categories, about which again I had expressed some initial unease as to the risk of over-simplification: emotional words (those reflecting the feelings generated out of, during, or in response to the sessions) or cognitive words (those reflecting the thinking, ideas, or approach generated out of, during, or in response to the sessions). Of the Shard Reading descriptors, fifty-four per cent were emotional, compared to twenty-one per cent for the Built Environment; but where the other seventy-nine per cent of key words for Built Environment were cognitive, the percentage figure of cognitive words for Shared Reading was still forty-six per cent, suggesting, to my delight, greater possibility of movement across the two categories in the act of reading. The broader conclusions are perhaps unsurprising but useful in adding further evidence to the distinction between different activities for the same participants. Thus, the vocabulary in Shared Reading was more to do with the the personal, the emotional, the introspective, and a sense of meaning or purpose; whereas for the Built Environment, the emphasis was on the external, the co-operative, and the applied, in the acquisition of knowledge and skills. The word 'open' in relation to Shared Reading also played into results taken from a standard mental health questionnaire, the Positive and Negative Affect Scale (PANAS), to explore the endorsement of positive and negative feelings following each session. In this there was some initial evidence to suggest that Shared Reading prompted and tolerated the experience of negative affect to a greater extent than did the environmental study. This is consistent with the thought that some of the intrinsic value of the shared reading of literature lies in its capacity to open individuals up to experience a broader range of emotional states without ill effect; and, further, that the description of emotions in polar terms of negative and positive is questionable and unhelpful in relation to the value of literature for thinking about life.

But it was the rough urgency of some of the single words that struck me, as though they were shorthand messages arising, distinctively, out of the activities and their differences. Our most recent research work is in a secure psychiatric hospital for those who present a grave danger to themselves and/or other people. The majority of the patients come there from prison, or through the court system, or from other secure units. Their defences in the reading group are stronger than we have found anywhere else. There are blocks and resistances that seem to do with what the participants cannot feel or do not want to feel; there often seems to be a lack of connection and the want of an emotional vocabulary. A group member might describe a feeling but not actually put himself in it: that is the opposite of what a literary language should prompt. It is a slow process over months, but still in the later sessions of the reading group there are breakthroughs in the capacity to be touched and moved; only—and this is my point here—they are much more to do with single words than in any other group, in any other setting, that we have ever analysed. The anthology poem by the late nineteenth-century American poet Robert Browning Hamilton, entitled 'Along the Road', describes in its first stanza a walk with an allegorical figure of Pleasure: 'She chattered all the way,/But left me none the wiser/For all she had to say'; in its second, a walk with Sorrow, 'and ne'er a word said she':

> But oh, the things I learned from her
> When Sorrow walked with me!

After reading it aloud and waiting, a group leader asked what 'thing' it might be that you could learn from Sorrow... After a silence, one of the men in the group just said, very quietly,'Regret', and then after a long and full pause, changed it to— 'Remorse'. We could somehow see on the film that everyone in the room, around the small group of five, felt what was in that pause before and after the single words. Suddenly the authority in the group had shifted from the group leader, and the weight of meaning had landed instead on a group member. At such moments, a group is never a fixed entity, it moves and morphs with the responses to the text. For these men, 'remorse' is usually a word that is much bandied about in therapy sessions: they do not always know what it is, reports one of the clinicians, but they know they ought to feel it. And in the research team we ourselves usually dislike the blanket use of noun-labels that seem to be pigeon-holing. But here it is felt otherwise: behind those bare, blurted one-word articulations, and in the movement from one to another, seemed the cry of unspoken years of suffered experience. 'Remorse.' Poetry would want to work that way, in what lies behind words.

So in light of the above—of words such as 'moved', 'open', 'sorrow'—I have decided to try for a few such single words or phrases, here in afterword. They are meant to describe not the sessions but, more cumulatively, what in simplified impact this book has shaken down to, for its often over-finicky or wordy writer, at the point of leaving it. One of the OUP readers of my manuscript had already picked out 'Risky': 'the words "risk" and "risky" recur throughout the book—for the way in which both writing and reading itself might be inherently risky.' Here are four of my own words or phrases.

From passive to active. That is one phrase to describe a real movement of the readers in this book, in the act of reading, when a breakthrough occurs. It sometimes seems to me perhaps the most important human shift of all. The shift from being distant from a text or lying helpless under an emotion, or compliant with the given and the norm; to being closer to a felt experience, made alive by it whatever its content for good or ill, and, almost at the same time as being more *in* it, also rising a degree *above* it, for being able to think of it. I hate the diminishment that passivity and pain and suffering cause and constitute, but it is not just that here as described in these pages is action, feeling, thought, instead, in sudden response. In the model for thinking about life that reading literature offers, it is the process and movement *from* passive to active, the invisible transition *between* the two, that is the astonishing achievement of which humans can be at least temporarily capable.

Literary. I hate the word, and love the thing, compared to the deadness of the merely literal and normative. But the real-world cases and examples in this book make me believe in literature more than ever, in the power of a literary language to release the individual, the human and the emotional, the buried memory; to trigger life and the translation of meaning. For shorthand: the difference between the literal and the literary is between a participant saying 'Well, I just think that . . . ', with all the force of pre-set opinion, and offering instead, "It is almost as if, it"s as though . . .' Reading literature makes for a more creative form of human thinking, related to feeling, which people who are not writers themselves can still have, even so, by being readers, and becoming deeper thinkers as a result of their reading. And this helps create at least temporarily—single word again—a *warmer* world, more honest and more innerly-turned-out, in place of customary defaults and defences. '*Literary*' then: just a name for qualities of thinking and feeling and being that can and ought to exist outside literature, and which literature seeks to transfer and re-call there.

Middle. So this book exists where readers exist—between art and life, for want of better terms, in the mess and midst of things. Not ending in some clear therapeutic cure or definite solution or easy answer. This book is a hybrid work that needs art in order to trigger life, but needs life to take art and to show art outside itself.

Small. The tiny catalytic words in a text, unheralded; the transient moment when a reader picks up and manages something deep but specific; the uncertainty as to how important or lasting this can be.

And connected to the challenge of 'small', here is a final move, again related to what I have learnt from the example of ordinary readers in this book. It is to do with interviews, particularly when we showed participants filmed excerpts of themselves and others in action in shared reading, but also when we read excerpts of texts together again with all the readers, whether or not they attended reading groups. We thought at first the interview would be no more and no less than a research tool for the elicitation of evidence—in particular, to test out hypotheses on shared-reading groups, seeing if the people themselves saw or did not see what we thought was happening in seemingly key moments. But actually these interviews became a further part of the process. They enabled the group members, more individually, in aftermath, to see better what they had done, to feel and consolidate what they had accomplished, when what otherwise would have remained too quick and too little was reproduced in film and talked over at interview. Again, it was as though the filmed excerpt and the subsequent reflective one-to-one conversation were like a little bit of art, of ur-art, of what art comes out of in the effort to rescue meaning from time. The interviewers were like readers in real-life, trying to understand the meaning of people they were looking at and talking to. And it felt to me that the interviews helped the less experienced readers to be more as the practised ones were able to be in this book: in further absorbing and extending what a powerful literary moment had meant for them.

So I asked one of our team of research interviewers to turn it around and put to me one simple question, for the sake of this afterword, as if in interview myself at the end of a long, long session. The question that she came up with was: Why bother writing this book?

What I have found in reply began with a fact we had both noticed about the interviewees: that almost invariably they turned up early for their meeting with us, to see and to talk about the sessions, or about their reading notes and favoured works. This may be merely because people like attention—that would be the easiest default mode of explaining it away. But it felt more than that, more as though they wanted *this* to become important, to be picked up. 'This happened to me' was the feeling: what happened in the reading seemed in its unexpected or anomalous force to need confirmation or completion or further realization. Why was it important? And if important, what was to be done with it? As one group member said, with surprise, 'We don't usually talk about stuff like this. Most of our conversations are about trivia.' 'This' referred to the reading group as something special, something that in interview needed to be taken seriously, in order to be made more, as it were, believable. It might otherwise be only a passing thought, but someone turns up and confirms that it's important, worth keeping and somehow using. This is why this book is written, as an extended interview of varied readers and readings. But this is also one of the great reasons why the literature itself exists, why poems and novels are written, to pick up what would be lost or neglected or incomplete, and to say, often against the odds and the norms and the troubles, that it *is* important if only by putting it into more words. This is always the basic challenge, arising afresh out of the experience of the apparently less practised readers, which the teacher, the doctor, the poet, the anthologist, and the novelist take up in themselves, though never wholly to resolve: namely, what to *do* with what comes out of literature; how and where to find a place for it in a life or a world.

If the less experienced readers needed the recognition of the interview, there was also one final turn, to do with the side-effect on the interviewers themselves. In that context sometimes, or too often, people do not appreciate what they have done. When the man in the secure unit managed just to say, 'Remorse', and feel it, it is likely that we the researchers valued this much more, as witnesses, than he himself was able to. Why? Not because of our (say) sentimentality, the easiest default explanation of them all, dismissive of emotion. But rather perhaps, because to him his response was only brief, and never much or long acknowledged in the minutes around and after it; because to be able to say it, authentically, must have felt to him far more painful than admirable and remarkable, as we felt it to be; because amidst the ruin his situation was still ongoing, and this was only one moment within it, with years behind, and doubtful if not unrewarding outcomes ahead. But this is what vicariousness is for: to feel for others what they cannot feel for themselves when—so ironically or paradoxically—they most need or deserve to. This also is what literature is for, in which reading itself is vicariousness—moved, surprised, connecting self to imagined others, others to hidden self. So in this book I end feeling gratefully proud of being, vicariously, part of a people who are capable of all that these readers have shown here; feeling moved and buoyed by the thought of them, and the poems and novels that helped make it so. Beyond the reading groups, *shared* reading means this finally: that what is shared in these pages, from these people, is something tentatively in between the private and the public, which literature exists to bring out, in place of isolating secrets or social denials.

READING LIST

Key reading texts

Those most central to the chapter are marked with an asterisk; many of the individual poems may also be found freely available on the internet. See also the anthologies Philip Davis (ed.), *All the Days of My Life* (J. M. Dent, 1999), and Angela Macmillan (ed.), *A Little Aloud* (Chatto and Windus, 2010).

Introduction

Raymond Carver, 'Happiness' in *All of Us: The Collected Poems* (Vintage, 1996).
Thomas Hardy, *Complete Poems*, ed. James Gibson (Macmillan, 1976).
William James, *The Varieties of Religious Experience*, 1902, ed. M. E. Marty (Penguin, 1986).

Chapter 1

The Bible: Authorized King James Version, 1611, ed. R. Carroll and S. Prickett (Oxford World's Classics, 2008).
Edward FitzGerald, *Rubaiyat of Omar Khayyam*, 1859, revised 1879, ed. D. Karlin (Oxford World's Classics, 2010).
Robert Frost, 'Revelation' in *Collected Poems* (Vintage Classics, 2013).
Paul Gallico, *The Snow Goose*, 1941 (Penguin, 2001).
George Herbert, 'The Flower' in *Complete Poetry*, ed. J. Drury (Penguin, 2015).
Somerset Maugham, *The Painted Veil*, 1925 (Vintage Classics, 2001).
*William Shakespeare, sonnet 29 in *The Sonnets and A Lover's Complaint*, ed. J. Kerrigan (Penguin, 1986).

Chapter 2

*Robert Burns, 'Remorse', in *Complete Poems and Songs*, ed. A. Noble and P. Scott Hogg (Canongate, 2003).
George Eliot, *Middlemarch*, 1871–2, ed. D. Carroll (Oxford World's Classics, 2008).
Douglas Oliver, *In The Cave of Suicession* (Street Editions, Cambridge, 1974).
Edmund Spenser, 'Lacking my love', *Amoretti and Epithalmion*, sonnet 78, in *The Shorter Poems*, ed. R. McCabe (Penguin, 1999).
Leo Tolstoy, *Childhood, Boyhood, Youth*, 1852, 1854, 1857, trans. J. Rosengrant (Penguin, 2012).
*Leo Tolstoy, *Anna Karenina*, 1877, trans. Louise and Aylmer Maude, 1918 (Oxford World's Classics, 1980).
*Leo Tolstoy, *War and Peace*, 1869, trans. Louise and Aylmer Maude, 1922, rev. Amy Mandelker (Oxford World's Classics, 2010).
William Wordsworth, *The Prose Works*, ed. W. J. B. Owen and J. W. Smyser, 3 vols (Clarendon Press, 1974).

Chapter 3

*Charles Dickens, *Great Expectations*, 1861, ed. M. Cardwell (Oxford World's Classics, 2008).

*Robert Frost, 'The Road Not Taken' in *Collected Poems* (Vintage Classics, 2013).

**Invictus: Selected Poems of W. E. Henley*, ed. J. Howlett (Sussex Academic Press, 2017).

Elizabeth Jennings, 'Friendship' in *Selected Poems* (Carcanet, 1979).

D. H. Lawrence, 'Trust' in *Pansies, Complete Poems of D. H. Lawrence*, ed V. de Sola Pinto and W. Roberts, 2 vols (Heinemann, 1964).

William Wordsworth, *Home at Grasmere*, composed 1800–6, ed. Beth Darlington (Cornell University Press, 1979).

Chapter 4

John Bunyan, *Grace Abounding to the Chief of Sinners*, 1666, ed. John Stachniewski (Oxford World's Classics, 2008).

*John Clare, 'I Am' in *Major Works*, ed. E. Robinson, D. Powell and T. Paulin (Oxford University Press, 2008); 'Now comes the bonny May' is most conveniently found in *Complete Works* (Delphi, 2013) or edited by F. Martin (Everlasting Flames, 2018).

**Invictus: Selected Poems of W. E. Henley*, ed. J. Howlett (Sussex Academic Press, 2017).

George Herbert, 'Love III' and 'The Flower', in *Complete Poetry*, ed. J. Drury (Penguin, 2015).

*Derek Walcott, 'Love After Love' in *Collected Poems, 1948–1984* (Faber & Faber, 1992).

Chapter 5

*Elizabeth Bishop, 'Cape Breton', 'In the Waiting Room' in *Poems: the Centenary Edition* (Chatto & Windus, 2011).

*Emily Dickinson, 'Tell all the truth', 'This Consciousness that is aware', 'How adequate unto itself' in *The Complete Poems* (Faber & Faber, 2016).

George Eliot, *Silas Marner*, 1861, ed. J. Atkinson (Oxford World's Classics, 2017).

*Robert Lowell, 'Epilogue' in *Day by Day, Collected Poems*, ed. Frank Bidart and David Gewanter (Farrar, Straus and Giroux, 2007).

*Marianne Moore, 'The Camperdown Elm' in *Complete Poems* (Faber & Faber, 2003).

Vladimir Nabokov, *Speak Memory*, 1951 (Penguin, 2000).

Frank O'Hara, 'The Day Lady Died' in *Lunch Poems* (City Lights, 2001).

*James Schuyler, 'The Bluet' in *Collected Poems* (Farrar, Straus and Giroux, 1994).

*Henry Van Dyke, 'Life' in *The Poems* (Quontro Classic Books, 2010).

**Words in Air; the complete correspondence between Elizabeth Bishop and Robert Lowell*, ed. T. Travisano and S. Hamilton (Faber & Faber, 2008).

Chapter 6

John Banville, *The Untouchable* (Picador, 1997).

*John Berger, *A Fortunate Man*, 1967 (Vintage, 1997).

e. e. cummings, 'maggie and milly and molly and may' in *Complete Poems 1904–62* (Liveright, 2016).

Charles Dickens, *A Christmas Carol*, 1843, ed. Robert Douglas-Fairhurst (Oxford World's Classics, 2018).

George Eliot, *Silas Marner*, 1861, ed. J. Atkinson (Oxford World's Classics, 2017).

*W. S. Graham, 'Implements in their Places' in *New Collected Poems*, ed. M. Francis (Faber & Faber, 2005).

Thomas Hardy, *Complete Poems*, ed. James Gibson (Macmillan, 1976).

Gerard Manley Hopkins, 'Felix Randal' in *The Major Works*, ed. C. Phillips (Oxford World's Classics, 2009).

Henry James, Prefaces to *The Awkward Age* and *The Spoils of Poynton* in *The Art of the Novel* (University of Chicago, 2011).

*Ben Jonson, 'To the Immortal Memory and Friendship of That Noble Pair, Sir Lucius Cary and Sir Henry Morison' in *Complete Poems*, ed. G. Parfitt (Penguin, 1981).

*Brendan Kennelly, 'Begin' in *The Essential Brendan Kennelly* (Bloodaxe, 2011).

Denise Riley, *Say Something Back* (Picador, 2016).

Christina Rossetti, 'Remember', 'Later Life, 6, 17' in *Complete Poems*, ed. B. Flowers (Penguin, 2001).

William Shakespeare, *Hamlet*, 1609, ed. Harold Jenkins (Arden, 2001).

Chapter 7

*Berthold Brecht, 'Everything Changes', 'Beds for the night' in *Collected Poems*, trans. D. Constantine and T. Kuhn (Liveright, 2018).

Samuel Taylor Coleridge, *Biographia Literaria*, 1817, ed. J. Engell and W. Jackson Bate, 2 vols (Princeton University Press, 1983).

David Constantine, 'Watching for Dolphins' in *Collected Poems* (Bloodaxe, 2004).

Samuel Daniel, 'Are They Shadows?' in *The New Oxford Book of Seventeenth-Century Verse*, ed. A. Fowler (Oxford University Press, 2008).

Samuel Daniel, *A Defence of Rhyme*, 1603, in *Sidney's 'The Defence of Poesy' and Selected Renaissance Literary Criticism*, ed. Gavin Alexander (Penguin, 2004).

Charles Dickens, *Little Dorrit*, 1855–7, ed. H. P. Shucksmith (Oxford World's Classics, 2012).

William Hazlitt, *An Essay on the Principles of Human Action*, 1805, in *Complete Works*, ed. P. P. Howe, 21 vols (J. M. Dent, 1932), vol 1.

*Robert Herrick, 'To Anthea, Who May Command Him Anything' in *The New Oxford Book of Seventeenth-Century Verse*, ed. A. Fowler (Oxford University Press, 2008).

Charles Lamb, *Specimens of English Dramatic Poets Who Lived About the Time of Shakespear*, 1808 (Leopold Classic Library, 2016).

William Shakespeare, *Coriolanus*, ed. P. Brockbank (Arden, 1976).

*William Shakespeare, *King Lear*, ed. R. Weis (Longman, 2019).

William Shakespeare, *Love's Labour's Lost*, ed. H. R. Woudhuysen (Arden, 1998).

William Shakespeare, *Macbeth*, ed. A. R. Braunmuller (Cambridge University Press, 2008).

William Shakespeare, *Two Noble Kinsmen*, ed. L. Potter (Arden, 1997).

*Tobias Wolff, 'Bullet in the Brain' in *Our Story Begins* (Bloomsbury, 2008).

William Wordsworth, *The Prose Works*, ed. W. J. B. Owen and J. W. Smyser, 3 vols (Clarendon Press, 1974).

Chapter 8

*Matthew Arnold, 'The Buried Life' in *Poems*, ed. K. and M. Allott (Longman, 1979).

*Philip Booth, 'First Lesson' in *Lifelines* (Viking, 1999).

*John Bunyan, *The Pilgrim's Progress*, 1678, ed. W. R.Owens (Oxford World's Classics, 2008).

T. S. Eliot, *Four Quartets*, 1941 (Faber & Faber, 2001).

Kim Stafford, *Early Morning: Remembering My Father, William Stafford* (Graywolf Press, Minnesota, 2002).

*William Stafford, 'Ask Me' in *The Way It Is: New and Selected Poems* (Graywolf Press, Minnesota, 2016).

William Stafford, *Writing the Australian Crawl* (University of Michigan Press, 1978). William Stafford, *You Must Revise Your Life*, (University of Michigan Press, 1986).

*Baron Wormser, 'A Quiet Life' in *Scattered Chapters: New & Selected Poems* (Sarabande Books, 2008).

Chapter 9

*Joseph Conrad, *Lord Jim*, 1899, ed. C. Watts and R. Hampson (Penguin, 1986).

*Joshua Ferris, *The Unnamed* (Penguin, 2011).

Thomas Hardy, *The Mayor of Casterbridge*, 1886, ed. D. Kramer (Oxford World's Classics, 1987).

Henry James, *The Beast in the Jungle* (Penguin, 2011).

Marilynne Robinson, *Home* (Virago, 2008).

William Shakespeare, *The Winter's Tale*, ed. J. Pitcher (Arden, 2010).

Chapter 10

Samuel Beckett, *Textes pour rien* in *Texts for Nothing and Other Shorter Prose, 1950–76* (Faber & Faber, 2010).

*Wendell Berry 'The Slip' in *The Peace of Wild Things: And Other Poems* (Penguin, 2018).

Charles Dickens, *David Copperfield*, ed. Nina Burgis (Oxford World Classics, 2008).

George Eliot, *Adam Bede*, ed. C. A. Martin (Oxford World's Classics, 2008).

George Eliot, *Daniel Deronda*, ed. G. Handley (Oxford World's Classics, 2014).

George Eliot, *Middlemarch*, 1871–2, ed. D. Carroll (Oxford World's Classics, 2008).

George Eliot, *The Mill on the Floss*, ed. G. S. Haight (Oxford World's Classics, 2015).

T. S. Eliot, *Four Quartets*, 1941 (Faber & Faber, 2001).

Elizabeth Gaskell, *Wives and Daughters*, ed. A. Easson (Oxford World's Classics, 2008).

George Herbert, 'The Flower' in *Complete Poetry*, ed. J. Drury (Penguin, 2015).

Angela Macmillan (ed.), *A Little Aloud* (Chatto & Windus, 2010).

Angela Macmillan (ed.), *A Little Aloud, for Children* (Doubleday, 2014).

Angela Macmillan (ed.), *A Little Aloud, With Love* (Chatto and Windus, 2016).

Vladimir Nabokov, *Speak Memory*, 1951 (Penguin, 2000).

John Henry Newman, *University Sermons*, 1826–43 (SPCK, 1970).

Norman Nicholson, 'Old Man at a Cricket Match', *Collected Poems* (Faber & Faber, 2009).

Christopher Reid, 'A Scattering' in *A Scattering* (Arete, 2009).

*Alfred, Lord Tennyson, *In Memoriam*, 'Tears, Idle Tears', 'Tithonus' in *Poems*, ed. C. Ricks (Longman, 1969).

*Thomas Traherne, 'The Salutation' in *Selected Poems and Prose*, ed. A. Bradford (Penguin, 1991).

Anthony Trollope, *The Duke's Children*, ed. K. Mullin and F. O'Gorman (Oxford World's Classics, 2011).

Chapter 11

Jane Austen, *Emma*, 1815, ed. A. Pinch and J. Kinsley (Oxford World's Classics, 2008).

Joseph Conrad, *The Rescue*, 1920 (Penguin, 1995).

*Henry James, *The Awkward Age*, 1899, ed. R. Blythe (Penguin, 1987).
Tove Jansson, *Moomins Collectors' Editions* (Sort of Books, 2017–18).
*Philippa Pearce, *Tom's Midnight Garden*, 1958 (Oxford University Press, 2005).
Rosemary Sutcliff, *Warrior Scarlet*, 1958 (Farrar, Straus and Giroux, 1994).
Salley Vickers, *Cousins* (Penguin, 2017).
Salley Vickers, *Miss Garnett's Angel* (HarperCollins, 2000).
Salley Vickers, *The Librarian* (Viking, 2018).
*Salley Vickers, *The Other Side of You* (Harper Perennial, 2007).
William Wordsworth, 'Ode: Intimations of Immortality from recollections of Early Child-hood', 'Old Man Travelling, Animal Tranquillity and Decay', 'Resolution and Independence' in *Selected Poems*, ed. S Gill (Penguin, 2004).
William Wordsworth, *The Prelude: the four texts*, ed. J. Wordsworth (Penguin, 1995).

Other Reading

Hannah Arendt, *The Human Condition* (University of Chicago, 1998).
Hannah Arendt, *The Life of the Mind*, 2 vols (Harcourt, 1978).
John Berger, *Confabulations* (Penguin, 2016).
John Berger, *The White Bird* (Chatto & Windus, 1985).
Josie Billington, *Is Literature Healthy?* (Oxford University Press, 2016).
David Bleich, *Subjective Criticism* (Johns Hopkins University Press, 1978).
Christopher Bollas, *Being a Character* (Routledge, 1993).
Christopher Bollas 'Mind Against Self' in *The Mystery of Things* (Routledge, 1999).
Karl Bühler, *Theory of Language*, 1934, trans. D. F.Goodwin (John Benjamins, 2011).
Robert Burton, *The Anatomy of Melancholy* 1628, ed. F. Dell and P. Jordan-Smith (Tudor, 1927).
Philip Davis (ed.), *Real Voices: On Reading* (Macmillan, 1997).
Christopher Dowrick, *Beyond Depression* (Oxford University Press, 2009).
Mark Edmundson, *Why Read?* (Bloomsbury, 2005).
Eugene Gendlin, *Experience and the Creation of Meaning* (Northwestern University Press, 1962).
Joseph Gold, *Read for Your Life* (Fitzhenry & Whiteside, 2002).
Joseph Gold, *The Story Species* (Fitzhenry & Whiteside, 2002).
William James, *The Principles of Psychology*, 2 vols (Henry Holt, 1890).
William James, *The Varieties of Religious Experience*, 1902, ed. M. E. Marty (Penguin, 1986).
Daniel Kahneman, *Thinking Fast and Slow* (Farrar, Straus and Giroux, 2011).
Iain McGilchrist, *The Master and his Emissary* (Yale University Press, 2009).
Marion Milner, *A Life of One's Own* (Routledge, 2011).
Marion Milner, *An Experiment in Leisure* (Routledge, 2011).
Iris Murdoch, *Metaphysics as a Guide to Morals* (Chatto & Windus, 1992).
Les Murray, *The Paperbark Tree* (Carcanet, Minerva, 1993).
John Henry Newman, *An Essay in Aid of a Grammar of Assent* (Burns, Oats, 1870).
John Henry Newman, *University Sermons*, 1826–43 (SPCK, 1970).
Tim Parks, *Out of My Head* (Harvill, 2018).
Catherine Pickstock, *After Writing* (Blackwell, 1998).
Catherine Pickstock, *Repetition and Identity* (Oxford University Press, 2013).
Marcel Proust, *On Reading Ruskin*, trans. J. Autret, W. Burford, and P. J. Wolfe (Yale University Press, 1987).
George Puttenham, *The Art of English Poesy*,1589, ed. Frank Whigham and Wayne A. Rebhorn (Cornell University Press, 2007).

Galen Strawson, 'Against Narrativity', *Ratio* 17.4 (2004), pp. 428–52.

Jane Tompkins, *Reading through the Night* (University of Virginia, 2018).

Roberto Mangabeira Unger, *Passion* (The Free Press, Macmillan, 1984).

Bessel Van der Kolk, *The Body Keeps the Score* (Penguin, 2014).

Maryanne Wolf, *Reader, Come Home* (HarperCollins, 2018).

Michael Wood, *Literature and the Taste of Knowledge* (Cambridge University Press, 2005).

NOTES

Introduction

1. John Berger, *Confabulations* (Penguin, 2016), pp. 3–4: I am indebted to Josie Billington, *Is Literature Healthy?* (Oxford University Press, 2016), pp. 119–20.
2. William James, *The Varieties of Religious Experience*, 1902, ed. M. E. Marty (Penguin, 1986), pp. 55–6; hereafter cited as *Varieties*.
3. In *The Limits of Critique* (University of Chicago Press, 2015), Rita Felski offers (what remains) a theoretical argument against the dominance of any one theoretical model of reading, in particular, the socio-political ideologies encouraged by the hermeneutics of suspicion. She makes the case for the encouragement of what she calls 'postcritical reading' in which 'the reader' is not an abstract concept, as in reader-response theory, but, more empirically, a specific autonomous individual capable of a range of responses besides the default of intelligent suspicion: 'We need ways of thinking about individual readers that does not flatten and reduce them, that grasps their idiosyncrasy as well as their importance. Texts cannot influence the world by themselves, but only via the intercession of those who read them, digest them, reflect on them, rail against them, use them as points of orientation, and pass them on' (pp. 171–2).
4. I am indebted to Charlotte Christiansen for reference to Luigi Muzzetto's 'Time and Meaning in Alfred Schutz', *Time and Society* (2006, vol. 15, no. 1, pp. 16–17).
5. The Risk of Reading', *New York Times*, 1 August 2004.
6. Beginning as a small outreach unit at the University of Liverpool in 1997, *The Reader* was established as a national charity in 2008: see http://www.thereader.org.uk.
7. Felski argues that the readers we think about should not be restricted to those trained within the professionalized confines of a single approach, as for example historical and socio-political context; but should be allowed to offer from within themselves riskily generous, personal, and imaginative responses that arise prior to formalization: 'The import of a text is not exhausted by what it reveals or conceals about the social conditions that surround it. Rather, it is also a matter of what it sets alight in the reader—what kind of emotion it elicits, what changes of perception it prompts, what bonds and attachments it calls into being. One consequence of this line of thought is a perspective less dismissive of lay experiences of reading (which also precede and sustain professional criticism)' (p. 179).
8. This account first appeared in *The Reader* magazine, and is reproduced more fully in Josie Billington, *Reading and Mental Health* (Palgrave Macmillan, 2019).
9. Stanley Middleton, *An After-Dinner's Sleep* (Hutchinson, 1986), p. 98.
10. See Talbot Brewer, 'What Good Are the Humanities?' in *Raritan*, 37.4 (Spring 2018), pp. 99–118.
11. Hannah Arendt, *The Life of the Mind*, 2 vols (Harcourt, 1978), vol. 1, p. 78 ('thinking always involves remembrance; every thought is strictly speaking an after-thought').

12. Preface to *The Ambassadors*: John Plotz, *Semi-Detached* (Princeton University Press, 2018), p. 138.
13. Arthur Schopenhauer, *The World as Will and Idea*, trans. R. B. H. Haldane and J. Kemp, 3 vols (Routledge & Kegan Paul, 1883–6), vol. 1, p. 404.
14. https://www.huffpost.com/entry/depressed-your-seeking-sy_b_3616967. Accessed July 2019.
15. See chapter 7, pp. 180–1 on Bayesian prediction errors.
16. Tim Parks, *Out of My Head* (Harvill, 2018), p. 88.
17. https://www.liverpool.ac.uk/humanities-social-sciences-health-medicine-technology/reading-literature-and-society/

Chapter 1

1. See Martin Buber, *The Knowledge of Man*, trans. M. Friedman and R. G. Smith (Harper & Row, 1965) on the two-way movement between 'distance and relation'. In move 1, 'distance': 'Only man gives distance to things…he sets them in their independence as things which from now on continue to exist ready for a function', and this applies to speech also: 'Man sets also his calls at a distance and gives them independence, he stores them like a tool he has prepared, as objects which are ready for use, he makes them into words which exist by themselves'. But then in move 2, 'relation' for which distance itself is the pre-supposition: for this distancing of speech into word-objects is made only 'in order that they should come again and again to life', the written turned back to the spoken it came out of, but spoken now in silent inner address to its reader. Even when seemingly soundless, the written word 'does not want to remain with its speaker. It reaches out toward a hearer' (pp. 65, 68, 112).
2. Baron Wormser, *The Road Washes Out in Spring* (University Press of New England, 2006), p. 177.
3. George Puttenham, *The Art of English Poesy* (1589), ed. Frank Whigham and Wayne A. Rebhorn (Cornell University Press, 2007), p. 285 (book 3, chapter 24).
4. It is what Walker Percy calls the delta factor, a triadic rather than dyadic relationship, in *The Message in the Bottle* (Farrar, Straus and Giroux, 1975), chapter 1.
5. Karl Bühler, *Theory of Language* (1934), trans. D. F.Goodwin (John Benjamins, 2011). Bühler's argument is that the evolution of language is from simple deixis, directly pointing outwardly to things themselves in the places of actual perception, to the creation of a silent symbolic field of language on the page where the linguistic representation substitutes itself by the internal pointing of relations through grammar. See also chapter 3 in this present work.
6. Les Murray, *The Paperbark Tree* (Carcanet, Minerva, 1993), p. 259.
7. The formulation is that of another of the CRILS team, Dr Grace Farrington, who like many others with us has been both a group leader and a researcher, combining practice and analysis.
8. Don Paterson, *Reading Shakespeare's Sonnets* (Faber, 2010), p. 88.
9. About which see more in chapter 7.
10. See also chapter 7, pp. 157–8, and the summary force of *Little Dorrit*.
11. I owe this thought to another researcher associated with our group, Thor Magnus Tangeras.
12. Though see Michael Wood, *Literature and the Taste of Knowledge* (Cambridge University Press, 2005), pp. 8–9 on how literary works should be personified, should be thought of as though it were a sort of person, a life-form offering deep knowledge and seeking transmission of itself.

Chapter 2

1. Leo Tolstoy, *War and Peace*, 1867, trans. Louise and Aylmer Maude, revised Amy Mandelker (Oxford University Press, 2010).
2. See Joseph Luna, 'The Poetics and Poetry of Douglas Oliver, 1973–91', PhD thesis, University of Sussex, 2015, http://sro.sussex.ac.uk/55079/ (p. 65); from Douglas Oliver Archive, Albert Sloman Library, University of Essex (box 9).
3. William James, *Talks to Teachers on Psychology and to Students on Some of Life's Ideals* (Henry Holt, 1925), xii 'Memory' (http://www.gutenberg.org/files/16287/16287-h/16287-h.htm).
4. Samuel Johnson, *Life of Savage*, 1744, ed. Clarence Tracy (Oxford University Press, 1971), p. 140.
5. Hannah Arendt, *The Life of the Mind*, 2 vols (Harcourt, 1978), vol. 1, pp. 179–93; hereafter cited as 'Life of the Mind'.
6. See Adam Phillips, 'On Getting Way with It' in *On Balance* (Hamish Hamilton, 2010): 'these not-having-been-punished experiences from childhood—these times when we got away with it, and which stayed with us; these miniature death-of-God experiences when we were abandoned to our transgressions...', p. 205.
7. *The Prose Works of William Wordsworth*, ed. W. J. B. Owen and J. W. Smyser, 3 vols (Clarendon Press, 1974), vol. 3, pp. 118–20; hereafter cited as 'Wordsworth Prose Works'.
8. F. D. Maurice, *The Conscience*, third edition (Macmillan, 1883), p. 13.
9. In *Elizabethan Critical Essays*, ed. G. Gregory Smith, 2 vols (Oxford University Press, 1904), vol. 1 p. 157.
10. John Updike, 'The Man Within', *New Yorker*, 26 June 1995.

Chapter 3

1. This excerpt like other texts often used in Shared Reading is printed in *A Little Aloud* (Chatto and Windus, 2010), an anthology compiled by Angela Macmillan who features in chapter 10 of this book.
2. See William James, 'We are expectant of a "more"... we cannot, it is true, *name*...' (*Essays in Radical Empiricism*, 1912, p. 9, 'Is Radical Empiricism Solipsistic?'); 'I am only aware as of a terminal MORE existing in a certain direction, to which the words might lead but do not lead yet' (*The Meaning of Truth*, 'The Sanction of the Illative Sense', 1909, p. 1 'The Function of Cognition').
3. David Constantine, 'Finding the Words' in *In Other Words*, Autumn/Winter 1999/2000 no. 13/14, pp. 10–22, p. 11.
4. David Bleich, *Subjective Criticism* (Johns Hopkins University Press, 1978), p. 72
5. William Wordsworth, *Home at Grasmere*, ed. Beth Darlington (Cornell University Press, 1979), pp. 94–5.
6. *The Prelude: A Parallel Text*, ed. J. C. Maxwell (Penguin, 1971), 1805 version, book 12, lines 368–9 (my italics).
7. See Adam Phillips, 'The Conversions of William James', in *Raritan*, 37.1, (Summer 2017), pp. 20–39.
8. John Henry Newman, *University Sermons*, 1826–43 (SPCK, 1970), p. 259.
9. John Henry Newman, *An Essay in Aid of a Grammar of Assent* (Burns, Oats, 1870), p. 347 (chapter 9, section 1, 'The Sanction of the Illative Sense').
10. Christopher Bollas, *Being a Character* (Routledge, 1993), pp. 54, 59–60.

11. See for example at https://richardepetty.files.wordpress.com/2019/01/2013-revista-metacognitive-confidence-luttrell-et-al.pdf: A. Luttrell, P. Briñol, R. E. Petty, W. Cunningham, and D. Díaz, 'Metacognitive Confidence: A neuroscience approach', *Revista de Psicologia Social*, 28 (2013), pp. 317–32; https://richardepetty.files.wordpress.com/2019/01/2010-brinol-demarree-petty-uncertain-self.pdf: P. Briñol, K. G. DeMarree, and R. E. Petty, 'Processes by which Confidence (vs. Doubt) Influences the Self' in R. M. Arkin, K. C. Oleson, and P. J. Carroll (eds.), *Handbook of the Uncertain Self* (New York: Psychology Press, 2010), pp. 13–35.

12. 'We deliberately tried to collect just isolated fragments of their experience—particular images, sounds and feelings—rather than the entire story, because that is how trauma is experienced', Bessel Van der Kolk, *The Body Keeps the Score* (Penguin, 2014), p. 40.

Chapter 4

1. Florian Cova and Julien A. Deonna, 'Being Moved', *Philosophical Studies*, 169 (July 2014), pp. 447–66 (pp. 450–1).

2. Madelijn Strick and Jantine van Soolingen, 'Against the Odds: human values arising in unfavourable circumstances elicit the feeling of being moved', *Cognition and Emotion* 32.6, (2017), pp. 1–16 (pp. 1–2).

3. See chapter 5 on Frances and chapter 7 on brain-imaging experiments with Shakespeare.

4. George Puttenham, *The Art of English Poesy*, 1589, ed. Frank Whigham and Wayne A. Rebhorn (Cornell University Press, 2007), p. 47 (book 1, chapter 24); hereafter cited as 'Art'.

5. Robert Burton, *The Anatomy of Melancholy*,1628, ed. F. Dell and P. Jordan-Smith (Tudor, 1927), pp. 468–9, 477 (second partition, section 2, member 6, subsections 1–2).

6. Guillaume Thierry, Clara D. Martin, Victorina Gonzalez-Diaz, Roozbeh Rezaie, Neil Roberts, and Philip Davis, 'Event-related Potential Characterisation of the Shakespearean Functional Shift in Narrative Sentence Structure', *NeuroImage*, 40 (2008), pp. 923–31; Guillaume Thierry, James Keidel, et al., 'How Shakespeare Tempests the Brain', *Cortex*, 49 (2013), pp. 913–19; N. O'Sullivan, P. Davis, J. Billington, V. Gonzalez-Diaz, and R. Corcoran,'"Shall I Compare Thee": The neural basis of literary awareness, and its benefits to cognition', *Cortex*, 73 (2015), pp. 144–57.

7. Respectively, Jaak Panksepp, *Affective Neuroscience* (Oxford University Press, 1998), p. 262; William James, *The Varieties of Religious Experience*, 1902 (Penguin, 1986), p. 162 (lecture 7); Peter Hobson, *The Cradle of Thought* (Pan, 2004), p. 3.

8. Clive Sinclair, interview in *The Independent*, Friday 2 October 1998.

9. See Christopher Bollas's fine chapter 'Mind Against Self' in his collection *The Mystery of Things* (Routledge, 1999), pp. 75–87; hereafter cited as 'Bollas'.

10. On this sense of impossibility, see, for example, Darian Leader, *The New Black* (Penguin, 2009), p. 187–99; Hubertus Tellenbach, *Melancholy*, trans. Erling Eng (Duquesne University Press, Pittsburgh, 1980), pp. 165–9.

11. See Andrew H. Miller, *The Burdens of Perfection* (Cornell University Press, 2008) on 'implicative criticism' in which literature's latent and resonant implications are performed, drawn out and realized in its readers' minds and inner voices: 'historical and ideological criticism...I could find no way to respond creatively to them' (p. 28).

12. Clive Sinclair, *A Soap Opera from Hell* (Picador, 1998), p. 39.

Chapter 5

1. Vladimir Nabokov, *Speak, Memory*, 1951 (Penguin, 2000), p. 91.
2. Lota de Macedo Soares, Brazilian landscape gardener and architect who had a lesbian relationship with Elizabeth Bishop from 1957 until Lota committed suicide in 1967.
3. *Words in Air; the complete correspondence between Elizabeth Bishop and Robert Lowell*, ed. T. Travisano and S. Hamilton (Faber and Faber, 2008) pp. 225–6; hereafter cited as '*Words in Air*'.
4. *Day by Day* in Robert Lowell, *Collected Poems*, ed. Frank Bidart and David Gewanter (Farrar, Straus & Giroux, 2007).
5. See, for example, John D. Salamone and Mercè Correa, 'The Mysterious Motivational Functions of Mesolimbic Dopamine' in *Neuron*, 76.3 (2012), pp. 470–85; Ian Robertson, *The Stress Test* (Bloomsbury, 2016).
6. E. T. Gendlin, 'The New Phenomenology of Carrying Forward', *Continental Philosophy Review*, 37.1 (2004), pp. 127–51 (pp. 132–4), http://www.focusing.org/gendlin/docs/gol_2228.html.
7. In D. H Lawrence, *Phoenix*, ed. E. D. McDonald (Heinemann, 1936), pp. 398–516 (p. 431).
8. Mal Waldron, American jazz pianist (1925–2002), her regular accompanist from 1957 until her death in 1959.
9. John Jay Chapman, *Emerson and Other Essays*, 1898 (Jefferson Press reprint, 2015) pp. 47–8.
10. Paul Valéry, *The Art of Poetry*, trans. Denise Folliot (Bollingen Series, Princeton University Press, 1958), p. 174.

Chapter 6

1. Christina Rossetti, 'Sonnets of Later Life', 6, 17.
2. John Berger, *A Fortunate Man* (Vintage, 1997), p. 116; hereafter cited as 'Fortunate Man'.
3. See R. M. Epstein, 'Whole Mind and Shared Mind in Clinical Decision-Making', *Patient Education and Counselling*, 90.2 (2013), pp. 200–6; R. M. Epstein and R. L. Street, Jr, 'Shared Mind', *Annals of Family Medicine*, 9.5 (2011), pp. 454–61.
4. Ralph Waldo Emerson, *Essays and Lectures*, ed. J. Porte (Library of America, 1983), p. 249.
5. In Hester Lynch Piozzi, *Anecdotes of Samuel Johnson*, ed. S. C. Roberts (Cambridge University Press, 1925), p. 57.
6. Ola Sigurdson (ed.), https://core.ac.uk/download/pdf/43560080.pdf: 'Medicine and technology combined as a component of our modern ambitions to create happier human beings and a happier civilisation have resulted in physical health becoming a vital aspect of the meaning of life, far more important than, for example, economic fairness, self-realisation or faith in God... In brief, this means that health as the absence of disease has come to be synonymous with health as well-being, as in the saying "at least I have my health!" The risk of such an identification, however, is that it becomes difficult to argue that one can be healthy even though one has so many ailments, or that the multidimensionality of health will be lost' (pp. 45–6).
7. Daniel Pennac, *Diary of a Body*, trans. Alyson Waters (MacLehose Press, 2016), p. xxx.
8. Iona Heath's lecture, 'Divided We Fail': http://www.clinmed.rcpjournal.org/content/11/6/576.full. See also Christopher Dowrick, *Beyond Depression* (Oxford University Press, 2009).
9. See William Ker Muir, *Police: Streetcorner Politicians* (University of Chicago Press, 1979), pp. 178–9.
10. John Berger, *The White Bird* (Chatto and Windus, 1985), p. 249; reprinted in *Selected Essays*, ed. G. Dyer (Bloomsbury, 2001), p. 450.

11. William Stafford, 'Believer' in *Stories That Could Be True: New and Collected Poems* (Harper, 1977).
12. See, for example, J. M. G. Williams 'Depression and the Specificity of Autobiographical Memory' in David C. Rubin (ed.), *Remembering Our Past* (Cambridge University Press, 1995), pp. 244–67.
13. Alison Liebling, 'Political Theory, Prison Moral Climates and Human Growth: Why Environments Matter', delivered at conference on 'Moral Understandings, Criminal Careers and Societal Responses to Criminal Careers', Cambridge, 24–6 September 2018.
14. Liebling's reference is to the American sociologist, C. Wright Mills on polar types.
15. See Galen Strawson, 'Against Narrativity', *Ratio* 17.4 (2004), pp. 428–52.
16. Compare D. H Lawrence's review of Frederick Carter, *The Dragon of the Apocalypse*, where Lawrence says he doesn't care if the book doesn't uniformly prove its point, is sometimes confused and inconsistent and ill-formed, or in some parts actually dull—if in other parts 'it suddenly open doors, and lets out the spirit into a new world, even if it is a very old world!', *Apocalypse*, first published 1931 (Penguin, 1995), p. 54.
17. John Banville *The Untouchable* (Picador 1997), p. 220; hereafter cited as 'Untouchable'.

Chapter 7

1. On what he thinks of as the revitalization of the right hemisphere in the history of Western culture see Iain McGilchrist, *The Master and his Emissary* (Yale University Press, 2009), especially pp. 200ff., 365.
2. *Prose Works of William Wordsworth*, ed. W. J. B. Owen and J. W. Smyser, 3 vols (Oxford University Press, 1974), vol. 1, p. 149; hereafter cited as 'Prose Works'.
3. On non-identical repetition I am indebted to Catherine Pickstock, *Repetition and Identity* (Oxford University Press, 2013) in the 'Literary Agenda Series' of which, as part of the project described in this current work, I am general editor.
4. *Selected Renaissance Literary Criticism*, ed. Gavin Alexander (Penguin, 2004), p. 216.
5. See chapter 1, pp. 37–8 and n. 10.
6. Saul Bellow, *Herzog* (Penguin, 1965), p. 34.
7. In *Bertolt Brecht Poems 1913–1956* (Methuen, 1987), p. 400.
8. The *Collected Poems of Bertolt Brecht*, trans. David Constantine and Tom Kuhn (Liveright, 2018).
9. Cf. in Shakespeare's *The Comedy of Errors*, 2.2.125–9: 'For know, my love, as easy mayst thou fall/ A drop of water in the breaking gulf,/ And take unmingled thence that drop again/ Without addition or diminishing,/as take from me thyself, and not me too.'
10. On unfreezing, see Hannah Arendt, *The Life of the Mind*, 2 vols (Harcourt, 1978), vol. 1, p. 171; Ralph Waldo Emerson writes in his essay 'The Poet' of language as 'fossil poetry', the poetry ossified in being taken for granted; see also R. C Trench, *On the Study of Words* (J. W. Parker, 1851), following Coleridge in thinking of words as living powers and concentrated poems.
11. Hannah Arendt, *The Human Condition* (University of Chicago, 1998), p. 246; hereafter cited as 'Arendt, *Human Condition*'.
12. S. T. Coleridge in *Biographia Literaria* (1817), chapter 7.
13. 'For in art the process of perception is an aim in itself and should be prolonged as much as possible; art is a means of experiencing a process of "becoming"; that which is already "become" is unimportant for art' (Shklovsky in S. Shlomith Rimmon-Kenan, *The Concept of Ambiguity—the Example of James* (University of Chicago, 1977), p. 229.

14. Maryanne Wolf writes of the reading brain's connectedness: 'at least as many things are happening in zigzagging, feed-forward, feed-backward interactivity as are occurring linearly', *Reader, Come Home* (HarperCollins, 2018), p. 34.
15. William James, *Varieties of Religious Experience*, ed. Martin E. Marty (Penguin, 1985), p. 197.
16. For example, William Davies, *Nervous States: How Feeling Took Over the World* (Penguin 2018).
17. William Hazlitt, *Complete Works*, ed. P. P. Howe, 21 vols (J. M. Dent, 1932), vol. 1, pp. 1–45; hereafter cited as 'Hazlitt'.
18. Charles Lamb's *Specimens of English Dramatic Poets Who Lived About the Time of Shakespear* (Routledge and Kegan Paul, 1808), pp. 341, 328. I am indebted to Pauline Kiernan for this example.
19. Peter Holland (ed.), *Garrick, Kemble, Siddons, Kean: Great Shakespeareans*, vol. 2 (Bloomsbury, 2014), p. 18. I am indebted here to James Harriman-Smith, Newcastle University.
20. Aaron Hill and William Popple, *The Prompter: A theatrical paper (1734–6)*, ed. W. W. Appleton and K. A. Burmin (Benjamin Blom, 1966), p. 85. I am indebted here to Dr James Harriman-Smith, Newcastle University. A version of parts of this chapter appears in Katharine Craik (ed.), *Shakespeare and Emotion* (Cambridge University Press, 2020).
21. William James, *The Principles of Psychology*, 2 vols (Henry Holt, 1890), vol. 1, p. 243; hereafter cited as 'Principles'.
22. George Puttenham, *The Art of English Poesy*, 1589, ed. Frank Whigham and Wayne A. Rebhorn (Cornell University Press, 2017), p. 255 (book 3, chapter 15).
23. To give more detail: With functional shift, non-usual activation appeared in the anterior and posterior cingulate cortices, which routinely are not much associated with language-processing but here are stimulated in the act of so-called error-detection because they are involved in the relation between *emotion* and new learning. The finding of increased activation in the inferior frontal and inferior temporal gyrus (normally associated with memory and visual recognition) bilaterally is consistent with this account of updating meaning. The involvement of the right fusiform gyrus is even more surprising, since it is to do with various forms of non-verbal recognition including the often emotional recognition of faces or the individuation of objects, while again it is the left that is more usually associated with language. What may be involved here is what Hamlet calls the *mind's* eye.
24. See chapter 4, pp. 96–7.
25. See Introduction, pp. 13–16 on second life.

Chapter 8

1. Kim Stafford, *Early Morning: Remembering My Father, William Stafford* (Graywolf Press, 2002), pp. 165, 4, 136; hereafter cited as 'Early Morning'.
2. William Stafford, *You Must Revise Your Life* (University of Michigan Press, 1986), p. 3; hereafter cited as 'Revise Your Life'.
3. R. L. Carhart-Harris, R. Leech, P. J. Hellyer, et al., 'The Entropic Brain: a theory of conscious states informed by neuroimaging research with psychedelic drugs', *Frontiers in Human Neuroscience*, 8 (2014), pp. 140–61; Z. Wang, Y. Li, A. R. Childress, and J. A. Detre, 'Brain Entropy Mapping Using fMRI', *PLOS ONE*, 9.3 (2014), e89948; V. Priesemann, M. Valderrama, M. Wibral, and M. Le Van Quyen, 'Neuronal Avalanches Differ from Wakefulness to Deep Sleep—evidence from intracranial depth recordings in humans', *PLOS Comput Biol*, 9.3 (2013), e1002985.

4. Hannah Arendt, *The Life of the Mind*, 2 vols (Harcourt, 1978) vol. 1, pp. 205, 208.
5. John Ruskin, *The Stones of Venice*, vol. 3 (1853), ch. 4, para. 23, *Modern Painters* vol. 3 (1856), ch. 10, para. 19.
6. John Ruskin, *The Stones of Venice*, vol. 2 (1853), ch. 6, paras. 11, 24.
7. Marcel Proust, *On Reading Ruskin*, trans. J. Autret, W. Burford, and P. J. Wolfe (Yale University Press, 1987), p. 114.
8. The Improving Access to Psychological Therapies (IAPT) programme began in 2008 for the treatment of adult anxiety disorders and depression in England.
9. See James W. Pennebaker on these function words in *The Secret Life of Pronouns* (Bloomsbury, 2011).
10. William James, *Varieties of Religious Experience*, 1902, ed. Martin E. Marty (Penguin, 1985), p. 111; hereafter cited as 'Varieties'.
11. William Stafford, *Writing the Australian Crawl* (University of Michigan Press, 1978), pp. 22–3.

Chapter 9

1. Joshua Ferris, *The Unnamed* (Penguin, 2011), pp. 36–7, 234–6; hereafter cited as 'Unnamed'.
2. Joseph Conrad, *Lord Jim* (Penguin, 1986), p. 187; both chapter and page numbers are given in the main text hereafter, cited as 'Lord Jim'.
3. Bertrand Russell, *Portraits from Memory* (Allen & Unwin, 1956) p. 87.
4. What Michael Burke helpfully calls 'sign-fed' and 'mind-fed' information in *Literary Reading, Cognition and Emotion* (Routledge, 2011), p. 151.
5. Marilynne Robinson, *Home* (Virago, 2008), p. 160.
6. See also chapter 6, p. 00, Pennac on acceleration in the race to burn up of a life.

Chapter 10

1. Iris Murdoch, *Metaphysics as a Guide to Morals* (Chatto & Windus, 1992), p. 335.
2. Tim Parks, *Out of My Head* (Harvill Secker, 2018), pp. 4, 9.
3. Vladimir Nabokov, *Speak, Memory*, 1951 (Penguin, 2000), p. 5.
4. Boswell's *Life of Johnson* (1791), entry for Thursday 26 October 1769.
5. Paul Englemann, *Letters from Ludwig Wittgenstein, with a Memoir* (Blackwell, 1967), p. 143.
6. John Henry Newman, *University Sermons*, 1826–43 (SPCK, 1970), p. 322 (sermon 15); hereafter cited as 'University Sermons'.
7. Luigi Muzzetto, 'Time and Meaning in Alfred Schutz', *Time and Society*, 15.1 (2006), pp. 16–17.

Chapter 11

1. Salley Vickers, 'I felt he wasn't my real father', *The Guardian*, 24 November 2012, https://www.theguardian.com/lifeandstyle/2012/nov/24/salley-vickers-mother-lost-legs; hereafter cited as 'The Guardian'.
2. *The National*, https://www.thenational.ae/arts-culture/salley-vickers-on-her-new-book-reflected-tragedy-is-something-i-ve-always-been-fascinated-by-1.181939.
3. Salley Vickers, *The Other Side of You* (Harper Perennial, 2007), p. 149; hereafter cited as 'TOSOY'.
4. Philippa Pearce, *Tom's Midnight Garden* (Oxford University Press, 2015), p. 170; hereafter cited as 'TMG'.

5. 'Nothing lawless can show the least reason why it should exist, or could at best have more than an appearance of life ... The mind of man is the product of live Law; it thinks by law, it dwells in the midst of law, it gathers from law its growth ... ': George MacDonald on the fantastic imagination in *A Dish of Orts*, 1893 (Johannesen, 1996), pp. 314–15.

6. Salley Vickers, *The Librarian* (Viking, 2018), p. 288.

7. Sally Vickers, *Cousins* (Penguin, 2016), p. 102.

8. See Roberto Mangabeira Unger, *Passion* (The Free Press, Macmillan, 1984), pp. 145–56.

9. Salley Vickers, *Miss Garnett's Angel* (HarperCollins, 2000), p. 330.

INDEX